Study Guide to accompany Gitman's

Principles of Managerial Finance

Sixth Edition

Thomas M. Krueger
University of Wisconsin
at LaCrosse

D. Anthony Plath
University of North Carolina
at Charlotte

HarperCollins*Publishers*

STUDY GUIDE To Accompany PRINCIPLES OF MANAGERIAL FINANCE, 6/E
By Krueger/Plath

Copyright © 1991 by HarperCollins *Publishers*, Inc.

ISBN: 0-06-043810-X
   91 92 93 94 9 8 7 6 5 4 3 2

Study Guide to accompany Gitman's

Principles of Managerial Finance

Sixth Edition

CHAPTER 1

THE ROLE OF FINANCE AND THE FINANCIAL MANAGER

SUMMARY

This chapter defines finance, describes the major areas and opportunities in finance, explains the finance function, and presents the goal of the financial manager. This text deals with the duties of the financial manager in the firm. Although the textbook does not overlook the sole proprietorship and partnership forms of business organization, the primary emphasis of the textbook is on corporations.

Larger firms often organize the financial activities of cash, capital expenditure, credit, financial planning and fund raising, and investment portfolio management under the treasurer. The accounting activities are under the controller. Accounting and finance are closely related, but finance is more concerned with cash flow while accounting is based on the accrual method of recognizing revenue at the point of sale and matching expenses to sales. A second difference is that the accountant's responsibility is generally data collection and presentation; the financial manager uses such data for decision making.

The financial manager must analyze and plan, manage the firm's asset structure, and control the capital structure with the overall long-run objective of maximization of the owner's wealth. This objective is not necessarily consistent with that of profit maximization. For corporations, maximizing owner's wealth means maximizing share price. A manager's personal goals may conflict with those of shareholders, creating an agency problem which gives rise to agency costs. Over sixty percent of business and political leaders believe that businesses reduce their value by acting in an unethical manner.

The chapter concludes with a preview of the eight sections of the textbook.

CONCEPT OUTLINE

I.   **Finance is a broad, dynamic field that affects everyone.**

    A. Finance is the art and science of managing money.

    B. There are two major areas of finance.

        1. Financial services is concerned with the design and delivery of advice and financial products. This fast-growing area includes banking and related institutions, personal financial planning, real estate and insurance.

2. Managerial finance, and this text, is concerned with the duties of the financial manager. Duties include budgeting, financial forecasting, cash management, credit administration, investment analysis, and funds procurement.

II.   **Three basic forms of organization are available to a business.**

A. Sole proprietorships are the most common form, accounting for 75 percent of all firms.

   1. The earnings of a sole proprietorship are taxed as personal income.

   2. Advantages of sole proprietorships include ownership of all profits, low organizational costs, tax savings, secrecy, and ease of dissolutions.

   3. Disadvantages include unlimited liability, which means that the proprietor can lose more than the investment, and the inability to grow large.

B. Partnerships consist of two or more individuals doing business together.

   1. There are large partnerships with many partners in public accounting, law and some brokerage firms.

   2. Advantages of partnerships include the ability to raise larger amounts of capital and obtain higher credit standing.

   3. Disadvantages include unlimited liability and limited life, because the death of a partner dissolves a partnership.

   4. A limited partnership allows the limited partners to have limited liability as long as a general partner has unlimited liability.

C. Corporations account for about 15 percent of all business firms but provide nearly ninety percent of business receipts.

   1. A corporation is a legal entity that can make contracts and be sued.

   2. Corporate owners, or stockholders, may represent a large, diverse group.

   3. The Board of Directors, who set the policy, are elected by the stockholders.

   4. The president, or chief executive officer, is responsible for ongoing operations and for following the Board's policies.

5. Advantages of corporations include limited liability, ability to grow large, transferability of ownership, long life, professional management, easy to expand, and certain tax advantages.

6. Disadvantages include possibly higher taxes, higher organizational expenses, and stricter government regulation.

III. **An understanding of the role of the financial manager is important.**

A. The role of the finance function is largely dependent on the size of the business firm.

1. Small firms typically house the finance function within the accounting department.

2. In large-scale operation, the finance function is explicitly recognized as a separate area.

3. This area is commonly headed by the treasurer, who is linked directly to the firm's president and Chief Executive Officer (CEO) through a vice-president of finance.

B. Finance is closely related to economics.

1. From economics, the tools of marginal analysis used in a profit maximization context are drawn.

2. Marginal analysis states that an action should be made only when the added benefits exceed the added costs.

C. Finance and accounting are closely related functions within the business firm.

1. The accounting function is best viewed as an input to the finance function.

2. The primary function of the accountant is to develop logically and provide data for measuring the firm's performance, for assessing its financial position, and for paying taxes.

3. The accountant uses accrual concepts, which recognize revenues at the point of sale and expenses when incurred, while the financial manager is more concerned with when the actual cash flows associated with these actions take place.

4. The financial manager is more concerned with maintenance of the firm's solvency, while the accountant primarily gathers and presents data.

5. The financial manager devotes more attention to decision making than does the accountant.

D. The financial manager performs three basic functions within the firm.

1. The financial manager must undertake financial analysis and planning.

2. The financial manager must manage the firm's asset structure.

3. The financial manager must manage the firm's financial structure.

E. The overall goal of the financial manager should be to maximize the long-run wealth of the firm's owners.

1. Profit maximization is a short-run approach, while wealth maximization considers the long-run approach.

2. Wealth maximization tends to reflect differences in the timing of returns, while profit maximization fails to do so.

timing

3. The owner of a share of stock receives a return in the form of periodic cash dividend payments or increase in the stock price, or both.

4. Profit maximization does not consider risk, while the use of wealth maximization gives explicit consideration to differences in risk.

risk

5. Risk and return are the key determinants of stock price.

F. The agency issue considers the potential conflict between managers' personal goals and shareholders' goal of maximum stock price.

1. Agency problems may results from this conflict.

2. Agency costs are incurred to monitor, bond, and streamline organizational decision-making to reduce conflicts.

3. Potential agency problems have resulted in the recent emergence of large private corporations. These business organizations often result from mergers, takeovers, and leveraged buyouts.

4. Excessive purchase prices suggest that privatization may allow managers to unlock corporate value by eliminating "undermanaged" corporations.

G. Unethical activities of business leaders has resulted in renewed interest in developing standards of business conduct.

1. Survey respondents believe that businesses strengthen their competitive position by maintaining high ethical standards.

2. Increasing numbers of firms require employees to abide by ethics policies.

3. Implementation of an ethics program is expected to enhance share price by reducing potential litigation and judgement costs and building a positive corporate image.

IV. **The text is organized using a valuation approach, with emphasis on how financial decisions affect the firm's market value. The eight areas covered are:**

A. The goals and environment of managerial finance.

B. Basic financial concepts.

C. Financial analysis and planning.

D. Long-term investment decisions.

E. Cost of capital, leverage, and capital structure.

F. Long-term financing decisions.

G. Short-term financing decisions.

H. Special managerial finance topics.

APPLICATIONS

DEFINITIONS

1. *Finance* is defined as the art and science of managing money.

2. The *Financial services* area is concerned with the design and delivery of financial advice and products.

3. The *Financial manager* actively manages the financial affairs of any type of business.

4. Sole proprietors and at least one partner have *unlimited liability*, which means that the owner can lose more than his or her investment.

5. A *partnership* is similar to a sole proprietorship, but it involves two or more owners.

6. Corporations are sometimes referred to as *legal entities*

7. Corporate ownership is represented by *stock*

8. The firm's officer responsible for financial planning, fund raising, managing capital expenditure decisions, and similar matters is the *Treasurer*

9. The micro-economic principle of *marginal analysis* states that an action should be taken only when added benefits exceed added costs.

10. Revenues are recognized at the point of sale and expenses when incurred in the *accrual method*

11. The key determinants of stock price are *risk* and *return*.

12. Modern corporations are frequently controlled by professional managers, or *agents* of the stockholders.

13. Agency costs have spurred the recent emergence of *large private corporations* which are closely monitored by persons or institutions with major equity or debt interests in the firm.

14. *Ethics training* is expected to enhance share price as it improves the corporation's image and loyalty, while reducing potential litigation and judgement costs.

15. *Owner wealth maximization* is assumed to be the primary focus of the financial manager.

MULTIPLE CHOICE

1. Finance can be defined as:
    a. equivalent to accounting.
    b. the art and science of managing money.
    c. the design and delivery of financial products.
    d. the relationship of business and government.

2.   Managerial finance concerns the duties of the:
      a. chief executive officer.
      b. financial manager.
      c. investment banker.
      d. marketing director.

3.   The principle that financial decisions should be made and actions taken only when the
      added benefits exceed the added costs is called:
      a. asset structure management
      b. financial planning
      c. marginal analysis
      d. the accrual method

4.   The primary activities of a financial manager include all but which of the following:
      a. financial analysis and planning.
      b. management of the firm's asset structure.
      c. managing the firm's financial structure.
      d. the design and delivery of banking advice and products.

5.   The likelihood that managers may place personal goals ahead of corporate goals is called
      a(n):
      a. agency problem.
      b. opportunity cost.
      c. poison pill.
      d. none of the above.

6.   The individual or group elected by shareholders with ultimate authority to guide corporate
      affairs is the:
      a. board of directors.
      b. chief executive officer.
      c. executive board
      d. financial managers.

7.   Wealth maximization is superior to profit maximization as the goal of financial
      management because:
      a. profits do not represent cash flow.
      b. profit ignores the timing of returns.
      c. profit maximization disregards risk.
      d. all of the above.

8.   About ____ percent of all business firms are sole proprietorships.
    a. 9
    b. 16
    c. 75
    d. 88

9.   The minimum number of partners that must assume unlimited liability in a limited partnership is:
    a. 0.
    b. 1.
    c. 2.
    d. a number equal to the number with unlimited liability.

10.   Financial activities organized under the controller include:
    a. accounting.
    b. cash management.
    c. credit management.
    d. fund raising.

11.   The method that recognizes revenues and expenses only with respect to actual inflows and outflows of cash is the:
    a. accrual method.
    b. agency method.
    c. cash method.
    d. limited method.

12.   Risk is defined in finance as the:
    a. chance that actual returns differ from expected returns.
    b. chance that agency costs will result in lower earnings.
    c. range of returns over an extended period of time.
    d. variance of earnings per share.

13.   We assume that most shareholders are:
    a. risk-averse.
    b. risk-loving.
    c. risk-neutral.
    d. risk-seekers.

14.   Payments to managers designed to minimize agency problems included all of the following, <u>except</u>:
    a. cash bonuses.
    b. fidelity bonds.
    c. performance shares.
    d. stock options.

15.   Ethics policies cover employee interaction with:
    a. all corporate constituents.
    b. customers.
    c. other employees.
    d. suppliers.

PROBLEM

1.   Michael Thompson has invested $35,000 in the Northern Development Company. This firm has recently become bankrupt and has $75,000 in unpaid bills. Explain the nature of payments, if any, by Mr. Thompson in each of the following situations.

    a. The Northern Development Company is a sole proprietorship owned by Mr. Thompson. *Liable for $75,000 due to unlimited liability*

    b. The Northern Development Company is a 50-50 partnership of Mr. Thompson and Deborah Lynn. ($20,000 of the debt was incurred by Ms. Lynn.) *Liable for $75,000*

    c. The Northern Development Company is a corporation. *Limited liability — could lose up to $35,000.*

SOLUTIONS

DEFINITIONS

1.   Finance
2.   financial services
3.   financial manager
4.   unlimited liability
5.   partnership
6.   "legal entities"
7.   stock
8.   treasurer
9.   marginal analysis
10.   accrual method

11.   risk; return
12.   agents
13.   large private corporations
14.   Ethics training
15.   Owner wealth maximization

MULTIPLE CHOICE

1.	b	6.	a	11.	c
2.	b	7.	d	12.	a
3.	c	8.	c	13.	a
4.	d	9.	b	14.	b
5.	a	10.	a	15.	a

PROBLEM

1.
    a. Mr. Thompson would be liable for the $75,000 liability of Northern Development Company, because a sole proprietor has unlimited liability.

    b. Mr. Thompson would still be liable for the $75,000 liability of Northern Development Company, even if the bills were incurred by Ms. Lynn, because a partner has unlimited liability.

    c. Mr. Thompson cannot lose more than the $35,000 invested, because a corporation's stockholder has limited liability.

CHAPTER 2

THE OPERATING ENVIRONMENT OF THE FIRM

SUMMARY

Financial decision-making relies heavily on the estimation and analysis of the cash flows associated with alternative courses of action. These cash flows are affected by a variety of environmental factors -- including income taxes, the price and availability of funds in financial markets, and the number of borrowing and lending options available to financial managers.

It is important that financial managers understand and anticipate the tax consequences resulting from their decisions. In the United States, ordinary income and capital gains represent the major sources of taxable income to corporations. While interest expense represents a tax-deductible cost to the firm, dividends paid to holders of the firm's common stock are not tax deductible.

Financial markets provide organized forums in which the suppliers and demanders of various types of funds can come together and make transfers. Financial managers seeking to borrow funds or invest idle corporate resources can execute these transactions by dealing with financial institutions, entering financial markets directly, or negotiating a private placement with another party.

In each case, the interest rate paid by borrowers to lenders represents the price of exchange for money. In efficient financial markets, this interest rate allocates funds to their most productive uses and insures that investors receive the highest possible returns for a given level of risk. Because lenders do not like risk, they must be compensated for greater uncertainty with the expectation of greater financial returns.

CONCEPT OUTLINE

I. **Businesses, like individuals, must pay taxes on the income they receive.**

A. Ordinary corporate income, or income earned through the sale of a firm's products and services, is currently taxed at the following rates:

1. 15 percent on the first $50,000;
2. 25 percent on the next $25,000;
3. 34 percent on the next $25,000;
4. 39 percent on income between $100,000 and $335,000; and
5. 34 percent on income in excess of $335,000.

B. The average tax rate paid on a firm's ordinary income can be calculated by dividing its taxes by its taxable income, while the firm's marginal tax rate represents the tax rate paid on the last dollar of taxable income.

70% Exclusion

C. All interest income received by a corporation is taxed as ordinary income. Only 30 percent of the dividends received by a corporation on its investment in the common and preferred stock of other firms is taxed as ordinary income.

D. In calculating their taxes, corporations are allowed to deduct operating expenses (including advertising expenses, sales commissions, and bad debt losses) and interest expense. Dividends paid by the firm are not tax-deductible.

E. Capital gains occur when corporations sell a depreciable asset for more than its initial purchase price. Under current tax law, capital gains are taxed at the same rate as the firm's ordinary income.

F. Corporations which suffer losses on the sale of capital assets first carry these losses back 3 years, and then carry any remaining losses forward for up to 15 years to offset taxable income. This procedure evens out the annual tax payments made by firms which experience particularly volatile income patterns.

G. Subchapter S of the Internal Revenue Code allows corporations with 35 or fewer shareholders to be taxed like partnerships. The key advantage of this form of organization is that stockholders receive all of the benefits from being a corporation, and escape the double taxation normally associated with the distribution of corporate earnings.

H. Corporations normally pay estimated taxes four times each year on April 15, June 15, September 15, and December 15. They must settle any additional tax payments or refunds resulting from the under- and over-payment of estimated taxes by March 15 of the following calendar year.

II. **Firms that require funds from external sources can obtain them in three ways: (1) through a financial institution that accepts deposits and transfers them to individuals and businesses needing funds, (2) through financial markets where the suppliers and demanders of various types of funds can make an exchange, or (3) through a private placement between individual borrowers and lenders.**

A. Financial institutions are intermediaries that channel the savings of individuals, businesses, and governments into loans and investments.

1. The main suppliers of funds are individuals, while the main demanders of funds are businesses and governments.

2. The primary financial institutions in the United States are commercial banks, savings banks, savings and loan associations, credit unions, life insurance companies, pension funds, and mutual funds.

3. Changes in the regulation of financial institutions, resulting from the Depository Institutions Deregulation and Monetary Control Act of 1980 (DIDMCA), have increased the level of competition between different institutions. This competition has led to the development of firms known as financial supermarkets, where customers can obtain a wide variety of different financial services. In addition, increased competition between financial institutions helped promote the savings and loan crisis of the late 1980s.

B. Financial markets provide a means by which suppliers of funds and demanders of credit can come together and execute transactions directly. These markets include:

1. The primary market, where new securities are traded;

2. The secondary market, where pre-owned securities are traded;

3. The money market, where short-term debt instruments (marketable securities) are traded; and

4. The capital market, where long-term securities (stocks and bonds) are traded.

C. Financial institutions actively participate in the money and capital markets as both suppliers and demanders of funds.

D. The money market is created by the financial relationship between suppliers and demanders of funds which have maturities of one year or less.

1. The market's organization is considered intangible, because it has no formal structure. Transactions are made by finding and then contacting the people who deal in a given marketable security. Large banks, government security dealers, and the Federal Reserve actively participate and make markets in the money market.

2. The key participants in the money market include individuals, businesses, financial institutions, and governments.

3. The key money market instruments, or marketable securities, include Treasury bills, negotiable certificates of deposit, and commercial paper.

III. **The capital market is created by the financial relationship between suppliers and demanders of long-term funds, or funds that have maturities of more than one year.**

A. Major securities traded in the capital market include bonds (long-term debt), and both common and preferred stock (equity, or shares in corporate ownership).

B. Securities exchanges provide the marketplace in which firms can raise funds through the sale of new securities, and investors can maintain liquidity by being able to resell the securities they own.

1. Organized securities exchanges are tangible organizations where outstanding securities can be resold.

2. Organized securities exchanges include the New York Stock Exchange and the American Stock Exchange headquartered in New York City, as well as a number of regional exchanges such as the Midwest Stock Exchange (in Chicago) and the Pacific Stock Exchange (in San Francisco).

3. Trading is carried out on the floor of organized securities exchanges through an auction process in which the forces of supply and demand determine the price of securities.

4. The Over-the-Counter (OTC) securities exchange is an intangible market for the purchase and sale of securities not listed by organized exchanges. OTC dealers are linked with buyers and sellers of securities through the National Association of Securities Dealers Automated Quotations System (NASDAQ), which represents a telecommunications system that provides current price information on thousands of actively traded OTC securities.

5. Unlike the auction process used by organized securities exchanges, the prices at which OTC securities trade result from competitive bidding and negotiation between buyers and sellers.

C. Securities exchanges create efficient markets that allocate funds to the most productive uses of capital.

D. In order to raise money in the capital market, firms can also make private placements which involve the direct sale of a new security; or a public offering that represents the nonexclusive issue of either bonds or stock to the general public.

1. Most firms raise money through a public offering.

2. In offering new securities to the market, most firms hire an investment banker to find buyers for these securities.

IV. **Interest rates and required returns represent the costs of obtaining various types of financing.**

A. When funds are lent, the cost of borrowing these funds is the interest rate. When funds are invested in stock, the cost to the seller of this equity is called the required return.

B. The real rate of interest represents the rate of return earned in a world where there is no inflation, no liquidity preference associated with investments, and no uncertainty.

    1. The real rate of interest creates an equilibrium between the supply of savings and the demand for investment.

    2. The annual real rate of interest in the United States is stable and equal to about 2 percent.

C. The nominal rate of interest is the actual rate of interest charged by the suppliers of funds and paid by the demanders of funds. Ignoring risk, the actual cost of funds results from the real interest rate adjusted for inflation and liquidity preferences.

    1. The nominal interest rate differs from the real rate due to inflation expectations and issuer and issue characteristics:

$$k_i = k^* + IE + IC_i$$

    where k_i = the nominal rate of interest for security i;

                k^* = the real rate of interest;

                IE = inflation expectations; and

                IC_i = the risk premium.

    2. Inflation expectations concern future inflation, not the present rate of inflation.

D. For any class of similar-risk securities, the term structure of interest rates, or yield curve, relates the interest rate or rate of return to the length of time until maturity.

    1. The yield curve reflects the general supply-demand conditions for funds, the general preference of fund suppliers toward more liquid securities, and the general expectations of investors about future interest rate levels.

    2. An upward-sloping yield curve indicates expectations of higher interest rates in the future, a flat yield curve is consistent with expectations for stable interest rates, and a downward-sloping yield curve indicates expectations of falling interest rates.

E. The shape of the yield curve can be explained by three different theories:

    1. The expectations hypothesis suggests that the yield curve reflects investor expectations about future inflation. When the rate of inflation is expected to decline, the yield curve will be downward-sloping; when the rate of inflation is expected to rise, the yield curve will be upward-sloping.

E-L-ms

2. Liquidity preference theory suggests that long-term interest rates are higher than short-term rates because (1) investors view short-term securities as less risky, and (2) borrowers are generally willing to pay a higher rate for long-term financing.

3. Market segmentation theory suggests that the market for funds is segmented based on maturity, and interaction between the supply and demand for funds in each segment determines the prevailing interest rate in that segment.

F. All three term structure explanations have merit, and the actual shape of the yield curve is affected by each one.

G. Risky securities carry higher rates of interest than riskless securities, because investors must be compensated for bearing risk.

1. The nominal rate of interest for security i, k_i, is:

$$k_i = R_F + IC_i$$

where R_F = the risk-free rate of interest; and

IC_i = the risk premium.

2. The size of the risk premium depends upon the following factors:

D   a. Default risk, or the probability that the issuer of debt securities will not pay the contractual interest and/or principal payments as scheduled. The greater the uncertainty concerning the borrower's ability to meet these payments, the greater the risk premium.

m   b. Maturity risk, or the chance that a change in interest rates will cause the value of the security to change. The longer the time until maturity for a given security, the greater the maturity risk, and the larger the risk premium.

L   c. Liquidity risk, or the ease with which securities can be converted into cash without loss of value. Less actively traded securities have higher liquidity risk, and these securities carry a larger risk premium.

CP   d. Contractual provisions which protect the lender or investor reduce the risk premium, while provisions that favor the borrower increase the risk premium.

T   e. Tax treatment of various securities. Because the earnings on certain types of securities are exempt from taxes, these securities will carry lower nominal interest rates so that their after-tax returns are equivalent to the after-tax yields on fully taxable securities with similar risk.

APPLICATIONS

DEFINITIONS

1. A _Capital gain_ occurs when the price at which an asset is sold exceeds the purchase price of the asset.

2. An _S Corporation_ represents a tax reporting entity whose earnings are taxed not as a corporation, but as the incomes of its stockholders.

3. A forum in which suppliers and demanders of funds can transact business directly is known as a _financial market_

4. The financial market in which securities are initially issued is known as the _primary market_ , while pre-owned securities are traded in the _secondary market_

5. _Bonds_ represent long-term instruments used by businesses and governments to raise money, while _Common stock_ represents the ownership interests in a corporation.

6. Stockholders receive periodic distributions of corporate earnings in the form of _dividends_ , while bondholders receive periodic _interest_ payments from their investments.

7. The New York Stock Exchange represents an _organized security exchange_ , while the NASDAQ is an _over-the-counter_ market.

8. An _investment banker_ is a financial middleman engaged by a firm to solicit purchasers for new security issues.

9. The _real_ rate of interest is that rate that creates an equilibrium between the supply of savings and the demand for investment funds in a world without inflation. In contrast, the _nominal_ rate of interest represents the actual interest rate charged by suppliers of funds and paid by borrowers.

10. The required rate of return on a U.S. Treasury bill is known as the _risk free_ rate of interest.

11. The _term structure_ of interest rates shows the relationship between the rate of return on securities of similar risk and the time remaining until these securities mature.

(upward-sloping)
12. A _normal_ yield curve occurs when long-term interest rates are greater than short-term rates, while an _inverted_ yield curve occurs when long-term rates are below short-term rates.

(downward-sloping)

13.   The *expectations hypothesis* explains an upward-sloping yield curve by suggesting that investors expect higher rates of inflation in the future.

14.   According to the *risk-return tradeoff*, in exchange for accepting greater risk, investors must be compensated with higher returns.

15.   *Preferred stock* dividends must be paid prior the payment of any common stock dividends.

MULTIPLE CHOICE

1.   An important difference between interest and dividends is that:
       a.   interest is tax-deductible, while dividends are not.
       b.   dividends are tax-deductible, while interest is not.
       c.   long-term interest is tax-deductible, while dividends and short-term interest are not.
       d.   corporations rarely pay dividends, while they frequently pay interest.

2.   The major financial institutions in the U.S. economy include all but which of the following?
       a.   commercial banks.
       b.   life insurance companies.
       c.   the U.S. Congress.
       d.   mutual funds.

3.   Key net suppliers of funds to the financial markets include:
       a.   business.
       b.   state and local governments.
       c.   the federal government.
       d.   individuals.

4.   The nominal rate of interest differs from the real rate of interest as a result of:
       a.   inflation expectations.
       b.   issue characteristics.
       c.   both a and b.
       d.   none of the above.

5.   A downward-sloping yield curve reflects:
       a.   more buyers than sellers in financial markets.
       b.   expectations of higher inflation and interest rates in the future.
       c.   expectations of lower inflation and interest rates in the future.
       d.   general uncertainty in the financial markets.

6. Income earned through the sale of a firm's goods and services is known as:
    a.   primary income.
    b.   capital gains income.
    c.   ordinary income.
    d.   marginal income.

7. Under current tax law, corporations may carry tax losses back up to ____ years and forward for as many as ____ years.
    a.   3, 10.
    b.   10, 5.
    c.   3, 15.
    d.   3, 3.

8. Corporations that expect to have an annual tax liability of $40 or more are required to make estimated tax payments:
    a.   monthly.
    b.   quarterly.
    c.   annually.
    d.   semi-annually.

9. A financial institution that obtains funds through the sale of shares and uses the proceeds to acquire stocks and bonds issued by various businesses and governments is known as a:
    a.   mutual fund.
    b.   commercial bank.
    c.   life insurance company.
    d.   savings bank.

10. The annual real rate of interest in the U.S. is approximately:
    a.   7 percent.
    b.   15 percent.
    c.   10 percent.
    d.   2 percent.

11. Which of the following is not an external source through which firms can obtain funds?
    a.   financial institutions.
    b.   federal financing bank.
    c.   private placements.
    d.   financial markets.

12.   A financial supermarket represents a:
    a.   stock exchange located in New York City.
    b.   financial institution at which consumers can obtain a wide variety of financial services.
    c.   grocery store that also contains an automated teller machine.
    d.   a large consumer finance company.

13.   Marketable securities include:
    a.   common stock.
    b.   savings accounts.
    c.   long-term bonds.
    d.   commercial paper.

14.   Corporate bonds typically pay interest _____, and have a par value equal to $_____.
    a.   annually, $1000.
    b.   quarterly, $5000.
    c.   semiannually, $1000.
    d.   semiannually, $5000.

15.   Which of the following is not an explanation for the term structure of interest rates?
    a.   rational investors theory.
    b.   expectations theory.
    c.   market segmentation theory.
    d.   liquidity preference theory.

PROBLEMS

1.   Use the tax rates given in the text to calculate the taxes on corporate income of $180,000. What is the average tax rate? What is the marginal tax rate? — 39%

$22,250 + [.39(180,000 - 100,000)]$ 53450

$22,250 + 31,200 = 53,450$ $\frac{53450}{180000} = 29.7\%$

2.   The Wichita Company has operating earnings before tax of $101,000 and has just sold for $18,000 an asset not used in the business. Wichita purchased this asset three years ago for $15,000. Use the tax rates shown in the chapter to calculate:
    a.   The capital gain from the asset's sale; $18,000 - 15,000$ 3,000
    b.   Wichita's total tax liability;
    c.   Wichita's average tax rate; and   39%
    d.   Wichita's marginal tax rate.   39%

c.) $\frac{23810}{104,000} = 22.9\%$

101,000
3,000
——————
104,000

b.) $22,250 + [.39(104,000 - 100,000) =$
$22,250 + 1,560 = 23,810$

a.) 60,000
− 8,000 interest .40·52,000 = 20,800 taxes
52,000 taxable 52,000
− 20,800
31,200 net profit + available to stockholders

b.) 60,000·.40 = 24,000 taxes   60,000 − 24,000 = 36,000 net profits
8,000 dividends

3. The KLX Corporation anticipates earnings before interest and taxes to be $60,000 for the current year. Using the assumption of a 40 percent tax rate on ordinary income, what are the firm's after-tax net profits and earnings available for common stockholders if:
    a.   The firm pays $8,000 in interest expense and no common stock dividends.
    b.   the firm pays $8,000 in common stock dividends and no interest expense.

4. The interest rate data shown below is presented for securities within a given risk class for three different points in time. Based on these data:
    a.   Describe the yield curve for each point in time as upward-sloping, downward-sloping, or flat.
    b.   Describe the general inflation and interest rate expectations existing at each point in time.

Time Remaining Until Maturity (Months)	Point-In-Time #1 (Percent)	Point-In-Time #2 (Percent)	Point-In-Time #3 (Percent)
1	8.1	9.2	10.6
3	8.2	9.3	10.3
6	8.3	9.4	10.0
12	8.5	9.3	9.7
18	8.7	9.2	9.5
24	8.9	9.3	9.4

upward   flat   downward

5. The real rate of interest is currently 3 percent, and inflation expectations and risk premiums for four different securities are shown below. Based on this information:
    a.   Find the risk-free rate of interest, R_F, applicable to each security.
    b.   Find the nominal rate of interest for each security.

(R_E)
Risk Free Rate = $K^* + IE$ Nominal Rate: $K_i = R_F + IC_i$

Security	Inflation Expectations	Risk Premium
A	5%	2%
B	6	3
C	4	5
D	7	1

$R_F = K^* + IE$

	R_F	Nominal
A	8	10
B	9	12
C	7	12
D	10	11

6.   Rebecca Bunch needs to find the nominal rate of interest for each of two securities, P and Q, issued by different firms at the same point in time. She has the following information available to help her:

Characteristic	Security P	Security Q
Time Until Maturity	6 years	15 years
Inflation Expectations	5.0%	8.0%
Risk Premium for Default	1.0%	1.5%
Interest Rate Risk Premium	2.0%	2.5%
Liquidity Risk Premium	0.5%	1.5%
Other Risk Premium	1.0%	0.5%

   a. If the real rate of interest is 2 percent, find the risk-free rate of interest for each security. *7%*   *10%*
   b. What is the total risk premium attributable to each security? *4.5% & 6.0%*
   c. What is the nominal rate of interest for each security? *11.5% and 16.0%*

SOLUTIONS

DEFINITIONS

1.   capital gain
2.   S corporation
3.   financial market
4.   primary market; secondary market
5.   Bonds; common stock
6.   dividends; interest
7.   organized security exchange; over-the-counter
8.   investment banker
9.   real; nominal
10.   risk free
11.   term structure
12.   normal (or upward-sloping); inverted (or downward-sloping)
13.   expectations hypothesis
14.   risk-return tradeoff
15.   Preferred stock

MULTIPLE CHOICE

1. a	9. a
2. c	10. d
3. d	11. b
4. c	12. b
5. c	13. d
6. c	14. c
7. c	15. a
8. b	

PROBLEMS

1. Taxes on corporate income:

(.15)($50,000)	=	$7,500
(.25)($25,000)	=	$6,250
(.34)($25,000)	=	$8,500
(.39)($180,000 - $100,000)	=	$31,200
		$53,450

To find the firm's average tax rate, divide the total tax liability of $53,450 by its total taxable income of $180,000:

$$\$53,450 \: / \: \$180,000 \; = \; 29.7\%$$

To find the firm's marginal tax rate, note that the tax rate on the *last* dollar of taxable income is 39 percent.

2. a. There is a capital gain because the sale price of the machine is greater than its initial purchase price. Since the asset is not used in business, its book value equals its purchase price, and the capital gain represents the difference between the selling price and book value, or $18,000 - $15,000 = $3,000.

    b. The firm's total tax liability is based upon its total taxable income, including both ordinary income and capital gains:

Ordinary Income:	$101,000
Capital Gain:	3,000
Total Taxable Income:	$104,000

Total taxes equal:

(.15)($50,000) + (.25)($25,000) + (.34)($25,000) + (.39)($104,000 - $100,000)
= ($7,500) + ($6,250) + ($8,500) + ($1,560)

= $23,810.

c. The firm's average tax rate is equal to its total tax liability ($23,810) divided by its total taxable income ($104,000):

($23,810) / ($104,000) = 22.89%.

d. The firm's marginal tax rate represents that tax rate applied to its last dollar of taxable income, or 39 percent.

3. This problem requires the construction of a simple income statement under each of the financing options:

Income Statement Item	Option (a) Payment of Interest	Option (b) Payment of Dividends
EBIT	$60,000	$60,000
Less Interest Expense	8,000	0
Earnings Before Taxes	52,000	60,000
Taxes (40%)	20,800	24,000
Earnings After Tax	31,200	36,000
Dividends	0	8,000
Earnings Available to Common Shareholders	$31,200	$28,000

Because interest is tax-deductible while dividends are not, earnings available for common shareholders are higher under option (a). The $8,000 interest expense under this option reduces the firm's corporate tax liability by $3,200.

4. a. Time period #1 has a upward-sloping yield curve, the yield curve in time period #2 is almost flat, and time period #3 has a downward-sloping yield curve.

b. In period #1 market participants expect rising inflation and interest rates, in period #2 the expectation is for stable interest rates and inflation, and in period #3 the market expects falling interest rates and inflation.

5.   The equation for the risk-free rate of interest is:

$$R_F = k^* + IE$$

Security	(1) k^*	(2) IE	(3) (1) + (2) R_F
A	3%	5%	8%
B	3	6	9
C	3	4	7
D	3	7	10

The equation for the nominal rate of interest is:

$$k_i = R_F + IC_i$$

Security	(1) R_F	(2) IC_i	(3) (1) + (2) k_i
A	8%	2%	10%
B	9	3	12
C	7	5	12
D	10	1	11

6.   a.   Since $R_F = k^* + IE$,

      for Security P: $R_F = 0.02 + 0.05 = 0.07$, or 7%

      for Security Q: $R_F = 0.02 + 0.08 = 0.10$, or 10%

   b.   Since the total risk premium, IC_i, is equal to the sum of the default risk, interest rate risk, liquidity risk, and other risk premiums:

      for Security P: $IC_P = 0.01 + 0.02 + 0.005 + 0.01 = 0.45$ or 4.5%

      for Security Q: $IC_Q = 0.015 + 0.025 + 0.015 + 0.005 = 0.06$ or 6%

c.   Since $k_i = R_F + IC_i$,

for Security P: $k_P = 0.07 + 0.045 = 0.115$ or 11.5%

for Security Q: $k_Q = 0.10 + 0.06 = 0.16$ or 16%

CHAPTER 3

FINANCIAL STATEMENTS, DEPRECIATION, AND CASH FLOW

SUMMARY

Financial managers must know how to read, understand, and evaluate a variety of financial statements. The stockholders' annual report contains a great deal of important financial information that managers use. This report is published by publicly held corporations according to the requirements of the Securities and Exchange Commission (SEC). The report summarizes and documents the firm's financial activities for the year according to generally accepted accounting principles (GAAP).

The stockholders' report begins with a management letter from the chairman of the board or the president of the firm. Following this review of corporate performance and summary of business strategy, the shareholders' report contains four important financial statements: the balance sheet, the income statement, the statement of retained earnings, and the statement of cash flows.

The income statement presents operating results over a specified period of time, while the balance sheet summarizes the level of assets, liabilities, and net worth at a point in time. Income earned over a period and cash dividends paid during that period are reconciled in the statement of retained earnings. The statement of cash flows is a summary of the flow of funds (best thought of as cash) through the firm during a specified period.

Depreciation is the allocation of historical (fixed) cost over time. It is the most common type of non-cash expense. When estimating cash flow, depreciation and any other non-cash charges are added back to operating profits. Firms often use a different depreciation method for financial reporting than for tax purposes. Depreciation for tax purposes is determined using the Accelerated Cost Recovery System (ACRS), which was modified in the Tax Reform Act of 1986. ACRS classifies assets other than real estate into property classes based on recovery period (or lives) of: 3,5,7,10,15, and 20 years. Each recovery period has a schedule of depreciation percentages for each year of the recovery period.

Sources of funds increase the cash flow of a firm, while uses of funds decrease cash flow. Managers must identify all corporate sources and uses of funds, and then classify these items as operating, investment, or financing cash flows. The statement of cash flow allows managers and investors to analyze the firm's past and future cash flows by identifying the major sources and uses of corporate cash within a given period of time.

CONCEPT OUTLINE

I.   **A stockholders' report summarizes and documents a publicly held corporation's financial activities over the past year.**

A.   The guidelines used to prepare and maintain financial records and reports are known as generally accepted accounting principles (GAAP). These accounting principles are authorized by the Financial Accounting Standards Board (FASB).

B.   Publicly held corporations are those whose stock is traded on either an organized securities exchange or in the over-the-counter market. These corporations are required by the Securities and Exchange Commission (SEC) to provide their shareholders with an annual stockholders' report.

C.   The stockholders' report begins with a letter to the shareholders from management. This letter describes events having the greatest impact on the firm during the year.

D.   Four key financial statements follow the president's letter in the annual report.

  1. the income statement;
  2. the balance sheet;
  3. the statement of retained earnings; and
  4. the statement of cash flows.

II.   **As noted above, there are four basic financial statements contained in the shareholders' report.**

A.   The income statement provides a financial summary of the firm's operating results during a specific time period (usually a year).

  1. Sales revenue and business expenses are shown in this statement.

  2. The statement concludes with a "bottom line" earnings per share figure available to common shareholders.

B.   The balance sheet provides a summary statement of the firm's financial position at a given point in time.

  1. Assets, which are owned by the firm, are balanced against debt (that is owed to the firm) and equity (that is provided by the firm's owners).

  2. Current assets and liabilities are short-term accounts that are expected to be converted into cash within one year or less.

3. All other assets and liabilities, along with shareholders' equity, are considered long-term or fixed because they are expected to remain on the firm's books for more than one year.

4. Stockholders' equity represents the owners' claims against the firm. Stockholders' equity includes preferred stock, the par value of common stock, paid-in capital in excess of par, and retained earnings.

C. The statement of retained earnings reconciles the net income earned during a given year and any cash dividends paid with the change in retained earnings between the beginning and end of the year.

D. The statement of cash flows provides a summary of the firm's cash inflows and outflows over the course of the year. This statement is sometimes called a "source and use statement".

III. **Depreciation is the allocation of the historical cost of fixed assets over time.**

A. For tax purposes, the depreciation of corporations' fixed assets is determined using the Accelerated Cost Recovery System (ACRS).

B. To transform net income into cash flow from operations, one must add back depreciation and any other non-cash charges to net profits after taxes.

1. Non-cash charges are added back to net profits because these charges do not involve any cash outlay by the firm.

2. Depreciation and other non-cash charges shield the firm's income from taxes by lowering taxable income.

C. Under ACRS, the depreciable value of an asset (the amount that can be depreciated) is its full cost, including outlays for installation. No adjustment is required for expected salvage value.

1. The time period over which an asset is depreciated is called its depreciable life.

2. Under ACRS, there are six different depreciation recovery periods: 3,5,7,10,15 and 20 years.

D. For tax purposes, assets in the four shortest recovery periods are depreciated using the double-declining balance method.

1. Because ACRS uses a half-year convention, assets are assumed to be acquired in the middle of the year, so that only one-half of the first year's depreciation is recovered in the first year.

2. Given the half-year convention, the first half-year of depreciation is recovered in the year immediately following the asset's stated recovery period.

E. For financial reporting purposes, a variety of depreciation methods -- including straight-line, double-declining balance, and sum-of-years' digits -- can be used.

IV. **The statement of cash flows provides a summary of the firm's cash flows over a period of time.**

A. For reporting purposes, corporate cash flows are divided into three parts: operating flows, investing flows, and financing flows.

1. Operating cash flows are directly related to the production and role of the firm's products and services.

2. Investment cash flows are associated with purchases and roles of fixed assets and business interests.

3. Financing cash flows result from debt and equity financing transactions.

B. Sources of cash flow include decreases in assets, increases in liabilities, net profits after taxes, depreciation and other non-cash charges, and proceeds from the sale of stock.

C. Uses of cash flow includes increases in assets, decreases in liabilities, net losses, dividends paid, and funds spent on the repurchase or retirement of stock.

D. The statement of cash flows is developed in three steps:

1. Prepare a statement of sources and uses of cash.
2. Obtain necessary income statement data.
3. Properly classify and present the relevant data from Steps 1 and 2.

E. The sources and uses of cash statement requires three steps to prepare:

1. Calculate the balance sheet charges in assets, liabilities, and stockholder equity over the period of concern.

2. Classify and charge calculated in Step 1 as either a source or use of cash.

3. Separately sum all sources and all uses found in Steps 1 and 2. If the statement is prepared correctly, total sources will equal total uses.

F. Income statement data necessary to prepare the statement of cash flows include three items.

   1. Net profits after taxes.
   2. Depreciation and other non-cash charges.
   3. Cash dividends paid on common and preferred stock.

G. The statement of cash flows is completed by classifying each cash flow identified in (E) and (F) above with one of three categories.

   1. cash flows from operating activities;
   2. cash flows from investment activities; or
   3. cash flows from financing activities.

H. The net change in cash flows -- representing the sum of the cash flows from operating, investing and financing -- should equal the net increase (decrease) in cash and marketable securities for the accounting period in question.

I. The statement of cash flows allows financial managers to analyze the firm's past and future cash flow. Managers can prepare and evaluate the statement of cash flows from historical financial statements as well as projected (pro forma) financial information.

APPLICATIONS

DEFINITIONS

FASB

1. The _Financial Accounting Standards Board_ represents the rule-setting body in the accounting profession that authorizes generally accepted accounting principles.

2. Corporations whose stock is traded in either an organized security exchange or the over-the-counter exchange are known as _publicly held_.

3. The _Stockholder's report_ is a document required of publicly held corporations that summarizes for stockholders the firm's financial activities of the past year.

4. The _income_ statement provides a financial summary of the firm's operating results during a specified period.

5. _Current_ assets represent those accounts likely to be converted into cash within one year or less.

6. The cumulative total of all earnings reinvested in a corporation since its inception is known as _____.
    retained earnings

7. The statement of cash flows reconciles the firm's operating, investment, and financing cash flows with changes in the _cash_ and _balance sheet_ _marketable sec._ accounts.

8. _Depreciation_ represents the systematic charging of a portion of the costs of fixed assets against annual revenues.

9. The method used to determine the depreciation of assets for tax purposes is known as _accelerated cost recovery system_   _ACRS_

10. The _depreciable life_ of an asset represents the period of time over which it can be depreciated.

11. The value arbitrarily assigned to an issue of common stock for accounting purposes is _par_ value.

12. The _balance sheet_ is an accounting statement that summarizes the firm's position at a given point in time.

13. Expenses that are related to after-tax income that produce cash flow are known as ___ _non cash_ charges.

14. Short-term liabilities expected to be converted into cash within one year or less are known as _current_ liabilities.

15. The federal regulatory body that governs the role and listing of securities is known as the _Securities + Exchange Commission_

MULTIPLE CHOICE

1. The primary communication from management to the firm's owners is the:
   - a. president's letter.
   - b. dividend declaration.
   - c. SEC letter.
   - d. greenmail report.

2. Which of the following is not a current asset?
   - a. cash.
   - b. inventory.
   - c. accounts receivable.
   - d. machinery and equipment.

3.   Cephus Cement purchased a new machine for $40,000. It cost the company $5,000 to install the equipment. The new machine has an expected useful life of 5 years and is expected to have a salvage value of $8,000 at that time. What is the depreciable value of the new machine?
     a. $40,000.
     b. $45,000.
     c. $32,000.
     d. $37,000.

*4. Which of the following is not a use of cash?
     a.   an increase in the asset cash.
     b.   a decrease in accounts payable.
     c.   payment of dividends.
     d.   an increase in accumulated depreciation.

5.   Which of the following items is not part of the annual stockholders' report?
     a.   statement of shareholder ownership.
     b.   income statement.
     c.   statement of cash flows.
     d.   statement of retained earnings.

6.   The allocation of the historical cost of owing assets is known as:
     a.   reconciliation.
     b.   job costing.
     c.   depreciation.
     d.   amortization.

*7. Federal tax regulations that specify the depreciable life of various assets are knows as:
     a.   FASB.
     b.   SEC.
     c.   ACRS.
     d.   IRS.

8.   The statement of cash flows does not include:
     a.   cash flows from financing activities.
     b.   cash flows from marketing activities.
     c.   cash flows from operating activities.
     d.   cash flows from investment activities.

*9. Operating profit is often called:
     a.   net income.
     b.   net receipts.
     c.   earnings after tax.
     d.   earnings before interest and taxes.

10.   Which of the following accounts do not appear in the income statement?
    a.   accumulated depreciation.
    b.   interest expense.
    c.   sales revenue.
    c.   cost of goods sold.

11.   The Lap Tech Company began the year with $100,000 in retained earnings, had net profits after taxes of $20,000, and paid $15,000 in dividends. What amount of retained earnings did the firm show at the end of the year?
    a. $120,000.
    b. $105,000.
    c. $115,000.
    d. $ 95,000.

12.   According to current ACRS requirements, assets are assumed to be purchased in the _____ of the year for depreciation purposes.
    a.   beginning.
    b.   last quarter.
    c.   middle.
    d.   end.

13.   For financial reporting purposes, firms must use which of the following depreciation methods?
    a.   straight-line.
    b.   double declining balance.
    c.   sum-of-years' digits.
    d.   any of the above.

14.   The statement of cash flows should reconcile with the actual change in which of the following accounts?
    a.   net income.
    b.   cash and marketable securities.
    c.   current assets.
    d.   accumulated depreciation.

15.   The first step in preparing the statement of cash flows requires:
    a.   preparing the income statement.
    b.   examining the firm's retained earnings account.
    c.   preparing the sources and uses of cash statement.
    d.   reading the president's letter.

PROBLEMS

1.   For each of the accounts listed below, indicate in column A whether it is an income statement (IS) or balance sheet account (BS). Indicate in Column B whether the account is a current asset (CA), current liability (CL), expense (E), fixed asset (FA), long-term debt (LTD), revenue (R), or stockholder's equity (SE).

	(A) Statement	(B) Type of Account
Cash	BS	CA
Common Stock (at par)	BS	SE
Taxes	IS	E
Preferred Stock	BS	E ??
Cost of Goods Sold	IS	E
Long-Term Debt	BS	LTD
Marketable Securities	BS	CA
Sales Revenue	IS	R
Interest Expense	IS	E
Accumulated Depreciation	BS	FA ??
Common Stock Dividends	Neither	—
Inventories	BS	CA
Notes Payable	BS	CL or LTD

2.   Select the required items among those listed below to prepare the income statement for RKO Cement for the year ending December 31, 1990.

ITEM	VALUE ($000) AT OR FOR YEAR ENDED 12-31-90
Tax Rate (percent)	40
Cost of Goods Sold	$200
Depreciation	$45
Accounts Receivable	$250
Sales Revenue	$500
Selling Expense	$20
Interest Expense	$25
Accumulated Depreciation	$103
General and Administrative Expense	$40
Preferred Stock Dividends	$14
Stockholders' Equity	$200
Number of Common Shares Outstanding	50,000

440,000
- 176,000 Taxes
264,000

264,000
- 34,000 Pre.
230,000

CHAPTER 3   FINANCIAL STATEMENTS, DEPRECIATION, AND CASH FLOW   PAGE 3-10

3.   Toko Co. ended 1990 with a net profit before taxes of $440,000. The company is subject to a 40 percent tax rate and must pay $34,000 in preferred stock dividends prior to distributing any earnings on the 115,000 shares of common stock currently outstanding.

a. Calculate Toko Co.'s 1988 earnings per share (EPS). $\frac{230,000}{115,000} =$ $2.00

b. If the firm paid common stock dividends of $.80 per share, how many dollars would go to retained earnings?   230,000
- 92,000
138,000

4.   Use the appropriate items from those listed below to prepare in good form Fred Brown Company's balance sheet at December 31, 1990.

Accounts payable	$ 200
Accounts receivable	410
Accruals	45
Accumulated depreciation	200
Buildings	200
Cash	180
Common stock (at par)	70
Cost of goods sold	2,000
Depreciation expense	40
Equipment	125
Furniture and fixtures	145
General Expense	290
Inventories	340
Land	100
Long-term debts	400
Machinery	375
Marketable securities	50
Notes payable	400
Paid-in capital in excess of par	200
Preferred stock	100
Retained earnings	310
Sales	3,000

(handwritten: 2,800,000 / 200,000 = 13 x 1.14 / share)

5.   Tulsa Corporation has one issue of preferred stock and one issue of common stock outstanding. Given the items from Tulsa's stockholders' equity account shown below, determine the original price per share at which the firm sold its single issue of common stock.

Preferred stock	$125,000
Common stock ($1.00 par, 200,000 shares outstanding)	200,000
Paid-in capital in excess of par on common stock	2,600,000
Retained earnings	500,000
Total stockholders' equity	$3,425,000

6.   At the beginning of 1990, ABC Ltd. had a retained earnings balance of $600,000. During 1990 the firm earned $377,000 after taxes. From this amount, preferred stockholders were paid $47,000 in dividends. At year-end 1990 the firm's retained earnings totaled $700,000. The firm has 50,000 shares of common stock outstanding during 1990.

(handwritten: 600,000 / 377,000)

   a.   Prepare a statement of retained earnings for the year ended December 31, 1990 for the firm.

(handwritten: 977,000 / 47,000 / 930,000 / 760,000)

   b.   Calculate the firm's 1990 per share (EPS).

   c.   How large a per-share cash dividend did the firm pay on common stock during 1990?

(handwritten: 230,000)

7.   Assume that a firm had earnings after taxes of $80,000 in 1990. Depreciation charges were $28,000, and a $12,000 charge for amortization on a bond discount was incurred. What was the actual cash flow from operations?

(handwritten: 80,000 earnings + 40,000 non cash charges = 120,000)

8.   Assume that a firm expects to have earnings before depreciation and taxes (EBDT) of $320,000 in each of the next six years. It is considering the purchase of an asset costing $280,000 requiring $20,000 in installation costs, and having a recovery period of five years.

   a.   Calculate the annual depreciation for the asset purchase using the ACRS depreciation percentages in Table 3.6 in the textbook.

   b.   Calculate the annual operating cash flows for each of the six years. Assume a 40 percent ordinary tax rate.

   c.   Compare and discuss your findings in a and b.

9.   Given the information below, identify each of the following balance sheet charges as either a source (S) or use (U) of funds.

Account	1989	1990	Change
ASSETS			
Cash	$12,000	$13,000	$-1,000
Accounts Receivable	20,000	28,000	-8,000
Inventory	28,000	30,000	-2000
Net Plant and Equipment	140,000	120,000	20,000
LIABILITIES AND EQUITY			
Accounts Payable	$20,000	$15,000	$5,000
Notes Payable - Bank	25,000	26,000	-1,000
Long-term Debt	60,000	60,000	0
Common Stock	70,000	68,000	2,000
Retained Earnings	25,000	22,000	3,000

10.   An income statement and balance sheet for the Kennedy Tool and Die Company is given below. Using this information, prepare:

(A) A statement of sources and uses of cash for the period between 12/31/89 and 12/31/90; and

(B) A statement of cash flows for the year ended December 31, 1990, including:

1. Cash flow from operating activities,
2. Cash flow from investment activities, and
3. Cash flow from financing activities.

KENNEDY TOOL AND DIE COMPANY
BALANCE SHEETS
FOR YEARS 1989 AND 1990
(IN THOUSANDS)

S   *U*

ASSETS:	*Change*	1990	1989		
Cash	+100	$ 800	$ 700		100
Accounts Receivable	−100	300	400	100	
Inventory	− 300	200	500	300	
Total Current Assets		1,300	1,600		
Property, Plant and Equipment	+ 500	3,200	2,700		500
Accumulated Depreciation	+ 200	1,500	1,300	200	
Net Fixed Assets		1,700	1,400		
Total Assets		$3,000	$3,000		

LIABILITIES AND STOCKHOLDERS' EQUITY:

		1990	1989		
Accounts Payable	+100	$ 300	$ 200	100	
Notes Payable	− 200	500	700		200
Accruals	−100	200	300		100
Total Current Liabilities		1,000	1,200		
Long-term Debt	+100	1,100	1,000	100	
Total Liabilities		$2,100	$2,200		
Common Stock		$ 200	$ 200		
($1.00 par value, 200,000 shares outstanding)					
Additional paid-in-capital		400	400		
Retained earnings	+ 100	300	200	100	
Total Stockholders' Equity		900	800		
Total Liabilities and Stockholders' Equity		$3,000	$3,000		

900 900

KENNEDY TOOL AND DIE COMPANY
INCOME STATEMENT
FOR YEAR ENDING DECEMBER 31,1990

Sales Revenue	$1,900
Cost of Goods Sold	1,100
Gross Profit	800
Operating Expenses	
Selling Expense	100
General and Administrative	100
Depreciation	200
Total Operating Expense	400
Net Operating Income	400
Interest Expense	100
Profit Before Taxes	300
Taxes (at 50 percent)	150
Profit After Tax	150
Earnings per share of common stock	$0.75

SOLUTIONS

DEFINITIONS

1.   Financial Accounting Standards Board
2.   publicly held
3.   stockholders' report
4.   income
5.   current
6.   retained earnings
7.   cash; balance sheet
8.   depreciation
9.   accelerated cost recovery system
10. depreciable life
11. par
12. balance sheet
13. noncash
14. current
15. Securities and Exchange Commission

MULTIPLE CHOICE

1.	a	9.	d
2.	d	10.	a
3.	b	11.	b
4.	d	12.	c
5.	a	13.	d
6.	c	14.	b
7.	c	15.	c
8.	b		

PROBLEMS

1.

	(A) Statement	(B) Type of Account
Cash	BS	CA
Common Stock (at par)	BS	SE
Taxes	IS	E
Preferred Stock	BS	E
Cost of Goods Sold	IS	E
Long-Term Debts	BS	LTD
Marketable Securities	BS	CA
Sales Revenue	IS	R
Interest Expense	IS	E
Accumulated Depreciation	BS	FA
Common Stock Dividends	Neither	*
Inventories	BS	CA
Notes Payable	BS	CL or LTD

*   Reduces retained earnings on balance sheet

2.

Collins Cement
Income Statement
Year Ended 12/31/90

Sales Revenue		$500,000
Less: Cost of goods sold		200,000
Gross Profit		300,000
Less: Operating expenses		
Selling expense	20,000	
General and administrative	40,000	
Depreciation	45,000	
Total operating expense		105,000
Operating profit		195,000
Less: Interest expense		25,000
Net profits before taxes		170,000
Less: Taxes		68,000
Net profits after taxes		102,000
Less: Preferred dividends		14,000
Earnings per share (EPS) (50,000 shares)		$1.76

3.

a.	Net profit before taxes	$440,000
	Less: Taxes	176,000
	Income after taxes	264,000
	Less: Preferred dividends	34,000
	Earnings available to common shareholders	230,000
	EPS (115,000 shares)	$2.00
b.	Earnings available to common shareholders	$230,000
	Less: Common stock dividend	92,000
	Contribution to retained earnings	138,000

4.

Balance Sheet
Fred Brown Company
12/31/90 in ($000)

Current Assets	
Cash	$180
Marketable securities	50
Accounts receivable	410
Inventory	340
Total Current Assets	980
Gross Fixed Assets (at cost)	
Land	100
Buildings	200
Equipment	125
Machinery	375
Furniture and fixtures	145
Total fixed assets at cost	945
Less: Accumulated depreciation	200
Net Fixed Assets	745
Total Assets	$1,725

Liabilities and Stockholders' Equity

Current Liabilities	
Accounts payable	$200
Notes payable	400
Accruals	45
Total current liabilities	645
Long-term debt	400
Total Liabilities	$1,045

Stockholders' Equity	
Preferred stock	$100
Common stock (at par)	70
Paid-in capital in excess or pay	200
Retained earnings	310
Total stockholders' equity	680
Total Liabilities and Stockholders' Equity	$1,725

5.   Total paid-in capital = $200,000 + $2,600,000

                             = $2,800,000

      Price per share   = $2,800,000/200,000

                          = $14.00

6.   ABC LTD. Statement of Retained Earnings
                               Year Ended (12/31/90)

      a. Retained earnings balance (1/1/90) $600,000
          Plus: net profits after taxes (1990)   377,000
          Less: cash dividends (paid during 1990)
            Preferred stock   47,000
            Common stock   230,000
          Retained earnings balance (12/31/90) $700,000

      b. EPS = ($377,000 - $47,000)/50,000 = $6.60

      c. Dividends per share = $230,000/50,000 = $4.60

7.   Net profits after taxes $80,000
      Plus: non-cash charges
          Depreciation   28,000
          Amortization   12,000
            Total Cash Flow $120,000

8.   a. Depreciation schedule:

YEAR	COST* (1)	PERCENTAGES (FROM TABLE 3.6) (2)	DEPRECIATION [(1) x (2)]
1	$300,000	20	$60,000
2	300,000	32	96,000
3	300,000	19	57,000
4	300,000	12	36,000
5	300,000	12	36,000
6	300,000	5	15,000

    * $280 asset cost + $20,000 installation cost.

b. Cash flow schedule:

YEAR	EBDT (1)	DEPR. (2)	NET PROFIT BEFORE TAXES [(1) - (2)] (3)	TAXES [.4 x (3)] (4)	NET PROFIT AFTER TAXES [(3) - (4)] (5)	OPERATING CASH FLOWS [(2) + (5)] (6)
1	$320,000	$60,000	$260,000	$104,000	$156,000	$216,000
2	320,000	96,000	224,000	89,000	134,400	230,400
3	320,000	57,000	263,000	105,200	157,800	214,000 214,800
4	320,000	36,000	284,000	113,600	170,400	206,400
5	320,000	36,000	284,000	113,600	170,400	206,400
6	320,000	15,000	305,000	122,000	183,000	198,000

c. If the firm purchases the machine, the annual depreciation expenses will reduce net profits before taxes (Col. 3), but actually increase operating cash flow. This is because the firm will use the depreciation expense as a tax shield against income.

9.

	1989	1990	Change	Class (S) or (U)
ASSETS				
Cash	$12,000	$13,000	-$1,000	S
Accounts receivable	20,000	28,000	- 8,000	S
Inventory	28,000	30,000	- 2,000	S
Net plant and equipment	140,000	120,000	20,000	*
LIABILITIES AND EQUITY				
Accounts payable	$20,000	$15,000	$5,000	S
Notes payable - bank	25,000	26,000	- 1,000	U
Long-term debt	60,000	60,000	0	-
Common stock	70,000	68,000	2,000	S
Retained earnings	25,000	22,000	3,000	*

* Indicates items that are not directly entered, but require special adjustments.

10.   A.   A statement of sources and uses of funds is shown below. This statement lists the changes in the balance sheet accounts between 1989 and 1990. Sources and uses of cash are determined as follows:

Sources:
  1. Decrease in an asset account
  2. Increase in a liability account

Uses:
  1. Increase in an asset account
  2. Decrease in an liability account

STATEMENT OF SOURCES AND USES OF CASH FOR
KENNEDY TOOL AND DIE COMPANY
BETWEEN YEAR-END 1989 AND 1990

ACCOUNT	1990	1989	CHANGE	SOURCE	USE
ASSETS:					
Cash	$800	$700	+$100		$100
Accounts Receivable	300	400	-100	$100	
Inventory	200	500	-300	300	
Property, Plant, and Equipment	3,200	2,700	+500		500
Accumulated Depreciation	1,500	1,300	+200	200	
LIABILITIES:					
Accounts Payable	500	700	-200		200
Notes Payable	500	700	-200		200
Accruals	200	300	-100		100
Long-term Debt	1,100	1,000	+100	100	
EQUITY:					
Common Stock (at par)	200	200			
Additional Paid-in Capital in excess of par	400	400			
Retained Earnings	300	200	+100	100	
TOTALS				900	900

B. Before completing a statement of cash flows, several items of interest must be taken from the firm's balance sheet. These are:
  1. Profit after tax,
  2. Depreciation and other noncash charges (amortization and/or depletion), and
  3. Cash dividends paid to stockholders.

In this case:

	(Thousands)
1. Profit after tax	$150
2. Depreciation	200
3. Dividends paid	50

This amount is found using the following formula:

Dividends = profit after tax - change in retained earnings
= $150 - 100
= $50

Using this information, a statement of cash flows can be assembled as shown below:

KENNEDY TOOL AND DIE COMPANY
STATEMENT OF CASH FLOWS FOR 1990
(IN THOUSANDS OF DOLLARS)

Cash flow from operating activities:

Profit after taxes	$150
Depreciation	200
Decrease in accounts receivable	100
Decrease in inventory	300
Increase in accounts payable	100
Decrease in accruals	(100)
Cash provided by operating activities	$750

Cash flow from investment activities:

Increase in property, plant and equipment	($500)
Changes in business interests	0
Cash used for investment	($500)

Cash flow from financing activities:

Decrease in notes payable	($200)
Increase in long-term debt	100
Changes in stockholders' equity	0
Dividends paid	(50)
Cash used for financing activities	(150)

Net increase in cash	$100

Notice that the net increase in cash figure from the statement of cash flows concurs with the change in the cash account on the firm's balance sheet.

CHAPTER 4

THE TIME VALUE OF MONEY

SUMMARY

The time value of money represents an important concept that is used repeatedly in finance. This concept suggests that a dollar received today is worth more than a dollar received at a later date, because the recipient of today's dollar can obtain immediate satisfaction from consumption or earn a rate of return from investment.

Because dollars received today can be invested to yield returns, the future value of a given amount exceeds its present value. The relationship between present and future value is described by compound interest, where the interest earned on a given principal balance is computed and added to the principal balance at the conclusion of the compounding period. As the principal balance grows larger through time with the repeated application of compound interest, the future value of today's dollars grows larger and larger.

The concept of present value, which involves discounting future cash flows back to the present, represents the inverse of compounding. Because today's dollars can be invested to earn interest through time, the receipt of cash at some point in the future is necessarily worth less in the present period. The procedure for finding the present value of a future amount involves discounting future cash flows at an appropriate interest rate back to the present.

In addition to finding the present and future values associated with individual cash flows, the time value of money is useful for evaluating streams of cash flow. These streams include mixed cash flows, or streams of cash that vary in amount from period to period; and annuity streams, which represent equal cash flows received period after period. In order to simplify financial calculations, these annuity streams can be treated as a group to find their present and future values.

Calculations involving the time value of money are made easier by the availability of financial calculators and interest factor tables. Both of these tools allow rapid computation of exponential equations for present and future values of annuities and individual cash flows. In addition, ordinary annuities, or streams of equal cash payments made at the end of each year, can be quickly converted to annuities due, or streams of cash payments made at the beginning of each year, on financial calculators and interest factor tables.

Aside from directly determining future amounts and present values, a number of important applications of compound interest and present-value techniques exist. The annual end-of-year payments necessary to accumulate a future amount can be found by dividing the interest factor for the future value of an annuity for the appropriate life and interest rate into the desired future sum. In order to amortize a loan (i.e., convert it into equal annual payments), the amount of the loan can be divided by the interest factor for the present value of an annuity for the appropriate life and interest rate. An interest or growth rate associated with a stream of cash flows can be determined by dividing the earliest value by the most recent value to obtain what is equivalent to the interest factor for the present value of one dollar. Indexing the table for the appropriate number of years and finding the interest factor closest to that calculated will indicate the approximate rate of growth.

Finally, the time value of money can be used to find the present value of a perpetuity, or annuity with an infinite life, by dividing the annual payment by the appropriate interest rate.

CONCEPT OUTLINE

I.   **Future value involves the application of compound interest to an initial principal balance to generate a future amount.**

    A.   Compounding refers to the fact that, after interest is earned on the amount initially deposited (i.e., initial principal) at the end of the first compounding period, it becomes part of the principal on which interest is earned in the next compounding period.

    B.   The formula for future value is

$$F_n = P(1 + k)^n,$$

Where F = the amount of money at the end of period n
      P = the initial principal
      k = the annual rate of interest paid on the account
      n = the number of periods the money is left in the account

    C.   A table of interest factors for the future value of one dollar deposited at the start of the year can be used to simplify compound-interest calculations.

        1.   The table gives the value of $FVIF = (1+K)^n$, which is indexed for a given interest rate, k, and a specified period of time, n.

        2.   The future-value interest factor for a single amount is always greater than one.

        3.   By multiplying the interest factor from the table for the future value of one dollar by the present amount, the future amount can be found.

        4.   The interest factor for the future value of one dollar increases as both interest rate and time increase.

D.   Sometimes one needs to find the future value when interest is being compounded more often than once a year (i.e., intrayear compounding).

   1.   The general formula for the future sum in this case is

$$F_n = P \left(1 + \frac{k}{n}\right)^{m \times n}.$$

   All variables are as defined earlier, and m represents the number of times per year interest is compounded.

   2.   As interest is compounded more frequently (i.e., m increases), the future value of a given sum will increase.

   3.   By indexing a table for the future value of one dollar (Table A-1 in the Appendix) for [k/m] percent and m x n years, an interest factor for use when interest is compounded m times per year at k percent for n years can be obtained.

E.   The nominal rate of interest represents the contractual rate charged by a lender or provided by a borrower. The effective rate of interest, or annual percentage rate (APR) represents the rate of interest actually paid or earned on a particular transaction.

   1.   The formula for calculating the effective rate of interest is

$$k_{eff} = \left(1 + \frac{k}{m}\right)^{m} - 1.$$

   2.   In consumer finance transactions, federal law requires the effective rate to be clearly stated for borrowers and depositors.

II.   **An annuity represents a stream of equal cash flows. These inflows can be inflows of returns earned on investments or outflows of funds invested in order to earn future returns.**

   A.   The two basic types of annuities are the ordinary annuity and annuity due

   1.   An ordinary annuity is an annuity for which the payments occur at the end of each time period.

   2.   An annuity due is an annuity for which the payments occur at the beginning of each time period.

B.   The future value of an ordinary annuity can be found using basic future-value interest techniques.

1. The formula for the future value of an ordinary annuity is

$$FVA_n = PMT \times (FVIFA_{k,n}) ,$$

where ($FVIFA_{k,n}$) represents the future value interest factor of an ordinary annuity at k percent for n periods).

2.   Table A-2 in the Appendix provides the interest factors for finding the future value of ordinary annuities.

3.   The formula for the future value interest factor of an ordinary annuity is

$$FVIFA_{k,n} - \sum_{t=1}^{n} (1 + k)^{t-1}$$

4.   The compound value of an annuity has similar properties to the compound value of one dollar, in that it increases as both interest and time increase.

C.   The future value of an annuity due can also be found by using basic future value interest techniques.

1.   A simple conversion of the future value interest factors for ordinary annuities provides the future value interest factors for annuities due. In this conversion, the ordinary annuity interest factors are multiplied by (1+k):

$$FVIFA_{k,n} \text{ (annuity due)} = FVIFA_{k,n} \times (1 + k).$$

2.   The formula for the future value of an annuity due is

$$FVIFA_s = PMT \times [FVIFA_{k,n}(\text{annuity due})].$$

3.   For a given number of payments (n) and interest rate (k), the future value of an annuity due is always greater than the future value of an ordinary annuity.

III.   **The calculation of present values is important in assessing a firm's value and other financial decisions.**

T

A.   Present value, as future value, is based on the general belief that money has time value.

1.   Present value is based on the fact that one dollar today is worth more than one dollar at some future date.

2.   The present value of a future amount depends on the earning opportunities of the recipient and on when the money is to be received.

B.   The process of finding present value is the opposite of that for future value.

1.   The present value represents how much a future amount is worth today if the decision maker has an opportunity to earn a certain return.

2.   This required return is often called the discount rate, the cost of capital, or the opportunity cost.

C.   The formula for the present value of dollar, P, is

$$P - \frac{F_n}{(1 + k)^n} - F_n \times \left[\frac{1}{(1 + k)^n} \right],$$

where the variables are the same as those defined earlier.

D.   In order to simplify present-value calculations, a table for the present-value interest factors for one dollar is available in Table A-3.

1.   The table presents values for $1/(1+k)^n$ at various discount rates, k, and periods of time, n.

2.   The present-value factor for a single amount is always less than one.

3.   By indexing the table for the appropriate discount rate, k, and number of years, n, the appropriate present-value interest factor is obtained, which when multiplied by the future amount, F_n, yields its present value, P.

4.   The present-value interest factor decreases as both the discount rate and the number of years increase.

E. In comparing the equations for present and future value interest factors, notice that these factors are inverse expressions of one another.

IV **Finding the present value of cash flow streams is an important activity to financial managers.**

T

A. A mixed stream of cash flows reflects no particular pattern, whereas an annuity stream is a pattern of equal annual cash flows.

B. The present value of a mixed stream of cash flows can be found by determining and then summing the present value of each of the individual cash flows.

C. The present value of an annuity stream can be found by using the present value interest factors for an annuity. These factors are shows in Table A-4 in the Appendix.

1. The formula for the present value of an annuity is

$$PVA_n = PMT \times (PVIFA_{k,n}),$$

where $(PVIFA_{k,n})$ represents the present value interest factor for an annuity at k percent for n periods.

2. The formula for the present value interest factor of an annuity is

$$PVIFA_{k,n} - \sum_{t-1}^{n} PVIF_{k,n},$$

where $(PVIF_{k,n})$ represents the present value interest factor for a single sum.

D. The present value interest factor of an annuity decreases with increases in the interest rate (k), and increases with increases in the number of time periods for the annuity (n).

V. **Future-value and present-value techniques can be used to solve a variety of problems in personal and managerial financial management.**

T

A. The annual end-of-year payments necessary to accumulate a given future amount can be determined by dividing the future amount by the appropriate future value interest factor of an ordinary annuity:

$$PMT \ - \ \frac{FVA_n}{FVIFA_{k,n}} \ .$$

B.   The annual payment necessary to amortize a loan (i.e., convert it to equal annual payments) can be found by dividing the principal balance of the loan by the present value interest factor of an annuity:

$$PMT \ - \ \frac{PVA_n}{PVIFA_{k,n}} \ .$$

C.   The interest rate or growth rate associated with a stream of cash flows can be found in two steps.

     1.   The first step is to divide the earliest value by the most recent value to obtain what is equivalent to an interest factor for the present value of one dollar.

     2.   By indexing the present value of one dollar table for the appropriate number of years, the interest rate associated with the interest factor closest to the calculated interest factor is the interest or growth rate for the stream.

     3.   When the computed factor falls between two table factors, interpolation may be used to get a more exact answer.

D.   The present value of a perpetuity, which is an infinite-lived annuity, can be found by multiplying the amount of the annuity by the interest factor for the present value of a perpetuity, which is calculated by dividing the discount rate into 1:

$$PV \ (perpetuity) \ - \ PMT \times \left[\frac{1}{k} \right] \ .$$

APPLICATIONS

DEFINITIONS

1.   The value of a present sum at a future date found by applying compound interest over a specified period of time is known as *future value*

2.   _Compounded interest_ represents interest earned on a given deposit that has become part of the principal at the end of a specified period.

3.   A _principal_ balance is the amount of money on which interest is paid.

4.   The multiplier used to calculate the future value of a present amount is known as a _future value interest factor_

5.   When interest is compounded an infinite number of times each year, a _continuous_ compounding interval exists.

6.   The contractual rate of interest charged by a lender or promised by a borrower is the _nominal_ interest rate.

7.   A stream of equal annual cash flows is called an _annuity_

8.   Consumer lenders are required by law to express borrowing costs in the form of an _annual percentage rate_ of interest.

9.   Annuities for which the payments occur at the beginning of the year are called _annuities due_ annuities, while annuities for which payments occur at the end of the year represent _ordinary_ annuities

10.   An annuity with an infinite life is known as a _perpetuity_

11.   The rate of interest actually paid or earned in a financial transaction is known as an _effective_ rate of interest.

12.   The multiplier used to calculate the future value of an _ordinary_ annuity is known as the future value interest factor of an annuity.

13.   The process of finding the present value of a future amount is known as _discounting_ cash flows.

14.   A loan _amortization schedule_ shows the equal payments necessary to repay the loan.

15.   A group of unequal cash flows that reflect no particular pattern represents a _mixed_ stream.

MULTIPLE CHOICE

(Do not use calculators or tables on questions 1 through 10).

1.   The concept of compound interest refers to:
      a.   earning interest on a single deposit from more than one source.
      b.   adding interest to principal at the end of a specified period.
      c.   receiving interest more than once a year.
      d.   earning a rate of interest of 10 percent or higher.

2.   The future value of an initial deposit _____ both with increases in the interest rate and with the passage of time.
      a.   increases.
      b.   decreases.
      c.   first increases, then decreases.
      d.   first decreases, then increases.

3.   The compound value of $1 earning 10 percent interest would be _____ in 3 years?
      a. $1.30.
      b. $0.83.
      c. $1.33.
      d. $3.30.

4.   Which of the factors below is the compound value interest factor of $1 for 8 years at 3 percent?
      a.   1.000.
      b.   1.267.
      c.   0.839.
      d.   0.789.

5.   Sam deposited $1,000 in the Collinsville State Bank on January 1, 1975. December 31, 1987, that deposit had grown to $2,000. What was the approximate annual rate of return on his investment?
      a.   12 percent.
      b.   100 percent.
      c.   3 percent.
      d.   6 percent.

6.   The more frequently interest is compounded, the _____ the effective interest rate.
      a.   safer.
      b.   higher.
      c.   lower.
      d.   less predictable.

7.   An ordinary annuity is a stream of _____ payments that come at the _____ of each
      period.
      a.   equal, end.
      b.   cash, end.
      c.   expected, beginning.
      d.   equal, beginning.

8.   The current value of a future sum is called?
      a.   an annuity.
      b.   the opportunity cost.
      c.   the present value.
      d.   a delayed payment.

9.   For a given discount rate, the present value of a dollar _____ with the passage of time.
      a.   increases.
      b.   remains constant.
      c.   decreases.
      d.   none of the above.

10.   Which of the following is the present value interest factor for a five year annuity at 8
      percent?
      a.   40.00.
      b.   1.32.
      c.   5.08.
      d.   3.99.

(You may use calculators or tables on the remaining questions).

11.   According to the data below, at what annual rate has the price of Blug Laundry Powder's
      common stock been growing?

Year	Price
1988	$2.50
1987	2.20
1986	1.95
1985	1.65
1984	1.25

      a.   100 percent.
      b.   50 percent.
      c.   72 percent.
      d.   18 percent.

12.   The effective rate of interest associated with a 6 percent nominal rate of return when interest is compounded monthly is:

   $$K_{eff} = \left(1 + \frac{.06}{12}\right)^{12} - 1$$

  a. 6.14 percent.
  b. 6.09 percent.
  c. 6.17 percent.
  d. 6 percent.

13.   Given the same interest rate (k), number of payments (n), and compounding interest (m), the future value interest factor of an annuity due is _____ _____ the future value interest factor of an ordinary annuity.

  a. smaller than.
  b. larger than.
  c. equal to.
  d. unrelated to.

14.   A loan _____ schedule shows the equal annual loan payments necessary to provide a lender with a specified interest return and repay the loan principal over a specified period of time.

  a. repayment.
  b. payoff.
  c. review.
  d. amortization.

15.   A perpetuity provides a specific cash payment for how many years?

  a. 10.
  b. $(1.10)^{10}$.
  c. infinite number.
  d. impossible to determine.

in three years

PROBLEMS

Comp. every 6 mo.

Periods	%	Factor
6	6%	1.419 — 4257
9	4%	1.423 — 4269
12	3%	1.426 — 4278
18	2%	1.428 — 4284

1. Daniel Busch is attempting to evaluate each of the following situations. Help him answer each of the following questions.

a. If I deposit $3,000 today into an account paying interest of 12 percent, compounded annually, and leave my money on deposit for three years, how much will I have?

3% → $4,214.78$

b. If the interest is compounded every six months, four months, three months, or two months, how much would the future amounts be? Why?

6% = 4257

c. If, instead of depositing $3,000 now, I were to deposit $3,000 at the end of each year for the next three years into the same account paying 12 percent, compounded annually, how much would I have at the end of the three years?

$3.374 \cdot 3000 = 10,122$

2. Suppose Boone Phillips were to deposit $1,000 into a savings account one year from now, $2,000 two years from now, $3,000 three years from now, and $1,000 four years from now. How much would be in the account, which pays annual interest of 8 percent, at the end of five years?

1000	4	1.360 =	1360
2000	3	1.260	2520
3000	2	1.166	3498
1000	1	1.080 —	1080

3. Calculate the present value of $10,000 to be received 14 years from now if the decision maker's opportunity cost is 10 percent.

$10,000 \cdot .263 = 2630$

4. Determine the present value at 9 percent of each of the following five-year cash inflow streams. Assume that cash inflows occur at the end of the year.

Year	Stream A	Stream B
1	$8,000	$10,000
2	9,000	10,000
3	10,000	10,000
4	11,000	10,000
5	12,000	10,000

$10,000 \cdot .389 = 38,900$

5. Use the formula given in the text to solve for the future-value interest factor of an annuity for 10 percent for 5 years. Check your answer with the FVIFA$_{k,n}$ table.

6. Use the formula for the present-value interest factor of an annuity to solve the PVIFA$_{8,3}$. Compare this number with the table value.

7. Compute the effective interest rate if the nominal rate is 12% and the amount is compounded:

$$K_{eff} = \left(1 + \frac{k}{m}\right)^m - 1$$

   a. semi-annually.
   b. quarterly.
   c. monthly.

T

8. If an individual wishes to accumulate $15,000 in six years by making equal annual end-of-year deposits into an account paying 7 percent interest, how large should the deposits be?

$$PMT = \frac{FVA_n}{FVIFA_{k,n}} = \frac{15,000}{7.153} = 2097$$

Future Value of an Annuity

T

9. A lender wishes to determine the size of the equal annual end-of-year payments necessary to fully amortize a $4,000 loan at 11 percent interest over three years. How large should the payments be?

T

T

Present Value of an annuity

$$\frac{4000}{2.444} = 1636.66$$

10. Find the compound annual growth rate associated with the following cash flows:

   a. To the nearest 1 percent.
   b. Interpolate to the nearest 1/100 of 1 percent.

T

Year	Cash Flow
1988	$298
1987	275
1986	260
1985	227
1984	209
1983	200

11.   Determine the present value of a perpetuity of $1,000 discounted at the firm's opportunity rate of 8 percent.

T

12.   Your younger sister will be attending Hibbard College 19 years from today. It will cost $20,000 per year, payable at the beginning of each year, for each of her four years in college, how much will your family need to save for the next 19 years at 6 percent to pay for your sister's education?

T

SOLUTIONS

DEFINITIONS

1.   future value
2.   compounded interest
3.   principal
4.   future value interest factor
5.   continuous
6.   nominal or stated
7.   annuity
8.   annual percentage rate
9.   ordinary; annuities due
10.   perpetuity
11.   effective
12.   ordinary
13.   discounting
14.   amortization schedule
15.   mixed

MULTIPLE CHOICE

1.	b	9.	c
2.	a	10.	d
3.	c	11.	d
4.	b	12.	c
5.	d	13.	b
6.	b	14.	d
7.	a	15.	c
8.	c		

PROBLEMS

1.

a. In order to find the future sum, the interest factor for the future value of one dollar deposited for three years at 12 percent must be obtained (Table A-1 in the Appendix) and multiplied by the amount of the deposit (i.e., $3,000). From Table A-1, the interest factor for the future value of one dollar at 12 percent for three years is 1.405:

Future sum = (1.405) x ($3,000) = $4,215.

b. In order to evaluate the four alternate compounding periods, the appropriate interest factors to use in indexing the future value of one dollar table (Table A-1) must be found:

Compounding Period (months) (1)	Frequency of Compounding [12/(1)] (2)	Number of Periods (years) (3)	Period Factor [(2) x (3)] (4)	Stated Interest Rate (5)	Interest Factor [(5)/(2)] (6)
6	2	3	6	12%	6%
4	3	3	9	12	4
3	4	3	12	12	3
2	6	3	18	12	2

Finding the interest factor in the table for the future value of one dollar (Table A-1), using the year factor given in column (4) and the interest factor given in column (6), and multiplying this factor by the $3000 deposit yields the future sum for each case. The calculation is given in tabular form:

Compounding Period (months) (1)	Period Factor (2)	Interest Factor (3)	Future Value Interest Factor (Table A-1) (4)	Deposit (5)	Future Sum (End of Year 3) [(4) x (5)] (6)
6	6	6%	1.419	$3,000	$4,257
4	9	4	1.423	3,000	4,269
3	12	3	1.426	3,000	4,278
2	18	2	1.428	3,000	4,284

Comparing the future sum of $4,215 calculated in part (a) for annual compounding with the results obtained in column (6), it can be seen that the shorter the compounding period (or the more often interest is compounded, the greater the future sum realized for a given annual interest rate (i.e., 12 percent) and time horizon (i.e., three years).

c.   If $3,000 were deposited into an account paying 12 percent annual interest over a three-year-period, the future sum could be found with the aid of a table for the compound-value interest factors for a one dollar annuity (Table A-2 in the Appendix). The future amount could be found by identifying the interest factor for 12 percent and three years for the future value of an annuity, and multiplying this interest factor by the $3,000 annuity. From Table A-2, the interest factor for the future value of an annuity at 12 percent for three years is 3.374:

Future sum of the annuity = (3.374) x ($3,000) = $10,122.

2.   The deposits can be viewed as having been made at the end of the first, second, third, and fourth year. The important point to keep in mind in evaluating this problem is that the deposits will earn interest for four, three, two, and one year, respectively. The required calculations are presented in tabular form:

Deposit (1)	Deposited at End of Year (2)	Number of Years Earning Interest [5 years - (2)] (3)	Interest Rate (4)	Future Value Interest Factor (Table A-1) (5)	Sum at End of Year 5 [(1) x (5)] (6)
$1,000	1	4	8%	1.360	$1,360
2,000	2	3	8	1.260	2,520
3,000	3	2	8	1.166	3,498
1,000	4	1	8	1.080	1,080
TOTAL					$8,458

3.　　To find the present value of the future amount, the present-value interest factor for 10 percent and 14 years must be obtained from a table for the present-value interest factors for one dollar (Table A-3 in the Appendix) and multiplied by the $10,000 to be received in the future. From Table A-3, the interest factor for the present value of one dollar discounted at 10 percent for 14 yrs is 0.263:

Present value = (0.263) x ($10,000) = $2,367.　??

2630

4.　　Cash-inflow stream A is a mixed stream, whereas cash-inflow stream B is an annuity. Because B is an annuity, a shortcut is available, using a table for the present-value interest factors for a one dollar annuity (Appendix Table A-4). The present value of the mixed stream must be found by finding the present value of each cash inflow for the appropriate number of years and the 9 percent rate, using the interest factors for the present value of one dollar (Table A-3). The required calculations for stream A are as follows:

Year	Cash Inflow (1)	Present Value Interest Factor (Table A-3) (2)	Present Value [(1) x (2)] (3)
1	$8,000	0.917	$7,336
2	9,000	0.842	7,578
3	10,000	0.772	7,720
4	11,000	0.708	7,788
5	12,000	0.650	7,800
TOTAL			$38,222

The present value of stream B can be found by multiplying the interest factor for the present value of a five-year annuity discounted at 9 percent by the amount of the annuity ($10,000). From Table A-4, the interest factor for the present value of a five-year annuity discounted at 9 percent is 3.890:

Present value of stream B = (3.890) x ($10,000) = $38,900.

5.

$$FVIFA_{10,5} - \sum_{t-1}^{5} (1.10)^{t-1}$$

Time (t)	$(1.10)^{t-1}$	Factor Value
1	$(1.10)^0$	1.000
2	$(1.10)^1$	1.100
3	$(1.10)^2$	1.210
4	$(1.10)^3$	1.331
5	$(1.10)^4$	1.461
TOTAL		6.105

Notice that the value of $FVIFA_{10,5}$ from Table A-2 is also 6.105.

6.

$$PVIFA_{8,3} \ - \ \sum_{t=1}^{3} (1 + k)^t$$

Time (t)	$1/(1.08)^t$	Factor Value
1	$1/(1.08)^1$	0.9259
2	$1/(1.08)^2$	0.8573
3	$1/(1.08)^3$	0.7938
TOTAL		2.5770

Notice that the value of $PVIFA_{8,3}$ from Table A-3 is also 2.5770.

7.   Using the equation given in the text:

$$k_{eff} \ - \ \left(1 + \frac{k}{m}\right)^m - 1 \ .$$

a.

$$k_{eff} \ - \ \left(1 + \frac{.12}{2}\right)^2 - 1 \ - \ 12.36\%$$

b.

$$k_{eff} = \left[1 + \frac{.12}{4}\right]^4 - 1 = 12.55\%$$

c.

$$k_{eff} = \left[1 + \frac{.12}{12}\right]^{12} - 1 = 12.68\%$$

8.   The size of the deposits can be found by dividing the interest factor for the future value of an annuity (Table A-2) for six years, 7 percent into the desired future sum (i.e., $15,000). According to Table A-2, the interest factor for the future value of an annuity for six years, 7 percent is 7.153:

$$\text{Annual Deposit} = \frac{\$15,000}{7.1530} = \$2,097.02$$

9.   The loan payments can be determined by dividing the interest factor for the present value of an annuity (Table A-4) at 11 percent for three years into the $4,000 loan principal. From Table A-4, the interest factor for the present value of a three-year annuity at 11 percent is 2.444:

$$\text{Annual Loan Payment} = \frac{\$4,000}{2.444} = \$1,636.66$$

10.   a.   A number equivalent to an interest factor for the compound value of one dollar can be obtained by dividing the earliest value ($200 in 1983) by the most recent value ($295 in 1988):

$$\text{Factor} = \frac{\$200}{\$295} = 0.678$$

Because the six years shown represent five years of growth, using the table for the present value interest factor for one dollar, the interest factor closest to .678 is (.681), which occurs at 8 percent. The growth rate of the stream to the nearest 1 percent, therefore, is 8 percent.

b.   Since .678 does not equal the table value (.681) exactly, the actual growth rate is not 8 percent. Because the computed factor lies between the table factors for 8 and 9 percent, the actual interest rate is between 8 and 9 percent. To get a more exact rate using interpolation:

Step 1:   The difference between the 8 and 9 percent table factors is

$0.681 - 0.650 = 0.031.$

Step 2:   The absolute difference between the calculated factor and the 8 percent table factor is:

$0.681 - 0.678 = 0.003.$

Step 3: $0.003/0.031 = 0.10.$

Step 4:   The growth rate is $(8 + 0.10)$ percent, or 8.1 percent.

11.   The present-value interest factor for a perpetuity, which is an infinite-lived annuity, is found by dividing the discount rate into 1:

$$PVIV_{8,infinite} = \frac{1.00}{0.08} = 12.5$$

Multiplying the present-value interest factor for the perpetuity by its amount (i.e., $1,000) yields its present value:

Present value of perpetuity of $1,000 at 8% = (12.5)($1,000) = $12,500.

12.   First find the sum necessary in year 19 to provide $20,000 per year, for each of the four years your sister will attend college. Notice that this represents $20,000 for her first year's tuition, followed by a $20,000 annuity for three years:

Needed sum = $20,000 x $(PVIFA_{6\%,3years})$ + $20,000

= $20,000 x (2.673) + $20,000 = $73,460.

In 19 years, your family must have $73,460.

Second, what sum deposited each year and earning 6% will grow to $73,460?

$73,460 = PMT x $(FVIFA_{6\%, 19 years})$

$73,460 = PMT x (33.769)

$$PMT = \frac{\$73,460}{33.760} = \$2,176 \text{ per year.}$$

CHAPTER 5

RISK AND RETURN

SUMMARY

In this chapter the two determinants of share price, risk and return, are defined, and the concepts of diversification and portfolios are explained. Because of the importance and complexity of the concepts covered in this chapter, students should plan to give this material extra time and attention.

 Risk is considered present when the probability distributions of returns are known, whereas uncertainty is considered present when the probability distributions are unknown. Return is measured as the total gain or loss from an investment over a given time period from both changes in market value and cash distributions. Return is frequently stated as a percentage. Managers may have risk-indifferent, risk-averse, or risk-taking behaviors; most are risk averse, meaning they require an increase in return for accepting a given increase in risk.

Approaches commonly used to get a feel for asset risk include evaluating estimates of potential asset returns, such as pessimistic, most likely, and optimistic, graphic representations such as a bar chart or probability distribution, and statistical measures including the standard deviation and the coefficient of variation. The farther into the future returns are to be received, the greater the variability of these returns.

The correlation between assets in a portfolio greatly affects the overall risk of the portfolio. Assets with negatively correlated returns provide the best combination for minimizing overall risk, but as long as assets have less than perfect correlation, there are portfolio gains available through diversification.

A trade-off exists between risk and return. In a perfect world of efficient markets, the only relevant risk is the nondiversifiable risk, which cannot be eliminated since it is attributed to changes in the economy. The diversifiable risk can be eliminated through diversification. The nondiversifiable risk can be measured by beta. The capital asset pricing model (CAPM) uses beta to relate an asset's risk relative to the market to the asset's required return. The capital asset pricing model is given by the following equation:

$$k_j = R_F + b_j \times (k_m - R_F)$$

 The required return on asset j, k_j is the sum of the return on a risk-free asset, R_F, plus a risk premium, $b_j \times (k_m - R_F)$, which reflects the asset's (relevant) risk relative to the market. The security market line (SML) graphically illustrates the associated required return for each level of nondiversifiable risk (i.e., beta).

CONCEPT OUTLINE

I.   **Financial decisions affect the risk and return characteristics of the firm; therefore, one must understand risk and return and related risk preference concepts.**

A. Risk and return are the two primary determinants of share price, and, hence, owner wealth.

B. Risk can be defined as the chance of loss. Assets which have greater chances of loss are considered more risky.

C. Return is measured as the total gain or loss experienced on behalf of the owner over a given period of time. Stated as a percentage, it can be computed for a specific holding period as:

$$k_t = \frac{P_t - P_{t-1} + C_t}{P_{t-1}}$$

where: k_t =   actual, expected, or required rate of return during period t.
P_t =   price (value) of stock at time t (ending price).
P_{t-1} =   price (value) of stock at time t-1 (beginning price).
C_t =   cash dividends paid in the time period t-1 to t.

1. Return is measure as the total gain or loss from an investment over a given time period from both changes in market value and cash distributions.

2. In an efficient market, price is continuously adjusting so that the expected return equals the required return.

3. Actual returns may be calculated with this model after the ending price is known; it is an ex post value.

4. After the period, one may compare actual to required returns.

5. By dividing by the beginning price, P_{t-1}, one is calculating the return as a percentage of the original investment.

6. There is a positive relationship between risk and return. As risk increases return also increases.

D. Three different behavioral attitudes toward risk are:

1. Risk-indifferent which requires no increase in return for given increases in risk.

2. Risk-averse which requires an increase in return for a given increase in risk.

3. Risk-taking which is satisfied with a decrease in return for given increase in risk.

4. Most investors are risk-averse.

5. Although agency theory suggests managers may have different attitudes toward risks, the managers should make decisions as if their risk preferences were the same as the firm's owners.

II. **One must understand basic risk concepts in order to evaluate financial alternatives.**

A. The terms risk and uncertainty are used interchangeably to refer to the variability of possible returns associated with an asset.

1. If future returns were know with certainty, there would be no risk.

2. One measures the risk of a single asset in a portfolio in the same way one measures the risk of a portfolio, or collection of assets.

3. Special diversification advantages accrue to those who hold portfolios.

B. Sensitivity analysis is a simple, behavioral view of risk. It allows one to get a feel for the variability of returns.

1. Using sensitivity analysis forces the decision maker to consider the sensitivity of the asset to various changes in the company, industry, and economy, plus the likelihood of the various conditions.

2. Often the worst, most likely, and best (pessimistic, expected, and optimistic) returns are estimated.

3. The range - the difference between the best and the worst returns - provides the most basic measure of risk. (The larger the difference or range, the greater the risk).

C. Probabilities more accurately assess the risk involved in an asset. The probability that an event will occur may be viewed as the percentage chance of occurrence.

1. The expected value of return, or mean, of a probability distribution is indicative of the most likely outcome. It is computed using the following equation:

$$\bar{k} = \sum_{i=1}^{n} (k_i \times Pr_i)$$

where k   = expected value of return
      k_i = outcome or return i
      Pr_i = probability of outcome i actually occurring
      n   = number of outcomes considered

and

$$\sum_{i=1}^{n} (Pr_i) = 1$$

the sum of all probabilities is 1.

2. The simplest probability distribution is the discrete distribution, which can be illustrated with a bar chart. The continuous probability distribution shows the probability for each possible outcome.

3. The standard deviation from the mean, σ, is the most commonly used measure of risk. It is given by the following equation:

$$\sigma_k = \sum_{i=1}^{n} (k_i - \bar{k})^2 \, Pr_i$$

where the variables are as defined earlier.

4. The coefficient of variation, CV, allows one to assess the relative riskiness of assets with differing expected values. This value is calculated by dividing the standard deviation by the expected return:

$$CV = \frac{\sigma_k}{\bar{k}}$$

5. Risk can be viewed not only with respect to the current time period, but as an increasing function of time. The farther in time one forecasts asset returns, the more variable, and thus the more risky, the forecast values are.

D. Holders of assets should be viewed as having a portfolio of assets selected in a manner consistent with the goal of wealth maximization.

   1. The return on a portfolio is the weighted average of returns on the individual assets. It is calculated as follows:

$$k_p = \sum_{j=1}^{n} (w_j \times k_j)$$

   2. Assets selected must be those that best diversify (reduce) the risk while generating an acceptable return.

   3. This will result in portfolio risk that is less than the sum of the risks of the separate assets.

   4. Correlation, a measure of the statistical relationship between series of numbers (such as two probability distributions), must be understood in order to create efficient portfolios - those that achieve a maximum return for a given amount of risk.

   5. The correlation coefficient, the statistical measure of correlation, has a range from +1 to -1. Projects with positive correlation coefficients move together, while those with negative correlation coefficients move counter-cyclically.

 E. To diversify and reduce risk and create an efficient portfolio, the assets that are best combined are those that have negative (or low positive) correlation with existing assets.

   1. By combining less than perfectly positive correlated assets, the overall variability of returns can be reduced.

 2. The combination of two perfectly correlated assets cannot lower portfolio risk below the least of the separate risks.

 3. Combining two assets with perfect negative correlation (correlation coefficient = -1) can result in a zero risk investment.

4. For each pair of assets, there is some combination that will result in the lowest possible risk.

5. The best strategy is to diversify a firm's or stockholder's risk across assets in order to either maximize the return for a given level of risk or minimize the risk for a given level of return. A portfolio which meets these objectives is referred to as an efficient portfolio.

III. **A key consideration in financial decision making involves the trade-off between risk and return.**

A. The basic theory with respect to the risk-return trade-off is the capital asset pricing model (CAPM).

   1. The CAPM was developed primarily to explain the behavior of security prices and to provide a mechanism whereby investors could readily assess the impact of a proposed security investment on their portfolio risk and return.

   2. The most important aspect of risk is the overall risk of the firm as perceived by investors in the marketplace. Thus, an understanding of this risk is important, since it affects the owner's wealth.

   3. Alternatively, arbitrage pricing theory suggests that equity returns are a function of a number of unidentified factors in addition to the systematic risk and the return on the market.

B. The CAPM relies on a number of assumptions related to the efficiency of the markets and investors' preferences.

   1. All investors are assumed to have accurate information with respect to securities, and the marketplace is assumed to be highly efficient.

   2. Investors are assumed to prefer to earn higher (versus lower) returns and at the same time, to be averse to risk, preferring lower (versus higher) risk.

C. A security's (or asset's) risk is said to consist of two components - diversifiable and nondiversifiable risk.

$$
\begin{array}{c}
\text{Total} \\
\text{Security} \\
\text{Risk}
\end{array}
=
\begin{array}{c}
\text{Nondiversifiable} \\
\text{Risk}
\end{array}
+
\begin{array}{c}
\text{Diversifiable} \\
\text{Risk}
\end{array}
$$

1. Diversifiable risk, or unsystematic risk, which is attributed to the firm itself and results from the occurrence of uncontrollable or random events, can be eliminated through diversification.

2. Nondiversifiable risk, or systematic risk, is inescapable, since it is attributable to changes in the economy.

3. Systematic risk is the only relevant risk in a perfect world, since any investor can create a portfolio of assets that will diversify away all unsystematic risk.

4. Each security relates to the market differently, so each security has a different level of systematic risk.

D. The beta coefficient is a measure of the systematic risk. It can be found by examining the asset's historical returns relative to the returns for the market.

1. Beta is a index of comovement of an asset's return relative to that of the market.

   a. Beta can be estimated using least-squares regression.

   b. The "characteristic line" is the graphic portrayal of the relationship between security and market returns.

2. The market returns are measured by the average return on the Standard and Poor' s 500 Stock Composite Index or some other broad stock index.

3. The market beta is equal to 1; all other beta values are viewed in relation to that value. A beta of 2 thus indicates that the stock is twice as volatile as the market.

4. Betas can be positive or negative. Most are positive and between .2 and 2.

5. Stocks with betas of -2.0 and 2.0 are twice as risky as the market, but the former assets' returns move in direction opposite to that of the market.

E. The CAPM equation uses beta to relate risk and return for all assets.

1. The equation for the required (or expected) return on an asset is as follows:

$$k_j = R_F + b_j \times (k_m - R_F)$$

where: k_j = the required (or expected) return on asset j
        R_F = the risk-free rate of return
        b_j = the index of nondiversifiable risk (or beta) for asset j
        k_m = the required return on the market portfolio

2. The model can be broken into two parts: the risk-free rate, R_F; and the risk premium, $b_j \times (k_m - R_F)$, which reflects the asset's risk relative to the market.

3. The value $(k_m - R_F)$ can be viewed as the market risk premium.

F. The Security Market Line (SML) graphically depicts the capital market line. For each level of nondiversifiable risk as measured by beta, it reflects the required return in the marketplace.

1. A change in expectations concerning inflation will result in a parallel change in the SML - up if inflation worries increase and down if inflation worries decline.

2. The slope of the SML will increase if investors become more risk averse--require more return for any given level of risk.

G. Although some assumptions used in developing the CAPM may not seem realistic, the key concept is that a risk-return trade-off, which may be difficult to quantify, exists.

1. The model relies on historical data to estimate required returns, and so the required returns specified by the model can only be viewed as rough approximations.

2. Analysts often make subjective adjustments to historically computed betas when they anticipate a change in the risk-return relationship of a stock.

3. The model is most commonly used as a conceptual framework rather than a quantitative measure of the link between risk and required return.

APPLICATIONS

DEFINITIONS

1. A collection or group of assets is referred to as a _portfolio_

2. The _characteristic line_ graphically depicts the relationship between the market return and an asset's return.

3. Total risk consists of _diversifiable risk_ and _nondiversifiable risk_

4. The _Arbitrage Pricing Theory_ suggests that the risk premium on securities may result from a number of factors in addition to the market return.

5. Correlation coefficients can range from +1 for _perfectly positive_ correlated series to -1 for _perfectly negative_ correlated series.

6. A(an) _efficient portfolio_ maximizes return for a given level of risk or minimizes risk for a given level or return.

7. The _range_ measures the difference between the worst and best possible outcomes.

8. A measure of relative dispersion that is useful in comparing the risk of assets with different expected returns is the _coefficient of variation_

9. A normal probability distribution resembles a _bell shaped_ curve.

10. The chance of a given outcome occurring is its _probability_

11. An approach that uses a number of possible return estimates to obtain a sense of the variability among outcomes is _sensitivity analysis_

12. A manager with a _risk indifferent_ preference will not require a change in return as risk changes.

13. Nondiversifiable risk is also called _systematic risk_.

14. Assets with betas equal to _0.5_ and _-0.5_ are only half as responsive, or risky, as the market portfolio.

15. _Portfolio betas_ are a weighted average of the betas of the individual assets in the group.

MULTIPLE CHOICE

1. The more variable the returns, the _____ their risk.
    a. higher
    b. less important
    c. lower
    d. none of the above

2. _____ managers require return increases for an increase in risk.
    a. Risk-averse
    b. Risk-indifferent
    c. Risk-neutral
    d. Risk-taking

3. Which of the terms in the following equation is inappropriate:

    $$k_t = \frac{P_t - P_{t-1} + C_t}{P_t}$$

    a. The first P_t
    b. P_{t-1}
    c. C_t
    d. The second P_t

    $$k_t = \frac{P_t - P_{t-1} + C_t}{P_{t-1}}$$

4. Given the following probability distribution, what is the expected return?

Probability	Outcome
.20	10 percent
.30	12 percent
.40	14 percent
.10	18 percent

    2.0
    3.6
    5.6
    1.8
    ———
    13.0

    a. 13.50 percent
    b. 13.80 percent
    c. 14.00 percent
    d. none of the above

5. Which of the following statements is <u>not</u> true about a normal probability distribution?
    a. Ninety-nine percent of all outcomes lie within two standard deviations of the expected value.
    b. From the peak, the curves are mirror images of each other.
    c. Greater risk is represented by a "less peaked" curve.
    d. Half of the curve's area lies to the left of the peak and half to the right of the peak.

6. The most commonly used indicator of an asset's risk is the:
    a. expected value.
    b. loss level.
    c. range.
    d. standard deviation.

7. Security risk is a(an) _____ function of time.
    a. constant
    b. decreasing
    c. increasing
    d. volatile

8. Given the following information, use the coefficient of variation to determine which asset is most risky.

	Assets		
	X	Y	Z
Expected Return in percent	10	8	16
Standard Deviation in percent	14	12	20

$\frac{14}{10} = 1.4$

$\frac{12}{8} = 1.5$

$\frac{20}{16} = 1.25$

    1.4   1.5   1.25

    a. Asset X
    b. Asset Y
    c. Asset Z
    d. Not enough information is given to answer

9. If two return series move in the same direction, they are:
    a. diversified.
    b. negatively correlated.
    c. positively correlated.
    d. none of the above.

10. Risk can be reduced to zero if two securities have:
    a. perfect negative correlation.
    b. perfect positive correlation.
    c. zero correlation.
    d. any of the above.

11. There definitely are gains from diversification when one combines two assets:
a. into a portfolio.
b. only if they are negatively correlated.
c. that are not perfectly positively correlated.
d. all of the above.

12. The relevant portion of an asset's risk attributable to factors that affect all firms is:
a. diversifiable risk.
b. firm specific risk.
c. marketability risk.
d. nondiversifiable risk.

13. A firm with a beta value of 1.5 has a required rate of return of _____ if the risk-free rate is 10 percent and the market rate of return is 15 percent.
a. 10 percent
b. 15 percent
c. 17.5 percent
d. 22.5 percent

$$10 + 1.5(15-10) = 17.5$$

14. A decline in investor risk aversion will result in:
a. a less steep SML slope.
b. a more steep SML slope.
c. a parallel shift downward in the SML.
d. a parallel shift upward in the SML.

15. A decline in inflation expectations due to recent economic events would result in:
a. a less steep SML slope.
b. a more steep SML slope.
c. a parallel shift downward in the SML.
d. a parallel shift upward in the SML.

$$A \quad \frac{11,000 - 10,000 + 2,000}{10,000} = \frac{3000}{10000} = 30\%$$

PROBLEMS

1. Terri Harris, a financial analyst for Collins Cement, wishes to estimate the rate of return for two similar risk investments - A and B. Her best data will be the performance of the two during the past year. At the beginning of the year, A had a market value of $10,000 and B had a market value of $23,000. During the year, A paid a cash return of $2,000 while B paid $3,000. The current market values of A and B are $11,000 and $25,000, respectively.
a. Calculate the actual rates of return on the two investments for the past period.
b. Assuming the coming year will equal the previous year, and that the two investments are equally risky, which would Terri prefer, and why?   A

$$B \quad \frac{25 - 23 + 3}{23} = \frac{5}{23} = 21\%$$

2. Martin Owens, the financial manager at Tri-County Hi-Tech, must evaluate three proposed investments, A, B, and C. The firm currently earns 14 percent on its investments which have a risk index measure of 10 percent. The investments under consideration are:

Investment	Expected Return (%)	Expected Risk Index (%)
A	21	16
B	14	8
C	10	17

high returns a. Which investment would Owens select if he were risk-indifferent? Why? *A*
   b. Which investment would Owens select if he were risk-averse? Why? *B*
High Risk c. Which investment would Owens select if he were a risk-taker? Why? *C*
   d. Which investment would he select if his preference were those of the typical financial manager? Explain.

3. The Burgess Corporation is attempting to evaluate the risk of each of two assets. Management has made pessimistic, most likely, and optimistic estimates of annual returns as given below:

Annual rate of return

	Asset A	Asset B
Pessimistic	.14	.08
Most Likely	.16	.16
Optimistic	.18	.24

a. Calculate the range, using the estimates above. *A - .04   B - .16*
b. Discuss and compare the risk of the projects. *B is riskier*
c. If the probabilities of the pessimistic, most likely, and optimistic events are 25 percent, 60 percent, and 15 percent, respectively, what is the expected value of the asset returns? *multiply & then add.*

4. Use the table below to do the following:
a. Calculate the standard deviation for each asset.
b. Calculate the coefficient of variation for each asset.
c. Compare and contrast the risk of the two projects, using the findings from parts a and b.

Asset R		Asset Q	
Outcome	Probability	Outcome	Probability
10 %	.10	9 %	.20
11 %	.20	11 %	.30
12 %	.40	13 %	.30
13 %	.20	15 %	.20
14 %	.10		

5.   Using the standard deviation values for Assets R and Q calculated above and information on their portfolio weightings and correlation information given below, calculated the standard deviation of a portfolio containing both assets.

	Asset R	Asset Q
Portfolio Weighting	45 %	55%
Correlation		.50

C. $.09 + 1.5(x-.09) = 15$
$.09 + 1.5x - .135 = .15$ $1.5x = .15 + .135 - .09$ $1.5x = .195$ $x = .13$

6.   Use the basic equation for the capital asset pricing model (CAPM) to solve each of the following:
   - a. Find the required return of an asset with a beta of 1.2 when the risk-free rate and market rata are 8 percent and 12 percent, respectively.
   - b. Find the beta for an asset with a required rate of return of 16 percent when the risk-free rate and market return are 10 percent and 14 percent, respectively.
   - c. Find the market return for an asset with a required return of 15 percent and a beta of 1.5, when the risk free rate is 9 percent.

b.) $.10 + \beta(.14-.10) = 16$
$.10 + \beta(.04) = .16$
$.10 + \beta(.04) = .16$
$-.10 + .04\beta = .16$
$.04\beta = .06$ $\beta = (1.5)$

a.) $.08 + 1.2(.12-.08) = .08 + .048 = .128 = 12.8\%$

7.   Sagi Industries wishes to determine the required return on a project using the capital asset pricing model (CAPM) and its graphical representation, the security market line (SML).
   - a. Use the information given below to calculate the required (or expected) return and the risk premium the project must earn, given its level of nondiversifiable risk.
     - (1)   The risk-free rate of interest is 12 percent.
     - (2)   The beta coefficient or measure of nondiversifiable risk is 1.5.
     - (3)   The rate of return on the market portfolio is 16 percent.

$\bar{K} = .12 + 1.5(.16-.12)$
$\bar{K} = .12 + 1.5(.04)$
$\bar{K} = .12 + .06$ $\bar{K} = .18$

$\dfrac{-1.5\ RF}{.06 - \text{Risk prem.}}$

8.   Assume the beta measures of firms X, Y, and Z are as given below.
   a. Calculate the approximate change in return for each firm if the market experiences an increase in its rate of return of 10 percent over the next period.
   b. Calculate the approximate changes in expected returns if the market experiences a decrease of 5 percent.
   c. Rank and discuss the relative risk of each firm. Which would be expected to perform best in an economic downturn?

Firm	Beta
X	1.30
Y	75
Z	-.95

9.   Reedsburg, Inc., has four divisions. Each division's beta and percentage of the entire corporation is given below. What is the company's beta?

Division	Division's Beta	Percentage of Firm
Electronic processing	1.10	10%
Iron castings	1.20	30%
Paints and coatings	0.80	20%
Plastic moldings	0.90	40%

SOLUTIONS

DEFINITIONS

1. portfolio
2. characteristic line.
3. diversifiable risk, nondiversifiable risk.
4. Arbitrage Pricing Theory
5. perfectly positively; perfectly negatively
6. efficient portfolio
7. range
8. coefficient of variation.
9. "bell-shaped"
10. probability.
11. sensitivity analysis
12. risk-indifferent
13. systematic risk
14. 0.5; -0.5
15. Portfolio betas

MULTIPLE CHOICE

1. a
2. a
3. d
4. d $.2(.1) + .3(.12) + .4(.14) + .1(.18) = .13$ or 13 percent
5. a
6. d
7. c
8. b $CV_X = 1.4$, $CV_Y = 1.5$, $CV_Z = 1.25$; Y's CV is largest.
9. c
10. a
11. c
12. d
13. c $10 + 1.5(15-10) = 17.5$ percent
14. a
15. c

PROBLEMS

1.   a. The equation for the rate of return over a given period is:

$$k_t = \frac{P_t - P_{t-1} + C_t}{P_{t-1}}$$

For A: $k = \dfrac{\$11,000 - \$10,000 + \$2000}{\$10,000} = \dfrac{\$3,000}{\$10,000} = 30\%$

For B: $k = \dfrac{\$25,000 - \$23,000 + \$3000}{\$23,000} = \dfrac{\$5,000}{\$23,000} = 21.74\%$

b. Based on rates of return, Terry should prefer A because it has a higher rate of return for a given level of risk.

2. a. The risk-indifferent manager would select investment A because it has the highest return.

    b. The risk-averse manager probably would select investment B because it offers the highest return for a given risk.

    c. The risk-taking manager would select investment C because it offers the highest risk.

    d. Most financial managers are risk averse and would select investment B.

3. The range is found by simply subtracting the pessimistic estimate from the optimistic estimate.

    a.

	Annual rate of return	
	Asset A	Asset B
Optimistic	.18	.24
Less: Pessimistic	-.14	-.08
Range	.04	.16

    b. Since asset A has a range of only .04, while asset B has a range of .16, asset B is more risky.

    c. The expected value is the sum of outcome times probability for each outcome.

Potential Outcome	Asset A (outcome X probability)	Asset B (outcome X probability)
Pessimistic	.14 X .25 = .035	.08 X .25 = .02
Most Likely	.16 X .60 = .096	.16 X .60 = .096
Optimistic	.18 X .15 = .027	.24 X .15 = .036
	Expected Value 0.158	Expected Value .152

4.   a. **Asset R**: First compute the expected return:

Outcome X Probability =
.10 X .10   = .01
.11 X .20   = .022
.12 X .40   = .048
.13 X .20   = .026
.14 X .10   = .014
Expected return of R   .12

Sum the deviations squared times the probabilities:

(Actual - Expected)^2 Return Return	X	Probability		
$(.10 - .12)^2$	X	0.10	=	.00004
$(.11 - .12)^2$	X	0.20	=	.00002
$(.12 - .12)^2$	X	0.40	=	.00
$(.13 - .12)^2$	X	0.20	=	.00002
$(.14 - .12)^2$	X	0.10	=	.00004
			Sum	.00012

Take the square root of the sum:

$$\sigma_r = \sqrt{.00012} = .011$$

Asset Q: First compute the expected return:

Outcome X Probability =
.09 X .20   = .018
.11 X .30   = .033
.13 X .30   = .039
.15 X .20   = .03
Expected return of Q   .12

Sum the deviations squared times the probabilities:

(Actual - Expected)^2 X Probability
Return   Return

$(.09 - .12)^2$	X	0.20	=	.00018
$(.11 - .12)^2$	X	0.30	=	.00003
$(.13 - .12)^2$	X	0.30	=	.00003
$(.15 - .12)^2$	X	0.20	=	.00018

Sum   .00042

Take the square root of the sum:

$$\sigma_Q = \sqrt{.00042} = .0205$$

b. The coefficient of variation is the standard deviation divided by the expected return.

The coefficient of variation for asset R is:

$$CV_R = \frac{\sigma_{K_R}}{\overline{k}_R} = \frac{0.011}{0.12} = .0917$$

The coefficient of variation for asset Q is:

$$CV_Q = \frac{\sigma_{K_Q}}{\overline{k}_Q} = \frac{0.0205}{0.12} = .1708$$

c. Project R has less risk, as shown by a lower standard deviation and lower coefficient of variation.

5.   The standard deviation for this two-asset portfolio can be calculated using the following formula:

$$\sigma_{RQ} = \sqrt{w_R^2 \sigma_R^2 + w_Q^2 \sigma_Q^2 + 2w_R w_Q r_{1,2}\, \sigma_R \sigma_Q}$$

Applying the information given:

$$\sigma_{RQ} = \sqrt{.45^2 \times .011^2 + .55^2 \times .020^2 + 2(.45)(.55).50(.011)(.020)}$$

$$\sigma_{RQ} = \sqrt{.000024 + .000121 + .000055} = \sqrt{.0002}$$

$$= .014 \text{ or } 1.4\,\%$$

This is less than the arithmetic average of the two standard deviations, or 1.55% [(.011+.020)/2], despite investing a greater proportion in the riskier asset.

6.   All parts of this solution are the basic CAPM model:

$$k_j = R_F + b_j \times (k_m - R_F)$$

a. $k_j = 0.8 + 1.2\,(.12 - .08)$

   $k_j = 12.8$ percent

b. $.16 = .10 + b_j\,(.14 - .10)$

   $06 = b_j\,(.04)$

   $b_j = 1.5$

c. $.15 = .09 + 1.5\,(k_m - .09)$

   $.06 = 1.5\,(k_m - .09)$

   $.04 = k_m - .09$

   $k_m = 13$ percent

7.   a. The required return on the project can be calculated using the CAPM given in the
            equation:

$$k_j = R_F + b_j \times (k_m - R_F)$$

where: k_j = the required (or expected) return on asset j
         R_F = the risk-free rate of return
         b_j = the index of nondiversifiable risk (or beta) for asset j
         k_m = the required return on the market portfolio

Substituting R_F = 12%, b_j = 1.5, and k_m = 16% into the CAPM equation:

$$k_j = 12\% + 1.5 \times (16\% - 12\%)$$

$$= 12\% + 6\%$$

$$= 18\%$$

The CAPM can be broken into two parts: the risk-free rate, R_F, and the risk
premium, $b_j \times (k_m - R_F)$. Substituting the values of R_F = 12%, b_j = 1.5, and k_m =
16% into the second part of the equation:

$$\text{Risk premium} = 1.5 \times (16\% - 12\%)$$

$$= 6\%$$

Sagi Industries' risk-free rate, R_F was 12 percent, and the required return on the
market portfolio, k_m, was 16 percent. Since the betas associated with R_F and k_m are
by definition zero and one, respectively, the security market line can be plotted using
these two sets of coordinates. For assets with beta greater than 1, the risk premium
is greater than that for the market, for assets with betas less than 1 the risk
premium is less than that for the market.

8.   a. | Firm | Beta x Market Change | = | Expected Return Change |
            |------|---------------------|---|------------------------|
            | X | 1.30 x (+ 10.0) | = | 13.0% |
            | Y | .75 x (+ 10.0) | = | 7.5% |
            | Z | -.95 x (+ 10.0) | = | -9.5% |

        b. | | | | |
            |------|---------------------|---|------------------------|
            | X | 1.30 x (- 5.0) | = | -6.5% |
            | Y | .75 x (- 5.0) | = | -3.75% |
            | Z | -.95 x (- 5.0) | = | 4.75% |

c. Higher beta values have more risk, regardless of their sign. So ranking would be: X = most risky, Z = intermediate risk, Y = least risk.

Since firm Z has a negative beta it would be expected to earn a positive return during an economic downturn while the others would not.

9. The following equation can be used to calculate portfolio beta:

$$b_p = \sum_{j=1}^{n} (w_j \times b_j)$$

Applying this equation to Reedsburg's situation:

Division	w_j	x	b_j	=	Division's Contribution
Electronic processing	.10	x	1.10	=	0.11
Iron castings	.30	x	1.20	=	0.36
Paints and coatings	.20	x	0.80	=	0.16
Plastic moldings	.40	x	0.90	=	0.36
Firm Beta					0.99

CHAPTER 6

VALUATION

SUMMARY

Valuation, determining the worth of income/cash flow-generating assets, couples the time value techniques presented in Chapter 4 with the risk and return factors developed in Chapter 5. The key inputs to the valuation process include cash flows (returns), timing, and the discount rate (risk). The value of any asset is the present value of all future cash flows from the asset.

The value of a bond, a certificate indicating that a corporation has borrowed a certain amount of money, is the present value of the periodic interest payments plus the present value of its par, or maturity, value. The discount rate used to determine the bond value is a required return, which may differ from the bond's coupon rate, and is determined by money availability and risk. When the required return is greater than the coupon interest rate on a bond, the bond will sell at a discount below its par value; when the required return is less than the coupon rate, it will sell at a premium above par value. When the required return on a bond is constant, the value of the bond approaches its par value as time to maturity grows closer. The shorter the time period to a bond's maturity, the less responsive it is to changes in the required rate of return. The rate of return to maturity, or yield to maturity, (YTM), can be estimated using time value techniques or the approximate yield equation. Calculators simplify bond value and stock value estimation.

Popular stock valuation approaches include book value, liquidation value, and price/earnings (P/E) multiples. The best approach is the dividend approach, whereby the share value equals the present value of all expected future dividends over an infinite time horizon. Three different dividend models are presented in the text: the zero growth, constant growth, and variable growth models. The constant growth model can be expressed as:

$$P_o = D_1 \div (k_s - g)$$

where P_o = current stock price
D_1 = the per share dividend expected at the end of one year
k_s = the required rate of return on equally risky common stock
g = the expected annual rate of dividend increase

Changes in D_1 and g (returns) or changes in k_s (risk) greatly affect P_o. According to CAPM, if beta increases, k_s increases, and P_o, current stock value, falls. Similarly, as g or D_1 increase, P_o will rise. In making financial decisions, the combined effects on both risk and return must be considered, so that actions taken will protect or increase the wealth of the firm's owners.

CONCEPT OUTLINE

I.   **The valuation process involves determining the worth of income-generating assets.**

   A. Key inputs to the valuation process are cash flows, timing, and the discount rate.

      1. For an asset to have value, it must provide at least one cash flow to its owner.

      2. The timing of cash flows must be known as earlier cash flows have greater present value.

      3. The level of risk associated with a cash flow significantly affects its value. More risky cash flows must be discounted using a higher, risk adjusted, discount rate, reducing the value of the return.

   B. The value of any asset is its present value: the present value of all future cash flows from that asset discounted at the rate appropriate for the risk level of the cash flows.

      1. The model may be applied to any asset.

      2. At this point, we apply the model only to bonds and stocks.

II. **Corporate bonds are certificates evidencing that a firm has borrowed a fixed sum, which it has promised to repay at a specified future time. Periodic interest payments, usually semiannual, are also specified.**

   A. The value of a bond is equal to the present value of all cash payments it must make from the current time until it matures. This includes both interest and principal.

      1. The cash payments are discounted at the required rate of return, k_d, which depends on both prevailing interest rates and risk.

      2. The equation for the value of a bond is

$$B_0 = I \sum_{t=1}^{n} \frac{1}{(1 + k_d)^t} + M \frac{1}{(1 + k_d)^n} = I(\text{PVIFA}_{k_d,n}) + M(\text{PVIF}_{k_d,n})$$

   where B_0 = value of bond
           I = annual interest payments, in dollars
           M = par or face value, in dollars
           n = years to maturity or repayment

NOTE: The chapter provides many examples of using a hand-held calculator to simplify computations.

3. When the coupon or stated rate of interest is equal to the required rate of return, the bond's market value will equal its par value.

B. The value (or price) of an outstanding bond often differs from its par value.

1. Changes in the supply-demand relationship for money cause the level of interest rates to rise or fall, thus changing k_d.

2. Changes in the firm's risk will affect the required return on the security.

3. If k_d increases, because of either higher interest rates or market participants' perceptions of higher security risk, the value of the bond (and its price) will fall.

4. If k_d decreases, because of either lower interest rates or market participants' perceptions of lower security risk, the value of the bond will increase.

5. If k_d exceeds the bond's coupon rate, the bond's value is less than its par value, and will sell at a discount.

6. If k_d is less that the bond's coupon rate, the bond's value is greater than its par value, and it will sell at a premium.

7. In practice, bond purchase prices include bond value and interest accrued since the last interest payment date.

C. The amount of time to maturity impacts bond values even if the required return remains constant.

1. When the required return is different from the coupon rate and assumed constant until maturity, the value of the bond will approach its par value as time approaches the maturity date.

2. The shorter the amount of time until a bond's maturity, the less responsive is its market value to a given change in the required return. In other words, short maturities have less interest rate risk than long maturities.

D. Investors evaluate and trade bonds based on rates such as yield to maturity (YTM), the rate of return which would be earned by purchasing a bond and holding it to maturity.

1. Assuming interest is paid annually, the YTM can be found by solving the equation specified in part II, A, 2 above for the value of k_d. One often must interpolate between two interest rate factors.

2. A simple approach to estimating the YTM is the approximate yield formula:

$$\text{approximate yield} = \frac{I + \dfrac{M - B_o}{n}}{\dfrac{M + B_o}{2}}$$

where all variables are defined as in Section II, A, 2, above.

E. Most corporate bonds pay interest semiannually rather than annually.

1. To evaluate a bond paying semiannual interest, follow the procedure for intrayear compounding:

a. Convert I to semiannual interest by dividing by 2.

b. Convert n to the number of six-month periods by multiplying by 2.

c. Convert k_d to a semiannual rate by dividing by 2.

d. Use the bond valuation equation with these changes.

2. The value of a bond paying semiannual interest is given by the following equation:

$$B_o = \frac{I}{2} \sum_{t=1}^{2n} \frac{1}{\left(1 + \dfrac{k_d}{2}\right)^t} + M \frac{1}{\left(1 + \dfrac{k_d}{2}\right)^{2n}}$$

$$= \frac{I}{2}(\text{PVIFA}_{k_d/2,2n}) + M(\text{PVIF}_{k_d/2,2n})$$

F. Perpetual bonds and preferred stock are securities with no maturity dates. They pay interest or dividends, respectively, over an infinite horizon.

1. Assuming annual cash flows, the value of a perpetual security (P_o) is:

$$P_o = I\left(\frac{1}{k_d}\right) = \frac{I}{k_d}$$

where I is the annual cash flow.

2. More frequent cash flows require adjustments such as those made for semi-annual bond coupons (presented in II, E, 2 above).

III. **Owners, prospective owners, and security analysts attempt to assess the value of the firm's common stock. It is this value with which a financial manager attempts to maximize shareholder wealth.**

A. In an efficient market the expected return equals the required return.

1. Prices in an efficient market quickly and fully reflect all new important information. They are seldom far from the true value of the asset.

2. If expected return exceeds required return, there will be additional demand for the asset. The additional demand will drive up price, reducing the expected return to subsequent buyers.

3. Excess returns are not available in efficient markets, since undervalued stocks do not exist.

4. Several studies, however, indicate that the even the stock market, with its active trading, is not perfectly efficient.

B. The basic common stock valuation model views the value of a share of common stock as the present value of an infinite stream of dividends.

1. With zero growth, this model is identical to the perpetual bond and preferred stock models and is expressed as

$$P_o = D_1 \div k_s$$

where P_o = the value (or price) of the common shares
           D_1 = the annual dividend to be received
           k_s = the required rate of return

2. With constant growth in dividends and earnings, the model is expressed as

$$P_o = D_1 / (k_s - g)$$

where g is the constant rate of growth expected in dividends.

    a. This model is sometimes called the Gordon growth model.

    b. The required return must exceed the growth rate. The growth rate may exceed the required rate of return for short periods of time, requiring use of the variable dividend model.

3. The dividend growth rate, g, can be estimated by using historical dividend-per-share values to calculate their compound annual growth rate.

4. When growth is not constant, a multi-step model can be used. The present value of the dividends in the initial period is added to the present value of the stock price at the end of the initial growth period. The model is:

$$P_o = \sum_{t=1}^{N} \frac{D_t}{(1 + k_s)^t} + \left(\frac{1}{(1 + k_s)^N} \times \frac{D_{N+1}}{(k_s - g)} \right)$$

5. If multiple growth rates exist, one may either discount the dividends during each year leading up to the point of constant growth or identify the present value of dividends received during each nonconstant period.

6. The basic theoretical underpinning and ease of application make the constant growth model the most widely accepted valuation model.

C. Several simple valuation approaches exist.

1. Book value per share represents the accounting valuation of an owner's shares.

2. Liquidation value, is the amount each shareholder would actually receive if the firm were liquidated.

3. The average price/earnings (P/E) ratio for the industry multiplied by the expected earnings of the firm is an estimate of the share's market value.

4. Of these three approaches, the P/E approach is superior to the other two because it uses expected earnings.

IV. **The decisions of financial managers affect expected returns (D_1 and g) and risk (k_s).**

A. Managerial actions that cause existing or prospective shareholders to raise their expectations of future dividends should increase the firm's value, so long as these actions do not raise the required rate of return (by increasing risk).

    1. Actions that increase perceptions of D_1 or g raise the value of shares.

    2. Actions that decrease D_1 or g lower the value of shares.

B. Managerial actions that affect nondiversifiable risk (measured by beta) affect k_s, the required rate of return, according to CAPM:

$$k_s = R_F + b_s \times (k_m - R_F)$$

    1. An action that increases b_s will increase k_s and lower the value of shares.

    2. An action that decreases b_s will lower k_s and increase the value of shares.

C. Most actions affect both risk and expected return. Actions that increase expected returns usually raise the level of nondiversifiable risk, and those that lower expected returns usually lower the level of nondiversifiable risk.

    1. One must consider the combined effect of a managerial action on both risk and return to estimate properly the effect of an action on share price.

    2. The economic environment also affects share price through R_F, the risk-free rate, or through the market return k_m. These effects also must be considered in evaluating the effects of financial decisions.

APPLICATIONS

DEFINITIONS

1. Valuation is the process that links _risk_ and _return_ to determine the worth of an asset.

2. A bond selling at a _discount_ has a market price that is less than its par value.

3. A bond's _premium_ is the amount by which a bond's value exceeds its face value.

4. The _yield to maturity_ is the rate of return earned if a bond is held to maturity.

5.   Yield to maturity can be obtained using the ___-___-___ approach, the _____ _yield_ formula, or a _calculator_.

6.   The required return is the specified return require for a given _level of risk_.

7.   The return anticipated over a specified period of time is the _expected return_.

8.   Securities are fairly priced in an _efficient_ market.

9.   In an efficient market stock prices _fully reflect_ all public information.

10.   The appropriate dividend valuation model when dividends are constant is the _zero_ growth model.

11.   The constant growth model, or _Gordon model_, assumes dividends will grow at a steady rate that is less than the required rate.

12.   When dividends are not constant a _variable_ growth model is required.

✗ 13. Assets minus liabilities, divided by the number of shares outstanding provides the _book_ value per share.

14.   _Liquidation_ value is the actual amount per share received if the firm is put on the auction block.

15.   The _price/earnings ratio_ reflects the amount investors are willing to pay for each dollar of earnings.

MULTIPLE CHOICE

✗ 1.   The value of any asset is the _____ value of all future _____.
       a. expected, operating profits.
       b. future, cash flows.
       c. future, earnings per share.
       d. present, cash flows.

✗ 2.   Key inputs to the valuation process includes _____ information.
       a. cash flow
       b. discount rate
       c. timing
       d. all of the above

3. For an asset to have value it must provide:
    a. a single cash flow.
    b. an annual cash flow.
    c. an intermittent cash flow.
    d. any of the above.

4. Which of the terms in the following basic valuation model is inappropriate.

$$V_o = \sum_{t=1}^{\cdot} \frac{CF_t}{(1 + g)^t}$$

    a. CF
    b. g
    c. t
    d. Σ

    $(1 + K)$

5. Bond value will equal par if:
    a. the required return equals the coupon interest rate.
    b. the required return exceeds the coupon interest rate.
    c. the required return is less than the coupon interest rate.
    d. the required return is unknown.

6. When using a hand-held calculator to calculate the present value of a bond, the last key punched is the _____ key.
    a. CPT
    b. N
    c. PV
    d. %i

7. A $1,000 face value, 10 year, bond pays a coupon of $100 a year (paid annually). If the required rate of return on equally risky bonds is 10 percent, what is the value of the bond?
    a. $850.
    b. $1,056.
    c. $1,107.
    d. none of the above.

8. Which of the following bonds would have the greatest price response to a one percent change in the required rate of return?
    a. 5 year, 10 percent coupon.
    b. 8 year, 8 percent coupon.
    c. 10 year, 10 percent coupon.
    d. 12 year, zero coupon.

9.   When calculating yield to maturity with a hand-held calculator, the last key punched is
      the _____ key.
            a. CPT
            b. N
            c. PV
            d. %i

10.   The annual bond valuation model can be adjusted for semiannual payments by doing all
      of the following, except:
            a. dividing the annual required rate of return, k_d, by 2.
            b. multiplying years to maturity, n, by 2.
            c. multiplying annual interest, I, by 2.
            d. a and b.

11.   The best method to value common stock is:
            a. book value.
            b. liquidation value.
            c. present value of dividends.
            d. price-earnings ratios.

12.   The _____ model is appropriate for preferred stock.
            a. constant growth
            b. preferred growth
            c. variable growth
            d. zero growth

13.   If a firm pays a $2.00 dividend and that is expected to remain constant, what is the value
      of the firm's common stock, if the firm's required rate of return is 16 percent?
            a. $2.00.
            b. $12.50.
            c. $32.
            d. none of the above.

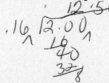

14.   A firm's common stock sells for $20 because it has a required return of 18 percent and
      an expected constant growth in dividends of 4 percent (the coming year's dividend will be
      $2.80). The firm is considering a decision that will increase its growth to 6 percent after
      this year, but increase its required return to 19 percent. What should the firm do?
            a. accept, increasing share value by $1.54
            b. accept, increasing share value by $2.84
            c. reject, avoid decreasing share value by $1.33.
            d. not enough information is give to accept or reject.

15. A firm owning a substantial amount of valuable property, which was purchased many years ago, that is used in profitable production would find the lowest valuation estimate provided by the _____ approach.
    a. book value
    b. dividend discount model
    c. liquidation value
    d. price/earnings multiple

PROBLEMS

1.
T
Prior to making the decision to purchase a small truck, assume you can purchase the vehicle with funds you would have on deposit earning 8 percent after taxes. The truck should provide after tax benefits of $1500 per year, and you expect to sell the truck at the end of five years to net $2000.
   a. Is the truck a financial or real asset?
   b. Identify the cash flows, their timing, and the discount rate to be used in valuing the truck.
   c. What is the maximum price you would pay for the truck? Why?

2.
T
Judd Fisher must estimate the value of an asset expected to provide cash inflows of $10,000 per year at the end of years 1 through 4 and $25,000 at the end of year 5. His firm requires an 8 percent return on low risk assets, a 14 percent return on average risk assets, and a 20 percent return on high risk assets.
   a. What is the maximum price Judd should pay for the asset if he considers it (1) low, (2) average, or (3) high risk?
   b. What effect does increasing risk have on the value of an asset (holding all other factors constant)? Use your answers in (a) above to explain.

3.
T
Determine the value of a bond having a $1000 par value, paying annual interest at a coupon rate of 8 percent, and having twelve years remaining to maturity, if the required rate of return is 14 percent paid annually.

4.
T
Rework problem 3 above assuming the coupon and required returns are annual rates but interest is paid (compounded) semiannually.

5.   Ed's Company bonds currently sell for $945, have a 13-percent coupon, pay interest
 annually, and a $1000 par value, and 10 years to maturity.
      a. Calculate the yield to maturity using the more precise trial-and-error present-value
         based approach.
      b. Use the approximation formula to estimate the yield to maturity.
      c. Compare the yields in a and b above.
      d. Explain the relationship between coupon rate and yield to maturity and between
         par value and current value of a bond.

6.   What is the value of a share of preferred stock if the annual dividend is $12 and the
     required rate of return is 15 percent?

7.   The balance sheet for the M. McKenna Company is as follows:

<table>
<tr><td colspan="4" align="center">M. McKenna Company
Balance Sheet
Year Ending December 31</td></tr>
<tr><td colspan="2" align="center">Assets</td><td colspan="2" align="center">Liabilities and Net Worth</td></tr>
<tr><td>Cash</td><td>$80,000</td><td>Accounts payable</td><td>$ 150,000</td></tr>
<tr><td>Marketable securities</td><td>120,000</td><td>Notes payable</td><td>200,000</td></tr>
<tr><td>Accounts receivable</td><td>100,000</td><td>Accrued wages</td><td>50,000</td></tr>
<tr><td>Inventory</td><td>200,000</td><td>Total current debt</td><td>$400,000</td></tr>
<tr><td>Total current assets</td><td>$ 500,000</td><td>Long-term debt</td><td>300,000</td></tr>
<tr><td></td><td></td><td>Preferred stock</td><td>100,000</td></tr>
<tr><td>Fixed assets</td><td>500,000</td><td>Common Stock</td><td>200,000</td></tr>
<tr><td>Total assets</td><td>$1,000,000</td><td>Total liabilities and net worth</td><td>$1,000,000</td></tr>
</table>

The following additional information about the firm is available.

(1) The firm has 5000 shares of common stock outstanding.
(2) Preferred stock can be liquidated for its book value.
(3) Accounts receivable can be liquidated for 95 percent of book value.
(4) Inventory can be liquidated for 85 percent of book value.
(5) The fixed assets can be liquidated for 80 percent of book value.
(6) All others items, except common stock equity, can be liquidated for book value.
(7) All dividends and interest are currently paid up.
(8) No administrative costs would be incurred in liquidation.

Given this information:
    a. Calculate the book value par share.
    b. Calculate the liquidation value per share.
    c. If the firm is expected to earn $2.50 per share in the future and its stock is currently selling for twenty times earnings (i.e., price/earnings ratio), using the price/earnings multiple approach, determine the stock value.
    d. Briefly compare and discuss the preceding results.

8. Grandview Mining Corporation is known to pay a fixed percentage of its earnings as dividends. Over the past six years, the firm has exhibited the following dividend-payout pattern.

Year	Dividend per share
1991	$2.50 (expected)
1990	2.30
1989	2.20
1988	2.05
1987	1.95
1986	1.82
1985	1.72

    a. The firm is expected to pay a dividend of $2.50 par share in the coming year, and the required rate of return is 10 percent. Determine the theoretical value of the firm, using the dividend model, assuming constant growth.
    b. How will the value of the firm change, using the model, if actions are taken that cause g to be 8 percent and k_s to be 15 percent. (Hint: D_1 should still be $2.50.)

9. Round One Sports Center has had great success since first going public and issued
T common stock three years ago. Earnings and dividends have increased by 50 percent in
each year and are expected to do so for two more years. Starting with the third year,
growth (g^*) is expected to fall to a more normal 6 percent. During the year just
completed, the firm paid dividends of $1.00 per share. The required rate of return on
Round One is 15 percent.
   a. What is the maximum price an investor should pay for a share of Round One?
   b. What would the answer be for a. above, if the 50 percent growth would last only
      one year rather than two?
   c. What does the difference between a. and b. above, illustrate?

SOLUTIONS

DEFINITIONS

1.   risk, return
2.   discount
3.   premium
4.   yield to maturity
5.   trial-and-error; approximate yield; calculator
6.   level of risk
7.   expected return
8.   efficient
9.   fully reflect
10. zero
11. Gordon model
12. variable
13. book
14. Liquidation
15. price/earnings ratio

MULTIPLE CHOICE

1.   d
2.   d
3.   d
4.   b
5.   a
6.   c
7.   d; interest payment equals required return
8.   d; zero coupon bonds of a given maturity have more interest rate risk than coupon bonds

---

9. d
10. c
11. c
12. d
13. b; $2 ÷ .16 = $12.50
14. a; $2.80 ÷ (.19-.06) - $20 = $21.54 - $20 = $1.54
15. a

PROBLEMS

1. a. The truck is a real asset.

    b. | Time | Cash Flow |
        | --- | --- |
        | Year 0 | + ? |
        | Year 1 | + $1500 |
        | Year 2 | + $1500 |
        | Year 3 | + $1500 |
        | Year 4 | + $1500 |
        | Year 5 | + $3500 ($1500 + $2000) |

    discount rate = k_d = 8 percent

    This is the opportunity cost of the funds. We are assuming the cash flows from the truck are equally risky with our alternative (deposit) use of funds. If cash flows from the truck are more risky than other opportunities, a higher discount rate should be applied.

    c. The present value of these cash flows, at 8 percent is:

    V = $1500 (PVIFA$_{4 \text{ years, } 8\%}$) + $3500 (PVIFA$_{5 \text{ yrs, } 8\%}$)

    = $1500 (3.312) + $3500 (.681) = $4968 + $2384 = $7352

    so $7,352 is the maximum price you should pay. At this price the rate of return would be 8%.

2. a. In each case, the value is found using the following equation:

    V = PVIFA$_{kd, 4\text{yrs}}$ X ($10,000) + PVIF$_{kd, 5\text{yrs}}$ X ($25,000)

low risk: V = 3.312 ($10,000) + .681 ($25,000)
$(k_d = 8\%)$

= $33,120 + $17,025 = $50,145

avg. risk: V = 2.914 ($10,000) + .519 ($25,000)
$(k_s = 14\%)$

= $29,140 + $12,975 = $42,115

high risk: V = 2.589 ($10,000) + .402 ($25,000)
$(k_d = 20\%)$

= $25,890 + $10,020 = $35,940

b. Higher risk, and higher discount rates, correspond to lower present values of assets.

3. The solution uses the bond valuation equation using annual interest payments. The present value factors for 14 percent and 12 years are used here.

$B_0 = I (PVIFA_{14\%,12yrs}) + M(PVIF_{14\%,12\ yrs})$

$I = \$1000 \times .08 = \$80$

$P_0 = \$80 (5.660) + \$1000 (.208) = \$452.80 + \$208 = \$660.80$

4. The formula for semi-annual interest is presented in section II, E, 2 above. One simply multiplies the periods by 2 and divides the required rate and annual interest by two, then reworks the problem as in 3 above.

$B_0 = \$40 (PVIFA_{7\%,24periods}) + \$1000(PVIF_{7\%,24periods})$

= $40(11.469) + $1000(.197) = $458.76 + $197 = $655.76

5. a. Solve for k_d in the following formula using trial and error:

$B_0 = I (PVIFA_{kd,n}) + M(PVIF_{kd,n})$

$\$945 = \$130 (PVIFA_{kd,10yrs}) + \$1000(PVIF_{kd,10yrs})$

Since Ed's is selling at a slight discount, we know that the yield to maturity is close but over 13 percent.

Try 14%:

$$\$945 \; = \; \$130 \; (5.216) + \$1000(.270)$$
$$= \; \$678.08 + \$270$$
$$\$945 \; \neq \; \$948.08 \;\; \text{(but very close)}$$

Try 15%:

$$\$945 \; = \; \$130 \; (5.019) + \$1000(.247)$$
$$= \; \$652.47 + \$247$$
$$\neq \; \$899.47 \;\; \text{(further away and smaller)}$$

So YTM is approximately 14%. Actually the rate is slightly above 14% and through interpolation a more precise answer of 14.06% could be obtained.

b. A simple approach to estimating the YTM is the approximate yield formula:

$$\frac{I + \dfrac{M - B_o}{n}}{\dfrac{M + B_o}{2}} = \frac{\$130 + \dfrac{\$1000 - \$945}{10}}{\dfrac{\$1000 + \$945}{2}} = \frac{\$130 + \$5.5}{\$972.5} = 13.93\%$$

c. Obviously, the answer in (a) is more correct, but it is also more difficult to compute. The difference between the two answers (.07 percent) may be large enough to justify the extra work. Selection of a YTM approach depends on the precision required.

d. When the coupon rate is less than (greater than) the required rate, the bond sells at a discount (premium). When a bond sells at a discount (premium) from its par value, it has a yield to maturity above (below) its coupon rate.

6. Substituting the numbers from the problem, $I = \$12$ and $k_p = 15\%$, results in a price of $80.00.

$$P_o \; = \; I \, / \, k_p \; = \; \$12 \, / .15 \; = \; \$80$$

7. a. The book value per share can be found by dividing the amount of common stock equity by the number of shares of common stock outstanding.

$200,000 ÷ 5000 shares = $40/share

b.   Liquidation value per share can be found by adjusting the firm's assets to their liquidation value, subtracting all liabilities and preferred stock, and dividing by the number of shares of common stock outstanding. Using the percentages given, the liquidation value of assets is calculated as follows:

Cash	$ 80,000
Marketable securities	120,000
Accounts receivable (0.95)($100,000)	95,000
Inventory (0.85) ($200,000)	170,000
Fixed assets (0.80) ($500,000)	400,000
Liquidation Value of Assets	$ 865,000

Subtracting the firm's liabilities and preferred stock from the liquidation value of assets leaves the amount of money available to common stockholders:

Liquidation value of assets	$ 865,000
Less: Current liabilities	-400,000
Long-term debt	-300,000
Preferred stock	-100,000
Funds Available to Common Stockholders	$ 65,000

Dividing the amount available to common stockholders ($65,000) by the number of shares of common stock outstanding (5,000) yields the liquidation value per share.

$65,000 ÷ 5000 shares = $13/share

c.   To find the stock value using the price/earnings multiple approach, the expected eps must be multiplied by the price/earnings ratio. Using the values given for eps ($2.50) and the price/earnings ratio (20), the share value is calculated:

Value per share: (20)($2.50) = $50/share

d.   The book value per share of $40 and the liquidation value per share of $13 are rather static values obtained by viewing the firm as dead rather than alive. From this point of view, the liquidation value per share is the best measure, because it recognizes that the dead value of the firm amounts to what the firm can actually be liquidated for - not the account's historical book value. The price/earnings multiple approach, which views the firm as a stream of earnings - not as dead - indicates that the firm is worth $50 per share. If the firm is expected to continue operating and is believed to be a going concern, this value is a better measure than the other two.

8.   a.   To apply the dividend model, assuming constant growth, to these data, g must be estimated from the historical dividend data. This can be done in three steps:

(1) Dividing the earliest dividend ($1.72) by the most recent dividend yields a factor of .748 (i.e., $1.72 ÷ $2.30)

(2) Using the table for the present-value factor for one dollar, the five-year growth period, and the factor calculated in step (1), the factor closest to .748 for five years is found: .747.

(3) The growth rate to the nearest 1 percent is 6 percent. Substituting the expected dividend, D_1, which equals $2.50, the growth rate, g, which equals 6 percent, and the required rate of return, k_s, which equals 10 percent, into the model results in the theoretical value of the firm's stock, P:

$$P = \frac{D_1}{k_s - g} = \frac{\$2.50}{.10 - .06} = \frac{\$2.50}{.04} = \$62.50/share$$

b.   The model now shows:

$$P = \frac{D_1}{k_s - g} = \frac{\$2.50}{.15 - .08} = \frac{\$2.50}{.07} = \$35.71/share$$

This illustrates that both the risk and return of a decision must be considered, along with their effects on share price.

9.   a.   Step 1:   Find the value of the cash dividends at the end of each year during the initial growth period. (Cols. 1 and 2 below).

         Step 2:   Find the present value of the dividends during the initial growth period. (Col. 4 below).

(1)	(2) Dividend $D_o(1.5)^t$	(3) PVIF	(4) PV
Year			
t=1	$1.50	.870	$1.30
t=2	$2.25	.756	$1.70
			$3.00

Step 3:   Find the value of the stock at the end of the initial growth period, year 2 (using the constant growth model):

$$P_2 = \frac{D_{n+1}}{k_s - g^\bullet} = \frac{\$2.25(1.06)}{.15 - .06} = \frac{\$2.385}{.09} = \$26.50$$

The present value of the price in two years is:

$$P_2 \times \frac{1}{(1 + k_s)^2} = \$26.50 \times \frac{1}{(1.15)^2} = \$26.50 \times .756 = \$20.03$$

Step 4:   Add the present value components:

$$P_0 = \$3.00 + \$20.03 = \$23.03$$

b. Repeat the steps for the revised initial growth period of year one:

(1) Year	(2) Dividend $D_0(1.5)^t$	(3) PVIF	(4) PV
t=1	$1.50	.870	$1.30

$$P_2 = \frac{D_{n+1}}{k_s - g^\bullet} = \frac{\$1.50(1.06)}{.15 - .06} = \frac{\$1.59}{.09} = \$17.67$$

$$P_2 \times \frac{1}{(1 + k_s)} = \$17.67 \times \frac{1}{(1.15)} = \$17.67 \times .87 = \$15.37$$

$$P_0 = \$1.30 + \$15.37 = \$16.67$$

c. Longer periods of high growth, other things equal, increase the value of the firm.

CHAPTER 7

THE ANALYSIS OF FINANCIAL STATEMENTS

SUMMARY

Managers use financial statement analysis, or ratio analysis, to compare a firm's performance and status to that of other firms or to itself over time. This activity requires calculating and interpreting financial ratios in order to assess performance and status. The basic inputs to ratio analysis include a firm's balance sheet and income statement, while the output is a relative comparison of the firm's condition to that of its historical condition and to its industry peers.

Financial statement analysis takes two different forms: cross-sectional analysis and time series analysis. Cross-sectional analysis requires a comparison of different firms' performance and condition at a given point in time, while time series analysis reviews one particular firm's financial condition across different time periods. In both cases, managers rely upon external sources of financial information such as *Robert Morris Associates Statement Studies* to provide comparative ratios from a variety of different evaluations.

Ratios can be divided into four groups: liquidity, activity, debt, and profitability. Liquidity, or the ability of the firm to pay its bills as they come due, can be measured by the firm's net working capital, its current ratio, or quick ratio. Activity ratios are used to measure the speed with which various accounts are converted into sales or cash. The activity or inventory can be measured by its turnover, that of accounts receivable by the average collection period, and that of accounts payable by the average payment period. The fixed asset turnover measures how efficiently the firm has been using its fixed assets to generate sales. The total asset turnover measures the efficiency with which the firm has utilized all its assets. Activity ratios may reflect seasonality, so caution should be applied to their use.

Debt ratios measure both the degree of indebtedness and the ability to service debts. Generally, higher use of debt results in greater financial leverage, which increases the potential for return and the financial risk of the firm. The debt ratio and the debt-equity ratio measure indebtedness. The ability to service fixed contractual obligations such as interest, principal or sinking-fund payments, lease payments, and preferred dividends is measured with coverage ratios, such as times interest earned and fixed payment coverage. The higher these coverage ratios, the better able the firm is to meet its fixed payment obligations.

Several measures of profitability exist. Common size statements such as the percent income statement show each item on the statement as a percentage of sales. From the percent income statement, one can determine the gross profit margin, the operating profit margin, and the net profit margin. Other measures of profitability include the return on investment, the return on equity, earnings per share, and the price/earnings P/E ratio. The relationship between a firm's net profit margin, total asset turnover, and return on investment may be shown with the DuPont formula. The Modified DuPont formula adds the interaction of leverage -- the degree of indebtedness -- on the return on investment in order to determine the return on equity.

DuPont = npm, tat, roi
modified adds leverage - degree of indebtedness

CONCEPT OUTLINE

I.   Financial ratios are used to compare a firm's performance and status to that of other firms or to itself over time. Ratio analysis involves calculating and interpreting financial ratios to assess the firm's performance and status.

A.   Financial ratios provide important information to the firm's shareholders, creditors, and managers.

B.   Financial ratios are relative values that relate one financial value to another in the form of a quotient.

C.   Ratio analysis requires more than simply applying a particular formula to financial data -- interpretation of the ratio value is important.

D.   When using financial ratio analysis to analyze past, current, or projected firm performance, two different types of comparisons are made.

   1.   The cross-sectional approach compares similar financial ratios for differing firms at the same time. Industry-average ratios, which are available from such sources as Dun and Bradstreet, often are used for cross-sectional comparisons.

   2.   The time-series approach, which compares the performance of the same firm at different points in time, may be based on past or projected operations. Time-series analysis is used to evaluate the firm's present performance in light of its past or future performance in order to isolate any developing trends.

E.   The most informative approach to ratio analysis is one that combines cross-sectional and time-series analyses.

F.   Accurate ratio analysis depends upon several important ingredients:

   1.   A single ratio observed in isolation provides incomplete information for judging the overall performance of the firm.

   2.   Financial statements being compared should be dated at the same point in time during the year.

   3.   Audited financial statements provide the most accurate source of financial information.

4.   Financial data being compared should follow a similar accounting convention.

5.   Analysts should consider the impact of inflation on nominal accounting data.

G.   Financial ratios are divided into four basic categories:

1.   Liquidity ratios,
2.   Activity ratios,
3.   Debt ratios, and
4.   Profitability ratios.

H.   At minimum, the inputs to an effective financial analysis include the income statement and balance sheet.

II.   **Liquidity ratios measure the firm's ability to satisfy short-term obligations as they come due.**

A.   Net working capital (current assets minus current liabilities) measures the absolute level of liquidity.

T

B.   The current ratio (current assets ÷ current liabilities) measures liquidity on a relative basis.

C.   The quick ratio or acid-test ratio [(current assets minus inventory) ÷ current liabilities] measures the firm's ability to cover current obligations with its very liquid current assets. Inventory is not included in this measure because inventory is considered the least liquid current asset.

III.   **Activity ratios measure the speed with which various accounts are converted to cash or sales.**

A.   Inventory turnover (cost of goods sold ÷ inventory) measures the activity of a firm's inventory.

T

B.   Average collection period (accounts receivable ÷ average sales per day) measures the length of time an average account receivable is outstanding.

C.   Average payment period (accounts payable ÷ average purchases per day) measures the length of time an average account payable is outstanding.

D.   Fixed asset turnover (sales ÷ net fixed assets) measures the efficiency of fixed assets in generating sales.

E.   Total asset turnover (sales ÷ total assets) indicates the efficiency with which the firm is able to use its assets to generate sales.

IV.   **Debt measures include the degree of indebtedness and the ability to service debts. Measures of the ability to service debts and other contractual obligations are provided by coverage ratios.**

A.   Greater use of debt results in greater financial leverage, which increases both the potential returns and the financial risk of the firm.

T

B.   Debt ratios covering the degree of indebtedness include the debt ratio and the debt-to-equity ratio.

1.   The debt ratio (total liabilities ÷ total assets) indicates the proportion of assets financed by the firm's creditors.

2.   The debt-equity ratio (long-term debt ÷ stockholders' equity) indicates the relationship between the long-term funds provided by creditors and those provided by owners.

C.   The ability to serve debts means the readiness of a firm to meet its fixed contractual payments on a scheduled basis over the life of a debt. Measures of indebtedness include the times interest earned ratio and the fixed payment coverage ratio.

1.   Times interest earned (earnings before interest and taxes ÷ interest) measures the firm's ability to meet its contractual interest payments.

    2.   The fixed-payment ratio, or the overall coverage ratio [(earnings before interest, lease payments, and taxes) ÷ (interest, lease expense, pretax principal, and pretax preferred dividends or sinking-fund requirements)], measures the firm's ability to meet lease payments as well as preferred stock dividend payments and service debt as contractually required.

V. Profitability ratios measure the returns of the firm with respect to either sales, assets, or equity. A common size statement such as the percent income statement, in which each entry is stated as a percentage of sales, is useful in evaluating a firm's profitability in relation to sales.

A. The gross profit margin (gross profit ÷ sales), operating profit margin (operating profits ÷ sales), and net profit margin (net profits after taxes ÷ sales) may be directly obtained from the percent income statement.

B. Return on investment, or ROI (net profits after taxes ÷ total assets), measures the overall effectiveness of management in generating profits from available assets.

C. Return on equity, or ROE (net profits after taxes ÷ stockholders' equity), measures the return earned on the owners' investment (for holders of both preferred and common stock).

D. Earnings per share, or EPS (earnings available for common stockholders ÷ number of outstanding shares of common stock), indicates the number of dollars earned on behalf of each outstanding share.

E. The price-earnings (P/E) ratio (market price per share of common stock ÷ earnings per share) represents the amount investors are willing to pay for each dollar of the firm's earnings.

VI. Comprehensive ratio analysis includes a large number of liquidity, activity, debt, and profitability ratios. Popular frameworks which organize these data into a coherent picture of financial performance include the DuPont system of analysis and the summary analysis of ratio data.

A. The DuPont system of analysis allows analysts to subdivide financial statement data for quick analysis.

B. ~~The DuPont formula calculates a firm's return on investment~~ by multiplying the net profit margin by the total asset turnover: $ROI = NPM \cdot TAT$

C. The summary analysis of ratio data provides a written evaluation of the firm's financial performance and condition on the basis of the ratio data obtained from financial statement analysis.

APPLICATIONS

DEFINITIONS

1. *Cross Sectional* analysis compares different firms' financial ratios at the same point in time, while ____ ____ analysis evaluates financial performance over several time periods. *time series)*

2. A firm that is easily able to satisfy its short-term obligations as they come due maintains a high degree of *liquidity*

3. The difference between current assets and current liabilities is known as *Net working capital*

4. The *average collection period* measures the average amount of time needed to collect accounts receivable.

5. The efficiency with which a firm has been using its fixed assets is measured by the *fixed asset turnover* ratio.

6. In order to calculate the quick ratio, it is necessary to subtract *inventory* from *current assets* and then divide this sum by current liabilities.

7. A common-size income statement expresses each financial quantity as a *percentage* of the firm's sales.

8. The return on *investment* measures the overall effectiveness of management in generating profits with its available assets, while the return on ____ measures the return expected on the owners' investment in the firm. *equity*

9. The liquidity associated with a firm's investment in inventory is measured by the *inventory turnover* ratio.

10. One particular ratio that measures the ability of a firm to service its debt obligations is the *times interest* earned ratio.

11. The proportion of total assets financed by a firm's creditors is measured by the *debt* ratio.

12. The debt-equity ratio is calculated by dividing *long term debt* by *stockholder equity*

13. *Operating* profits show the firm's ability to generate returns from sales before interest and taxes are considered.

14.   The DuPont formula for return on investment (ROI) shows that increasing either the _net profit margin_ or _total asset_ _turnover_ results in improved financial performance.

15.   At minimum, financial analysts require the financial statement data contained in a firm's _balance sheet_ and _income statement_ to perform accurate ratio analysis.

MULTIPLE CHOICE

1.   The two methods of ratio analysis are called:
   a.   cross-sectional and time-series.
   b.   long-range and short-range.
   c.   cross-sectional and financial planning.
   c.   none of the above.

2.   The total asset turnover ratio measures the efficiency with which the firm is able to use all its assets to generate sales. It is computed using which formula?
   a.   sales/(total assets).
   b.   (profits after taxes)/sales.
   c.   (total assets)/sales.
   d.   (current assets)/(fixed assets).

   S/TA

3.   One measure of financial leverage is the debt ratio, which is:
   a.   (current assets)/(current liabilities).
   b.   (current liabilities)/(total assets).
   c.   (total liabilities)/(total assets).
   c.   (total liabilities)/(stockholders' equity).

   $\dfrac{TL}{TA}$

4.   The ratio that represents what are often called the pure profits earned on sales is:
   a.   the net profit margin.
   b.   the operating profit margin.
   c.   the gross profit margin.
   d.   all of the above.

   $\dfrac{OP.P.}{S}$ OPM

5.   The DuPont system allows an analyst to break return on equity into all but which of the following?
   a.   a profit-on-sales component.
   b.   a managerial-efficiency component.
   c.   a use-of-leverage component.
   c.   an efficiency-of-asset-use component.

6.   Inflation can seriously distort which of the following financial ratios?
     a.   gross profit margin.
     b.   operating margin.
     c.   inventory turnover.
     d.   return on equity.

7.   Which of the following ratios does not help analysts evaluate a firm's liquidity position?
     a.   inventory turnover ratio.
     b.   net working capital.
     c.   current ratio.
     d.   quick ratio.

8.   Firms that exhibit current ratios substantially above the industry average may be holding _____ amounts of cash, accounts receivable, or inventory.
     a.   insufficient.
     b.   excessive.
     c.   adequate.
     d.   uncertain.

9.   A particularly low gross profit margin may indicate either a _____ cost of merchandise sold or a _____ selling price.
     a.   low; high.
     b.   high; high.
     c.   low; low.
     d.   high; low.

10. Analysts seeking industry averages for various financial ratios can find this information in each of the following sources except:
     a.   Dun & Bradstreet's Key Business Ratios.
     b.   Robert Morris Associates Statement Studies.
     c.   the New York Times Financial Reporter.
     d.   the Almanac of Business and Industrial Financial Ratios.

11. Seasonal selling patterns can seriously distort the accuracy of which of the following financial ratios?
     a.   debt ratio.
     b.   average collection period.
     c.   return on equity.
     d.   price-earnings ratio.

12. Increased financial leverage implies that a firm will experience _____ potential returns and _____ risk.
   a. higher; greater.
   b. higher; smaller.
   c. lower; greater.
   d. lower; lower.

13. A firm that shows a particularly high inventory turnover ratio may experience:
   a. a reduced return on investment.
   b. stockouts and lost sales.
   c. a sudden increase in sales.
   d. a reduction in average outstanding receivables.

14. The _____ is the product of the net profit margin and the total asset turnover.
   a. return on sales.
   b. return on net worth.
   c. return on inventory.
   d. return on investment.

15. Activity ratios are used to measure:
   a. the ability of the firm to pay its debts upon short notice.
   b. the ability of the firm to withstand a prolonged sales slump.
   c. the ability and speed of the firm in converting assets to cash.
   d. the amount of employee turnover within the firm.

PROBLEMS

1. Gulf and Northern's total current assets, net working capital, and inventory for each of the past four years are as follows:

T

Financial Statement Item	1986	1987	1988	1989	1990
Total Current Assets	$27,000	$24,000	$22,000	$17,000	$16,500
Net Working Capital	9,600	9,900	9,300	7,950	7,550
Inventory	7,200	6,900	6,900	6,000	6,100

   a. Calculate the firm's liquidity ratios for each year. Compare the resulting time series of each measure of liquidity (i.e., net working capital, current ratio, and quick ratio).

b. Comment on the firm's liquidity over the period.

c. Do the following inventory turnover ratios for Gulf and Northern each year in the period and industry averages support or conflict with your evaluation in part b? Why?

Inventory Turnover Ratios	1986	1987	1988	1989	1990
Gulf and Northern	11.1	10.8	11.2	10.6	10.8
Industry Average	6.4	7.0	6.8	6.3	6.1

$$IT = \frac{CGS}{I} \qquad 4 = \frac{384000}{I} \qquad 4\frac{I}{I} = 384,000 \qquad 96,000$$

2. Given the following information, along with the partially completed balance sheet, fill in the balance sheet. Assume a 360-day year.

Debt-to-Equity Ratio	=	1.5
Average Payment Period	=	45 days
Quick Ratio	=	0.80
Annual Credit Purchases	=	$400,000
Total Asset Turnover	=	1.6
Gross Profit Margin	=	20%
Inventory Turnover	=	4

$\frac{LTD}{80000} = 1.5$

$LTD = 120,000$

$\frac{AP}{400000} \cdot 360 = 45$

$AP = 45$

$\frac{AR}{100,000} \quad 15000+X = .8$

$15000+X = 80,000$

$\frac{80,000}{15000}$

$65,000$

$TAT = \frac{S}{Assets} \quad X = 480,000$

$1.6 = \frac{X}{300000}$

$\frac{480,000}{96,000}$ S or PR

384000 CGS

$AP = 50,000$

ASSETS		LIABILITIES	
Cash	$15,000	Accounts Payable	50000
Accounts Receivable	65000	Notes Payable	$40,000
Inventory	96000	Accruals	10,000
Fixed Assets	124,000	Long-Term Debt	120000
		Stockholders' Equity	80,000
TOTAL	300,000	TOTAL	300,000

3. The Midwest City Bank is evaluating the Telaxe Corporation, which has requested a $2,000,000 loan, in order to determine its leverage and the financial risk involved in the loan request.

a. Based on the debt ratios for Telaxe and following financial information given to the bank, evaluate and recommend appropriate action on the loan request.

T

Balance Sheet
Telaxe Corporation
December 31, 1990

ASSETS:

Current Assets	$ 1,000,000
Cash	3,000,000
Marketable securities	12,000,000
Inventory	7,500,000
Total current assets	$23,500,000
Fixed Assets	$11,000,000
Land and buildings	20,000,000
Machinery and equipment	8,000,000
Furniture and fixtures	$39,500,000
Less: Accumulated depreciation	13,000,000
Net fixed assets	$26,500,000
Total Assets	50,000,000

LIABILITIES AND STOCKHOLDERS' EQUITY:

Current Liabilities	
Accrued liabilities	$ 500,000
Notes payable	8,000,000
Accounts payable	8,000,000
Total current liabilities	$16,000,000
Long-term debts[1]	$20,000,000
Stockholders' equity	
Preferred stock[2]	$ 2,500,000
Common stock	
(1 million shares at $5 par)	5,000,000
Additional Paid-In Capital	4,000,000
Retained earnings	2,000,000
Total stockholders' equity	$13,500,000

Total Liabilities & Stockholders' Equity $50,000,000

1. Required annual principal payments are $800,000.
2. 12,500 shares of $8.00 cumulative preferred stock outstanding.

Income Statement
Telaxe Corporation
December 31, 1990

Net Sales		$30,000,000
Less: Cost of goods sold		12,000,000
Gross Profits		$ 9,000,000
Less: Operating expenses		
Selling expense	$2,500,000	
Gen. and admin. expense	1,500,000	
Depreciation expense	1,000,000	
Total operating expense		5,000,000
Earnings before interest and taxes		$ 4,000,000
Less: Interest		2,000,000
Earnings before taxes		2,000,000
Less: Taxes (40%)		800,000
Earnings after taxes		$1,200,000

Industry Average - Selected Financial Ratios

Current ratio	1.95
Debt ratio	0.46
Debt-equity ratio	1.07
Times interest earned	7.30
Fixed-payment coverage ratio	1.85

b.   A common size statement for the Telaxe Corporation's 1989 operations is presented below. Develop and compare it to the 1990 year-end common size income statement. Which areas require further analysis or investigation?

Percent Income Statement
Telaxe Corporation
December 31, 1989

Net Sales ($35,000,000)	100.0%
Less: Cost of goods sold	65.9
Gross profit	34.1%
Less: Operating expenses	
Selling expense 12.8%	
Gen. and admin. expense 6.9	
Depreciation 3.5	
Total operating expense	23.2%
Earnings before interest and taxes	10.9%
Less: Interest	1.5
Earnings before taxes	9.4%
Less: Taxes (40%)	3.8
Earnings after taxes	5.6%

4.   Martha's Homestyle Baked Goods had the following income statements and balance sheets for the period 1988-1990:

T

Income Statement
Martha's Homestyle Baked Goods
Year-End December 31, 19XX

	1988	1989	1990
Sales	$600,000	$580,000	$680,000
Less: Cost of goods sold	450,000	460,000	550,000
Gross profit	$150,000	$120,000	$130,000
Less: Operating expense	60,000	50,000	70,000
Operating profit	$ 90,000	$ 70,000	$ 60,000
Less: Interest	10,000	12,000	12,000
Profits before taxes	$ 80,000	$ 58,000	$ 48,000
Less: Taxes	40,000	29,000	24,000
Net profits after taxes	$ 40,000	$ 29,000	$24,000

Balance Sheet
Martha's Homestyle Baked Goods
Year-End December 31, 19XX

Assets	1988	1989	1990
Cash	$ 30,000	$ 10,000	$ 10,000
Accounts Receivable	120,000	150,000	170,000
Inventory	150,000	160,000	210,000
Total current assets	$300,000	$320,000	$390,000
Fixed assets	450,000	520,000	480,000
Total Assets	$750,000	$840,000	$870,000

Liabilities and Equity			
Accounts payable	$ 80,000	$120,000	$130,000
Notes payable	50,000	40,000	40,000
Accruals	20,000	20,000	20,000
Total current liabilities	$150,000	$180,000	$190,000
Long-term debt	200,000	240,000	240,000
Stockholders' equity	400,000	420,000	440,000
Total Liabilities and Equity	$750,000	$870,000	$870,000

Assuming that 80 percent of the firm's cost of goods sold represents purchases, given the industry-average values:

a.   Develop a series of financial ratios for the firm and compare your results to the industry averages shown below.

b.   Evaluate the firm's performance on both a time-series and cross-sectional basis over the 1988-90 time period.

Historical Industry-Average Ratios
The Baked Goods Industry

	1988	1989	1990
	Industry Average	Industry Average	Industry Average
Current Ratio	1.90	1.85	1.95
Quick Ratio	0.95	0.95	0.95
Average Collection Period	65 days	70 days	71 days
Average Payment Period	70 days	75 days	75 days
Inventory Turnover	4.0X	3.8X	4.0X
Fixed Asset Turnover	1.50X	1.55X	1.60X
Total Asset Turnover	0.90X	0.93X	0.95X
Debt-Equity Ratio	0.48	0.49	0.49
Gross Profit Margin	24.0%	25.0%	27.0%
Operating Profit Margin	14.8%	14.9%	15.0%
Net Profit Margin	7.0%	6.7%	6.8%
Return On Investment	6.5%	6.5%	6.4%
Times Interest Earned	8.0X	8.0X	8.0X

5. Illustrate the DuPont Model using 1990 data for Martha's Homestyle Baked Goods as presented in Problem #4 above.

T

6. Given the following information, calculate the Galaxo Company's return on investment and return on equity using the Modified DuPont formula.

T

Debt ratio	=	0.39
Total asset turnover	=	2.20X
Net profits before taxes	=	$100,000
Tax rate	=	40%
Sales	=	$900,000

7. Use the given ratio information for Big DD Industries and the industry averages for Big DD's lines of business to do the following:

T

a. Construct the Modified DuPont model for both Big DD and the industry.

b. Evaluate Big DD (and the industry) over the three-year period.

c. For Big DD Industries, determine which areas require further analysis.

Ratio	1990 Big DD	1990 Industry Average	1989 Big DD	1989 Industry Average	1988 Big DD	1988 Industry Average
Debt Ratio	0.43	0.40	0.43	0.41	0.46	0.39
Net Profit Margin	0.061	0.054	0.058	0.049	0.046	0.041
Total Asset Turnover	2.04X	2.18X	2.18X	2.11X	2.38X	2.15X

8.   In 1990, Randi's Cookies-N-Cakes had sales of $800,000 and a gross profit margin of 50 percent. The firm's end-of-quarter inventories for 1990 are presented below:

T

Quarter	Inventory
1	$30,000
2	$50,000
3	$60,000
4	$20,000

a.   Use the end-of-year inventory to calculate the firm's inventory turnover ratio and average age of inventory.

b.   Find the average quarterly inventory and use it to calculate the firm's inventory turnover ratio and the average age of inventory.

c.   Discuss the difference between a and b.

d.   If the firm is in an industry with an average inventory turnover of 30, based on end-of-year data, how would you evaluate the activity of Randi's inventory?

SOLUTIONS

DEFINITIONS

1. cross-sectional; time series
2. liquidity
3. net working capital
4. average collection period
5. fixed asset turnover
6. inventory; current assets
7. percentage
8. investment; equity

9. inventory turnover
10. times interest
11. debt
12. long term debt; stockholders' equity
13. operating
14. net profit margin; total asset turnover
15. balance sheet; income statement

MULTIPLE CHOICE

1.	a	9.	d
2.	a	10.	c
3.	c	11.	b
4.	b	12.	a
5.	b	13.	b
6.	c	14.	d
7.	a	15.	c
8.	b		

PROBLEMS

1.

a. The following ratio equations are required:

Current ratio = current assets ÷ current liabilities

Quick ratio = (current assets - inventory) ÷ current liabilities

Net working capital = current assets - current liabilities

Current liabilities = current assets - net working capital

Year	Current Assets (1)	Net Working Capital (2)	Current Liabilities [(1)-(2)] (3)	Current Ratio [(1)÷(3)] (4)	Inventory (5)	Quick Ratio [(1)-(5)]÷(3) (6)
1990	$16,500	$7,550	$8,950	1.84	$6,100	1.16
1989	17,000	7,950	9,050	1.88	6,000	1.22
1988	22,000	9,300	12,700	1.73	6,900	1.19
1987	24,000	9,900	14,100	1.70	6,900	1.21
1986	27,000	9,600	17,400	1.55	7,200	1.14

Ratio	1986	1987	1988	1989	1990
Current Ratio	1.55	1.70	1.73	1.88	1.84
Quick Ratio	1.14	1.21	1.19	1.22	1.16
Net Working Capital	$9,600	$9,900	$9,300	$7,950	$7,550

b.   The pattern indicates a small reduction in liquidity in 1990, following three years of an improving liquidity position. Net working capital has fallen throughout the period.

c.   The high inventory turnover suggests that liquidity may be better than the liquidity measures indicate. High inventory turnover also may indicate inventory stockout possibilities, and should reviewed carefully.

2.   The order in which this problem is solved could vary, but the most straightforward approach is as follows.

a.   Find long-term debt:

debt-to-equity ratio = (long-term debt) ÷ (stockholders' equity),

thus, long-term debt = (debt-to-equity) x (stockholders' equity).

Long-term debt = (1.5) x ($80,000) = $120,000.

b.   Find accounts payable:

average payment period = (accounts payable) ÷ [(credit purchases) ÷ (360)],

thus, accounts payable = (average payment period) x [(credit purchases) ÷ (360)].

accounts payable = (45) x [($400,000) ÷ (360)] = $50,000.

c.   Find total assets. Using the results of parts (a) and (b), total liabilities and equities are found to equal $300,000, so total assets must also equal $300,000.

d.   Calculate sales, which is necessary for finding inventory:

total asset turnover = (sales) ÷ (total assets),

thus, sales = (total asset turnover) x (total assets).

Sales = (1.6) x ($300,000) = $480,000.

e.   Calculate the cost of goods sold, which also is necessary to find inventory:

cost of goods sold = (sales) x (1 - gross profit margin)

$$= (\$480,000) \times (1 - .20) = \$384,000.$$

f.   Calculate inventory:

inventory turnover = (cost of goods sold) ÷ (inventory),

thus, inventory = (cost of goods sold) ÷ (inventory turnover).

Inventory = ($384,000) ÷ (4) = $96,000.

g.   Calculate accounts receivable. Based on the given balance sheet information, cash plus accounts receivable would equal current assets minus inventory. Thus,

quick ratio = (cash + accounts receivable) ÷ (current liabilities), and

accounts receivable = [(quick ratio) x (current liabilities)] - cash.

In this problem, current liabilities equal the sum of accounts payable, notes payable, and accruals, or $50,000 plus $40,000 plus $10,000.

Accounts receivable = [(.80) x ($100,000)] - $15,000 = $65,000.

h.   By subtracting cash, accounts receivable, and inventory from the firm's total assets of $300,000, fixed assets are:

fixed assets = ($300,000) - ($15,000) - ($65,000) - ($96,000) = $124,000.

The completed financial statement is as follows:

ASSETS		LIABILITIES AND EQUITY	
Cash	$ 15,000	Accounts payable	$50,000
Accounts receivable	65,000	Notes payable	40,000
Inventory	96,000	Accruals	10,000
Fixed assets	124,000	Long-term debt	120,000
		Stockholders equity	80,000
Total	$300,000		$300,000

3.

    a. Telaxe's debt ratios (and the industry-average ratios) are as follows:

        1. Current Ratio = (current assets) ÷ (current liabilities)

$$= (\$23,500,000) \div (\$16,500,000) = 1.42.$$

        Industry Average = 1.95.

        2. Debt Ratio = (total liabilities) ÷ (total assets)

$$= (\$36,500,000) \div (\$50,000,000) = 0.73.$$

        Industry Average = 0.46.

        3. Debt-to-Equity Ratio = (long-term debt) ÷ (total equity)

$$= (\$20,000,000) \div (\$13,500,000) = 1.48.$$

        Industry Average = 1.07.

        4. Times Interest Earned = (EBIT) ÷ (interest)

$$= (\$4,000,000) \div (\$2,000,000) = 7.30X$$

        Industry Average = 7.30X.

        5. Fixed Payment Coverage Ratio =

(EBIT + Lease Payments) ÷ {Interest + Lease Payments + [Principal/(1-t)] + [Preferred Dividends/(1-t)]}

$$= (\$4,000,000) \div \{\$2,000,000 + [\$800,000/(1-0.4)] + [\$100,000/(1-0.4)]\} = 1.14$$

        Industry Average = 1.85.

Telaxe has a much higher degree of indebtedness and a much lower ability to service debt than the average firm in the industry. The firm has a low current ratio. Most likely, the bank would not want to make the loan. Further information could be obtained by restating the financial statements as if the firm now had the loan.

b. The common size income statements for 1989 and 1990 are as follows:

Common Size Income Statement
Telaxe Corporation
Year-End December 31. 19XX

Account	1989	1990
Net Sales	100.0%	100.0%
Less: Cost of Goods Sold	65.9	70.0
Gross Profit Margin	34.1%	30.0
Less: Operating Expenses		
Selling Expenses	12.8%	8.3%
General Expenses	6.9	5.0
Depreciation	3.5	3.3
Total Operating Expense	23.2%	16.6%
EBIT	10.9%	13.4%
Less: Interest Expense	1.5	6.7
Earnings Before Taxes	9.4%	6.7%
Less: Taxes	3.8	2.7
Earnings After Taxes	5.6%	4.0%

Sales have fallen and the cost of goods sold has risen as a percentage of sales. This may result from a loss of productive efficiency. Selling and general operating expenses have both fallen as a percentage of sales. Although this may be a result of cost control policies, it may be connected to the fall in sales. The significant increase in interest as a percentage of sales is also a key concern, and supports the findings regarding the firm's debt and debt service ratios.

4.

a. The values of the various ratios were calculated as follows:

Current Ratio = (current assets) ÷ (current liabilities).

Quick Ratio = (current assets - inventory) ÷ (current liabilities).

Average Collection Period = (accounts receivable) ÷ (average daily sales),

where average daily sales = (annual sales) ÷ (360).

Average Payment Period = (accounts payable) ÷ (average daily purchases),

where average daily purchases = (annual purchases) ÷ (360).

Inventory Turnover = (cost of goods sold) ÷ (inventory).

Fixed Asset Turnover = (sales) ÷ (net fixed assets).

Total Asset Turnover = (sales) ÷ (total assets).

Debt-to-Equity Ratio = (long-term debt) ÷ (stockholders' equity).

Gross Profit Margin = (gross profit) ÷ (sales).

Operating Profit Margin = (operating profit) ÷ (sales).

Net Profit Margin = (net profits after taxes) ÷ (sales).

Return on Investment = (net profits after taxes) ÷ (total assets).

Times Interest Earned = (earnings before interest and taxes) ÷ (interest).

Applying these ratios to the financial statements results in the completed table below. All the calculations requiring balance sheet values use the year-end balance.

Historical and Industry-Average Ratios
Martha's Homestyle Baked Goods

Ratio	1988 Martha's	1988 Industry	1989 Martha's	1989 Industry	1990 Martha's	1990 Industry
Current Ratio	2.00	1.90	1.78	1.85	2.05	1.95
Quick Ratio	1.00	0.95	0.89	0.95	0.95	0.95
Average Collection Period	72 days	65 days	93 days	70 days	90 days	71 days
Average Payment Period	80 days	70 days	117 days	75 days	106 days	75 days
Inventory Turnover	3.00	4.00	2.90	3.80	2.60	4.00
Fixed Asset Turnover	1.33	1.50	1.11	1.55	1.41	1.60
Total Asset Turnover	0.80	0.90	0.69	0.93	0.78	0.95
Debt-to-Equity Ratio	0.50	0.48	0.57	0.49	0.55	0.49
Gross Profit Margin	25%	24%	21%	25%	19%	27%
Operating Profit Margin	15%	14.8%	12%	14.9%	8.8%	15%
Net Profit Margin	6.7%	7.0%	5.0%	6.7%	3.5%	6.8%
Return on Investment	5.3%	6.5%	3.5%	6.5%	2.8%	6.4%
Times Interest Earned Ratio	9.0	8.0	5.8	8.0	5.0	8.0

b. Analysis:

The overall liquidity of the firm, as shown by the current and quick ratios, appears better than the industry average performance. The increasing trend in average collection period, which is considerably higher than the industry average, indicates the presence of collection problems. The firm's payables, on average, are being paid beyond the industry average age, and the trend appears to be deteriorating further. The firm's inventory also appears to be mismanaged, because it turns over less frequently than the average firm and has a deteriorating trend. Both fixed and total asset turnover ratios are well below industry averages.

The firm's debt-to-equity ratio is only slightly above the industry figures, and therefore does not appear to be problematic. The profitability of the firm in relation to sales (i.e., gross profit margin, operating profit margin and net profit margin) along with return on investment indicate poor profit performance, which seems to be deteriorating with the passage of time. Finally, the firm's ability to meet fixed interest charges, as indicated by the times interest earned ratio, is also deteriorating and remains below the industry average.

The firm's problems seem to result from excessive levels of accounts receivable, accounts payable, inventory, and from its inability to earn sufficient profits. A trend of rising costs and expenses without corresponding increases in the selling price may explain the declining returns on sales and assets.

5. DuPont Model: ROI = (Net Profit Margin) x (Total Asset Turnover)

$$= (3.5\%) \text{ x } (0.78 \text{ times}) = 2.7\%$$

The difference in this number and the 2.8% ROI reported above is due to rounding.

6. The DuPont formula states:

Return on Investment = (Total Asset Turnover) x (Net Profit Margin).

In order to find the net profit margin, profits after taxes can be obtained from net profits before taxes according to:

Net Profits After Tax = (Profits Before Tax) x (1 - t).

$$= (\$100,000) \text{ x } (1 - 0.40) = \$60,000.$$

Net Profit Margin = (Net Profits After Tax) ÷ (sales)

$$= (\$60,000) \div (\$900,000) = 6.67\%.$$

Since total asset turnover is equal to 2.2 times,

Return on Investment = (2.2) x (6.67%) = 14.67%.

Using the Modified DuPont formula:

Return on Equity = [(Net Profit Margin) x (Total Asset Turnover)] ÷ (1 - debt ratio).

= [(6.67%) x (2.2)] ÷ (1 - 0.39) = 24.05%.

Note: The value of the numerator used in calculating the Modified DuPont formula is the firm's return on investment.

7.

a.   The Modified Dupont model for Big DD and the industry yields the following:

(Net Profit Margin) x (Total Asset Turnover) = ROI + (1 - Debt Ratio) = ROE.

Year	Net Profit Margin (1)	Total Asset Turnover (2)	Return on Investment [(1) x (2)] (3)	[1 - debt ratio] (4)	Return on Equity [(3) ÷ (4)] (5)
1990 Big DD	0.046	2.38	10.95%	(1 - 0.46)	20.28%
1990 Industry	0.041	2.15	8.82	(1 - 0.39)	14.46
1989 Big DD	0.058	2.18	12.64	(1 - 0.43)	22.18
1989 Industry	0.049	2.11	10.34	(1 - 0.41)	17.53
1988 Big DD	0.061	2.04	12.44	(1 - 0.43)	21.83
1988 Industry	0.054	2.05	11.07	(1 - 0.40)	18.45

b. Analysis:

Profitability: Net profit margins are decreasing; Big DD's net profit margins have fallen an amount equivalent to those of the average firm in the industry.

Efficiency: Asset turnover has increased; Big DD's has increased more than that of the average firm in the industry.

Leverage: Big DD shows an increase in leverage higher than the industry.

As a result of these changes, the ROE has fallen for both Big DD and the industry, but Big DD has experienced a much smaller decline in its ROE.

c.   Areas requiring further analysis::

Profitability: An important question here is, are sales decreasing, or are costs increasing?

Leverage: Some management teams attempt to magnify returns by using financial leverage to offset declining margins. This strategy is effective only within a narrow range. A high-leverage strategy actually may result in a decline in stock price due to the increased risk.

8.

a.   Inventory Turnover = ($400,000) ÷ ($20,000) = 20 times.

Average Age of Inventory = (360) ÷ (20) = 18 days.

b.   Average Inventory = ($30,000 + $50,000 + $60,000 + $20,000 ÷ (4) = $40,000.

Inventory Turnover = ($400,000) ÷ ($40,000) = 10 times.

Average Age of Inventory = (360) ÷ (10) = 36 days.

c.   Seasonal industries may need to be averaged over the four quarters to get meaningful ratio data.

d.   The firm has less active inventory than the average firm, because its end-of-year inventory turnover ratio is only 20 times while the average firm turns its inventory 30 times a year.

CHAPTER 8

FINANCIAL PLANNING

SUMMARY

[handwritten notes in top right margin:]
Receipts
- Disbursements
─────────
Net Cash Flow
+ Beginning Cash
─────────
Ending Cash
- Minimum Cash Bal
─────────
Required Finan. or Excess Cash

Financial planning provides a key ingredient in formulating effective corporate strategy. Firms use financial plans to guide their actions toward achievement of immediate and long-run goals. The financial planning process begins with long-run, or strategic, financial plans that in turn guide the formulation of short-run, or operating, plans and budgets. Important inputs to the planning process include a sales forecast and various forms of operating and financial data. Outputs from the planning process include operating budgets, a cash budget, a pro forma income statement, and a pro forma balance sheet.

The cash planning process is concerned mainly with the preparation of the cash budget, or cash forecast. The cash budget relies heavily on the sales forecast as an input. Both external and internal sales forecast data are used to produce the cash budget. This budget is usually prepared for a one-year period divided into monthly intervals. In the cash budget, cash receipts and cash disbursements for each period are netted against one another to get that period's net cash flow. By adding beginning cash to the net cash flow, the ending cash can be estimated. After subtracting the minimum cash balance required from the ending cash, the required total financing or excess cash balance can be determined. Managers can then arrange to obtain required financing or invest surplus funds in marketable securities.

Within the cash budget, the use of sensitivity analysis or computer simulation is suggested. One common sensitivity analysis approach involves preparing separate cash budgets based upon pessimistic, most likely, and optimistic estimates. A carefully prepared cash budget is very valuable in determining the need for short-term financing or in planning uses for any excess cash balance. It must be recognized, however, that the cash budget does not insure that the firm will be able to meet its cash requirements on a day-to-day basis. Only by monitoring daily cash flows can this problem be managed effectively.

The profit-planning process involves preparation of pro forma statements, which are projected income statements and balance sheets. The financial manager usually prepares these statements using simple approximations, while the detailed procedures typically are left to accountants. Two approximation, or simplified, approaches to pro forma statement preparation include the percent-of-sales method and the judgment method.

The percent-of-sales method uses the relationship between certain cost and expense items and the firm's sales to forecast pro forma income statement accounts. This approach implies that all costs are variable -- a situation that is unlikely to exist. A pro forma balance sheet can be estimated with the percent of sales method by determining those assets and liabilities which spontaneously change with sales, and letting additional external funding required act as a balancing figure. The judgmental approach, preferred when a more detailed pro forma statement is required, relies on more specific and detailed assumptions and estimates of financial data.

Pro forma financial statements are used to assess the firm's likely performance in coming years, determine the amount of external financing the firm will require to support a given level of sales, estimate the level of profitability the firm is likely to achieve, and evaluate the firm's sources and uses of cash over time. In addition, pro forma statements allow financial managers to adjust planned corporate operations to achieve short-run financial goals.

CONCEPT OUTLINE

I. **Financial planning provides a key ingredient in formulating effective corporate strategy.**

    A. Planning provides a road map for achieving the objective of wealth maximization.

    B. Budgets and financial plans provide a structure to coordinate diverse activities of the organization.

    C. These plans provide a standard against which actual performance can be evaluated.

II. **The planning process begins with long-run plans. These dictate parameters reflected in the short-run plans and budgets.**

    A. Long-run plans are more general, while short-run plans are more specific.

        1. Long-run plans tend to focus on implementation of proposed capital expenditures, research and development activities, marketing and product development activities, and major sources of financing.

        2. These long-run plans cover two to ten years and are often supported by a series of annual budgets and profit plans.

    B. Short-run plans cover near-term actions.

        1. Key inputs include a sales forecast and various forms of operating and financial data.

        2. Key outputs include operating budgets, the cash budget, and pro forma financial statements.

        3. The total financial planning process begins with a sales forecast and results in a cash budget, a pro forma income statement, and a pro forma balance sheet.

III.   **The cash budget, or cash forecast, is a statement used by the firm to plan its short-term financing and investing.**

A.   The cash budget typically is prepared to cover a one-year period.

  1.   The cash budget is most commonly broken into monthly divisions.
  2.   For firms without highly seasonal sales patterns, less frequent time intervals are used.

B.   The key input to the cash budget is the sales forecast.

  1.   The sales forecast may be developed externally, using the relationship of sales to certain economic indicators.

  2.   An internal sales forecast, which is developed by using various sales estimates built-up within the organization, can also be used.

  3.   A good forecast generally combines external and internal sales forecasts.

C.   Once the sales forecast has been prepared, the firm must estimate cash receipts and disbursements.

  1.   Cash receipts include cash sales; collection of accounts receivable; dividends received; interest received; proceeds from the sale of equipment, bonds, or stock; and other items.

  2.   Cash disbursements include cash purchases; payment of accounts payable, cash dividends, rent, wages, and salaries; tax payments; capital additions; interest on debt; loan and sinking-fund payments; stock repurchase or retirement; and other items.

  3.   Collection of accounts receivable and payment of accounts payable are most difficult to estimate because of their close relationship to projected sales and purchases, respectively.

D.   The final step in preparing the cash budget is to determine the net cash flow and ending cash without financing.

  1.   Net cash flow for each period is found by subtracting the cash disbursements from the cash receipts of each period.

  2.   Adding the beginning cash for each period, which is the ending cash of the preceding period, to the net cash flow results in the ending cash without financing.

E.　　The financial manager can determine, for each period, the amount of financing required or any excess cash balance available for investment in marketable securities by using the ending cash without financing figure.

　　1.　By subtracting any minimum cash requirement from the ending cash without financing, the amount of short-term borrowing or investing can be determined.

　　2.　If ending cash is greater than the minimum cash balance, the excess cash is invested in liquid interest-paying vehicles. If ending cash is less than the minimum cash balance, financing is required.

F.　　To cope with uncertainty in these projected values, cash budgets are often prepared with sensitivity analysis or by computer simulation.

　　1.　A common sensitivity analysis approach involves preparation of cash budgets based on pessimistic, most likely, and optimistic estimates.

　　2.　By monitoring daily cash flows, a firm can better meet its day-to-day cash requirements.

IV.　**Profit planning involves the preparation of pro forma financial statements, which are forecast statements, typically prepared for one year into the future.**

A.　　The two most common pro forma statements are the pro forma income statement and the pro forma balance sheet.

　　1.　The pro forma income statement projects the firm's revenues and costs for the coming year.

　　2.　The pro forma balance sheet shows the firm's expected financial position at the end of the forecast period.

　　3.　Two inputs are required for preparing pro forma statements: financial statements for the preceding year, and the sales forecast for the coming year.

B.　　Two simplified approaches for developing pro forma statements are the percent-of-sales method and the judgmental approach.

　　1.　The percent-of-sales approach assumes all income statement and some balance sheet amounts can be forecast as their historical percentage of sales.

a. The pro forma income statement can be developed by using a percent-of-sales method, in which one forecasts sales and then uses values for the cost of goods sold, operating expense, and interest expense that are a certain percentage of projected sales. This approach implies that all costs are variable -- a situation that is not likely to exist.

b. The pro forma balance sheet can be prepared by using estimates of desired levels of certain accounts and the inputs from the simplified pro forma income statement, letting the firm's funds requirement act as the balancing figure.

2. The judgmental approach requires more specific inputs, but provides a more detailed pro forma balance sheet.

3. There are two basic weaknesses in simplified forecasting approaches.

a. The assumption that the past will accurately reflect the future is questionable.

b. Forcing certain variables to take on desired values can be very unrealistic.

4. After analyzing pro forma statements, financial managers can take steps to adjust planned operations in order to achieve short-run financial goals.

APPLICATIONS

DEFINITIONS

1. _Strategic_ financial plans represent long-run plans that guide in the formulation of short-run budgets.

2. A financial projection of a firm's short-term cash surpluses or shortages represents a _Cash budget_

3. The key input to the short-run financial planning process is the _Sales_ forecast.

4. A sales forecast that relates the firm's observed sales to market-related data such as the gross national product is known as an _external_ forecast.

5. If a firm's cash budget shows a positive required total financing balance, then the ending cash balance for the period is _less_ than the minimum cash balance maintained by the firm.

6.   Projected financial statements are known as ___ _pro forma_ financial statements.

7.   The external funds required account within the pro forma balance sheet is used as a _plug_ figure to bring this forecast financial statement into balance.

8.   The ending cash balance in a cash budget is obtained by adding the beginning cash balance to the _net cash flow_ from the budgeting period.

9.   Cash _receipts_ minus cash _disbursements_ produce net cash flow within the cash budget.

10.   The percent-of-sales forecasting method expresses the firm's _variable costs_ as a percentage of projected sales.

11.   The most common components of cash _receipts_ include cash sales, collections of accounts receivable, and other cash inflows.

12.   _Depreciation_ is excluded from cash disbursements in the cash budget because it is a noncash charge.

13.   If all costs are assumed to be variable costs within the percent-of-sales forecasting method, the pro forma income statement will _understate_ profits when sales are rising and _overstate_ profits when sales are falling.

14.   A sales forecast based on a buildup, or consensus of forecasts through the firm's own sales channels represents an _internal_ forecast.

15.   The _financial planning process_ includes both long-run strategic financial plans and the short-run operating plans and budgets necessary to achieve these long-run objectives.

MULTIPLE CHOICE

1.   The key input to short-run financial planning and the cash budget is:
        a.   The budget period.
        b.   return for investment forecasts.
        c.   sales forecasts.
        d.   none of the above.

2.   If the pro forma balance sheet, prepared using the judgment approach, shows an expected
      level of assets that exceeds expected liabilities and stockholders' equity:
      a.   external financing is required.
      b.   extra dividends should be paid to eliminate surplus funds.
      c.   there must be a mistake, the balance sheet has to balance.
      d.   the percent-of-sales method should be used to avoid this problem

3.   The strict percent-of-sales approach to pro forma income statement preparation assumes:
      a.   all costs are variable.
      b.   all costs are fixed.
      c.   all costs are constant.
      d.   all costs are marginal.

4.   A typical strategic financial plan covers a _____ year time period, while an operating
      financial plan looks _____ years into the future.
      a.   1, 5.
      b.   10, 5.
      c.   5, 10.
      d.   10, 2.

5.   Which of the following is <u>not</u> a key output from the short-run financial planning process?
      a.   cash budget.
      b.   pro forma balance sheet.
      c.   dividends budget.
      d.   pro forma income statement.

6.   Highly seasonal or uncertain corporate cash flows call for _____ time intervals within
      the annual cash budget.
      a.   fixed.
      b.   shorter.
      c.   variable.
      d.   longer.

7.   The purpose of the cash budget is to forecast:
      a.   short-run cash requirements.
      b.   corporate cash flows.
      c.   long-run cash requirements.
      d.   short-run profit potential.

8.   Internal sales forecasts depend upon which of the following inputs?
      a.   gross national product projections.
      b.   expected new housing starts.
      c.   disposable personal income forecasts.
      d.   estimated sales for each of the firm's products.

9.   Which of the following would not be considered a cash receipt?
      a.   collection of accounts receivable.
      b.   cash sales.
      c.   payment of accounts payable.
      d.   collection of past-due accounts.

10.   Which of the following would be considered a cash disbursement?
      a.   principal payments on loans.
      b.   depreciation expense.
      c.   amortization of bond premiums.
      d.   declaration of dividends.

11.   In order to adjust for the presence of fixed costs when preparing a pro forma income statement, managers will:
      a.   divide the firm's historical costs into fixed and variable components.
      b.   treat all costs as variables.
      c.   ignore fixed costs.
      d.   divide the firm's historical costs into operating and financing components.

12.   A plug figure added to the right-hand side of the pro forma balance sheet in order to bring this financial statement into balance indicates that:
      a.   the pro forma balance sheet is inaccurate.
      b.   the firm's total financing exceeds its needs.
      c.   the firm will be unable to achieve its projected sales.
      d.   the firm must obtain additional financing to support its projected sales level.

13.   A major weakness associated with the percent-of-sales forecasting technique is that:
      a.   this method requires extensive computing resources.
      b.   many managers do not know about this method.
      c.   the firm's past financial condition is assumed to be an accurate indicator of its future.
      d.   managers are frequently unable to obtain historical cost data for the firm.

14.   Uses of pro forma financial statements include:
      a.   analyzing in advance the level of profitability expected by the firm.
      b.   analyzing the firm's expected sources and uses of cash.
      c.   adjusting the firm's planned operations to achieve short-run financial goals.
      d.   all of the above.

15.   When a firm exhibits an excess cash balance within its cash budget, financial managers will typically plan to invest this balance in:
      a.   the firm's common stock.
      b.   property, plant, or equipment.
      c.   marketable securities.
      d.   the firm's research and development plans.

PROBLEMS

1.

The Newport Paper Company wishes to estimate the cash inflows from sales expected during the months of March, April, and May. The firm's actual sales during January and February were $30,000 and $40,000, respectively, while the forecast sales for March, April, and May are $50,000, $60,000, and $50,000, respectively. The firm makes 20 percent of its sales for cash, collects another 50 percent one month later, and receives the remaining 30 percent after a two-month wait. Calculate the firm's cash inflows for March, April, and May.

2.

Rodney Bell, Inc., had sales of $130,000 and $150,000 in July and August and projected sales of $150,000, $160,000, $180,000, and $200,000 for September through December, respectively. The following data represent the firm's historical and forecast funds behavior:

1. Twenty percent of the firm's sales is for cash, 40 percent is collected one month later, and the remaining 40 percent is collected two months later.

2. The firm expects to receive a monthly income of $5,000 attributable to interest, dividends, and lease payments.

3. The firm's purchases during July and August were $80,000 each month and are expected to be $90,000, $100,000, $110,000, and $130,000 during September through December, respectively.

4. Ten percent of the firm's purchases is for cash, 40 percent is paid one month later, and the remaining 50 percent is paid after a two-month lag.

5. Wages and salaries can be found for each month by adding 10 percent of the previous month's sales to a fixed $20,000 charge.

6. Monthly rent of $16,000 must be paid.

7. Cash dividends of $8,000 will be paid in September and December.

8. Taxes of $15,000 must be paid in September and December.

9. A loan payment of $30,000, principal and interest, must be made in November.

10. A $50,000 payment for purchase of a piece of capital equipment must be made in October.

11. The firm's cash balance at the end of August was $35,000.

12. The firm wishes to maintain a $20,000 minimum cash balance.

a. Based on these data, prepare a cash budget for September, October, November, and December.

b. Determine the amount of borrowing or investing the firm should undertake during this period.

3.

Durabright Industries expects to sell $200,000 worth of flashlights during each of the months of January, February, and March. Its monthly purchases during this time will be $140,000; wages and salaries will be $20,000 per month; and a monthly rent of $5,000 must be paid. Taxes of $30,000 are due in January. A $25,000 payment for the purchase of capital equipment is due in February. All sales are for cash, and beginning cash balances are assumed to be zero. The company maintains a $5,000 minimum cash balance.

a. Construct a cash budget for the months of January, February, and March.

b. Durabright is unsure of its sales level, but all other figures are certain. If the pessimistic sales figure is $180,000 per month and the optimistic figure is $220,000 per month, what are the minimum and maximum cash balances the company can expect for each of the three monthly periods?

4.

The Burgess Bath Corporation wishes to use the percent-of-sales shortcut method to prepare their 1991 pro forma financial statements. Use the operating statements below and the additional information given to:

a. Prepare a pro forma income statement.
b. Prepare a pro forma balance sheet.
c. Analyze these statements and discuss the financing changes required.

Income Statement
Burgess Bath Corporation
December 31, 1990
(in thousands)

Sales	$1,200
Less: Cost of goods sold	900
Gross profits	$ 300
Less: Operating expense	150
Profits before taxes	$ 150
Less: Taxes (40%)	60
Profits after taxes	$ 90
Less: Cash dividends	30
To retained earnings	$ 60

Balance Sheet
Burgess Bath Corporation
December 31, 1990
(in thousands)

ASSETS:		LIABILITIES AND EQUITY	
Cash	$ 48	Accounts Payable	$156
Marketable securities	36	Taxes Payable	15
Accounts receivable	216	Other current liabilities	0
Inventory	144	Total current liabilities	$171
Total current assets	$444	Long-term debt	300
Net fixed assets	540	Common stock	225
		Retained earnings	288
Total Assets	$984	Total Liabilities and Equity	$984

The following financial data are also available:

1. The firm has estimated that its sales for 1991 will be $1,350,000.
2. The firm expects to pay $52,000 in cash dividends in 1991.
3. Taxes payable will equal 1/4 the tax liability on the pro forma income statement.
4. All assets and all current liabilities change as a percentage-of-sales.
5. Long-term debt and common stock will not change spontaneously with sales.

5.

The Texas Tile and Drain Company has 1990 sales of $10 million. They wish to use a simplified method to analyze their expected performance and financing needs for the next two years. The following information is available:

1. The percentages of sales for items that vary directly with sales are as follows:

> Cash, 5%
> Receivables, 18%
> Inventory, 12%
> Net fixed assets, 39%
> Accounts payable, 13%
> Accruals, 5%
> Net profit margin, 5%
> No other accounts vary as a percent of sales.

2. No sale of common stock is expected.

3. The dividend payout of 60% is expected to continue.

4. Sales are expected to be $11 million in 1991 and $13 in 1992.

5. The December 31, 1990, balance sheet is as follows:

Balance Sheet
Texas Tile and Drain
December 31, 1990
(in thousands)

ASSETS:		LIABILITIES AND EQUITY:	
Cash	$ 500	Accounts payable	$1,300
Marketable securities	200	Accruals	500
Accounts receivable	1,800	Other current liabilities	80
Inventory	1,200	Total current liabilities	$1,880
Total current assets	$3,700	Long-term debt	2,000
Net fixed assets	3,900	Common equity	3,720
Total Assets	$7,600	Total Liabilities and Equity	$7,600

Use the above information to:

a. Prepare pro forma balance sheets dated December 31, 1991, and December 31, 1992.

b.   Discuss the financing needs that the firm will experience in these years.

SOLUTIONS

DEFINITIONS

1. strategic
2. cash budget
3. sales
4. external
5. less
6. pro forma
7. plug
8. net cash flow
9. receipts; disbursements
10. variable costs
11. receipts
12. depreciation
13. understate; overstate
14. internal
15. financial planning process

MULTIPLE CHOICE

1.	c.	9.	c
2.	a	10.	a
3.	a	11.	a
4.	d	12.	d
5.	c	13.	c
6.	b	14.	d
7.	a	15.	c
8.	d		

PROBLEMS

1. To determine the cash inflows from sales during a month, 20 percent of that month's sales, plus 50 percent of the previous month's sales, plus 30 percent of the sales two months earlier will provide the desired results, as shown:

Account	January	February	March	April	May
Sales	$30,000	$40,000	$50,000	$60,000	$50,000
Cash Sales (20%)	6,000	8,000	10,000	12,000	10,000
Collections of Accts. Receivable					
One Month Lag (50%)		15,000	20,000	25,000	30,000
Two Month Lag (30%)			9,000	12,000	15,000
Cash Inflows from Sales			$39,000	$49,000	$55,000

As the table shows, the resulting cash inflows from sales for March, April, and May are $39,000, $49,000, and $55,000, respectively.

2. a. The resulting cash budget is presented below. The only difficulties in its preparation are the alignment of the collections of accounts receivable and the payments of accounts payable according to the proper months.

Account	July	August	September	October	November	December
Sales	$130,000	$150,000	$150,000	$160,000	$180,000	$200,000
Cash Sales	26,000	30,000	30,000	32,000	36,000	40,000
Collection of Receivables						
One-Month Lag (40%)		52,000	60,000	60,000	64,000	72,000
Two-Month Lag (40%)			52,000	60,000	60,000	64,000
Other Cash Receipts			5,000	5,000	5,000	5,000
(1) TOTAL CASH RECEIPTS			$147,000	$157,000	$165,000	$181,000
Purchases	$ 80,000	$ 80,000	$ 90,000	$100,000	$110,000	$130,000
Cash Purchases (10%)	8,000	8,000	9,000	10,000	11,000	13,000
Payment of Payables						
One-Month Lag (40%)		32,000	32,000	36,000	40,000	44,000
Two-Month Lag (50%)			40,000	40,000	45,000	50,000
Wages and Salaries			35,000	35,000	36,000	38,000
Rent			16,000	16,000	16,000	16,000
Cash Dividends			8,000			8,000
Taxes			15,000			15,000
Principal and Interest					30,000	
Capital Equipment Purchased				50,000		
(2) TOTAL CASH DISBURSEMENTS			$155,000	$187,000	$178,000	$184,000
Net Cash Flow [(1) - (2)]			($8,000)	($30,000)	($13,000)	($3,000)
Add: Beginning Cash			35,000	27,000	(3,000)	($16,000)
Ending Cash			$27,000	($3,000)	($16,000)	($19,000)
Less: Minimum Cash Balance			20,000	20,000	20,000	20,000
Required Total Financing			---	$23,000	$36,000	$39,000
Excess Cash Balance			$7,000	---	---	---

The source of each entry in the cash budget has been noted in parentheses next to the entry. The required total financing figure in the final section of the statement represents the amount of money that must be borrowed in order to allow a $20,000 minimum ending cash balance.

b.   The financial manager may draw two conclusions from the cash budget:

(1)   The $7,000 excess cash balance during September could be invested in some interest-earning form during the month.

(2)   During October, November, and December, the firm's borrowings must increase from $23,000 to $36,000 to $39,000, respectively, in order to maintain the minimum required cash balance of $20,000. These figures do not represent additional borrowing for each month; rather they indicate the accumulated maximum amounts that must be obtained during the period. Therefore, if the firm arranges for borrowing power of slightly more than $39,000 (in order to allow a margin of safety because of the forecast nature of the statement), it should be able to complete the year successfully. Of

course, the firm's success is largely dependent on the accuracy of its forecast.

3.   a.   Durabright Industries cash budget is as follows:

Cash Budget
Durabright Industries

	January	February	March
Sales	$200,000	$200,000	$200,000
(1) Total cash receipts	$200,000	$200,000	$200,000
Disbursements:			
Purchases	$140,000	$140,000	$140,000
Wages	20,000	20,000	20,000
Rent	5,000	5,000	5,000
Taxes	30,000	-------	-------
Capital equipment	--------	25,000	-------
(2) Total cash disbursements	$195,000	$190,000	$165,000
Net cash flow [(1) - (2)]	$ 5,000	$ 10,000	$ 35,000
Add: Beginning cash	0	5,000	15,000
Ending cash	$5,000	$ 15,000	$ 50,000
Less: Minimum cash balance	5,000	5,000	5,000
Required total financing	-------	-------	------
Excess cash balance	-------	$ 10,000	$ 45,000

b.   Since total cash disbursements remain the same for each month, net cash flow for the pessimistic and optimistic sales figures of $180,000 and $220,000, respectively, are calculated and included in the sensitivity analysis table. The most likely figures are incorporated into the table from the cash budget in part (a).

A Sensitivity Analysis of Durabright Industries Cash Budget ($000's)

Cash Flows	January Pessi-mistic	January Most Likely	January Opti-mistic	February Pessi-mistic	February Most Likely	February Opti-mistic	March Pessi-mistic	March Most Likely	March Opti-mistic
Total Cash Receipts	$180	$200	$220	$180	$200	$220	$180	$200	$220
Less: Total Cash Disburse-ments	195	195	195	190	190	190	165	165	165
Net Cash Flow	($15)	$ 5	$ 25	($10)	$ 10	$ 30	$ 15	$ 35	$ 55
Add: Beginning Cash	$ 0	$ 0	$ 0	($15)	$ 5	$ 25	($25)	$ 15	$ 55
Ending Cash	($15)	$ 5	$ 25	($25)	$ 15	$ 55	($10)	$ 50	$110
Less: Minimum Cash Balance	5	5	5	5	5	5	5	5	5
Required Total Financing	$ 20	----	----	$ 30	----	----	$ 15	----	----
Excess Cash Balance	----	----	$ 20	----	$ 10	$ 50	----	$ 45	$105

During January, Durabright will need a maximum of $20,000 of financing, while at best, it will have $20,000 available for short-term investment. During February, the firm's maximum financing reqirement will be $30,000, however, it could experience a surplus between $10,000 and $50,000. The March projections reflect a borrowing requirement of $15,000, with a surplus between $45,000 and $105,000. By considering the extreme values reflected in the pessimistic and optimistic outcomes, Durabright should be able to plan its cash requirements more accurately.

4.   a.   The pro forma income statement is as follows:

Pro Forma Income Statement, 1991
Burgess Bath Corporation
(in thousands)

Sales	$1,350.00
Less: Cost of goods sold	1,012.50
Gross profits	$ 337.50
Less: Operating expense	$ 168.75
Earnings before taxes	$ 168.75
Less: taxes (.40)	$ 67.50
Earnings after taxes	101.25
Less: Cash dividends	52.00
To retained earnings	$ 49.25

   b.   The pro forma balance sheet is as follows:

Pro Forma Balance Sheet
Burgess Bath Corporation
December 31, 1991
(in thousands)

Cash (4%)	$ 54.00	Accounts payable	$175.50
Marketable securities (3%)	40.50	Taxes due	16.87
Accounts receivable (18%)	243.00	Other current liabilities	0.00
Inventory (12%)	162.00	Total current liabilities	$192.37
Total current assets	$499.50	Long-term debt	$300.00
Fixed assets (45%)	607.50	Common stock	225.00
		Retained earnings	337.25
		External funds required	52.37
Total assets	$1107.00	Total liabilities and net worth	$1107.00

   c.   Based on these pro forma statements, the firm will have an external funding requirement of $52,375 to support its planned 1991 sales level.

5.   a.   The pro forma balance sheets for 1991 and 1992 are as follows:

Pro Forma Balance Sheet
Texas Tile and Drain
December 31, 1991
(in thousands)

ASSETS		LIABILITIES AND EQUITY	
Cash	$ 550	Accounts payable	$1,430
Marketable securities*	200	Accruals	550
Accounts receivable	1,980	Other current liabilities*	80
Inventory	1,320	Total current liabilities	$2,060
Total current assets	$4,050	Long-term debt	2,000
Net fixed assets	4,290	Common equity**	
		Required financing	
		External funds required	340
Total Assets	$8,340	Total Liabilities and Equity	$8,340

Pro Forma Balance Sheet
Texas Tile and Drain
December 31, 1992
(in thousands)

ASSETS		LIABILITIES AND EQUITY	
Cash	$ 650	Accounts payable	$1,690
Marketable securities	200	Accruals	650
Accounts receivable	2,340	Other current liabilities*	80
Inventory	1,560	Total current liabilities	$2,420
Total current assets	$4,750	Long-term debt	2,000
Net fixed assets	5,070	Common equity*	4,200
		Required financing	
		External funds required	1,200
Total Assets	$9,820	Total Liabilities and Equity	$9,820

*Assuming no change, not directly related to sales.
**Common equity equals the 1990 figure, $3,720,000, plus $480,000 in additions to retained earnings over the two-year period: ($11.0 mil)(.4)(.05) = $220,000 in 1991; and ($13.0 mil)(.4)(.05) = $260,000 in 1992.

   b.   Since the changes are in permanent assets, the firm can expect to increase its long-term financing by $1,200,000 over the two year period. As the pro forma balance sheets show, $340,000 is needed in 1991 and another $860,000 in 1992.

CHAPTER 9

CAPITAL BUDGETING AND CASH FLOW PRINCIPLES

SUMMARY

Capital budgeting is the process of evaluating and selecting long-term investments consistent with the objective of shareholder wealth maximization. For manufacturing firms, the most common such investments are for fixed assets. Fixed assets are very important, because they represent the largest dollar investment and the key earning assets of a manufacturing firm. Fixed assets are considered to be earning assets because they provide the basis for the firm's earning power and value.

A capital expenditure is an outlay for which the resulting benefits are expected to accrue to the firm over a period of time greater than one year. Capital expenditures are commonly made to expand, replace, or renew fixed assets. The capital budgeting process is a five step process: idea generation, review and analysis, decision-making, implementation, and follow-up.

Capital budgeting projects can be either independent or mutually exclusive. The acceptance of independent projects does not eliminate other projects from further consideration. Mutually exclusive projects are those that perform the same function, so that the acceptance of one eliminates the others. A firm can have unlimited funds or can be in a situation of capital rationing, which means that the firm's projects are competing for a limited amount of funds. Capital budgeting decisions may result from an accept-reject analysis or from ranking of projects. Accept-reject decisions are made when a firm has independent projects and unlimited funds, while ranking is necessary when a firm must choose from mutually exclusive projects or when it is operating under capital rationing. Cash flow patterns may be classified as conventional (an initial cash outflow followed by a series of inflows) or nonconventional (all other cash-flow patterns).

To evaluate capital expenditure alternatives, the after-tax cash outflows and inflows associated with each project must be determined. The relevant flows to consider are the initial investment, operating cash inflows, and terminal cash flows. In order to determine the initial outflow, or initial investment, associated with a proposed replacement, all outflows and inflows occurring at time zero must be netted. The general procedure suggests that the cost of a new asset, plus any installation costs and changes in working capital, less the proceeds from the sale of the old asset adjusted for taxes, will yield the initial investment. The taxes on the sale will depend on whether the asset is sold above its initial purchase price, below its purchase price but above its book value, or below its book value.

Operating cash inflows in future years must be measured as incremental after-tax cash inflows. Because cash -- not accounting profit -- pays the firm's bills, an emphasis on cash flow is required. Care must be taken to make sure that depreciation and other noncash charges associated with each alternative are added back to the associated profits after taxes in order to obtain operating cash inflows. By using the difference between the operating cash inflows under proposed plans and those under the current plan, the relevant (i.e., incremental) cash inflows result.

Terminal cash flows occur when a project is liquidated at the end of its economic life. These are after-tax flows, exclusive of operating cash inflows, which occur in a project's last year. These flows can be found by calculating the after-tax proceeds expected from the sale of the fixed assets plus the cash inflow expected from the reversion of net working capital to the firm.

CONCEPT OUTLINE

I.   **Capital budgeting represents the process of generating long-term investment proposals; reviewing, analyzing, and selecting them; and implementing and following up on those proposals selected.**

A.   Fixed assets, which include plant and equipment, are the most common form of long-term investment made by a manufacturing firm.

1.   Fixed assets are the firm's earning assets.

2.   These long-term investments provide the basis for the firm's earning power and value.

B.   Capital expenditures, those present expenditures which yield benefits for more than one year, describe the purchase of fixed assets which, by definition, are expected to exist for more than one year.

1.   The basic motives for capital expenditures are for expansion, replacement, and renewal of fixed assets.

2.   Some capital expenditures, such as advertising and research and development, do not result in fixed assets on the firm's balance sheet.

C.   The capital budgeting process can be viewed as having five distinct, but inter-related, steps.

1.   Idea generation, or the development of capital expenditure proposals, can come from almost any area of a business organization.

2.   Proposals must be reviewed, to see if they are appropriate given the firm's overall objectives, and evaluated, to determine their economic validity.

3.   The decision on a proposed expenditure may come from one of several levels in the firm depending on the dollar outlay and strategic importance of the project.

4.   Implementation of a project is fairly routine but important. Those projects which require longer implementation periods require greater control.

5.   The follow-up stage represents a control function to monitor operating cash inflows relative to expectations.

D.   In order to understand the capital budgeting process, one must become familiar with capital budgeting terminology.

1.   Projects under consideration may be independent or mutually exclusive.

a.   Independent projects are projects whose cash flows do not depend on one another. The acceptance of one project does not eliminate the others from consideration.

b.   Mutually exclusive projects are projects that perform the same function. The acceptance of one project eliminates the others from further consideration.

2.   The capital expenditure decision-making environment is affected by the availability of funds.

a.   A firm may have unlimited funds, which means that all projects meeting some predetermined criterion can be accepted.

b.   A more common situation is capital rationing -- in which projects must compete for a limited amount of money.

3.   Two basic types of capital budgeting decisions may exist.

a.   Accept-reject decisions, which must be made for independent projects, indicate whether or not a project meets a firm's predetermined decision criterion.

b.   Ranking of projects based on some criterion must be done when a firm has mutually exclusive projects or is in a capital rationing situation.

4.   A project's cash flows can be classified as conventional or nonconventional, and as annuities or mixed streams.

a.   A conventional cash flow pattern consists of an initial outflow followed by a series of inflows.

       b.   Nonconventional cash flow patterns include all other cash flow patterns.

       c.   Streams of equal annual cash inflows are called annuities, and they have a conventional cash-flow pattern, unequal annual cash inflows are called mixed streams, and they have either conventional or nonconventional cash-flow patterns.

II.   The relevant incremental cash flows used to make capital budgeting decisions include the initial investment, operating cash flows, and a terminal cash flow.

    A.   Incremental cash flows represent the additional cash flows -- outflows and inflows -- expected to result from a proposed capital expenditure.

    B.   Cash flows, rather than accounting profits, are used to evaluate capital budgeting proposals.

    C.   The development of relevant cash flows is most straightforward for expansion projects, where all cash flows represent after-tax inflows and outflows associated with the proposed outlay.

    D.   The development of relevant cash flows for replacement projects is more complicated, because the firm must isolate the incremental cash flows that will result from the proposed replacement.

III.   The initial investment is the relevant cash outflow required at time zero to implement a proposed long-term project.

T

    A.   The initial investment in a fixed asset is found by adding to the cost of the new asset any installation cost, and subtracting from this total the tax-adjusted proceeds from the sale of any old assets retired by the new asset. Finally, any increase in net working capital is added to the initial investment.

    B.   In a replacement decision, taxes are sometimes difficult to determine, because the old asset could be sold for more than its initial purchase price, for less than the initial purchase price but more than book value, or for less than book value. Each scenario produces different tax consequences.

    C.   The difference between the change in current assets and the change in current liabilities brought about by the proposed project represents the change in net working capital. This change must be included in the initial investment.

IV.   **Operating cash inflows are the relevant cash flows resulting from the use of a proposed long-term investment during its life.**

A.   Operating cash inflows in each year can be calculated by (1) subtracting operating expenses, depreciation, and taxes from project revenues to obtain net profits after tax, and then (2) adding depreciation charges back to net profits to obtain cash inflows.

B.   Operating cash inflows represent incremental cash flows that determine how much more or less cash enters the firm as a result of the project.

V.   **The terminal cash flow represents the relevant cash flow attributable to liquidation of a long-term investment at the end of its life.**

A.   The terminal cash flow includes net proceeds from asset sales, taxes on the sale of assets, and changes in net working capital.

B.   Net proceeds from asset sales, after selling expenses and taxes, represent a cash inflow.

C.   The reduction in net working capital reflects the reversion of any net working capital investment at the end of the project's economic life, and represents a cash inflow to the firm.

APPLICATIONS

DEFINITIONS

1.   A _Capital expenditure_ represents an outlay of funds that is expected to produce benefits over a period of time greater than one year.

2.   Independent projects are projects whose cash flows are _unrelated_ to one another; the acceptance of one project does not eliminate the other from consideration.

3.   In cases where _Capital rationing_ exists, a firm has only a fixed number of dollars to allocate among competing capital expenditures.

4.   Conventional cash flow patterns contain an initial cash _outflow_ followed by a series of cash _inflows_.

5.   When the acceptance of project A eliminates projects B and C from further consideration, projects A, B, and C represent _mutually exclusive_ projects.

6.   An outlay of funds resulting in benefits within one year represents a *current* expenditure.

7.   Capital budgeting represents the process of selecting long-term investments that are consistent with the firm's goal of *owner wealth* maximization.

8.   In cases where project cash flows do not represent an initial expenditure followed by a series of cash inflows, the cash flow pattern is considered *unconventional*

9.   Recaptured depreciation represents that portion of a used asset's selling price which is *above* the asset's book value and *below* its initial purchase price.

10.   The incremental, after-tax cash flows resulting from the use of a project during its life are known as *operating* _____ cash inflows.

11.   Incremental cash flows represent the *additional* _____ cash flows -- including both inflows and outflows -- expected to result from a proposed capital expenditure.

12.   By subtracting *accumulated depreciation* _____ from the installed cost of an asset, financial analysts can obtain the book value of the asset.

13.   The difference between the change in current assets and the change in current liabilities represents the change in *net working capital*

14.   Positive changes in net working capital associated with a capital budgeting project *increase* the firm's initial investment in this project.

15.   The after-tax nonoperating cash flow occurring in the final year of a project, usually attributable to the liquidation of the project, represents the _____ cash flow. *terminal*

MULTIPLE CHOICE

1.   The basic motive(s) for capital expenditures is/are to:
      a.   expand fixed assets.
      b.   replace fixed assets.
      c.   renew fixed assets.
      d.   all of the above.

2.   The capital budgeting process includes all but which of the following steps?
      a.   proposal generation.
      b.   marketing plan.
      c.   follow-up.
      d.   review and analysis.

3.   A firm is considering two capital budgeting projects. If it accepts one, this acceptance does not eliminate the other from consideration. The two projects are called:
     a.   independent projects.
     b.   mutually exclusive projects.
     c.   socially desirable projects.
     d.   interdependent projects.

4.   When a firm has a financial situation such that it cannot accept all independent projects that provide an acceptable return, it is said to face:
     a.   bankruptcy.
     b.   capital rationing.
     c.   limited liability.
     d.   a cash flow crisis.

5.   The relevant cash flows to consider in capital budgeting decisions are:
     a.   incremental and after-tax.
     b.   incremental and before-tax.
     c.   initial and before interest and tax.
     d.   total and both before- and after-tax.

6.   The basic components of a conventional capital budgeting project contain all but which of the following?
     a.   operating cash inflows.
     b.   initial investment.
     c.   after-tax cash reversion.
     d.   terminal cash flow.

7.   If the implementation of a capital project requires an increase in net working capital, that increase should be considered:
     a.   as an outflow with the initial investment.
     b.   as an outflow with the terminal cash flow.
     c.   in the sources and uses of funds statement, but not in the capital budgeting cash flows.
     d.   as an outflow in each of the annual net cash flows.

8.   A firm is considering a capital project that requires the purchase of a new machine. The machine costs $200,000 and will require expenditures of $20,000 to install. The firm can sell the old machine which this project will replace to net $35,000 after-tax. The project requires a build-up in net working capital of $40,000. What is the project's initial investment?
     a. $295,000.
     b. $185,000.
     c. $225,000.
     d. $205,000.

9. To determine the relevant operating cash flows for a replacement capital budgeting project, one must:
    a. determine the total cash flow from the project without regard to the existing asset.
    b. determine the change in cash flows with and without the project.
    c. determine the after-tax profits of the project without regard to depreciation of the project.
    d. determine the difference in after-tax profits with and without the project.

10. Terminal cash flows refer to those which occur:
    a. at the end of the accounting period.
    b. at the beginning of a project.
    c. at the end of a project.
    d. when the projects is canceled ahead of schedule.

11. The terminal cash flow:
    a. can never be negative.
    b. can never be zero.
    c. can never be positive.
    d. none of the above.

12. Capital expenditures differ from current expenditures in that:
    a. current expenditures are always less than $1,000.
    b. capital expenditures are expected to produce benefits over a period of time exceeding one year, while current expenditures result in benefits received within one year.
    c. current expenditures are used to acquire current assets, while capital expenditures are used to fund property, plant, and equipment purchases.
    d. current expenditures are used to support expansion projects, while capital expenditures are used to support replacement projects.

13. Which of the following is not considered as part of the initial investment in a capital budgeting project?
    a. installation costs.
    b. the purchase price of new assets.
    c. the cost of the computer time used in developing the capital budgeting analysis.
    d. the after-tax proceeds from the sale of old assets replaced by the investment project.

14.   The portion of the selling price obtained for capital assets that exceeds the book value of the asset is known as:
      a.   excess value.
      b.   recaptured depreciation.
      c.   residual income.
      d.   a capital gain.

15.   Many expenditures for capital assets are capitalized, which means that:
      a.   these expenditures are treated as costs in the current accounting period.
      b.   these expenditures must be depreciated using an accelerated method.
      c.   the funds used to acquire these capital assets come from the firm's retained earnings account.
      d.   these expenditures are treated as fixed assets, and depreciated over time.

PROBLEMS

1.   Examine the following list of outlays, and indicate whether each would normally be considered a capital or current expenditure. Explain your answer.

      a.   A payment of $25,000 to purchase a fried chicken franchise.
      b.   A rental payment of $315 for use of a delivery truck to move equipment to a new facility.
      c.   Payment of $10,000 for the first year's tuition in Acme University's MBA program.
      d.   Expenses of $40,000 for research on a new manufacturing process.
      e.   A payment of $45 to acquire a hammer made with a graphite shaft.

2.   A local business is evaluating two opportunities:

    Alternative A: Adding convenience store operations to a self-service gas station in a high traffic area. The firm expects the building would cost $25,000 to construct and require $5,000 in new inventory. Estimated operating inflows are $15,000/year for 10 years.

<u>Alternative B</u>: Investing in any or all of the projects for which relevant cash flows are given below. The firm has a total of $15,000 to invest.

Year	Project #1	Project #2	Project #3
0	($8,000)	($15,000)	($7,000)
1	4,000	7,000	4,000
2	(1,000)	7,000	1,000
3	5,000	7,000	3,000

For each of the alternatives, indicate:

a.   Whether the alternative presents independent or mutually exclusive projects;

b.   Whether the availability of funds is limited or capital rationing exits;

c.   Whether accept-reject or ranking decisions are required;

d.   Whether each project's cash flows are conventional or unconventional.

3.

T

The R. Spurlock Corporation is contemplating selling an asset originally purchased for $100,000 three years ago. The asset is being depreciated under the Accelerated Cost Recovery System (ACRS) over its five-year recovery period. The firm pays taxes of 40 percent on ordinary income and capital gains. For each of the following asset sale prices, determine the amount of resulting tax liability, if any. The ACRS five-year recovery period used the following recovery schedule:

Recovery Year	ACRS Five-Year Recovery
1	20%
2	32
3	19
4	12
5	12
6	5

a.   The asset is sold for $120,000;
b.   The asset is sold for $ 80,000;
c.   The asset is sold for $ 29,000;
d.   The asset is sold for $ 20,000;

(handwritten margin notes)

40,000
30,000
5,000
75,000

10,000
18,000
28,000

75
28
47

4.

T

Big Bear Corporation is considering a facilities expansion. When the firm's new retail stores open Big Bear will carry $40,000 more in inventory, have $30,000 more in accounts receivable, and have $10,000 more in accruals. The firm also expects accounts payable to be up by $18,000 and plans to hold $5,000 more in cash.

    a.   What increase in net working capital would be included in the initial investment for this expansion? *47,000*

    b.   Why is this a relevant cash flow?

    c.   What terminal cash flow might one expect here?

5.

The J. Harris Company is contemplating replacing an old machine purchased two years ago for $90,000. The old machine is being depreciated using ACRS over its five-year recovery period. It is believed that it can be sold for $100,000. The new machine will cost $150,000 and will have a usable life of five years. It will be depreciated using ACRS over its five-year recovery period. The firm's ordinary income is taxed at 40 percent, as are any capital gains.

T

Use the ACRS factors for a five-year recovery, presented in Problem 3 above to:

    a.   Calculate the initial investment associated with the proposal as presented above;

    b.   Determine the amount of the initial investment if disposal costs of $6,000 are expected from the sale of the old machine;

    c.   Calculate the initial investment if the old machine is sold for $70,000;

    d.   Calculate the initial investment if the old machine is sold for $30,000 and the firm has earnings from operations of $50,000.

6.   The after-tax earnings for the J. Harris Company (presented in Problem 5) with the old machine and with the new machine for each of the next five years is given below. (Note that, although the old machine has only three years remaining in its ACRS recovery period, it has a useful life of five years).

T

Earnings After Taxes

Year	Old Machine	New Machine
1	$80,000	$90,000
2	90,000	100,000
3	100,000	110,000
4	80,000	110,000
5	80,000	110,000

a.   Calculate the remaining depreciation schedule associated with each machine;

b.   Determine the operating cash inflows associated with each machine;

c.   Determine the incremental operating cash flows associated with the replacement of the old machine with the new machine.

7.

T

The Solid Cement Company is considering the purchase of a new mixer to replace its old one, which was purchased three years ago for $160,000. The old mixer is being depreciated under the ACRS method with a five-year recoverable life and has a five-year remaining life, with zero salvage value expected at the end of its usable life. Solid has been offered $150,000 for the old mixer.

The new mixer, expected to streamline the firm's production process significantly, would cost $280,000 plus an additional $20,000 to install. The new mixer will be depreciated under the ACRS with a five-year recoverable life, and it will have a five-year usable life with an expected salvage value of $20,000 at the end of year 5. The firm has estimated its earnings before depreciation and taxes (EBDT), both with and without the new mixer, over each of the next five years, as given in the table below. The new mixer requires an increase of $20,000 in net working capital.

Solid Cement Company
Revenues and Expenses (excluding depreciation),
and Earnings Before Depreciation and Taxes

Year	Projected Revenue (1)	Projected Expenses (Excluding Depreciation and Taxes) (2)	Projected Earnings Before Depreciation and Taxes [(1) - (2)] (3)
With New Mixer			
1	$2,200,000	$1,960,000	$240,000
2	2,300,000	2,020,000	280,000
3	2,400,000	2,100,000	300,000
4	2,500,000	2,180,000	320,000
5	2,500,000	2,180,000	320,000
With Old Mixer			
1	$2,000,000	$1,780,000	220,000
2	2,000,000	1,780,000	220,000
3	2,000,000	1,780,000	220,000
4	2,000,000	1,780,000	220,000
5	2,000,000	1,780,000	220,000

The firm pays taxes at a rate of 40 percent on ordinary income and on capital gains. The prospective purchaser of the old mixer has agreed to pay for removing it.

a.   Calculate the initial investment associated with the purchase of the new mixer;

b.   Calculate the relevant or incremental operating cash inflows associated with the proposed purchase, using both the income statement approach and the alternative approach;

c.   Calculate the terminal cash flows associated with the proposed mixer;

d.   Prepare a table showing all incremental cash flows associated with this replacement project.

SOLUTIONS

DEFINITIONS

1. capital expenditure
2. unrelated
3. capital rationing
4. outflow; inflows
5. mutually exclusive
6. current
7 owner wealth
8. nonconventional
9. above; below
10. operating
11. additional
12. accumulated depreciation
13. net working capital
14. increase
15. terminal

MULTIPLE CHOICE

1.	d	9.	b
2.	b	10.	c
3.	a	11.	d
4.	b	12.	b
5.	a	13.	c
6.	c	14.	b
7.	a	15.	d
8.	c		

PROBLEMS

1. Expenditures a, c, d, and e are all capital expenditures, since each is a present expenditure expected to generate benefits for more than one year.

    Expenditure b is a current expenditure for the current use of a truck.

2. a. In Alternative A, the project is independent.
        In Alternative B, the projects are independent.

b.   In Alternative A, there is no capital rationing.
        In Alternative B, capital rationing exists.

c.   In Alternative A, one must make an accept-reject decision because it is an
        independent project with no limit on funds.
        In Alternative B, one must rank the projects due to capital rationing.

d.   In Alternative A, the project has conventional cash flows.
        In Alternative B, projects 1 and 3 have unconventional cash flows. Project 2 has
        conventional cash flows.

3.   In order to determine the taxes in each of the cases, one must first determine the asset's
      book value. Note that the asset has been in service for three years, so that

$$\text{accumulated depreciation} = (0.20 + 0.32 + 0.19) \times (100{,}000) = \$71{,}000, \text{ and}$$

$$\text{book value} = \$100{,}000 - \$71{,}000 = \$29{,}000.$$

a.   If the asset is sold for $120,000, which is above the initial purchase price, the firm
        would experience a capital gain:

$$\text{capital gain} = \$120{,}000 - \$100{,}000 = \$20{,}000.$$

The other component of income from the sale of the asset is the recaptured
depreciation, which is found by subtracting the asset's book value from its initial
purchase price:

$$\text{recaptured depreciation} = \$100{,}000 - \$29{,}000 = \$71{,}000.$$

The capital gain and the recaptured depreciation are treated as ordinary income
and taxed at the ordinary tax rate of 40 percent. The resulting taxes are:

$$(\$71{,}000 + \$20{,}000) \times 0.40 = \$36{,}400.$$

b.   If the asset is sold for $80,000, there would be no capital gain, but a portion of the
        depreciation would be recovered because the sale price exceeds the book value.

$$\text{Recaptured depreciation} = \$80{,}000 - \$29{,}000 = \$51{,}000.$$

Taxes on the recaptured depreciation would be levied at a rate of 40 percent:

$$\text{taxes} = (\$51{,}000) \times 0.40 = \$20{,}400.$$

c.   If the asset is sold for $29,000, the sale price would just equal the book value. In this case, there would be no tax liability associated with the transaction.

d.   If the asset is sold for $20,000, the firm would have a capital loss on the sale of a depreciable asset, because the asset is a depreciable one used in the firm's business and would be sold for less than its book value:

depreciable asset loss = $29,000 - $20,000 = $9,000.

The loss can be applied against the firm's operating income, and, if sufficient current income is not available, it may be carried back or forward. The value of the tax deduction would equal $3,600 [i.e., ($9,000) x (0.40)].

4.   a.   The following table allows easy computation of the changes in net working capital.

Increase in Current Assets (1)		Increase in Current Liabilities (2)		Increase in Net Working Capital [(1) - (2)] (3)
Cash	$5,000	Accounts Payable	$18,000	
Accts. Receivable	30,000	Accruals	10,000	
Inventory	40,000			
TOTAL	$75,000	TOTAL	$28,000	$47,000

b.   The change in net working capital of $47,000 is an outflow of funds which must be considered in evaluating this project.

c.   At the end of the project's economic life, the full $47,000 can be expected as a cash inflow.

5.   a.   A key step in determining the initial investment is to calculate the taxes on the sale of the old machine. In this case, there are two taxable components -- the capital gain (long-term) and the recaptured depreciation.

Book value = $90,000 - [(.20 + .32) x ($90,000)] = $90,000 - $46,800 = $43,200.

Capital gain = $100,000 - $90,000 = $10,000, and

recaptured depreciation = $90,000 - $43,000 = $46,800.

The taxes on the sale of the old machine would be:

($10,000 + $46,800) x 0.40 = $22,720.

Now the initial investment can be determined:

Cost of new machine	$150,000
Less: Proceeds for sale of old machine	-100,000
Taxes on sale of old machine	22,720
Initial investment	$ 72,720

b.   If the firm incurs disposal costs of $6,000 on the old machine, the proceeds on its sale would be:

Sale price, old machine	$100,000
Less: Removal cost	6,000
Net Sale Price	$ 94,000

Based on a sale price of $94,000, the taxes on the sale of the old machine must be calculated:

capital gain = $94,000 - $90,000 = $4,000, and

recaptured depreciation = $90,000 - $43,000 = $46,800.

The taxes resulting from this transaction would be:

($4,000 + $46,800) x 0.40 = $20,320.

The initial investment can now be determined:

Cost of new machine	$150,000
Less: Proceeds from sale of old machine	- 94,000
Taxes on sale of old machine	20,320
Initial investment	$ 76,320

c.   If the old machine is sold for $70,000, there would be no capital gain, but the recaptured depreciation would be:

$70,000 - $43,200 = $26,800.

Taxes on this recaptured depreciation would be:

($26,800) x 0.40 = $10,720.

The initial investment can now be determined:

Cost of new machine	$150,000
Less: Proceeds from sale of old machine	- 70,000
Taxes on sale of old machine	10,720
Initial investment	$ 90,720

d.   If the old machine is sold for $30,000, the firm would experience a capital loss on the sale of a depreciable asset:

$$\$43,200 - \$30,000 \ = \ \$13,200.$$

Because the firm has $50,000 of operating earnings, this loss can be deducted from the firm's operating income and it will reduce taxes by an amount equal to the amount of loss times the firm's marginal tax rate:

$$\text{reduction in taxes} \ = \ (\$13,200) \times 0.40 \ = \ \$5,280.$$

The initial investment can now be determined:

Cost of new machine	$150,000
Less: Proceeds from sale of old machine	- 30,000
Tax shield produced by sale of old machine	- 5,280
Initial investment	$114,720

6.   a.   The depreciable value of the new machine includes only the cost of the machine; there are no installation costs. Depreciable value is $150,000; recoverable life is 5 years.

ACRS Depreciation Schedule for New Machine

Year	Recovery Percentage (1)	Depreciable Value (2)	Annual Depreciation [(1) x (2)] (3)
1	0.20	$150,000	$30,000
2	0.32	150,000	48,000
3	0.19	150,000	28,500
4	0.12	150,000	18,000
5	0.12	150,000	18,000
6	0.05	150,000	7,500
TOTAL			$150,000

ACRS Depreciation Schedule for Old Machine

Year*	Recovery Percentage (1)	Depreciable Value (2)	Annual Depreciation [(1) x (2)] (3)
1	0.19	$90,000	$17,100
2	0.12	90,000	10,800
3	0.12	90,000	10,800
4	0.05	90,000	4,500
5	0.00	90,000	0
6	0.00	90,000	0
TOTAL			$43,200

*The machine is two years old and has three years remaining on its recovery period, but it has a remaining useful life of five years.

b.   The operating cash inflows associated with the old and the new machines can be determined by adding the depreciation under each alternative back to the profits after taxes.

Operating Cash Inflows - New Machine

Year	Profits After Tax (1)	Depreciation (2)	Operating Cash Inflows [(1) + (2)] (3)
1	$90,000	$30,000	120,000
2	100,000	48,000	148,000
3	110,000	28,500	138,500
4	110,000	18,000	128,000
5	110,000	18,000	128,000
6	0	7,500	7,500

Operating Cash Inflows - Old Machine

Year	Profits After Tax (1)	Depreciation (2)	Operating Cash Inflows [(1) + (2)] (3)
1	$80,000	$17,100	97,100
2	90,000	10,800	100,800
3	100,000	10,800	110,800
4	80,000	4,500	84,500
5	80,000	0	80,000
6	0	0	0

c.   The relevant initial investment for the new machine was found to be $72,720 in Problem 5a. The relevant operating cash inflows are found by subtracting the cash inflows connected with the old machine from the cash inflows for the new machine:

Year	Net Machine (1)	Old Machine (2)	Incremental [(1) - (2)] (3)
1	$120,000	$ 97,100	$22,900
2	148,000	100,800	47,200
3	138,500	110,800	27,700
4	128,000	84,500	43,500
5	128,000	80,000	48,000
6	7,500	0	7,500

7.   a.   A key step in calculating the initial investment is to find the taxes due on the sale of the old mixer:

book value of old mixer = $160,000 - [(.20 + .32 + .19)] x ($160,000)]

= $160,000 - $113,600 = $46,400.

Because the sale price of the old mixer is expected to be $150,000, there will be no capital gain, but some depreciation will be recaptured:

recaptured depreciation = $150,000 - $46,400 = $103,600.

The recaptured depreciation will be taxed as ordinary income at a rate of 40 percent:

taxes on sale of old mixer = ($103,600) x 0.40 = $41,440.

The initial investment can now be determined:

Cost of new mixer	$280,000
Installation cost	20,000
Less: Proceeds on sale of old mixer	-150,000
Taxes on sale of old mixer	41,440
Plus: Net working capital	+ 20,000
Initial Investment	$211,440

b. In order to find the incremental or relevant cash inflows, the cash inflows with both the old and new mixer must be determined. First, calculate the depreciation charges:

ACRS Depreciation Schedule for New Mixer

Year	Recovery Percentage (1)	Depreciable Value (2)	Annual Depreciation [(1) x (2)] (3)
1	0.20	$300,000	$60,000
2	0.32	300,000	96,000
3	0.19	300,000	57,000
4	0.12	300,000	36,000
5	0.12	300,000	36,000
6	0.05	300,000	15,000
TOTAL			$300,000

ACRS Depreciation Schedule for Old Mixer

Year*	Recovery Percentage (1)	Depreciable Value (2)	Annual Depreciation [(1) x (2)] (3)
1	0.12	$160,000	$19,200
2	0.12	160,000	19,200
3	0.05	160,000	9,000
4	0.00	160,000	0
5	0.00	160,000	0
TOTAL			$47,400

*Since the asset is three years old and has a five-year recoverable life, it has only three years of depreciable life even though it has five years of usable life remaining.

Next, to find the incremental or relevant operating cash inflows, the operating cash inflows with both the old and new mixer must be determined. The cash inflows are calculated in tabular form as follows:

Year	EBDT (1)	Depreciation (2)	EBT [(1) - (2)] (3)	EAT [(1 - 0.40) x (3)] (4)	Operating Cash Flow [(2) + (4)] (5)
Old Mixer					
1	$220,000	$19,200	$200,800	$120,480	$139,680
2	220,000	19,200	200,800	120,480	139,680
3	220,000	8,000	212,000	127,200	135,200
4	220,000	0	220,000	132,000	132,000
5	220,000	0	220,000	132,000	132,000
New Mixer					
1	$240,000	$60,000	$180,000	$108,000	$168,000
2	280,000	96,000	184,000	110,400	206,400
3	300,000	57,000	243,000	145,800	202,800
4	320,000	36,000	284,000	170,400	206,400
5	320,000	36,000	284,000	170,400	206,400

The basic calculations shown above involve subtracting depreciation from earnings before depreciation and taxes (EBDT) to obtain earnings before taxes (EBT). Multiplying EBT by one minus the firm's marginal tax rate of 40 percent produces earnings after taxes (EAT). Adding depreciation back to EAT yields the operating cash inflows. Subtracting the cash inflows associated with the old mixer from the cash inflows associated with the new mixer provides the incremental operating cash inflows for this replacement project:

Year	New Mixer (1)	Old Mixer (2)	Incremental [(1) - (2)] (3)
1	$168,000	$139,680	$28,320
2	206,400	139,680	66,720
3	202,800	135,200	67,600
4	206,400	132,000	74,400
5	206,400	132,000	74,400

Alternatively, the operating cash inflows calculated above can be determined directly by:

1. finding the changes in revenue, changes in expenses (excluding depreciation), and changes in depreciation;

2. adjusting these changes for taxes in order to determine the cash flows resulting from them; and

3. summing the after-tax changes in revenue and expense items to provide the relevant opearing cash inflows for each year of the project.

This alternative technique is demonstrated below.

Solid Cement Company
Determination of Annual Changes in Revenue and Expense
(Excluding Depreciation Expense)

Year	Revenue from New Mixer (1)	Revenue from Old Mixer (2)	Change in Revenue [(1) - (2)] (3)	Expenses from New Mixer (4)	Expenses from Old Mixer (5)	Change in Expense [(4) - (5)] (6)
1	$2,200,000	$2,000,000	$200,000	$1,960,000	$1,780,000	$180,000
2	2,300,000	2,000,000	300,000	2,020,000	1,780,000	240,000
3	2,400,000	2,000,000	400,000	2,100,000	1,780,000	320,000
4	2,500,000	2,000,000	500,000	2,180,000	1,780,000	400,000
5	2,500,000	2,000,000	500,000	2,180,000	1,780,000	400,000

Solid Cement Company
Determination of Annual Changes in Depreciation

Year	New Mixer (7)	Old Mixer (8)	Change [(7) - (8)] (9)
1	$60,000	$19,200	$40,800
2	96,000	19,200	76,800
3	57,000	8,000	49,000
4	36,000	0	36,000
5	36,000	0	36,000
6	15,000	0	15,000

Solid Cement Company
Alternative Computation of Relevant Operating Cash Inflows

Year	Item	Amount (1)	Factor (2)	Cash Flow [(1) x (2)] (3)
1	Changes in Revenue	$200,000	(1 - 0.4)	$120,000
	Less: Changes in Expenses	180,000	(1 - 0.4)	-108,000
	Plus: Changes in Depreciation	40,800	0.40	+ 16,320
	Equals: Relevant Operating Cash Inflow		----	$ 28,320
2	Changes in Revenue	$300,000	(1 - 0.4)	$180,000
	Less: Changes in Expenses	240,000	(1 - 0.4)	-144,000
	Plus: Changes in Depreciation	76,800	0.4	+ 30,720
	Equals: Relevant Operating Cash Inflow	----	----	$ 66,720
3	Changes in Revenue	$400,000	(1 - 0.4)	$240,000
	Less: Changes in Expenses	320,000	(1 - 0.4)	-192,000
	Plus: Changes in Depreciation	49,000	0.4	+ 19,600
	Equals: Relevant Operating Cash Flow	----	----	$ 67,600
4	Changes in Revenue	$500,000	(1 - 0.4)	$300,000
	Less: Changes in Expenses	400,000	(1 - 0.4)	-240,000
	Plus: Changes in Depreciation	36,000	0.4	+ 14,400
	Equals: Relevant Operating Cash Flow	----	----	$ 74,400
5	Changes in Revenue	$500,000	(1 - 0.4)	$300,000
	Less: Changes in Expenses	400,000	(1 - 0.4)	-240,000
	Plus: Changes in Depreciation	36,000	0.4	+ 14,400
	Equals: Relevant Operating Cash Flow	----	----	$ 74,400

A comparison of the operating cash inflows calculated above with the operating cash inflows calculated using the longer approach confirms the accuracy of the alternative approach.

c.   The terminal cash flow first requires calculation of the proceeds of the sale of the new asset, less taxes plus working capital recovery:

Proceeds from Sale	$20,000
Less taxes due on sale[1]	- 2,000
Recovery of net working capital[2]	20,000
Terminal cash flow	$38,000

Notes

1. Since the asset will have book value of $15,000 at the end of year five, $5,000 of the $20,000 sale proceeds represents recaptured depreciation taxed at the ordinary tax rate of 40 percent.

2. Assuming all the increase in net working capital is recaptured at the end of year 5.

d. The incremental annual cash flows associated with this replacement project are as follows:

Year	Annual Cash Flow
0	($211,440)
1	28,320
2	66,720
3	67,600
4	74,400
5	74,400 + 38,000 = 112,400

CHAPTER 10

CAPITAL BUDGETING TECHNIQUES:
CERTAINTY, RISK, AND SOME REFINEMENTS

SUMMARY

This chapter combines present value techniques and risk analysis with relevant cash flow techniques, in order to evaluate capital expenditures. The basic capital budgeting techniques under certainty and risk are described. Other refinements such as unequal lives and capital rationing are also considered. This is a key chapter and requires careful study.

The payback period is an unsophisticated capital budgeting technique that is calculated by determining the amount of time it will take the firm to recover its initial investment. The net present value (NPV) is the difference between the present value of cash inflows and the initial investment of a project. If NPV is greater than zero, the project is considered acceptable. The internal rate of return (IRR) is the discount rate that equates the net present value of a project with zero. If the IRR is greater than the firm's cost of capital, a project is acceptable.

Both sophisticated techniques consider the time factor in the value of money, use the cost of capital in the decision criterion, and provide the same accept-reject decisions for an independent project. There are often conflicts between the rankings of projects using NPV and IRR, resulting from the differences in the magnitude and/or timing of cash flows and from internal rate of return's implicit assumption that intermediate cash inflows are reinvested at the IRR. NPV assumes reinvestment at the firm's cost of capital. Although the NPV technique is theoretically more sound than the IRR, the latter is more commonly used by major firms, since it is consistent with the general preference of financial decision makers for using rates of return.

Several techniques for adjusting projects for risk are presented in the chapter. Subjective approaches to risk, such as estimating the probability of breakeven cash inflows (zero NPV), sensitivity analysis, and scenario analysis are frequently used to assess risk. Simulation provides a probability distribution of project returns. Certainty equivalents provide a mechanism whereby risky cash flows can be adjusted to certain amounts and then discounted at a risk-free rate in order to evaluate a project.

Risk adjusted discount rates (RADR), which are the discount rates required in the marketplace in order to compensate for project risk, are very useful. While the CAPM is appropriate for securities which trade in efficient markets, it is not appropriate for capital projects, which do not trade in efficient markets. Total risk, not systematic risk, is considered the appropriate risk measure for capital projects.

Mutually exclusive projects with unequal lives may be compared using the annualized net present value (ANPV) approach, which simply takes the computed NPV for each project and converts it to an equivalent (in NPV terms) annual amount. Under capital rationing, the firm must select the projects that maximize its overall NPV, given a fixed capital budget limit.

CONCEPT OUTLINE

I. **This chapter describes the key capital budgeting techniques available for evaluating capital expenditure alternatives under certainty and risk.**

A. The payback period represents the number of years required for a firm to recover its initial investment in a project.

1. By comparing the calculated payback period to the firm's maximum payback period, projects with paybacks shorter than the firm's maximum are accepted (i.e., short paybacks are preferable); other projects are rejected.

2. There are three key advantages of the payback method.

a. The use of cash inflows instead of accounting profits in the calculation of payback is viewed favorably.

b. Although it is not explicit, payback implicitly considers the timing of cash flows.

c. Payback is useful for measuring project risk exposure because it indicates how long it takes to recover an investment.

3. Three basic weaknesses are cited for not relying on payback to make capital budgeting decisions.

a. Payback values indicate when an investment is returned, without saying anything about increasing firm value in the interim.

b. Payback ignores any cash flows occurring beyond the payback period.

c. Payback does not give explicit consideration to the time value of money. If an investment costs $1,000, the timing of the return of the thousandth dollar is of paramount importance.

B. Both sophisticated capital budgeting techniques recognize the time value of money by discounting all project cash flows at a firm's discount rate, or cost of capital, and are consistent with the objective of maximization of stockholders' wealth.

1. Net present value (NPV) is calculated by, subtracting the initial investment, II, from the present value of future cash flows, CF, as shown below:

$$NPV = \sum_{t=1}^{n} \frac{CF_t}{(1 + k)^t} - II$$

   a. If the NPV is greater than zero, a project is acceptable; otherwise, it should be rejected.

   b. Projects can be ranked in descending order on the basis of NPV.

2. The internal rate of return (IRR) is the discount rate that equates a project's NPV with zero:

$$\$0 = \sum_{t=1}^{n} \frac{CF_t}{(1 + IRR)^t} - II$$

   a. A project is considered acceptable when its IRR is greater than its cost of capital; otherwise, the project should be rejected.

   b. The IRR can be found by using certain trial-and-error techniques or with the aid of a computer.

   c. Although the IRR agrees with the NPV with respect to accept-reject decisions, differences in ranking between NPV and IRR result from differences in magnitude or timing of project cash flows.

C. The relationship between the IRR and the NPV can best be illustrated by using a present-value profile, which is a graph showing the NPV associated with a broad range of discount rates.

D. The NPV is the theoretically preferable approach because it does not suffer from the deficiencies attributed to the IRR.

   1. Use of the NPV implicitly assumes that any intermediate cash flows generated by an investment are reinvested at the firm's cost of capital, while use of the IRR assumes reinvestment at the often unrealistic rate specified by the IRR.

2. Nonconventional patterns of cash flows have more than one IRR, which makes interpretation of the results difficult. A project with a cash outflow at maturity (i.e, salvage expenditure) will have two IRRs.

3. With low (high) discount rates, the IRR procedure will give preference to projects with lower (higher) early-year cash inflow patterns.

4. Although the NPV is theoretically preferable, the IRR is more popular, because financial decision makers can more readily relate it to the available decision data, which is often in percentage terms.

II. **The outcomes associated with most capital budgeting decisions are normally not known with certainty. A number of approaches for dealing with risk exist.**

A. With capital projects, one may define risk as the possibility that the project will be unacceptable.

1. One approach is to determine the probability of a negative NPV or an IRR less than the cost of capital. What is the probability of cash inflows not exceeding breakeven cash inflows?

2. More appropriate approaches consider the variability of future cash inflows.

B. Sensitivity techniques, such as pessimistic, most likely, and optimistic estimates of project returns, are subjective but allow managers to get a feel for the variability of returns.

1. The difference between optimistic and pessimistic outcomes is the range, another risk measure.

2. Scenario analysis permits adjustment of several factors that affect cash flows under specified conditions, such as a business recession.

C. Simulation is a process using random numbers and predetermined probabilities to simulate a project's outcome or payoff. The resulting outcomes represent a distribution, allowing the decision maker to view a continuum of outcomes rather than a single point.

D. Cash flow risk adjustment can be accomplished by adjusting the cash flows themselves or the discount rate.

1. Certainty equivalents, alpha in the following expression, are factors that reflect the percentage of a given cash flow that the financial decision maker would accept with certainty in exchange for the expected, but uncertain, cash flow.

$$NPV = \sum_{t=1}^{n} \frac{\alpha_t \times CF_t}{(1 + R_F)^t} - II$$

First, the cash flows are adjusted to their certainty equivalents using the certainty equivalent factor.

2. Second, the risk-free rate is applied as the discount rate.

3. If the NPV using certainty equivalent cash flows discounted at the risk-free rate is greater than zero, the project should be accepted.

4. The process of adjusting risky cash flows to certain cash flows is somewhat subjective, but the method is theoretically correct.

E. The risk-adjusted rate approach adjusts the discount rate to reflect risk, as shown below:

$$NPV = \sum_{t=1}^{n} \frac{CF_t}{(1 + RADR)^t} - II$$

1. Higher risk requires a higher discount rate to compensate the shareholder for the additional risk of a given project.

2. Since the market for real assets is seldom as efficient as the market for securities, the CAPM is not appropriate for this market.

3. The coefficient of variation (CV) is frequently used to measure relative risk, with the discount rate increasing with increases in CV. Estimating the market risk return function, the level of return required for each level of CV, is difficult.

4. Although the price of publicly-traded stock is not affected by diversification, if cash flows are enhanced more than risk, share price may increase.

5. Despite combining risk and time into one measure, implicitly assuming risk increases with time, RADRs are frequently used in practice.

        a. Firms frequently develop risk classes for certain types of projects.

        b. Alternatively, firms may assign divisional risk classes.

III. **Special circumstances may cause the capital budgeting process to differ from that previously discussed.**

A. Mutually exclusive projects with uneven lives must be brought to a common evaluative period. The efficient method presented is the annualized net present value method.

    1. First, compute the NPV of each project using the cost of capital. Only positive NPV projects should receive further consideration.

    2. Next, divide the NPV of each project by the present-value interest factor for the given cost of capital and the project's life to get the ANPV.

$$ANPV_j = NPV_j \div PVIFA_{k,nj}$$

    3. The project with the highest ANPV should be accepted.

    4. One key assumption is that each project could be repeated an infinite number of times. If this assumption is not acceptable, the manager must consider both the ANPV level and number of years the ANPV is earned.

B. Capital rationing is confronted by most firms in which there are more acceptable capital budgeting projects than available money.

    1. One way to select projects under capital rationing is the IRR approach. Projects are ranked by their IRR, and the projects are accepted in order of decreasing IRRs until the budget is exhausted or the IRR is less than the cost of capital.

    2. The NPV approach to capital rationing recognizes that the unused portion of a firm's budget does not increase the firm's value and in many cases may cause a decline in value. This approach uses trial-and-error techniques to find the group of projects that maximizes the present value of cash inflows.

APPLICATIONS

DEFINITIONS

1. The _Pay back Period_ is the exact amount of time required for a firm to recover its initial dollar investment.

2. The _profitability index_, or benefit-cost ratio, is obtained by dividing the present value of cash inflows by the initial investment.

3. _Net Present Value_ is a capital budgeting technique which subtracts the present value of cash outflow from the present value of cash inflows.

4. The NPV decision criterion is to _accept_ all projects with net present values greater than zero.

5. The internal rate of return equates the present value of _cash inflows_ and the _initial investment_

6. Discounting cash flows by the internal rate of return results in a net present value equal to _zero_

7. Graphs depicting the net present value of a project across different discount rates are known as _net present value profiles_

8. Conflicting rankings between NPV and IRR result from differences in _magnitude_ and _timing_ of cash flows.

9. Reinvestment assumptions become important when there are _intermediate_ cash flows.

10. While NPV has _theoretical_ strengths, IRR has _practical_ strengths.

11. At the _breakeven_ cash flow level, cash inflows equal the NPV-based criterion for acceptance.

12. _Scenario_ analysis is used to evaluate the impact on return of simultaneous changes in several variables.

13. The _risk-adjusted discount rate_ is the rate of return that must be earned on a given project in order to compensate for the project's risk.

14.   The annualized net present value approach is useful when evaluating _Unequal-lived_ - _____ projects.

15.   The objective of _Capital rationing_ _____ is to provide the highest overall net present value without requiring more dollars than budgeted.

MULTIPLE CHOICE

1.   Capital budgeting requires identification and consideration of:
      a. relevant cash flows.
      b. project risk.
      c. time value aspects.
      d. all of the above.

2.   A capital budgeting method that fails to consider the objective of wealth maximization is:
      a. internal rate of return.
      b. net present value.
      c. payback.
      d. all of the above.

3.   A capital budgeting technique similar to IRR in that it provides a return for invested dollar, but does not consider the time value of money is the:
      a. average rate of return.
      b. benefit-cost ratio.
      c. payback period.
      d. required rate of return.

4.   The net present value is found by subtracting _____ from the present value of the firm's cash inflows associated with the project.
      a. depreciation.
      b. initial investment
      c. taxes
      d. terminal value

5.   If the NPV is _____ zero, accept the project.
      a. equal to
      b. greater than
      c. less than
      d. no higher than

6. A project has an IRR of 14 percent and a required rate of return of 12 percent.
    a. Accepting the project will reduce share price.
    b. The project should be accepted.
    c. The project should be rejected.
    d. The project will have a negative NPV.

7. For conventional projects, NPV and IRR will _____ generate the same accept/reject decision.
    a. always
    b. cannot answer without more information.
    c. never
    d. sometimes

8. Hand-held calculators can be used to calculate:
    a. IRR
    b. NPV
    c. both a and b
    d. neither a or b

9. _____ assumes intermediate cash flow reinvestment at the cost of capital.
    a. IRR
    b. NPV
    c. Payback
    d. both a and b

10. Project risk generally arise from all of the following, except:
    a. cash inflows.
    b. initial costs.
    c. labor rates.
    d. sales levels.

11. Using probabilities, the project with the lowest probability of having a positive NPV:
    a. is most risky.
    b. will be ranked highest.
    c. will not be accepted.
    d. both a and c.

12. _____ is a sophisticated, statistical approach for analyzing project risk, which creates a probability distribution of net present values.
    a. Breakeven strategy
    b. Scenario analysis
    c. Sensitivity analysis
    d. Simulation

13.   The technique that adjusts risky cash flows to the proportion that investors would be satisfied to receive for sure is called:
a. certainty equivalent.
b. risk-adjusted discount rate.
c. scenario analysis.
d. sensitivity analysis.

14.   It is thought that total risk is a better measure of risk than non-diversifiable risk for evaluating capital assets, because:
a. only total risk can be measured.
b. the market for capital assets is relatively inefficient.
c. there are no gains from diversification of capital assets.
d. total risk is usually considered the relevant risk.

15.   The generally preferred technique for capital rationing is the:
a. annualized net present value.
b. initial rate of return approach.
c. net present value approach.
d. ranking rate of return approach.

PROBLEMS

1.   The Klein Company is contemplating two mutually exclusive projects. The data for each project are given below.

	Project A	Project B
Initial Investment:	$60,000	$ 70,000
Year	Annual Cash Inflow	
1	$ 10,000	$ 25,000
2	15,000	25,000
3	20,000	25,000
4	25,000	25,000
5	35,000	25,000

a. Calculate the payback period for each project.

b. If the firm has set a maximum payback period of three years, using the payback period, evaluate the acceptability of each project. Comment on which project is preferred.   *Project B*

2. Assume that a firm with an 11 percent cost of capital has identified two projects with the following cash flows.

	Project I	Project II
Initial Investment:	$100,000	$140,000
Year	Annual Cash Inflow	
1	$ 30,000	$ 53,000
2	35,000	53,000
3	40,000	53,000
4	45,000	53,000
5	55,000	53,000

a. Calculate the net present value for each of the projects.

b. Evaluate the acceptability of each project on the basis of net present value.

c. Select the best project, using net present value.

3. Perform the following operations on the firm presented in problem 2.

a. Calculate the internal rate of return (IRR) for each project.

b. Using discount rates of 0 percent, 10 percent, 20 percent, and the IRR calculated in part a., construct a table which could be used to draw the present-value profiles for each project on a common set of axes.

c. Comment on the acceptability and preferability of the projects. Discuss these results in light of the present value data table in part b.

4. Brenner's Buttons is evaluating three mutually exclusive projects: AA, BB, and CC. The relevant cash flows for each project are given below. The cost of capital to use in evaluating these equally risky projects is 18 percent. Use net present value to select the preferred project.

	Project		
	AA	BB	CC
Initial Investment:	$11,000	$12,000	$10,500
Year	Cash inflows		
1	$ 1,000	$ 6,000	$ 4,000
2	5,000	6,000	4,000
3	6,000	6,000	4,000
4	6,000	500	4,000
5	7,000	100	4,000

5. Sekely Steel accepts only projects with rates of return higher than the firm's 14 percent cost of capital. The firm is considering a nine-year project that provides annual operating cash inflows of $8,000 per year and requires an initial investment of $44,300.
   a. What is the IRR of this project?
   b. If the $8,000 operating cash inflows could continue beyond year 9, how many total years would the flows have to last for the project to be acceptable?
   c. Using the given life (9 years), initial investment ($44,300), and cost of capital (14 percent) what is the minimum operating cash inflow required to make this an acceptable project?

6. The Monroe Tile Company is considering purchasing a new machine that would last five years and require an initial investment of $250,000. Given below are the company's expected cash inflows and their associated certainty equivalents. The firm's management estimates the prevailing risk-free rate of return to be 8 percent. Calculate the net present value using certainty equivalents and explain whether or not the company should purchase the new machine.

Year	Cash Inflow	Certainty equivalent
1	$80,000	1.00
2	80,000	0.80
3	80,000	0.60
4	80,000	0.50
5	80,000	0.50

7. The Wood Company has investigated the market risk-return trade-offs and has gathered the following data:

Coefficient of variation (Total risk)	Market discount rate
0.0	6.0%
0.2	7.0
0.4	8.0
0.6	9.0
0.8	10.0
1.0	11.0
1.2	12.0
1.4	13.0
1.6	14.0
1.8	15.0
2.0	16.0

a. What is the riskless rate or return and what would be the risk premium for an asset with a coefficient of variation equal to 1.6.

b. Given the following data calculate the risk-adjusted net present value.

	Project	
	X	Y
Initial Investment	$100,000	$100,000
Project Life	8 years	8 years
Annual cash inflow	$ 25,000	$ 28,000
Coefficient of variation	0.4	1.4

c. Discuss the results of using a risk-adjusted discount rate. Do these results differ from those expected if both projects are considered equally risky? Explain.

8.   The Rich Candy Company must choose between two alternative candies - Tootie and Chicki - which it intends manufacturing for the summer. Tootie, a chocolate-coated candy, has higher initial costs but also has higher expected returns. Chicki, a peanut-caramel candy, has slightly lower initial costs but also has lower expected returns. The optimistic, most likely, and pessimistic cash inflows are listed below.

Candy	Initial investment	Present value of cash inflows under:		
		Optimistic Conditions	Most Likely Conditions	Pessimistic Conditions
Tootie	$ 150,000	$300,000	$200,000	- $100,000
Chicki	$ 120,000	$240,000	$160,000	- $ 60,000

     a. Use the NPV's of the alternatives to present a sensitivity analysis of the two candies. Which candy has the greatest risk?

     b. Assume furthermore that the probabilities of the alternatives are as follows:
         Optimistic: 25 %
         Most Likely: 55 %
         Pessimistic: 20 %

Combine this information with that presented above to calculate an anticipated NPV.

9.   The Philip's Pressure Cooker, a local restaurant, is evaluating three mutually exclusive projects: I, II, and III. The relevant cash flows for each project are given below. The cost of capital to use in evaluating these equally risky projects is 18 percent. Use the annualized net present value (ANPV) to select the preferred project.

	Project		
	I	II	III
Initial Investment:	$11,000	$12,000	$10,500
Year	Cash inflows		
1	$ 1,000	$ 6,000	$ 4,000
2	5,000	6,000	4,000
3	6,000	6,000	4,000
4	6,000	500	4,000
5	7,000		4,000
6			4,000

10. Joshua's Juices wishes to consider a proposed project, an apple juice press, using the NPV approach. The firm has a 13 percent cost of capital. The initial investment and relevant cash inflows for the project are summarized below.

Initial Investment: $50,000

Year	Cash Inflows
1	$16,000
2	16,000
3	16,000
4	16,000

a. Find the NPV for the project using the given data. Would you recommend the project be accepted? Why?

b. If the firm expects the cash inflows to increase by 5 percent per year, what would be the (inflation-adjusted) cash inflows?

c. Find the NPV based on b. Would you recommend the project be accepted considering inflation? (Note: The cost of capital includes any inflation-related premium.)

11. Shipping by Sarah is considering the following six investment projects. Each project's initial investment, IRR, and PV of subsequent cash inflows is also given, assuming the firm's cost of capital is 10 percent. Sarah is facing budgeting restrictions which limit the size of the firm's capital budget to $300,000. Which projects should Sarah accept?

Project	Initial Investment	IRR	PV of cash inflows discounted at 10 %
A	$132,000	12 %	$ 151,800
B	$ 72,000	16 %	94,800
C	$ 48,000	9 %	43,200
D	$120,000	17 %	174,000
E	$ 84,000	21 %	134,400
F	$ 96,000	13 %	120,000

SOLUTIONS

DEFINITIONS

1. payback period
2. profitability index
3. Net present value
4. accept
5. cash inflows; initial investment
6. zero
7. net present value profiles
8. magnitude; timing
9. intermediate
10. theoretical; practical
11. breakeven
12. Scenario
13. risk-adjusted discount rate
14. unequal-lived
15. capital rationing

MULTIPLE CHOICE:

1. d	6. b	11. a Risky projects with a
2. c	7. a	large potential cash
3. a	8. c	flow may be accepted
4. b	9. b	12. d
5. b	10. b	13. a
		14. b
		15. c

PROBLEMS

1.   a.   Payback for Project A is determined by summing the cash flow for each year.

Year	Sum	Total
1	$10,000	$ 10,000
2	15,000	25,000
3	20,000	45,000
4	25,000	70,000
5	35,000	105,000

Remaining shortage ($60,000 - $45,000) $15,000
Divided by: Cash inflow year 4   ÷ 25,000
     Portion of year required   =   .60

The project has an actual payback of about 3.6 years.

Payback for Project B can be determined by dividing the initial investment by the equal annual cash flows:

$$\$70,000/\$25,000 = 2.8 \text{ years}$$

   b.   Only Project B has a payback shorter the three years. It is the only acceptable project.

2. a. The net present value of each project can be calculated by finding the present value of cash inflows and subtracting the initial investments.

   The net present value (NPV) for project I can be calculated in tabular form:

Year	Cash Inflow (1)	11% PVIF (From Table A-3) (2)	Present Value [(1) X (2)] (3)
1	$ 30,000	.901	$ 27,030
2	35,000	.812	28,420
3	40,000	.731	29,240
4	45,000	.659	29,655
5	55,000	.593	32,615
Present value of inflows			$146,960

   NPV = $146,960 - $100,000 = $46,960

   Because Project II is an annuity, the interest factor for the present value of an annuity (from Table A-4) discounted at 11 percent for five years, which is 3.696, can be multiplied by the amount of the annuity to get the present value of cash inflows.

   Present value of inflows = (3.696) X ($53,000) = $195,888

   NPV = $195,888 - $140,000 = $55,888

   b. On the basis of net present value both projects are acceptable, because their NPVs are greater than zero.

   c. On the basis of NPV, project II is preferable to project I (i.e., NPV for II is $55,888 and NPV for I is $46,960).

3.   a. The IRR for project I must be determined using the step-by-step approach suggested
          for a mixed stream of cash flows.

     Step 1.   The average annual cash inflow must be determined as follows:

$$\frac{\$30,000 + \$35,000 + \$40,000 + \$45,000 + \$55,000}{5} = \frac{\$205,000}{5} = \$41,000$$

     Step 2.   The average cash inflow is divided into the initial investment to get the fake
               payback period:

          Fake payback = $100,000 ÷ $41,000 = 2.44

     Step 3.   In Table A-4 (PVIFA), the interest rate associated with the factor closest to
               2.44 for five years is found. The rate is at 30 percent (factor equals 2.436).

     Step 4.   Because the actual cash-flow stream is increasing, the fake annuity over-
               estimates the cash-flow stream. Therefore, the discount rate is subjectively
               adjusted to 26 percent.

     Step 5.   The NPV at a 26 percent rate is calculated:

Year	Cash Inflow (1)	26% PVIF (From Table A-3) (2)	Present Value [(1) X (2)] (3)
1	$ 30,000	.794	$ 23,820
2	35,000	.630	22,050
3	40,000	.500	20,000
4	45,000	.397	17,865
5	55,000	.315	17,325

Present value of inflows $ 101,060
Less: Initial investment   - 100,000
Net present value $ 1,060

     Step 6.   Because the resulting NPV is greater than zero (i.e., $1,060), the discount
               rate should be increased. Because the resulting NPV does not differ greatly
               from zero, a rate of 27 percent is used.

Step 7. The NPV is calculated using a 27 percent rate.

Year	Cash Inflow (1)	27% PVIF (From Table A-3) (2)	Present Value [(1) X (2)] (3)
1	$ 30,000	.787	$ 23,610
2	35,000	.620	21,700
3	40,000	.488	19,520
4	45,000	.384	17,280
5	55,000	.303	16,665

Present value of inflows	$ 98,775
Less: Initial investment	- 100,000
Net present value	$ 1,225

Because two consecutive discount rates have been found for which positive and negative NPVs result, the IRR to the nearest 1 percent can be determined. The discount rate for which the NPV is closest to zero must be selected (choosing between 26 percent and 27 percent). The IRR to the nearest 1 percent would therefore be 26 percent.

Because project II is an annuity, the IRR is much easier to estimate. Only two steps are required in this case:

Step 1. Calculate the payback period for the project, $140,000/$53,000 = 2.64 years.

Step 2. Using Table A-4 (PVIFA), find the interest rate associated with the factor closest to 2.64 for five years. This is the IRR to the nearest 1 percent for the project. This occurs at 26 percent, where the factor in Table A-4 for five years is 2.635, which is closest to 2.64. The IRR to the nearest 1 percent for project II is therefore 26 percent.

b. In order to draw the present value profiles for projects I and II as prescribed, the NPV at 0 percent, 10 percent, and 20 percent, and the IRR, which happens to be 26 percent for each project, must be calculated. For project I, the calculations are given below.

Project I						
		PVIF for one dollar (Table A - 3)			Present Values	
Year	Cash inflow (000s) (1)	0% (2)	10% (2)	20% (2)	0% (1)x(2)	10% (1)x(3)	20% (1)x(4)
1	$ 30	1.000	.909	.833	$ 30,000	$ 27,270	$ 24,990
2	35	1.000	.826	.694	35,000	28,910	24,290
3	40	1.000	.751	.579	40,000	30,040	23,160
4	45	1.000	.683	.482	45,000	30,735	21,690
5	55	1.000	.621	.402	55,000	34,155	22,110
Present value of inflows					$205,000	$151,110	$116,240
Less: Initial investment					100,000	100,000	100,000
Net present value					$105,000	$ 51,110	$ 16,240

The NPV at 26 percent was not calculated because it will be assumed to be zero at that point, which has been estimated as the IRR.

Because project II is an annuity, the NPV values for 0 percent, 10 percent, and 20 percent can be easily calculated with the aid of Table A-4.

Project II						
		PVIFA for a one dollar annuity (Table A - 3)			Present Values	
Amount of annuity (1)	0% (2)	10% (2)	20% (2)	0% (1)x(2)	10% (1)x(3)	20% (1)x(4)
$ 53,000	5.000	3.791	2.991	$265,000	$200,923	$158,523
Less: Initial investment				140,000	140,000	140,000
Net present value				$125,000	$ 60,923	$ 18,523

Because 26 percent is assumed to be project II's IRR, the NPV at 26 percent is assumed to be zero.

The following table summarizes the discount rates and associated NPVs:

Discount rate	NPV	
	Project I	Project II
0 %	$ 105,000	$ 125,000
10 %	51,110	60,923
20 %	16,240	18,523
26 %	0	0

c.　Both pr. s are acceptable because both have IRRs of 26 percent, which is greater than the firm's 11 percent cost of capital. Because both projects have IRRs of 26 percent, either project could be chosen. The present-value indicates that at discount rates below the IRR project II would always have a higher NPV. Although it does not occur in this case, present-value profiles sometimes intersect at rates below the IRR, thereby resulting in conflicting rankings.

4.　Compute the NPV for each project at 18 percent, the cost of capital. (The NPV of AA is computed for a mixed stream; for BB it is treated as a three-year annuity and single payments in years 4 and 5; and CC is treated as a five-year annuity.)

NPV(AA)　= [$1,000 X .847] + [$5,000 X .718] + [$6,000 X .609] + [$6,000 X .516] + [$7,000 X .437] - $11,000
　　　　　= $847 + $3,590 + $3654 + $3,096 + $3,059 - $11,000
　　　　　= $ 3,246

NPV(BB)　= [$6,000 X 2.174] + [$500 X .516] + [$100 X .437] - $12,000
　　　　　= $13,044 + $258 + $44 - $12,000
　　　　　= $ 1,346

NPV(CC)　= [$4,000 X 3.127] - $10,500 = $12,508 - $10,500
　　　　　= $ 2,008

Rank based on NPV:

   NPV (AA) = $3,246 preferred
   NPV (CC) = $2,008
   NPV (BB) = $1,348 (despite lowest payback)

5.   a.   Since this is an annuity, the IRR is determined by solving for the factor and checking in the PVIFA table for the rate.

$$0 = \$8000 \ (PVIFA)_{IRR\%, \ 9 \ yrs} - \$44,300$$

$$\$44,300/\$8000 = PVIFA_{IRR\%, \ 9 \ yrs}$$

$$5.538 = PVIFA_{IRR\%, \ 9 \ yrs}$$

$$IRR = 11\%$$

Because IRR is less than k, reject the project.

   b.   Here we solve for the factor and check the table for the number of years at 14 percent.

The ratio of cost of annual cash inflow is 5.538. In the PVIFA Table, the 14 percent column, this value is between the 11-year row and 12-year rows. Interpolation provides a value of 11.4 years. That is,

$$5.538 = PVIFA_{14 \ percent, \ 11.4 \ yrs}$$

The length of time required for $8,000 per year to yield 14 percent on an initial investment of $44,300 is 11.4 years.

   c.   Here solve for the payment, or annuity cash inflow, ACF:

$$\$44,300 = ACF \ X \ PVIFA_{14\%, \ 9 \ yrs} = ACF \ X \ 4.946$$

$$\$44,300/4.946 = ACF = \$8957$$

If the operating cash flows were $8957/year for 9 years, the project would be acceptable (have an internal rate of return of 14 percent).

6.   The certainty equivalent approach uses factors that reflect the percentage of a given cash inflow that the decision maker would accept in exchange for the expected cash inflow. The project is therefore adjusted for risk by first converting the expected cash inflows into certain amounts, using the certainty equivalents, and then discounting the certain cash inflows at a risk-free rate.

Year	Cash inflow (1)	Certainty equivalent (2)	Certain cash inflow (3)	8% PVIF (Table A-3) (4)	Present values [(3)x(4)] (5)
1	$80,000	1.0	$80,000	0.926	$ 74,080
2	80,000	0.8	64,000	0.857	54,848
3	80,000	0.6	48,000	0.794	38,112
4	80,000	0.5	40,000	0.735	29,400
5	80,000	0.5	40,000	0.681	27,240
	Present value of cash inflows				$ 223,680

NPV (@8%) = $223,680 - $250,000 = -$26,320

To gain acceptance of any project, the NPV should be greater than zero. Since the Monroe Tile Company's NPV is -$26,320, the company should not purchase the new machine.

7.   a.   The market indifference curve is drawn by plotting the coefficient of variation on the x-axis and the corresponding market discount rate on the y-axis. The market risk premium is the amount by which a given discount rate exceeds the risk-free discount rate, R_F, which in this case is 6 percent. The risk premium on an asset with a coefficient of variation equaling 1.6 would be 8 (14-6) percent.

     b.   Using the market indifference data, it can be seen that the cash inflows of project X should be discounted at 8 percent, and those of project Y at 13 percent. Using these rates to get the appropriate interest factors from Table A-4, the risk-adjusted NPV for each project is calculated as follows:

Project X NPV = ($25,000) X (PVIFA$_{8\%,8 \text{ yrs}}$) - $100,000

          = $143,675 - $100,000 = $ 43,675

Project Y NPV = ($28,000) X (PVIFA$_{13\%,8\,yrs}$) - $100,000

= $134,372 - $100,000 = $ 34,372

c. Comparing the risk-adjusted NPVs indicates that project X is preferable to project Y because its risk-adjusted NPV is larger ($43,675 versus $34,372). Had both projects been evaluated using the same discount rate, it is obvious that project Y would always be preferable, because its annual cash inflow is larger, while both projects have the same lives and initial investments. The importance of the risk adjustment should be clear from this comparison. When the risk of each project is considered, project X is found to be preferable to project Y.

8.   a. The sensitivity analysis is developed as follows:

Tootie:
   Optimistic NPV   = $300,000 - $150,000 = $150,000
   Most Likely NPV = $200,000 - $150,000 = $50,000
   Pessimistic NPV   = -$100,000 - $150,000 = -$250,000

Chicki:
   Optimistic NPV   = $240,000 - $120,000 = $120,000
   Most Likely NPV = $160,000 - $120,000 = $40,000
   Pessimistic NPV   = -$ 60,000 - $120,000 = -$180,000

This unsophisticated technique cannot always give a definite answer. Here the Chicki candy appears to have less risk per dollar of potential gain. The range for Chicki is $300,000, while that for Tootie is $400,000.

Multiplying each alternative's NPV by the anticipated likelihood of its occurrence reinforces the support of Chicki.
However, the difference has greatly narrowed.

Tootie:
   (.25)$150,000 + (.55)$50,000 + (.20)-$250,000 =
   $37,500 + $27,500 - $50,000 = $15,000

Chicki:
   (.25)$120,000 + (.55)$40,000 + (.20)-$180,000 =
   $30,000 + $22,000 - $36,000 = $16,000

Knowledge of both the likely cash flows during the various conditions and the likelihood of market conditions themselves are very important in sensitivity analysis.

9. Step 1. Compute the NPV for each project at 18 percent, the cost of capital. (The NPV of I is computed for a mixed stream, for II it is treated as a three-year annuity and one other single payment in year 4; and III is treated as a six-year annuity.)

NPV (I) = {$1,000 X .847} + {$5,000 X .718} + {$6,000 X .609}
{6,000 x .516} + {$7,000 X .437} - $11,000
= $847 + $3,590 + $3,654 + $3,096 + $3,059 - $11,000
= $ 3,246

NPV (II) = {$6,000 X 2.174} + {$500 X .516} - $12,000
= $13,044 + $258 - $12,000
= $1,302

NPV (III) = {$4,000 X 3.498} - $10,500
= $13,992 - $10,500
= $3,492

Step 2. Apply the following equation to the positive NPVs calculated in step 1:

$$ANPV_j = NPV_j \div PVIFA_{k,nj}$$

where k is the cost of capital and n_j it is the life in years for project j.

$$ANPV\ (I) = \frac{\$3246}{PVIFA_{18\%,5yrs}} = \frac{\$3246}{3.127} = \$ 1038.06$$

$$ANPV\ (II) = \frac{\$1302}{PVIFA_{18\%,4yrs}} = \frac{\$1302}{2.690} = \$ 484.01$$

$$ANPV\ (III) = \frac{\$3492}{PVIFA_{18\%,6yrs}} = \frac{\$3492}{3.498} = \$ 998.28$$

Step 3. Select the project with the highest ANPV, project I. This approach assumes each project may be repeated an infinite number of times.

10. a. Since this is a four-year annuity, the NPV may be easily found:

NPV = $16,000(PVIFA_{13%,4yrs}) - $50,000
= $16,000(2.974) - $50,000 = <u>-$2,416</u>

Reject the project, the NPV is less than zero.

b. Although you may first consider reducing the discount rate, an "inflation-adjusted" discount rate so to speak, this approach would give you the wrong answer. The relative relationship between numerator and denominator $16,800/1.13 versus $16,000/1.08, would not be the same. Cash flows are increasing, the required return is not decreasing. Annual Cash flows are multiplied by the respective FVIF, resulting in an adjusted cash flow.

Cash Flow without Inflation	X FVIF$_{5\%,n}$	= Cash Flow Adjusted
$ 16,000	1.050	$16,800
16,000	1.102	17,632
16,000	1.158	18,528
16,000	1.216	19,456

c. NPV = 16,800(.885) + 17,632(.783) + 18,528(.693) +
            $19,456(.613) - $50,000 =
        = 14,868 + 13,806 + 12,840 + 11,927 - 50,000 = $3441

The importance of considering inflation in future cash flows is exemplified by this problem. After adjusting for inflation, the present value of cash inflows rises $5758 ($3342 - (-$2416)). More importantly, the project is now estimated to have a positive NPV, and should be accepted.

11. Net present value is the technique that should be applied, since it seeks the combination of projects that provides the highest total value. NPVs would be obtained by subtracting the initial investment from the PV of cash inflows. The NPVs are listed in decreasing order below. (Since project C's return is less than the cost of capital, it is unacceptable and excluded from further analysis).

Project:	A	B	D	E	F
NPV:	$19,800	$22,800	$54,000	$50,000	$24,000

The highest NPVs, and IRRs, are derived from projects E and D, which have a combined initial investment of $204,000. Although the next highest IRR is that of project B (16%), its NPV is less than that of project F. In order to maximize NPV, Shipping by Sarah should invest in projects D, E, and F.

We are assuming that the unused portion of the budget will not gain or lose money. When investing in project B, $24,000 is left. Since the inclusion of project F fully uses the budget, Sarah is able to enhance NPV with a lower IRR project. (The answer would be different if the additional $24,000 could be invested to earn $1,200.)

CHAPTER 11

THE COST OF CAPITAL

SUMMARY

The cost of capital represents the rate of return a firm must earn on its investment projects to maintain the market value of its common stock. It can also be considered the rate of return required by the market suppliers of capital in order to invest funds in the firm. Accepting projects that earn less than the cost of capital will decrease the firm's value, while accepting projects that earn more than the cost of capital will increase it.

The cost of capital consists of the risk-free cost of financing, plus a business risk premium plus a financial risk premium. The risk-free cost varies with changes in the macroeconomy. The business risk premium is generally the same for firms within a given industry, while the financial risk premium varies among firms, depending on their financial structure. Suppliers of the various sources of capital add a premium to the risk-free cost for the business and financial risks they perceive in a given demander of capital.

The term capital in the context of this chapter refers to long-term financing. The key types of long-term funds available are long-term debt, preferred stock, common stock, and retained earnings. The cost of capital is calculated using a weighted average of all these sources of long-term financing. This avoids the acceptance of low-return projects based on the cost of debt, or the rejection of high-return projects based on the cost of common equity. To determine a firm's weighted average cost of capital, the cost of each specific type of capital contained within the average must be obtained using the formulas shown below.

The cost of debt, k_i, which represents the only type of capital that is tax-deductible, is given as:

$$k_i = k_d \times (1 - T),$$

where k_d is the before-tax cost of debt and T is the firm's marginal tax rate.

The cost of preferred stock, k_p, is obtained as:

$$k_p = \frac{D_p}{N_p},$$

where D_p is the annual preferred dividend in dollars and N_p is the net proceeds from the sale of the preferred stock, net of any flotation expenses incurred in marketing the new securities. The cost of preferred stock is normally higher than the cost of debt, because preferred stock dividends are not tax-deductible.

The cost of common stock equity, k_s, can be calculated using either the constant growth model or the capital asset pricing model (CAPM). The constant growth valuation model is based on the premise that the value of a share of stock is the present value of all anticipated dividends, where these dividends are assumed to grow at a constant rate over an infinite time horizon. The expression for the cost of common stock equity capital is given by the constant growth valuation model as:

$$k_s \ - \ \frac{D_1}{N_n} + g \ ,$$

where D_1 is the cash dividend expected in the coming year, P_o is the current price per share of common stock, and g is the expected growth rate for dividends and earnings.

The capital asset pricing model describes the relationship between the required return on common stock equity capital and the nondiversifiable risk facing the firm. This method of calculating the cost of equity capital is given by:

$$k_s \ = \ R_F + b \ x \ (k_m - R_F),$$

where R_F is the required rate of return on a risk-free security, k_m is the expected rate of return on the market portfolio of assets, and b is the level of nondiversifiable risk reflected by the firm. Because of problems in applying the CAPM, the constant growth model is generally used to obtain the cost of common stock equity.

In order to calculate the cost of new issues of common stock, k_n, the cost of equity is adjusted upward to reflect the flotation and issuance costs firms face in selling new stock. The formula for k_n is:

$$k_n \ - \ \frac{D_1}{N_n} + g \ ,$$

where N_n represents the current market price of the stock, less any underpricing and flotation charges.

In calculating the cost of retained earnings, k_r, it is commonly assumed that this capital source has a cost equal to the cost of equity capital, k_s. Retained earnings are not free; rather, they are treated as a fully subscribed new issue of common stock, for which all underpricing and flotation costs are avoided.

The weighted average cost of capital (WACC) is calculated by weighting the cost of each specific type of capital by the historical or target proportions of each capital source used. Historical weights, which are based on the firm's existing capital structure, can be calculated by using either book value or market value proportions. Market value weights typically result in a higher weighted average cost of capital, but these weights are preferred in calculating the WACC.

In contrast to historical weights, target weights are based on the proportions of the various types of capital the firm wishes to maintain. Because target capital structure weights are based on a desired capital structure that is believed to be optimal, they are preferred in calculating the WACC. The weighted average cost of capital, k_a, is shows as:

$$k_a = w_i k_i + w_p k_p + w_{s,\,r,\,or\,n} k_{s,\,r,\,or\,n} \, ,$$

where the sum of the weights (i.e. $w_i + w_p + w_{s,\,r,\,or\,n}$) must equal 1.0.

A firm's weighted marginal cost of capital (WMCC) can be developed by finding the weighted average cost of capital for various levels of new financing. The WMCC relates the weighted average cost of capital to each source of financing for various levels of use. Next, the breaking point for financing source j, BP_j, can be calculated using the relationship:

$$BP_j \; - \; \frac{AF_j}{w_j} \, ,$$

where AF_j is total new financing from source j at the breaking point, and w_j is the capital structure proportion (historical or target) for financing source j.

Once the breaking points have all been determined, the firm can use this information to construct a weighted marginal cost of capital schedule. This schedule relates the firm's WMCC to the different levels of total new financing it can obtain. By comparing this schedule to the firm's investment opportunity set, financial managers can determine the firm's optimal capital budget. This activity requires managers to select all investment projects for which the internal rate of project return exceeds the weighted marginal cost of capital.

CONCEPT OUTLINE

I.   **The cost of capital is the rate of return a firm must earn on its investments in order to leave its share price unchanged.**

A.   When calculating net present value, the cost of capital is the rate at which cash flows are discounted.

B.   When using the internal rate of return (IRR) to evaluate projects, the acceptability of a project is judged by comparing the IRR to the firm's cost of capital.

C.   In order to isolate the basic structure of the cost of capital, managers make important assumptions regarding risk and taxes:

1. The risk to the firm of being able to cover its operating costs -- known as business risk -- remains unchanged.

2. The risk to the firm of being able to cover required financing obligations -- known as financial risk -- remains unchanged.

3. The relevant cost of capital to the firm is its after-tax cost of capital.

D. The firm's nominal cost of capital is directly related to the riskless cost of a given type of financing, business risk, and financial risk:

$$k_1 \; = \; r_1 + b_p + f_p \, ,$$

where k_1 = the nominal cost of long-term financing option l;

r_1 = the risk-free cost of option l;

b_p = the firm's business risk premium; and

f_p = the firm's financial risk premium.

E. The cost of capital is measured at a given point in time.

F. Most firms maintain a deliberate, optimal mix of debt and equity financing. This mix, known as the target capital structure, is selected to maximize shareholder wealth by minimizing the firm's cost of capital.

G. A firm's cost of capital is obtained by first calculating the cost of specific sources of capital. The term capital used in this context refers to a firm's long-term funds, which may include long-term debt, preferred stock, common stock, and/or retained earnings.

II. **The cost of long-term debt is typically viewed as the after-tax cost to maturity of the firm's long-term bonds.**

T

A. The after-tax cost of long-term bonds includes flotation costs paid by the firm to sell new debt.

B. The before-tax cost of debt k_d, for a bond with a $1,000 par value can be approximated by:

$$k_d \; - \; \frac{I + \dfrac{1000 - N_d}{n}}{\dfrac{N_d + 1000}{2}} \; ,$$

where   I = annual interest in dollars;

         N_d = the net proceeds from the sale of a bond; and

         n = the number of years until the bond's maturity.

C.   The cost of debt, k_i, is the only source of capital with a cost that is tax-deductible; therefore, its calculation requires a tax adjustment. The after-tax cost of debt is calculated using the following formula:

$$k_i \; = \; k_d (1 - t) \, ,$$

where k_d = the before-tax debt cost; and

         t = the firm's marginal tax rate.

III.   **The cost of preferred stock is today's cost of issuing new preferred stock.**

T

A.   The cost of preferred stock, k_p, is found by dividing the annual preferred stock dividend, D_p, by the net proceeds from the sale of new preferred stock:

$$k_p \; - \; \frac{D_p}{N_p} \; .$$

B.   The cost of preferred stock is normally greater than the cost of debt.

C.   Since preferred stock dividends are paid from the firm's after-tax cash flows, no tax adjustment is required.

IV.   **The cost of common stock represents the level of return that the firm must provide to its shareholders to maintain its share price.**

T

A.   The cost of common equity, k_s, is the rate at which investors discount the firm's expected dividends to determine share value.

B.   The cost of common equity is calculated using the constant growth stock valuation model and the capital asset pricing model (CAPM).

1.   According to the constant growth model, the cost of common equity is found by dividing the dividend expected at the end of year 1, D_1, by the current price of the stock P_0, and adding the firm's expected growth rate:

$$k_s \;-\; \frac{D_1}{P_0} + g \;.$$

2.   Using the capital asset pricing model, the cost of common equity is found by adding a premium for the firm's nondiversifiable risk [$b \times (k_m - kr_f)$], to the risk-free rate of return:

$$k_s \;=\; R_F + b \times (k_m - R_F),$$

where R_F represents the required rate of return on a risk-free security, and k_m is the expected rate of return on the market portfolio of assets.

C.   Using the constant growth valuation model to find the cost of common stock equity capital is preferred over the capital asset pricing model because of the ready availability of data, and it can be easily adjusted for underpricing and flotation costs to find the cost of new issues of common stock.

D.   The cost of retained earnings, k_r, is normally assumed to equal the cost of equity capital, $k_r = k_s$. Retained earnings are normally viewed as fully subscribed new issues of common stock for which no underpricing or flotation costs are incurred.

E.   In order to calculate the cost of new issues of common stock, k_n, the net price of common stock, N_n, must be used. This net price adjusts the market price of the firm's stock according to the flotation costs the firm must pay to issue new stock:

$$k_n \;-\; \frac{D_1}{N_n} + g \;.$$

F.   Common stock typically is the most expensive type of capital.

G.   Since common stock dividends are paid from after-tax income, no tax adjustment is required for any of the cost of common stock measures.

V.   The weighted average cost of capital (WACC) reflects the average cost of the firm's long-term financing.

A.   A firm's weighted average cost of capital is calculated by weighting the cost of each specific type of capital by target proportions:

T

$$k_a = (w_i \times k_i) + (w_p \times k_p) + (w_s \times k_s),$$

where w_i = the proportion of long term debt used in the firm's capital structure;

           w_p = the proportion of preferred stock used in the firm's capital structure; and

           w_s = the proportion of common stock used in the firm's capital structure.

     1.   The sum of the weights must equal 1.0.

     2.   The common stock weight, w_s, is multiplied by either the cost of retained earnings, k_r, or the cost of new common stock, k_n. The specific cost used depends on whether the firm's common equity financing is obtained from retained earnings on new common stock.

   B.   Weights can be calculated as book value or market value weights.

     1.   Book value weights use accounting data to measure the proportion of each type of capital in the firm's financial structure.

     2.   Market value weights measure the proportion of each type of capital at its market value.

     3.   Market value weights are preferred over book value weights.

   C.   Weights can be calculated as historic or target weights.

     1.   Historic weights, in either book value or market value form, are based on actual capital structure proportions.

     2.   Target weights, also represented in either book value or market value form, reflect the firm's desired capital structure proportions.

     3.   Target weights are preferred to historic weights.

VI.   **The weighted marginal cost of capital (WMCC) is the weighted average cost of capital (WACC) associated with the firm's next dollar of new financing.**

   A.   In order to calculate the WMCC, the breaking points -- which represent the level of total new financing at which the cost of one of the financing components rises -- must be calculated:

$$BP_j - \frac{AF_j}{w_j} ,$$

where BP_j = the breaking point for financing source j;

AF_j = the amount of funds available from financing source j at a given cost; and

w_j = the capital structure proportion (historic or target) for financing source j.

B.   After the breaking points have been determined, the weighted average cost of capital over the range of total financing between breaking points must be obtained.

C.   Once the weighted average cost of capital for each range of total new financing has been determined, a schedule of these results is prepared.

D.   The WMCC shows that as the firm raises more new capital, the component costs associated with various financing sources will increase, leading to an increase in the WACC.

E.   The firm's investment opportunities schedule (IOS) represents a ranking of investment possibilities from best (highest returns) to worst (lowest returns).

F.   Using the IOS and WMCC in combination, the firm should accept all projects for which the internal rate of return exceeds the weighted marginal cost of funds used to finance the new project. Accordingly, the firm should accept all projects up to the point where the IOS curve intersects the WMCC schedule.

APPLICATIONS

DEFINITIONS

1.   The rate of return a firm must earn on its investments in order to maintain its market value and attract needed funds is called the ~~Cost of Capital~~

2.   ~~Net Proceeds~~ represent the funds actually received by the firm from its sale of new securities.

3. Because firms must pay _flotation_ _costs_ when they issue new securities, the net proceeds received from securities issuance is always less than the market value of these securities.

4. If a firm faces a high probability of being unable to cover its operating expenses, the firm has a high level of _business_ risk.

5. The constant growth stock valuation model assumes that the value of a share of stock equals the present value of all future _dividends_

6. The cost of _retained earnings_ is the same as the cost of a fully subscribed use of additional common stock.

7. Because issuing new equity requires the firm to underprice its new shares and bear flotation costs in connection with the stock sale, the cost of issuing new equity is _less_ than the cost of retained earnings.

8. In the determination of the weighted average cost of capital (WACC), weights that use accounting data to measure the proportion of each type of capital in the firm's capital structure represent _book-value_ weights.

9. In the determination of the WACC, weights that are based on actual capital structure proportions are known as _historic_ weights, while weights that are based on the firm's desired capital structure represent _target_ weights.

10. The specific WACC associated with the firm's next dollar of total new financing represents the _weighted marginal cost of capital_

11. The weighted marginal cost of capital schedule relates the firm's _WACC_ to the level of total new financing.

12. Ranking investment possibilities from best (highest returns) to worst (lowest returns) produces the _investment opportunities schedule_

13. The risk to a firm of being unable to cover its required financial obligations is known as _financial_ risk.

14. The firm's target capital structure provides the _optimal_ mix of debt and equity financing, because this particular mix maximizes shareholder wealth.

15. The after-tax cost of debt is _less_ than the before-tax cost of debt, because interest expense is tax deductible.

MULTIPLE CHOICE

1. The cost of capital is the rate of return a firm must earn on its project investments in order to:
    a.   maintain the market value of the stock.
    b.   remain competitive.
    c.   maintain its market share.
    d.   make a profit.

2. Select the true statement regarding the cost of capital:
    a.   it equals the cost of debt.
    b.   it is measured on a before-tax basis.
    c.   it equals the cost of a new issue of common equity.
    d.   it is measured on an after-tax basis.

3. Which of the following is not a basic source of long-term funds for the firm?
    a.   long-term debt.
    b.   preferred stock.
    c.   retained earnings.
    d.   accounts payable.

4. When new securities are sold in the market, the total costs of issuing and selling these are called:
    a.   margin costs.
    b.   flotation costs.
    c.   discounting costs.
    d.   effective interest costs.

5. Assume a bond with a $1,000 par value pays annual coupon interest of $100, has a 5 year maturity, and presently sells for $900. What is its approximate before-tax yield to maturity?
    a.   10%
    b.   20%
    c.   12.5%
    d.   8%

6. A firm with a before-tax cost of debt of 12 percent has a 40 percent tax rate. What is the firm's after-tax cost of debt?
    a.   12.00%
    b.   4.80%
    c.   7.20%
    d.   16.80%

    $.12(1-.4)$
    $.12 \cdot .6 = 7.2\%$

7.   A firm can issue preferred stock with a $10 annual dividend and expect net proceeds of
      $80 per share. If the firm has a 40 percent tax rate, what is the cost of preferred stock?
      a.   12.50%
      b.   7.50%
      c.   5.00%
      d.   17.5%

$$\frac{10}{80} = 12.5\%$$

no tax adjustment required

8.   The constant growth valuation model assumes the value of a share of stock equals:
      a.   the present value of its par value.
      b.   the present value of all future dividends.
      c.   dividends divided by the same dollar amount each period.
      d.   two of the above.

9.   A firm which has common stock selling at $60 per share, paying a dividend expected to
      be $3.00 this coming year, and expected to have a dividend growth of seven percent a
      year, has a cost of common stock equity of:
      a.   5.00%
      b.   3.00%
      c.   12.00%
      d.   6.00%

$$\frac{3}{60} + .07 =$$
$$.05 + .07 = .12 = 12\%$$

10.   A firm has a common stock price of $100. The risk free rate is 8 percent, the expected
      market return is 12 percent, and the firm's beta value is 1.5. Using the CAPM, what is
      the firm's required rate of return?
      a.   14.00%
      b.   13.50%
      c.   8.15%
      d.   21.00%

$$R_F + b(K_m - R_F)$$
$$.08 + 1.5(.12 - .08)$$
$$.08 + 1.5(.04)   .08 + 0.6 = .14$$

11.   Normally, in order to sell a new issue of common stock, it will have to be:
      a.   seasoned.
      b.   floated.
      c.   released after the close of the securities exchange.
      d.   underpriced.

12.   The cost of retained earnings is:
      a.   zero.
      b.   equal to that of a new issue of common stock.
      c.   less than the cost of debt.
      d.   equal to the cost of a fully subscribed issue of common stock.

13.   The weighted average cost of capital is normally based on _____ weights.
        a.   book value.
        b.   historical.
        c.   target.
        d.   equal.

14.   It is necessary to calculate break points in order to compute:
        a.   the cost of the components of the firm's capital structure.
        b.   the investment opportunity schedule.
        c.   weighted marginal cost of capital.
        d.   all of the above.

15.   As long as a project's internal rate of return is greater than the _____, the project
        should be accepted by the firm.
        a.   the weighted average cost of capital.
        b.   the weighted marginal cost of new financing.
        c.   firm's after-tax cost of debt.
        d.   the firm's cost of equity.

PROBLEMS

1.   The April Manufacturing Company wishes to determine its cost of debt. The firm, which
        is in the 40 percent tax bracket, has investigated the current market for debt and found
        that it could sell 12 percent, 20 year, $1,000 face-value bonds to obtain the needed
        financing. The interest on these bonds would be paid at the end of each year. In order
        to sell the entire issue, the firm believes that an average discount of $30 will have to be
        offered. The firm also expects to have to pay flotation costs of $20 per bond.

        a.   Calculate the firm's before-tax cost of debt to the nearest whole percent.

        b.   Interpolate the answer found in part (a) to the nearest .01 percent, and calculate
                the firm's after-tax cost of debt.

        c.   Calculate the firm's cost of debt by using the shortcut approximation formula.

2.   The April Manufacturing Company (presented in Problem 1) also wishes to determine its cost of preferred stock. Investigation has indicated that the firm could sell 11 percent preferred stock at $100 per share, the par value. The cost of issuing and marketing is expected to amount to $4 per share.

T

     a.   Calculate the firm's cost of preferred stock.

     b.   Compare the resulting cost of preferred stock to the cost of debt calculated in Problem (1-b).

3.   The April Manufacturing Company (presented in Problems 1 and 2) wishes to calculate the cost of new common stock. The firm has gathered the following information. The firm's common stock is currently selling for $83.33 per share. The firm expects to pay cash dividends of $5 per share next year (i.e., 1991). The firm's per-share dividends over the past five years are as follows:

T

Year	Dividend Per Share
1990	$4.63
1989	4.29
1988	3.97
1987	3.68
1986	3.40

If the firm sells new common stock, it will have to reduce its price by $10 per share, thereby causing it to reach the market at $73.33 per share. In order to market the stock, there will be flotation costs of $5.40 per share.

     a.   Calculate the firm's after-tax cost of equity capital, using the constant growth valuation model.

     b.   Calculate the firm's after-tax cost of new common stock equity, using the results from part (a).

4.   The April Manufacturing Company [presented in Problems (1) through (3)] has gathered data regarding book value, market value, and target weights. These values along with the specific costs computed in previous problems, are summarized in the following table:

T

Source of Capital	Book Value	Market Value	Target Weight	Specific Cost
Long-term debt	$1,000,000	$1,000,000	0.40	k_i = 7.54%
Preferred stock	800,000	500,000	0.10	k_p = 11.46%
Common equity	2,000,000	4,000,000	0.50	k_s = 14.00%
				k_n = 15.36%
TOTAL	$3,800,000	$5,500,000	1.00	

a.   Assume that all common stock equity is from retained earnings, and calculate the weighted average cost of capital using:

(1) Book value weights;
(2) Market value weights; and
(3) Target weights.

b.   Assume that all common stock equity is from new common stock, and calculate the weighted average cost of capital using:

(1) Book value weights;
(2) Market value weights; and
(3) Target weights.

c.   Review the answers in parts (a) and (b) and report on your observations regarding April's weighted average cost of capital.

5.   Kristal Industries wishes to determine its weighted marginal cost of capital. In preparing for this task, it has compiled the following data:

Source of Capital	Target Proportion (1)	Range of Financing (2)	After-Tax Cost (3)
Long-Term Debt	40%	$0 to $300,000 $300,001 to $600,000 $600,001 and above	6.5% 7.5 9.0
Preferred Stock	10%	$0 to $100,000 $100,001 and above	9.5% 10.0
Common Stock	50%	$0 to $500,000 $500,001 to $1,000,000 $1,000,001 and above	11.0% 12.5 14.0

a.   Determine the breaking points and ranges of total financing associated with each source of capital;

b.   Using the data developed in part (a), determine the levels of total financing at which the firm's weighted average cost of capital (WACC) will change;

c.   Calculate the weighted average cost of capital and the weighted marginal cost of capital (WMCC) for each range of total financing found in part (b);

d.   Using the results of part (c) along with the information on the available investment opportunities shown below, compile the firm's investment opportunities schedule (IOS), plot this schedule, and plot the weighted marginal cost of capital schedule.

Investment opportunity	Internal rate of return	Initial investment
A	14%	$200,000
B	12	300,000
C	11	500,000
D	10	300,000
E	9	600,000
F	8	100,000

e.   Which, if any of the available investments would you recommend that the firm accept? Explain your answer.

SOLUTIONS

DEFINITIONS

1. cost of capital
2. net proceeds
3. flotation costs
4. business
5. dividends
6. retained earnings
7. less
8. book value
9. historic; target
10. weighted marginal cost of capital
11. WACC
12. investment opportunities schedule
13. financial
14. optimal
15. less

MULTIPLE CHOICE

1.	a	9.	c
2.	d	10.	a
3.	d	11.	d
4.	b	12.	d
5.	c	13.	c
6.	c	14.	c
7.	a	15.	b
8.	b		

PROBLEMS

1. a. The first step in calculating the before-tax cost of debt, k_d, on the bond is to specify the bond's cash flows:

Year	Calculation	Cash Flow
0	$1,000 - $30 - $20	$950
1 through 20	Annual Interest = $1,000 x 0.12	($120)
20	Face Value	($1,000)

The preceding table indicates that the firm will initially receive $950, which represents the face value less the $30 discount and the $20 underwriting fee. The annual interest of $120 represents 12 percent of the bond's $1,000 face value.

To find the bond's before-tax cost of debt, cost to maturity, or internal rate of return, a trial-and-error approach is used. Because the cost to maturity is usually close to the bond's coupon rate (for small discounts), a 12 percent discount rate is tried initially.

Year	Cash Flow (1)	Table (2)	Factor (3)	Present Value [(1) x (3)] (4)
0	$ 950	None	1.000	$950.00
1-20	- 120	A-4, 12%, 20 yr	7.469	- 896.28
20	- 1,000	A-3, 12%, 20 yr	0.104	- 104.00
Net present value				-$ 50.28

Because the net present value obtained using a 12 percent discount rate produces a negative result, the bond's cash flows must be discounted at a higher rate in order to bring the NPV to zero. Because the present value tables are presented only in whole percentages, the discount rate will be raised to 13 percent and the NPV again calculated, as follows:

Year	Cash Flow (1)	Table (3)	Factor (3)	Present Value [(1) x (3)] (4)
0	$ 950	None	1.000	$950.00
1-20	- 120	A-4, 13%, 20 yr	7.025	- 843.00
20	-1,000	A-3, 13%, 20 yr	0.087	- 87.00
Net Present Value				$ 20.00

It should be clear that the before-tax cost of debt must lie between 12 and 13 percent, because at these consecutive discount rates the NPV is negative and positive, respectively. Because the NPV is closest to zero at the 13 percent discount rate (i.e., $20.00 away for 13 percent and $50.28 away for 12 percent), this rate represents the before-tax debt cost of cost to maturity to the nearest 1 percent.

b.   To interpolate the before-tax cost of debt, a step-by-step approach can be used.

Step 1. Find the difference in NPVs resulting from the use of the two consecutive discount rates for which the NPV is negative and positive, respectively.

$$\text{NPV @ 13\%} = \$20.00$$

$$\text{NPV @ 12\%} = \$50.28$$

$$\text{Difference} = \$70.28$$

Step 2. Find the absolute difference between the NPV at the lower rate and the desired NPV (zero in this case).

$$\text{NPV @ 12\%} \quad = \$50.28$$

$$\text{Desired NPV} \quad = \quad 0.00$$

$$\text{Absolute difference} = \$50.28$$

Step 3. Divide the result from step 2 by the result of step 1 to get the fraction in decimal form to the nearest one-hundredth.

$$\text{Fraction} \; - \; \$50.\frac{28}{\$70.28} \; - \; 0.715 \; - \; 0.72$$

Step 4. Add the fraction in step 3 to the lower of the two discount rates to obtain the interpolated value of the cost to maturity to the nearest 0.01 percent.

$$12\% + 0.72\% = 12.72\%$$

To convert the 12.72 percent before-tax debt cost into an after-tax debt cost, the before-tax cost must be multiplied by 1 minus the tax rate.

$$\text{After-Tax Cost of Debt} = (12.72) \times (1 - .40)$$

$$= (12.72) \times (.60) = 7.63\%$$

c.   As an alternative to the interpolation procedure described in part (b), the following formula can be used to calculate the firm's before-tax debt cost:

$$k_d = \frac{I + \dfrac{1000 - N_d}{n}}{\dfrac{N_d + 1000}{2}},$$

where

I = annual interest in dollars;
N_d = the net proceeds from the sale of a bond; and
n = the number of years until the bond's maturity.

Substituting I = $120, N_b = $950, and n = 20 into the preceding equation yields the following:

$$k_d = \frac{\$120 + \dfrac{\$1000 - \$950}{20}}{\dfrac{\$950 + \$1000}{2}} = 12.56\% .$$

Comparing the resulting before-tax cost of debt of 12.56 percent to the value calculated in part [b] (12.72 percent), it can be seen that only a small difference in values results from the use of the approximation technique.

Adjusting the before-tax debt cost for taxes produces:

After-Tax Cost of debt = (12.56%) x (1 -.40)

= (12.56%) x (.60) = 7.54%

Again, the similarity of the cost of debt calculated using the shortcut formula to the result found in part [b] (7.63 percent) demonstrates that the approximation technique provides a reasonable solution.

2.   a.   The cost of preferred stock, k_p, is calculated using the following formula:

$$k_p \ = \ \frac{D_1}{N_p} \ ,$$

where D_p = the annual preferred dividend in dollars, and

N_p = the net proceeds from the sale of preferred stock.

Before substituting into this formula, the dividends in dollars must be determined. Because the dividend is stated as a percentage, this percentage must be multiplied by the preferred stock's face value, $100:

$$d_p \ = \ (.11) \text{ x } (\$100) \ = \ \$11$$

Substituting d_p = $11 and Np = $96 (i.e., $100 - $4 issuance cost) into the equation for the cost of preferred stock yields:

$$k_p \ = \ \frac{\$11}{\$96} \ = \ 11.46\% \ .$$

b.   The 11.46 percent cost of preferred stock is greater than the after-tax cost of debt, which was found to be 7.63 percent. This relationship generally exists because the interest on debt is tax-deductible, while preferred stock dividends must be paid in after-tax dollars. The cost of debt, therefore, is frequently below the cost of preferred stock.

3.   a.   To calculate the cost of equity capital, k_s, using the constant growth valuation model, the following formula can be used:

$$k_s \ = \ \frac{D_1}{P_0} \ + g \ ,$$

where D_1 = the cash dividend expected in the coming year;
P_0 = the current price per share of common stock; and
g = the expected growth rate of dividends and earnings.

To apply this equation to the given data, we must calculate the growth rate of dividends using the historical data presented. The following steps are required:

<u>Step 1.</u> Divide the earliest value by the value expected:

$$\frac{D_{1986}}{D_{1991}} - \frac{\$3.40}{\$5.00} - 0.68 \ .$$

<u>Step 2.</u> Determine how many years of growth have occurred. In our case, we have six years of data that represent five years of growth.

<u>Step 3.</u> Using the table for the present value interest factor for one dollar (Table A-3), find the interest factor closest to the factor found in step 1 (0.68) and the period of time found in step 2 (five years). The interest factor for four years closest to .68 in Table A-3 occurs at 8 percent, where the table value is 0.681.

<u>Step 4.</u> The growth rate to the nearest 1 percent is equal to the interest rate associated with the table value. In this case, the growth rate, g, is 8 percent.

The values to be substituted into the equation for the cost of equity capital are:

$$D_1 \ = \ \$5.00;$$
$$P_0 \ = \ \$83.33; \text{ and}$$
$$g \ = \ 0.08.$$

Substituting these values yields:

$$k_s \ - \ \frac{\$5.00}{\$83.33} + 0.08 \ - \ 0.14 \ - \ 14\% \ .$$

b.   The after-tax cost of new common stock equity using the constant growth valuation model can be calculated in a similar fashion:

$$k_n \ - \ \frac{D_1}{N_n} + g \ ,$$

where N_n is the net price expected to be realized after underpricing and flotation charges. In this case:

$$N_n \ = \ \$83.33 - \$10.00 - \$5.40 \ = \ \$67.93,$$

and

$$k_n - \frac{\$5.00}{\$67.93} + 0.08 - .1536 - 15.36\% .$$

Note that common stock dividends are paid from after-tax income, so that no tax adjustment is required to the cost of new equity capital.

4.   a.   (1) Book Value Weights:

First, the weights must be determined:

$$w_i - \frac{\$1,000,000}{\$3,800,000} - 0.26 ,$$

$$w_p - \frac{\$800,000}{\$3,800,000} - 0.21 ,$$

$$w_s - \frac{\$2,000,000}{\$3,800,000} - 0.53 .$$

Next, multiply weights by the component capital costs, and sum:

$$k_a = w_i k_i + w_p k_p + w_s k_s$$

$$= [(0.26) \times (7.54)] + [(0.21) \times (11.46)] + [(0.53) \times (14)] = 11.79\%.$$

(2) Market Value Weights:

First, the weights must be determined:

$$w_i \; - \; \frac{\$1,000,000}{\$5,500,000} \; - \; 0.18 \;,$$

$$w_p \; - \; \frac{\$500,000}{\$5,500,000} \; - \; 0.09 \;,$$

$$w_s \; - \; \frac{\$4,000,000}{\$5,500,000} \; - \; 0.73 \;,$$

Next, multiply weights by the component capital costs, and sum:

$$k_a \; = \; w_i k_i \; + \; w_p k_p \; + \; w_s k_s$$

$= [(0.18) \times (7.54)] + [(0.09) \times (11.46)] + [(0.73) \times (14)] \; = \; 12.61\%.$

(3) Target Weights:

Here, the weights have been given, so multiply weights by the component capital costs, and sum:

$$k_a \; = \; w_i k_i \; + \; w_p k_p \; + \; w_s k_s$$

$= \; [(0.4) \times (7.54)] + [(0.1) \times (11.46)] + [(0.5) \times (14)] \; = \; 11.16\%.$

b.　　(1) Book Value Weights:

The weights have not changed from part (a-1), nor have the costs of debt or preferred stock. The only difference is in the cost of common equity. Thus:

$$k_a \; = \; w_i k_i \; + \; w_p k_p \; + \; w_s k_n$$

$= \; [(.26) \times (7.54)] + [(.21) \times (11.46)] + [(.53) \times (15.36)] \; = \; 12.51\%.$

(2) Market Value Weights:

Again the only change is in the cost of new common equity. Thus,

$$k_a = w_i k_i + w_p k_p + w_s k_n$$

$$= [(0.18) \times (7.54] + [(0.09) \times (11.46)] + [(0.73) \times (15.36) = 13.60\%.$$

(3) Target weights:

Again, the only change is in the cost of new common equity. Thus:

$$k_a = w_i k_i + w_p k_p + w_s k_n$$

$$= [(0.4) \times (7.54)] + [(0.1) \times (11.46)] + [(0.5) \times (15.36)] = 11.84\%.$$

c. Two observations are possible. First, the cost of capital is higher, regardless of the weights used, when the cost of new common equity rather than the cost of retained earnings is employed. Or, the choice of weights can make a significant difference in the estimation of the cost of capital. Book value weights yield the lowest WACC estimate, because the book value of common equity is often well below its market value. In this case, target weights (which reflect the firm's optimal weights) should be used, yielding a weighted average cost of capital of 11.84%.

5. a. The breaking points for each source of capital are calculated by dividing the upper limit of the financing ranges given in column (2) of the table in the problem by the target proportions given in column (1). The ranges of total financing are calculated using the breaking points and the corresponding financing ranges given in the problem.

Kristal Industries
Determination of Breaking Points

Source of Capital	Cost (1)	Range of New Financing (2)	Breaking Point (3)	Range of Total New Financing (4)
Long-Term Debt	6.5%	$0 to $300,000	($300,000) ÷ (0.40) = $750,000	$0 to $750,000
	7.5%	$300,001 to $600,000	($600,000) ÷ ((0.40) = $1,500,000	$750,001 to $1,500,000
	9.0%	$600,001 and above	-----	$1,500,001 and above
Preferred Stock	9.5%	$0 to $100,000	($100,000) ÷ (0.10) = $1,000,000	$0 to $1,000,000
	10.0%	$100,001 and above	-----	$1,000,001 and above
Common Stock	11.0%	$0 to $500,000	($500,000) ÷ (0.50) = $1,000,000	$0 to $1,000,000
	→12.5%	$500,001 to $1,000,000	($1,000,000) ÷ (0.50) = $2,000,000	$1,000,001 to $2,000,000
	14.0%	$1,000,000 and above	-----	$2,000,001 and above

b. An examination of columns (3) and (4) of the table in part (a) indicates that the firm's weighted average cost of capital will change at levels of total financing of $750,000, $1,000,000, $1,500,000, and $2,000,000. These are the breaking points in increasing order.

c. The weighted average cost of capital and the weighted marginal cost of capital for each range of total financing is calculated as follows:

Range of Total Financing	Type of Capital (1)	Target Proportion (2)	Cost* (3)	Weighted Cost [(2) x (3)] (4)
$0 to $750,000	Debt	0.40	6.5%	2.60%
	Preferred Stock	0.10	9.5	0.95
	Common Stock	0.50	11.0	5.50
Weighted Average Cost of Capital				9.05%
$750,001 to $1,000,000	Debt	0.40	7.5%	3.00%
	Preferred Stock	0.10	9.5	0.95
	Common Stock	0.50	11.0	5.50
Weighted Average Cost of Capital				9.45%
$1,000,001 to $1,500,000	Debt	0.40	7.5%	3.00%
	Preferred Stock	0.10	10.0	1.00
	Common Stock	0.50	12.5	6.25
Weighted Average Cost of Capital				10.25%
$1,500,001 to $2,000,000	Debt	0.40	9.0%	3.60%
	Preferred Stock	0.10	10.0	1.00
	Common Stock	0.50	12.5	6.25
Weighted Average Cost of Capital				10.85%
$2,000,001 and Above	Debt	0.40	9.0%	3.60%
	Preferred Stock	0.10	10.0	1.00
	Common Stock	0.50	14.0	7.00
Weighted Average Cost of Capital				11.60%

* The costs given for each range of total new financing were obtained from a comparison of columns (1) and (4) of the Table developed in part (a).

KRISTAL INDUSTRIES
WEIGHTED MARGINAL COST OF CAPITAL

Range of Total New Financing	Weighted Average Cost of Capital
$0 to $750,000	9.05%
$750,001 to $1,000,000	9.45
$1,000,001 to $1,500,000	10.25
$1,500,001 to $2,000,000	10.85
$2,000,001 and above	11.60

d.   The IOS is compiled as follows:

KRISTAL INDUSTRIES
INVESTMENT OPPORTUNITY SCHEDULE

Investment Opportunity	Internal Rate of Return (1)	Initial Investment (2)	Cumulative Investment* (3)
A	14%	$200,000	$ 200,000
B	12	300,000	500,000
C	11	500,000	1,000,000
D	10	300,000	1,300,000
E	9	600,000	1,900,000
F	8	100,000	2,000,000

* The cumulative investment represents the total amount invested in projects with higher internal rates of return, plus the investment required for the given investment opportunity.

Plotting the internal rates of return against the cumulative investment [i.e., column (1) against column (3)] on a set of axes showing total investment returns against total investment dollars traces the firm's investment opportunity schedule (IOS). Plotting the weighted average cost of capital against the range of total new financing, calculated in part (c), on the same set of axes pinpoints the firm's weighted marginal cost of capital (WMCC).

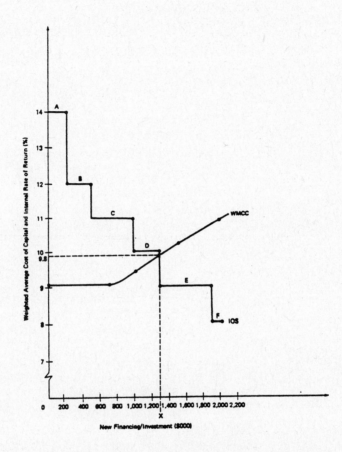

By raising $1,500,000 of new financing and investing these funds in projects A, B, C, and D; the wealth of the firm's owners will be maximized. With this particular investment budget, the 10 percent return on the last dollar invested in project D exceeds its 9.80 percent weighted average capital cost. Investment in project E is not feasible, since its 9 percent return is less than the cost of funds available to finance it.

CHAPTER 12

LEVERAGE AND CAPITAL STRUCTURE

SUMMARY

Leverage is a concept that describes a firm's ability to use fixed-cost assets or funds to magnify the returns to its owners. As leverage changes, the risk associated with the firm's ability to cover fixed-payment obligations also changes. This, in turn, affects the value of the firm. Thus, managers must carefully consider the relationship between leverage, risk, return, and value.

The three types of leverage that exist within most business firms are operating, financial, and total leverage. The concept of operating leverage is concerned with the effect of changes in a firm's sales revenues on earnings before interest and taxes; financial leverage is concerned with the effect of changes in earnings before interest and taxes on the earnings available for common stockholders; and total leverage is concerned with the combined impact of operating and financial leverage on the firm's earnings.

Operating breakeven analysis is a technique by which a firm determines the level of operations that must be maintained in order to cover all operating costs. The firm's cost of goods sold and its operating expenses contain fixed and variable operating cost components. Fixed costs are not a function of sales volume; variable costs vary in direct response to sales. The breakeven point in units can be found by dividing total fixed operating costs by the difference between price and variable cost per unit. The breakeven analysis for a firm (or product) is often presented graphically. Increases in fixed operating costs, decreases in sales price per unit, and increases in variable cost per unit result in increasing breakeven points.

Operating leverage results from the presence of fixed operating costs. As long as a firm has some fixed operating costs, it has operating leverage. The degree of operating leverage (DOL) measures the percentage change in a firm's earnings before interest and taxes (EBIT) resulting from a given percentage change in sales. The higher the firm's fixed operating costs, the higher its DOL. The higher a firm's operating leverage, the higher the business risk, or the greater the variability of EBIT.

Financial leverage results from the presence of fixed financial charges in the firm's income stream. These fixed financial charges of interest on debt and preferred stock dividends must be paid regardless of the amount of EBIT available. The degree of financial leverage (DFL) reflects the fact that the presence of fixed financial charges causes a greater-than-proportional change in earnings per share (EPS) to result from a given change in EBIT. In the same sense that high operating leverage is considered risky, high financial leverage is also considered risky, because a decrease in EBIT would result in a more than proportional decrease in EPS for the firm. The higher the level of fixed financial charges, the greater the DFL within the firm.

The total leverage of the firm is defined as its ability to use fixed costs - both operating and financial - to magnify the effects of changes in sales on earnings per share. The degree of total leverage (DTL) reflects the impact of a given percentage change in sales on the firm's EPS. The relationship between operating, financial, and total leverage is multiplicative, rather than additive. The total risk of the firm, which is associated with the ability to cover operating and financial costs, increases with increasing total leverage.

Financial risk depends upon a firm's capital structure. Capital structure is determined by the mix of long-term debt and equity the firm uses to finance its assets. The optimal capital structure for a particular firm represents the specific combination of debt and equity funding that minimizes the firm's weighted average cost of capital, and maximizes the value of the firm's stock. The optimal capital structures for different firms in different industries can be quite dissimilar, because operating characteristics differ between industries or lines of business.

According to capital structure theory, under the assumption of perfect markets the capital structure a firm selects does not affect its value. When this assumption is violated by (1) the tax deductibility of interest payments, (2) the increased probability of bankruptcy brought about by debt obligations, (3) the agency costs associated with monitoring and controlling the firm's actions by corporate lenders, and (4) the introduction of information asymmetries between managers and investors; a theoretical optimal capital structure *does* exist. For these more realistic cases, the optimal capital structure is one that balances the costs and benefits of debt financing.

The EBIT-EPS approach to capital structure focuses on selecting that particular capital structure which maximizes the firm's EPS over the expected range of EBIT. The EBIT-EPS approach can be used to graphically evaluate different capital structures in light of the financial risk these structures contain and the returns accompanying these risks. The major shortcoming of the EBIT-EPS approach is that this technique concentrates on maximization of corporate earnings rather than maximization of owners' wealth. Hence, this technique must be used cautiously by financial managers.

CONCEPT OUTLINE

I.   **Leverage results from the firm's use of fixed operating and financial (interest and preferred stock dividends) costs.**

    A.   Leverage and capital structure are closely related concepts linked to both the cost of capital and capital budgeting decisions.

    B.   Leverage results from the use of fixed cost assets or funds to magnify returns to a firm's owners.

        1.   Increases in leverage result in increased risk and return.
        2.   Decreases in leverage result in decreased risk and return.

    C.   There are three basic types of leverage: operating leverage, financial leverage, and total leverage.

1.   Operating leverage is concerned with the relationship between a firm's sales revenue and its EBIT.

2.   Financial leverage is concerned with the relationship between the firm's EBIT and the earnings available for common stockholders.

3.   Total leverage, which is concerned with the relationship between changes in sales and changes in EPS, considers the combined impact of operating and financial leverage.

II.   **Breakeven analysis (or cost-volume-profit analysis) is used to determine the level of operations necessary to cover all operating costs and to evaluate the profitability associated with various levels of sales.**

A.   The operating breakeven point is the level of sales necessary to cover all operating costs.

B.   The first step in finding the operating breakeven point is to divide the cost of goods sold and operating expenses into fixed and variable costs.

1.   Fixed costs are a function of time, not sales volume.
2.   Variable costs change in direct response to changes in sales volume.

C.   A firm's breakeven point can be determined either algebraically or graphically.

1.   Algebraically, a firm's breakeven point can be found by dividing fixed operating cost by the difference between sale price per unit and variable cost per unit:

$$Q - \frac{FC}{P - VC},$$

where   Q   =   sales volume in units;
VC   =   fixed operating cost per period;
P   =   selling price per unit; and
VC   =   variable operating cost per unit.

2.   Graphically, breakeven analysis may be plotted on a set of axes representing sales (x-axis) and dollar costs and revenue (y-axis).

D.   Changes in costs and revenues will affect the firm's breakeven point.

1.   An increase in fixed operating costs will increase the breakeven point, while a decrease in fixed operating costs will decrease the breakeven point.

2. An increase in unit sales price will decrease the firm's breakeven point, while a decrease in unit sales price will increase the firm's breakeven point.

3. An increase in variable operating costs per unit will increase the firm's breakeven point, while a decrease in these costs will decrease the firm's breakeven point.

III. **Leverage results from the use of fixed cost inputs, either operating inputs or financial inputs.**

A. Operating leverage results from the presence of fixed operating costs in the firm's income stream.

1. The degree of operating leverage (DOL) measures the percentage change in EBIT resulting from a given percentage change in sales.

2. The higher the amount of fixed operating costs relative to its variable costs, the greater the firm's operating leverage.

3. Because operating leverage works both ways (i.e., it magnifies losses as well as gains), a shift in cost structure toward more fixed costs tends to increase the magnitude of potential losses.

4. The degree of operating leverage at a given sales level Q is:

$$\text{DOL at Q} \ = \ \frac{Q(P - VC)}{Q(P - VC) - FC} \ ,$$

where P   =   sales price per unit;
       VC =   variable operating costs per unit; and
       FC =   fixed operating costs.

5. The higher a firm's operating leverage, the higher its business risk or sensitivity of EBIT to changes in sales.

6. As a firm increases its fixed operating costs, its operating risk increases, and the sales volume necessary to obtain breakeven increases. The opposite effect results from a decrease in fixed operating costs.

B. Financial leverage results from the presence of fixed financial charges (including interest and preferred stock dividends) in the firm's income stream.

1. Although preferred stock dividends can be passed, they are assumed to be

mandatory because the financial manager's goal is to maximize owner's wealth.

2.   Financial leverage uses the firm's fixed financial charges in order to magnify the effects of changes in EBIT on the firm's EPS.

3.   Financial leverage works in both directions, because a decrease in EBIT will result in a greater-than-proportional decrease in EPS.

4.   A direct method of calculating the degree of financial leverage at a base level of EBIT is:

$$\text{DFL for a given Q} = \frac{\text{EBIT}}{\text{EBIT} - I - \text{PD}\,[1\,/\,(1-T)]}\,,$$

where I   =   annual interest charges;
       PD =   annual preferred stock dividends; and
       T   =   the firm's marginal tax rate.

5.   Financial risk is directly related to financial leverage; the higher a firm's financial leverage, the worse the consequences on EPS of a drop in EBIT.

6.   The greater the level of fixed-cost financing (i.e., debt and preferred stock), the higher the firm's financial leverage.

C.   Total leverage can be defined as the firm's ability to use fixed costs (both operating and financial) to magnify the effect of changes in sales on the firm's EPS.

1.   The result of total leverage is to cause the percentage change in EPS to be greater than the percentage change in the sales initiating the action.

2.   Total leverage reflects the combined effect of operating and financial leverage on the firm.

3.   The degree of total leverage (DTL) can be found by taking the product (not the sum) of the firm's degree of operating leverage and its degree of financial leverage.

4.   The degree of total leverage at a given sales level, Q, can be calculated as:

$$\text{DTL at Q} = \frac{Q\,(P - VC)}{Q\,(P - VC) - FC - I - \text{PD}\,[1\,/\,(1-T)]}\,,$$

where the variables are defined as above.

5.   Total risk, which is related to the firm's ability to cover its operating and financial costs, increases with increasing total leverage and decreases with decreasing total leverage.

IV.   **The firm's optimal capital structure, representing a particular mix of debt and equity, results from balancing the benefits and costs of debt financing in order to minimize the firm's weighted average cost of capital.**

A.   The two basic types of capital are debt and equity.

1.   Debt capital includes all the long-term debts of the firm.

2.   Equity capital, which includes preferred stock, common stock, and retained earnings, represents ownership claims on the firm.

B.   An acceptable degree of financial leverage for one industry or line of business can be excessively risky in another, due to differing operating characteristics between industries or lines of business.

C.   Financial research suggests that there is an optimal capital structure range for a given firm.

1.   Modigliani and Miller demonstrated in 1958 that under the assumption of perfect markets, the capital structure a firm selects does not affect its value.

2.   Under less restrictive assumptions, however, researchers have shown that an optimal capital structure does exist. This optimal capital structure balances the benefits and costs of debt financing.

3.   The major benefit of debt financing is the tax shield provided by interest payments.

4.   The costs of debt financing include the increased probability of bankruptcy caused by debt obligations, the agency costs of the lender's monitoring and controlling the firm's actions, and the costs associated with managers having more and better information about the firm's prospects than do investors.

D.   The value of the firm is maximized when the firm's cost of capital is minimized.

1. The value of the firm, V can be defined as:

$$V = \frac{EBIT \times (1 - T)}{k_a},$$

where T = the firm's marginal tax rate; and
k_a = the firm's weighted average cost of capital.

2. Given a constant EBIT, V is maximized when k_a reaches its minimum value.

E. The relationship between the cost of debt, k_i, cost of equity, k_s, overall cost of capital k_o, and the firm's capital structure, [D/S], can be shown graphically.

1. The optimal structure occurs at point M, where the firm's overall cost of capital is at a minimum.

2. At point M, the value of the firm (V) is maximized for fixed EBIT.

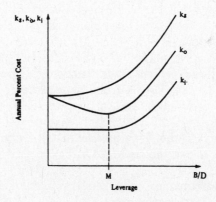

V. **The EBIT-EPS approach to capital structure focuses on selecting that particular mix of debt and equity that maximizes EPS over the expected range of EBIT.**

A. The main emphasis of the EBIT-EPS approach is on the effects of different capital structures on owners' returns.

B. Plotting various financing plans on a set of EBIT-EPS axes allows managers to compare the leverage, risk, and EPS for various levels of EBIT.

C. A financing plan can be graphed merely by finding the level of EPS associated with each of two EBIT values, and plotting these points.

D. One of the points could be the financial breakeven point, representing the level of EBIT for which EPS equals zero, which is calculated by adding the annual interest payment to the before-tax cost of preferred dividends.

E. The risk of the financing plan is reflected in its slope, its financial breakeven point, and its coverage ratio.

    1. The steeper the slope of the graph, the more highly levered the firm, and the greater the level of risk.

    2. The higher the financial breakeven point, the more risky the firm.

F. The EBIT-EPS technique concentrates on the maximization of earnings rather than the maximization of wealth. Users of the EBIT-EPS model must recognize that it does not fully capture the effects of risk on shareholder wealth.

VI. **The optimal capital structure is that particular mix of debt and equity which balances risk and return factors in order to maximize the market value of owners' wealth.**

A. To determine the value under alternative capital structures, the firm must identify the level of return that must be earned to compensate owners for the risks they incur.

B. The required return associated with a given level of financial risk can be estimated by the CAPM framework presented in Chapter 5, or the market risk-return function discussed in Chapter 10.

C. The value of the firm associated with alternative capital structures can be estimated using the standard valuation models introduced in Chapter 6.

D. The goal of financial managers is to maximize owners' wealth, which is not the same as maximization of profit.

APPLICATIONS

APPLICATIONS

1. *Leverage* results from the use of fixed-cost assets or funds to magnify returns to the firm's owners.

2. The level of sales at which EBIT equals zero is known as the *operating breakeven point*.

3. A firm's _Capital structure_ shows the mix of debt and equity maintained by the firm.

4. The effect of changes in sales on the firm's earnings per share is measured by the degree of ~~financial~~ _total ?_ leverage.

5. _Asymmetric_ information implies that the managers of a firm have more information about the firm's operations and future prospects than do investors.

6. Fixed financing costs include _interest_ as well as _preferred stock_ dividends.

7. ~~Increase~~ _Decreases_ in the sales price per unit of a firm's output will decrease its operating breakeven point.

8. The DOL is measured by dividing the percentage change in _EBIT_ by the percentage change in _Sales_

9. The DTL represents the product of a given firm's _DOL_ and _DFL_.

10. That particular capital structure which _Maximizes_ the value of a firm's common stock is known as the optimal capital structure.

11. The firm's capital structure directly affects its _financial_ leverage.

12. _Agency_ problems occur because shareholders hire managers and give them the authority to manage the firm in the shareholders' best interest.

13. The CAPM and the market risk-return function provide mechanisms which _link_ a firm's risk level with its appropriate level of return.

14. The goal of financial managers is to maximize _Owner wealth_.

15. Managers who are concerned about corporate control will prefer to issue new _debt_ securities rather than selling new ~~stock~~ _equity_

$$DOL = \frac{\% \Delta EBIT}{\% \Delta Sales} \qquad \frac{S}{EBIT}$$

$$DFL = \frac{\% \Delta EPS}{\% \Delta EBIT} \qquad \frac{}{EPS}$$

$$DTL = \frac{\% \Delta EPS}{\% \Delta Sales}$$

MULTIPLE CHOICE

1. Operating leverage results from the use of:
    a. fixed financing costs
    b. interest expense
    c. fixed operating costs
    d. dividend expense

2. A firm with fixed operating costs of $5,000 sells 2,000 units at $8.00 a unit. If the products have a variable cost of $6.00 a unit, at what output level is the firm at its operating breakeven?
    a. 2,000 units.
    b. 2,500 units.
    c. 3,000 units.
    d. 625 units.

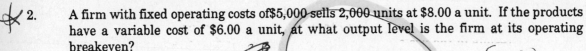

3. If a firm has a DOL of 4.00 and a DFL of 3.00 what is its DTL?
    a. 7.00
    b. 1.00
    c. 12.00
    d. none of the above.

4. A firm with a degree of financial leverage of four, experiences a drop in EBIT of ten percent. Holding other things constant, the firm will experience:
    a. a 40% drop in EPS.
    b. a 10% drop in operating profits.
    c. an increase in EPS of 4%.
    d. an increase in operating profits of 40%.

5. Debt financing is the source of a potential agency problem, because once a debt arrangement is in place:
    a. management may quit.
    b. management may sell the firm.
    c. management may increase the firm's level of debt.
    d. management may issue new equity securities.

6. A firm with $10,000 of interest payments, $10,000 of preferred dividend payments, and a tax rate of 40 percent, will have a financial breakeven point of:
    a. $20,000.
    b. $14,000.
    c. $26,667.
    d. $35,000.

7.   The EBIT-EPS approach to capital structure:
      a.   tends to concentrate on earnings maximization.
      b.   tends to concentrate on wealth maximization.
      c.   tends to concentrate on sales revenue maximization.
      d.   is most useful when used with the payback period.

8.   Selecting the capital structure that maximizes profits typically:
      a.   results in a structure that maximizes firm value.
      b.   results in a structure that minimizes firm risk.
      c.   does not result in a structure that maximizes firm value.
      d.   results in the use of less debt than the structure that maximizes firm value.

9.   A firm's operating breakeven point represents:
      a.   the level of profits necessary to cover all operating costs.
      b.   the level of profits necessary to cover all financing costs.
      c.   the point at which total sales will equal total interest expense.
      d.   the level of sales necessary to cover all operating costs.

10.   Fixed financing costs include:
      a.   interest expense
      b.   interest and depreciation expenses.
      c.   interest expense and preferred stock dividends.
      d.   interest expense, preferred stock dividends, and common stock dividends.

11.   As financial leverage increases, total leverage will:
      a.   decrease.
      b.   increase.
      c.   stay the same.
      d.   fall to zero.

12.   As a firm's debt ratio rises, the level of operating leverage:
      a.   remains unchanged.
      b.   rises.
      c.   falls.
      d.   begins to fluctuate.

13.   Which of the following does not represent a key difference between debt and equity capital?
      a.   debt has a senior claim against the firm's assets and income.
      b.   equity has no stated maturity, while debt has an explicit maturity date.
      c.   equity holders receive no contract rights with their investment, while debt holders are protected against losses.
      d.   debt service payments are tax-deductible to the firm, while dividend expense is not.

14.   According to the early work of Modigliani and Miller, under the assumption of perfect markets,
        a.   risk and return are directly related.
        b.   the capital structure chosen by the firm does not affect its value.
        c.   the value of the firm decreases as its financial leverage increases.
        d.   corporate capital structure is indirectly related to firm value.

15.   A firm with historically stable EBIT that shows a great deal of volatility in past EPS has
        a.   low financial leverage.
        b.   high operating leverage.
        c.   high financial leverage.
        d.   no total leverage.

PROBLEMS

1.   For each of the firms given below, calculate the operating breakeven point in units.

	Firm A	Firm B
Sale price per unit	$12	$15
Variable operating cost per unit	$8	$11
Fixed operating cost	$60,000	$40,000

2.   Given the following data for the Vitale Iron Company:

        EBIT = $60,000
        Sales = 25,000 units
        Sales price per unit = $9
        Fixed operating costs = $65,000

        a.   Calculate the operating breakeven point in units for the firm.

        b.   Graph the firm's cost and revenue functions, noting the operating breakeven point.

        c.   Determine the effect on the breakeven point from:

             (1) a decrease to $50,000 in fixed operating costs;
             (2) an increase in the sale price per unit to $10; and
             (3) a $1 per-unit increase in variable operating cost.

3.   Compare the operating leverage by calculating the EBIT associated with 20,000 and 30,000 units of sales for each of the following firms. Use 20,000 units as a base level in making the calculations. Calculate the degree of operating leverage (DOL) to make your comparison.

	Firm A	Firm B
Sale price per unit	$12	$15
Variable operating cost per unit	$8	$11
Fixed operating cost	$60,000	$40,000

4.   For each of the following firms, using EBIT levels of $40,000 and $50,000, and given the following information, calculate the following assuming a 40% tax rate:

   a.   the level of EPS associated with each EBIT for both firms;
   b.   the degree of financial leverage (DFL) for each firm, using the $40,000 EBIT base level; and
   c.   compare and contrast the financial leverage of each plan.

Capital Source	Firm A	Firm B
Debt	$75,000 at 12 percent	$100,000 at 10 percent
Preferred Stock	2,000 shares at $2.50 each	5,000 shares at $2.00 each
Common Stock	10,000 shares	7,000 shares

5.   Wesson Industries manufactures spark plugs. Each spark plug produced has a variable cost of $1.50 and sells for $2.00. The firm's total fixed costs are $30,000. Wesson has current annual interest charges of $8,000, and preferred stock dividends of $3,000 each year. The firm has a 40 percent tax rate, and currently sells 500,000 spark plugs per year. Calculate the degree of total leverage (DTL) for Wesson at its current level of sales.

6.   If a firm's degree of operating leverage is 8 and its degree of financial leverage is 10, identify the total leverage effect, or magnification of changes in sales on earnings per share.

7.   Micro-Widget is preparing to make a capital structure decision. They have obtained estimates of sales and the associated levels of EBIT. There is a 20 percent chance that EBIT will be $100,000. The firm has a capital structure of $2,000,000, presently funded with 80,000 shares of common stock (book value and market value are equal, at $25 per share). The following table represents the mix of debt and equity, as well as the number of shares of common stock outstanding under each capital structure alternative. Micro-Widget has a 40 percent tax rate.

Micro-Widget
Capital Structure

Debt-Equity Ratio	Total Financing ($000)	Debt ($000)	Equity ($000)	Common Stock Outstanding
0%	$2,000	$ 0	$2,000	80,000
10%	2,000	200	1,800	72,000
20%	2,000	400	1,600	64,000
30%	2,000	600	1,400	56,000
40%	2,000	800	1,200	48,000
50%	2,000	1,000	1,000	40,000
60%	2,000	1,200	800	32,000

Interest cost for each alternative capital structure is summarized as follows:

Debt-equity ratio	Borrowing ($000)	Interest rate on all debt	Interest ($000)
0%	$ 0	0%	$ 0
10%	200	9.0	18
20%	400	9.5	38
30%	600	10.0	60
40%	800	11.5	92
50%	1,000	14.0	140
60%	1,200	17.0	204

a.   Compute EPS for the expected level of EBIT ($300,000) for each capital structure. Which structure maximizes EPS?

b.   Compute the standard deviation and coefficient of variation of EPS for the 10 percent, 40 percent, and 60 percent capital structures. What conclusions can you draw from these measures of risk?

8.   The Fargo Well Company has EBIT of $200,000. The firm has $600,000 of debt outstanding at an average cost, k_i, of 8 percent. The firm's cost of equity capital, k_s, has been estimated as 12 percent.

a.   What is the value of the firm?
b.   What are the firm's overall capitalization rate and debt-equity ratio?

9.   The Fargo Well Company (presented in Problem 8) is considering decreasing its leverage by selling an additional $100,000 of stock and using the proceeds to retire an equal amount of bonds. As a result of this action, the firm's average cost of debt is expected to decrease to 7.5 percent, and its average cost of equity capital is expected to decrease to 11 percent.

a.   Using traditional capital structure analysis, determine the value of the firm, based on the proposed change;

b.   Determine the overall capitalization rate and debt-equity ratio associated with the proposed plan;

c.   Compare the present plan (from Problem 8) and the proposed plan, and indicate their status with respect to optimal capital structure.

10.   The C. Sanders Company, which is in the 40 percent tax bracket, is contemplating two possible financing plans. These alternative financing plans may be described as follows:

Source of Funds	Plan A	Plan B
Long-Term Debt	$200,000 at 10%	$600,000 at 12%
Preferred Stock	$100,000 at 9%	$300,000 at 10%
Common Stock	20,000 shares at $60.00	10,000 shares at $60.00

a.   Calculate the EPS for each plan for EBITs of $150,000 and $300,000;

b.   Calculate the financial breakeven point for each plan;

c.   Graph the plans on the same set of EBIT-EPS axes, and indicate the approximate value of EBIT at which you would be indifferent between the two plans;

d.   Calculate the fixed-payment ratio for each plan at EBITs of $150,000 and
        $300,000.

e.   Discuss the levels of EBIT at which each plan would be preferred, and briefly
        compare the leverage (i.e., risk) of each plan.

11.   The Micro-Widget Company (presented in Problem 7) has determined that the required
        rate of return on common stock, k_s, is related to its coefficient of variation of earnings per
        share. The following table summarizes that relationship:

Capital Structure (Debt-Equity Ratio)	Expected EPS	Coefficient of Variation for EPS	Estimated Required Rate of Return (k_s)
0%	$2.25	0.42	11.0%
10	2.35	0.45	11.2
20	2,46	0.48	11.4
30	2.57	0.53	12.0
40	2.60	0.61	13.5
50	2.40	0.79	15.5
60	1.80	1.32	18.0

a.   For each capital structure, what is the value of a share of stock?   Use the
        following earnings valuation model in your answer:

$$P_0 = \frac{EPS}{k_s} .$$

b.   Which capital structure maximizes shareholder wealth?

c.   Compare the capital structure selected in part (b) above to that selected in
        Problem (7-a)

SOLUTIONS

DEFINITIONS

1. leverage
2. operating breakeven point
3. capital structure
4. financial
5. asymmetric
6. interest; preferred stock
7. decreases
8. EBIT; sales
9. DOL; DFL
10. maximizes
11. financial
12. agency
13. link
14. owners' wealth
15. debt; equity

MULTIPLE CHOICE

1.	c	9.	d
2.	d ?	10.	c
3.	c	11.	b
4.	a	12.	a
5.	c	13.	c
6.	c	14.	b
7.	a	15.	c
8.	c		

PROBLEMS

1. The formula for the operating breakeven point (B/E) is:

$$BEP = \left(\frac{\text{Fixed Operating Costs}}{\text{Sales Price Per Unit} - \text{Variable Operating Costs Per Unit}} \right).$$

Substituting for each firm:

$$\text{Firm A BEP} \; - \; \frac{\$60,000}{\$12 - \$8} \; - \; 15,000 \text{ Units .}$$

$$\text{Firm B BEP} \; - \; \frac{\$40,000}{\$15 - \$11} \; - \; 10,000 \text{ Units .}$$

2.   In order to find the operating breakeven point, we must first determine the variable operating cost per unit. This may be done by substituting all known values into the income statement format and finding the unknown variable cost.

Sales (25,000 units)($9/unit) = $225,000	$225,000
Less: Variable operating cost [(25,000 units)($?/unit)]	?
Fixed operating cost	65,000
EBIT	$ 60,000

Variable operating cost = $225,000 - $65,000 = $100,000.

$$\text{Variable Operating Cost Per Unit} \; - \; \frac{\$100,000}{25,000 \text{ Units}} \; - \; \$4 \text{ Per Unit .}$$

Substituting into the equation for the operating breakeven point, we obtain:

$$\text{BEP} \; - \; \frac{\$65,000}{\$9 - \$4} \; - \; 13,000 \text{ Units .}$$

b: The cost and revenue functions appear as follows:

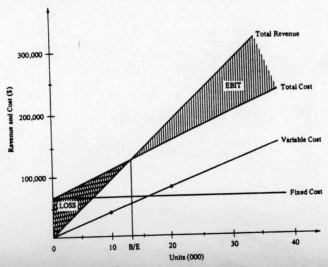

c.   (1) If fixed operating costs equal $50,000:

$$BEP \; - \; \frac{50,000}{\$9 - \$4} \; - \; 10,000 \; Units \; .$$

A decrease in fixed operating costs lowers the breakeven point.

(2) If sales price per unit is $10:

$$BEP \; - \; \frac{65,000}{\$10 - \$4} \; - \; 10,833 \; Units \; .$$

An increase in sales price per unit lowers the breakeven point.

(3) If variable operating costs per unit increase by $1.00, total variable operating costs will equal $5.00 per unit:

$$BEP \; - \; \frac{65,000}{\$9 - \$5} \; - \; 16,250 \; Units \; .$$

An increase in variable operating costs per unit increases the breakeven point.

3.   Firm A:

(a) Sales (Units)	$20,000	$30,000
(b) Sales Revenue [$12.00 x (a)]	240,000	360,000
(c) Less: Variable Operating Costs [$8.00 x (a)]	-160,000	-240,000
(d) Fixed Operating Costs	-60,000	-60,000
(e) EBIT [(b) - (c) - (d)]	$20,000	$60,000

$$DOL \; - \; \frac{\text{Percentage Change in EBIT}}{\text{Percentage Change in Sales}} \; :$$

$$\frac{\dfrac{\$60,000 - \$20,000}{\$20,000}}{\dfrac{\$30,000 - \$20,000}{\$20,000}} \; - \; \frac{200\%}{50\%} \; - \; 4 \; .$$

Firm B:

(a) Sales (Units)	$20,000	$30,000
(b) Sales Revenue [$15.00 x (a)]	300,000	450,000
(c) Less: Variable Operating Costs [$11.00 x (a)]	-220,000	-330,000
(d) Fixed Operating Costs	-40,000	-40,000
(e) EBIT [(b) - (c) - (d)]	$40,000	$80,000

$$\frac{\dfrac{\$80,000 - \$40,000}{\$40,000}}{\dfrac{\$30,000 - \$20,000}{\$20,000}} - \frac{100\%}{50\%} - 2 \; .$$

A more direct formula for calculating the degree of operating leverage at a base sales level is given by the formula:

$$\text{DOL at Base Sales Level } Q \; - \; \frac{Q\,(P - VC)}{Q\,(P - VC) - FC} \; ,$$

where Q = sales (units);
        P = sale price per unit;
    VC = variable operating cost per unit; and
    FC = fixed operating cost.

Substituting into the formula, we get:

Firm A: DOL at 20,000 Units $- \; \dfrac{20,000\,(\$12 - \$8)}{20,000\,(\$12 - \$8) - \$60,000} \; - \; \dfrac{\$80,000}{\$20,000} \; - \; 4 \; ,$

Firm B: DOL at 20,000 Units $- \; \dfrac{20,000\,(\$15 - \$11)}{20,000\,(\$15 - \$11) - \$40,000} \; - \; \dfrac{\$80,000}{\$40,000} \; - \; 2 \; .$

4.   a. Calculating the level of EPS for both firms:

Firm A:

EBIT	$40,000	$50,000
Less: Interest (.12 x $75,000)	-9,000	- 9,000
Earnings before taxes	$31,000	$ 41,000
Less: Taxes (.40)	-12,500	-16,000
Earnings after taxes	$18,600	$ 24,600
Less: Preferred dividends ($2.50/share		
x 2000 shares)		
Earnings available for common (EAC)	$13,600	$19,000
EPS [EAC ÷ No. of Shares Outstanding]	$1.36	$1.96

Firm B:

EBIT	$40,000	$50,000
Less: Interest (.12 x $75,000)	-10,000	-10,000
Earnings before taxes	$30,000	$40,000
Less: Taxes	-12,000	-16,000
Earnings after taxes	$18,000	$24,000
Less: Preferred dividends ($2/share		
x 5000 shares)	-10,000	-10,000
Earnings available for common (EAC)	$ 8,000	$14,000
EPS [EAC ÷ No. of Shares Outstanding]	$1.14	$2.00

b.   Calculating the Degree of Financial Leverage (DFL) for both firms, where

$$DFL - \frac{\text{Percentage Change in EPS}}{\text{Percentage Change in EBIT}}.$$

Firm A:

$$\frac{\dfrac{\$1.96 - \$1.36}{\$1.36}}{\dfrac{\$50,000 - \$40,000}{\$40,000}} - \frac{44\%}{25\%} - 1.76.$$

Firm B:

$$\frac{\dfrac{\$2.00 - \$1.14}{\$1.14}}{\dfrac{\$50,000 - \$40,000}{\$40,000}} - \frac{75\%}{25\%} - 3.00 \ .$$

A more direct formula for calculating the degree of financial leverage at a base level of EBIT is given by the formula:

$$\text{DFL for Given EBIT} - \frac{\text{EBIT}}{\text{EBIT} - I - \dfrac{\text{PD}}{(1 - T)}} \ ,$$

where   I = interest;
PD = preferred stock dividends; and
T = tax rate.

Substituting into the formula, we obtain

Firm A:

$$\text{DFL at \$40,000 EBIT} - \frac{\$40,000}{\$40,000 - \$9,000 - \dfrac{\$5,000}{(1 - 0.40)}} - 1.76 \ .$$

Firm B:

$$\text{DFL at \$40,000 EBIT} - \frac{\$40,000}{\$40,000 - \$10,000 - \dfrac{\$10,000}{(1 - 0.40)}} - 3.00 \ .$$

c.   Using a $40,000 base EBIT level, firm B has much higher financial leverage than firm A. The financial leverage ratio of 3 for B, as compared to 1.87 for A, indicates this. The higher financial leverage of firm B can also be observed by comparing the higher fixed financial charges of firm B to those of firm A.

5.   The degree of total leverage (DTL) is given by the formula:

$$\text{DTL at Base Sales } Q \ = \ \frac{Q(P - VC)}{Q(P - VC) - FC - I - \dfrac{PD}{(1 - T)}} \ ,$$

where   Q =   sales (units);
        P =   sales price per unit;
        VC =   variable operating cost per unit;
        FC =   fixed operating cost;
        I =   interest charges;
        PD =   preferred stock dividend; and
        T =   tax rate.

Substituting into the formula, we obtain

$$\text{DTL @ 500,000 Units} \ = \ \frac{50,000 \, (\$2.00 - \$1.50)}{500,000 \, (\$2.00 - \$1.50) - \$30,000 - \$8,000 - \dfrac{\$3,000}{(1 - 0.40)}} \ = \ 1.21 \ .$$

Total leverage is found by taking the product -- not the sum -- of the individual degrees of operating and financial leverage. Therefore, the total leverage effect would be 80 (i.e., 8 x 10), which means that a given change in sales would magnify changes in EPS by a factor of 80. If sales increase by 5 percent, EPS will increase by 400 percent under these circumstances.

7.   a.   First, compute EPS for each capital structure, assuming EBIT = $300,000:

Capital Structure
($000)

	0%	10%	20%	30%	40%	50%	60%
EBIT	$300.0	$300.0	$300.0	$300.0	$300.0	$300.0	$300.0
-Interest	- 0.0	- 18.0	- 38.0	-60.0	- 92.0	-140.0	-204.0
EBT	$300.0	$282.0	$262.0	$240.0	$208.0	$160.0	$96.0
-Taxes (40%)	120.0	112.8	-104.8	- 96.0	83.2	64.0	38.4
EAT	$180.0	$169.2	$157.2	$144.0	$124.8	$ 96.0	$57.6
No. Shares (000)	80	72	64	56	48	40	32
EPS	$2.25	$2.35	$2.46	$2.57	$2.60	$2.40	$1.80

According to the results, EPS is maximized at 40 percent, where it is $2.60.

b.   To compute the standard deviation and coefficient of variation of EPS, first compute each possible EPS outcome for each capital structure under consideration.

10% Structure ($000)

EBIT	$100.0	$300.0	$500.0
-Interest	- 18.0	- 18.0	- 18.0
EBT	$82.0	$282.0	$482.0
-Taxes (.40)	- 32.8	-112.8	-192.8
EAT	$ 49.2	$169.2	$289.2
No. of shares (000)	72	72	72
EPS	$49.2/72	$169.2/72	$289.2/72
	= $.68	= $2.35	= $4.02
Probability	20%	60%	20%

40% Structure ($000)

EBIT	$100.0	$300.0	$500.0
-Interest	- 92.0	- 92.0	- 92.0
EBT	$ 8.0	$208.0	$408.0
-Taxes (.40)	- 3.2	- 83.2	-163.2
EAT	$ 4.8	$124.8	$224.8
No. of shares (000)	48	48	48
EPS	$4.8/48	$124.8/48	$224.8/48
	= $.10	= $2.60	= $5.10
Probability	20%	60%	20%

60% Structure ($000)

EBIT	$100.0	$300.0	$500.00
-Interest	-204.0	-204.0	-204.0
EBT	-$104.0	$ 96.0	$296.0
-Taxes (.40)	+ 41.6	- 38.4	-118.4
EAT	-$62.4	$57.6	$177.6
No. of shares (000)	32	32	32
EPS	-$62.4/32 = $1.95	$57.6/32 = $1.80	$177.6/32 = $5.55
Probability	20%	60%	20%

For 10% Leverage:

Compute the standard deviation, given that the expected EPS of the 10% structure is $2.35:

Probability x $[EPS - E(EPS)]^2$:

0.20 x ($0.68 - $2.35)^2	=	.56
0.60 x ($2.35 - $2.35)^2	=	0
0.20 x ($4.02 - $2.32)^2	=	0.56
Total	=	1.12

Standard deviation (σ) = $(1.12)^{1/2}$
= $1.06

Coefficient of variation [$\sigma \div E(EPS)$] $1.06 \div $2.35 = 0.45

For 40% Leverage:

Compute the standard deviation, given that the expected EPS of the 40% structure is $2.60:

Probability x $[EPS - E(EPS)]^2$

0.20 x ($0.10 - $2.60)^2	=	1.25
0.60 x ($2.60 - $2.60)^2	=	0
0.20 x ($5.10 - $2.60)^2	=	1.25
Total	=	2.50

Standard deviation (σ) = $(2.50)^{1/2}$
= $1.58

Coefficient of variation [$\sigma \div E(EPS)$] $1.58 \div $2.60 = 0.61

For 60% Leverage:

Compute the standard deviation, given that the expected EPS of the 60% structure is $1.80:

Probability x [EPS - E (EPS)]^2

0.20 x ($1.95 - $1.80)^2	=	2.81
0.60 x ($1.80 = - $1.80)^2	=	0
0.20 x ($5.55 - $1.80)^2	=	2.81
Total	=	5.63

Standard deviation (σ)   =   (5.63)$^{\frac{1}{2}}$
                                  = $2.37

Coefficient of variation [σ + E(EPS)] $2.37 + $1.80 = 1.32

Clearly, the standard deviation and the coefficient of variation increase as financial leverage increases:

Capital Structure	Coefficient of Variation
10 Percent Debt	0.45
40 Percent Debt	0.61
60 Percent Debt	1.32

8.   a.   In order to determine the value of the firm, we must first calculate the market value of the stock, S. The calculation is as follows, where I equals the annual interest expense. It can be seen that the value of the stock is found by using the capitalization rate, k_s.

EAC	=	EBIT - I
EAC	=	$200,000 - ($600,000 x 0.08)
EAC	=	$200,000 - $48,000
	=	$152,000

S	=	EAC + k_s
	=	$152,00 + 0.12
	=	$1,266,666.67

Because the market value of debt is assumed equal to its book value, the value of the firm, V, is found by adding the value of debt, D, and stock, S:

$$V = D + S$$
$$= \$600,000.00 + \$1,266,666,67$$
$$= \$1,866,666.67$$

The current value of the firm is $1,866,666.67.

b.   The firm's overall capitalization rate, k_a, is found by dividing the EBIT by the firm's value, V:

$$k_a - \frac{EBIT}{V} - \frac{\$200,000.00}{\$1,866,666.67} - 10.71\% .$$

The debt-equity ratio, D/S, is found by dividing the market value of debt, D, by the market value of stock, S:

$$D/S - \frac{\$600,000.00}{\$1,266,666.67} - 0.47 .$$

9.   a.   Using the same framework used in Problem (8-a) yields:

$$EAC = EBIT - I$$
$$EAC = \$200,000 - (\$500,000 \times 0.075)$$
$$EAC = \$200,000 - \$37,500$$
$$= \$162,500$$

$$S = EAC \div k$$
$$= \$162,500 \div 0.11$$
$$= \$1,477,272.70$$

Using the value of the stock, the value of the firm under this plan can be calculated as follows:

$$V = D + S$$
$$= \$500,000.00 + \$1,477,272.70$$
$$= \$1,977,272.70$$

b.   The overall capitalization rate is calculated as follows:

$$k_a - \frac{EBIT}{V} - \frac{\$2,000,000.00}{\$1,977,272.70} - 10.11\% .$$

The debt-equity ratio is calculated as follows:

$$\frac{D}{S} = \frac{\$500,000.00}{\$1,477,272.70} = 0.34 .$$

c.   The key values calculated in Problem (8-a) and (8-b) and Problem (9-a) and (9-b) are summarized as follows:

Plan	Debt Ratio (D/S)	Capitalization Rate k_a	Firm Value (V)
Present	0.47	10.71%	$1,866,666,67
Proposed	0.34	10.11	$1,977,272.70

Analysis of these data indicate that by reducing leverage, the proposed plan will increase the value of the firm from $1,866,666,67 to $1,977,272.70 and decrease its overall capitalization rate from 10.71 percent to 10.11 percent. It is difficult to say if the proposed capital structure is optimal, but from the information developed, it is obvious that the optimal capital structure is at a less highly levered position than where the firm is presently. This is true because a less-levered proposed capital structure results in a higher corporate valuation than the current capital structure.

10.   a.   The first step in evaluating the plan is to calculate each plan's annual interest and preferred stock dividends. The annual interest is $20,000 for plan A (i.e., $200,000 x .10) and $72,000 for plan B (i.e., $600,000 x .12); the annual preferred dividends are $9,000 for plan A (i.e., $100,000 x .09) and $30,000 for plan B (i.e., $300,000 x 0.10). The EPS for EBITs of $150,000 and $300,000 is calculated for each plan as follows, where I equals annual interest, T equals taxes, PD equals preferred stock dividends, and n equals the number of shares outstanding:

	Plan A		Plan B	
EBIT	$150,000	$300,000	$150,000	300,000
I	- 20,000	- 20,000	- 72,000	- 72,000
EBT	$130,000	$280,000	$ 78,000	$228,000
-(.40)	- 52,000	-112,000	31,200	91,200
EAT	$ 78,000	$168,000	$ 46,800	$136,800
- PD	- 9,000	- 9,000	30,000	- 30,000
EAC	$ 69,000	$159,000	$ 16,800	$106,800

The next step requires calculation of the EPS figures associated with each of the plans, where:

$$EPS - \frac{EAC}{n} \, .$$

For Plan A:

When EBIT is equal to $150,000:

$$EPS_A - \frac{\$69,000}{20,000} - \$3.45 \, .$$

When EBIT is equal to $300,000:

$$EPS_A - \frac{\$159,000}{20,000} - \$7.95 \, .$$

For Plan B:

When EBIT is equal to $150,000:

$$EPS_B - \frac{\$16,800}{10,000} - \$1.68 \, .$$

When EBIT is equal to $300,000:

$$EPS_B - \frac{\$106,800}{10,000} - \$10.68 \, .$$

b.   The financial breakeven point for each project is found by substituting the annual interest, I, the annual preferred stock dividends, PD, and the tax rate, T, into the following equation:

$$\text{Financial Breakeven Point} - I + \frac{PD}{(1 - T)} \, .$$

For Project A:

Financial Breakeven Point$_A$ - $20,000 + $\dfrac{\$9,000}{(1 - 0.40)}$ - $35,000 .

For Project B:

Financial Breakeven Point$_B$ - $72,000 + $\dfrac{\$30,000}{(1 - 0.40)}$ - $122,000 .

c.   Parts (a) and (b) provide the following EBIT-EPS coordinates:

Plan	EBIT	EPS
A	$ 35,000	$ 0
	150,000	3.45
	300,000	7.95
B	$122,000	$ 0
	150,000	1.68
	300,000	10.68

Plotting these points on a set of EBIT-EPS axes yields the following graph:

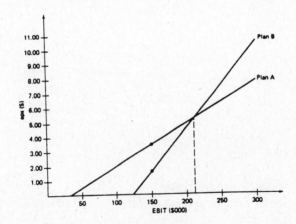

The point of indifference between Plans A and B occurs at the point where EBIT is equal to $209,000. This can be seen on the graph above, and by using the following equation:

$$\frac{(EBIT - I_A)(1 - T) - PD_A}{n_A} - \frac{(EBIT - I_B)(1 - T) - PD_B}{n_B}.$$

Solving for EBIT:

$$\frac{(EBIT - \$20,000)(1 - 0.40) - \$9,000}{20,000} - \frac{(EBIT - \$72,000)(1 - 0.40) - \$30,000}{10,000}.$$

$$- \frac{0.6\,EBIT - \$21,000}{20,000} - \frac{0.6\,EBIT - \$73,200}{10,000)},$$

$$0.60 \times EBIT = \$125,400$$

$$EBIT = \$209,000.$$

d.   The fixed-payment coverage ratios at EBITs of $150,000 and $300,000 can be calculated by substituting the annual interest, I, the annual preferred stock dividends, PD, and the tax rate, T, into the following equation.

$$Fixed\text{-}Payment\ Ratio - \frac{EBIT}{I + \dfrac{PD}{(1 - T)}}.$$

For Plan A:

Where EBIT is equal to $150,000:

$$Fixed\text{-}Payment\ Ratio_A - \frac{\$150,000}{\$20,000 + \dfrac{\$9,000}{(1 - 0.4)}} - 4.29.$$

Where EBIT is equal to $300,000:

$$\text{Fixed-Payment Ratio}_A = \frac{\$300,000}{\$20,000 + \dfrac{\$9,000}{(1 - 0.4)}} = 8.57 \ .$$

For Plan B:

Where EBIT is equal to $150,000:

$$\text{Fixed-Payment Ratio}_B = \frac{\$150,000}{\$72,000 + \dfrac{\$30,000}{(1 - 0.4)}} = 1.23 \ .$$

Where EBIT is equal to $300,000:

$$\text{Fixed-Payment Ratio}_B = \frac{\$300,000}{\$72,000 + \dfrac{\$30,000}{(1 - 0.4)}} = 2.46 \ .$$

e.   Analysis of the graph in part (c) indicates that, for the level of EBIT below the indifference point of $209,000, Plan A would be preferred because of its higher EPS, while, for levels of EBIT above $209,000, Plan B would be preferred because of its higher EPS over this range.

Plan B is more highly levered than Plan A because it has a steeper slope. Plan B is more risky than Plan A, not only because of its higher leverage but also because Plan B's financial breakeven point ($122,000) is greater than Plan A's breakeven point ($35,000). The higher risk of Plan B is rewarded once EBIT exceeds approximately $209,000.

The risk of the two plans also can be evaluated using fixed-payment coverage ratios. The higher the coverage ratios, the less risky the plans. A comparison of these ratios shows that Plan A is less risky than Plan B. When the firm's EBIT is equal to $150,000, Plan A shows a fixed-payment coverage ratio equal to 4.29, while Plan B's coverage ratio is only 1.23. Similarly, when the firm's EBIT is equal to $300,000 Plan A's coverage ratio is 8.57, while Plan B's coverage ratio is only 2.46.

11.   a.   The earnings valuation model suggests the following corporate values:

Structure			Value per share
0%	P_0 =	$2.25 ÷ 0.110 =	$20.45
10%	P_0 =	$2.35 ÷ 0.112 =	$20.98
20%	P_0 =	$2.46 ÷ 0.114 =	$21.58
30%	P_0 =	$2.57 ÷ 0.120 =	$21.42
40%	P_0 =	$2.60 ÷ 0.135 =	$19.26
50%	P_0 =	$2.40 ÷ 0.155 =	$15.48
60%	P_0 =	$1.80 ÷ 0.180 =	$10.00

   b.   The capital structure at which price per share is maximized is 20 percent, where EPS = $21.58.

   c.   Although EPS is maximized at a 40 percent debt structure ($2.60 per share), shareholder wealth -- as measured by price per share -- is lower at the 40 percent debt structure than at the 20 percent structure.   This indicates that EPS maximization does not consider risk, while wealth maximization does.

CHAPTER 13

LONG-TERM DEBT AND INVESTMENT BANKING

SUMMARY

The presence of debt in the firm's capital structure provides financial leverage, which magnifies the effects of increased operating profits on the owners' returns. Because the interest on debt is tax-deductible, the presence of long-term debt in the firm's capital structure is very desirable; it tends to lower the firm's cost of capital. Firms raise long-term debt either in the form of long-term loans or through the sale of bonds, which are negotiable long-term debt financing instruments.

Although long-term debt, by definition, has a maturity of more than one year, the long-term debt maturity for most corporate debt ranges from 5 to 20 years. The current portion of a long-term debt is often shown as a current liability on the firm's books. Most long-term debt agreements contain certain standard debt provisions, which are contractual requirements that assure the lender that the borrower will operate in a respectable and businesslike manner. These provisions may require that the borrower maintain satisfactory accounting records, render periodic financial statements to the lender, pay taxes and liabilities when due, and maintain facilities in good working order. These standard debt provisions assure the lender that the firm maintains liquidity and operates as a going concern, but they do not normally place a burden on a financially sound business.

Still other loan provisions often included in long-term debt agreements are known as restrictive debt provisions, or restrictive covenants. These items generally place certain contractual constraints on the borrower in order to provide the lender with adequate protection against financial loss. Restrictive covenants are largely dependent on the lender's evaluation of the riskiness of corporate borrowers. Common restrictive covenants require that the borrower maintain some minimum level of net working capital; prohibit the liquidation, acquisition, or encumbrance of fixed assets; prohibit subsequent borrowing, except subordinated loans; prohibit making financial lease agreements beyond a certain amount; prohibit combination through mergers or consolidation; prohibit or limit salaries of certain employees; require that the borrower maintain key employees; limit security investments; specify disposition of loan proceeds; and restrict dividends. Violations of any standard or restrictive provisions by the borrower are violations of a contract and provide certain recourse by the lender, which may include calling the loan or demanding immediate repayment.

The cost of long-term debt financing is generally greater than the cost of short-term financing because of the highly unpredictable nature of future interest rates. Higher rates compensate the lender for the expectation that future interest rates may rise. Other factors considered when the lender quotes a long-term rate are the maturity of the loan, the size of the loan, the business and financial risk of the borrower, and, of course, the basic cost of risk-free loans of similar maturity. This risk-free cost is typically considered to be that of a government issue.

Term loans, or long-term loans that typically have five- to twelve-year maturities, are made by financial institutions to business firms. These loan agreements are likely to include standard and restrictive covenants similar to those already described. Other term loan provisions include the specification of loan repayment dates, a description of any collateral if the loan is secured, and a description of any stock purchase options or warrants provided to the lender. Sometimes, term loans require lump-sum or balloon payments at maturity. The primary financial institutions making term loans are commercial banks, insurance companies, pension funds, regional development companies, commercial finance companies, and equipment manufacturers.

A bond is a certificate indicating that a corporation has borrowed a certain amount of money and promises to repay it at a future date. The issuing corporation agrees to pay bondholders the stated interest at specified time intervals (usually semiannual). Most bonds have ten- to thirty-year maturities and a $1,000 par value. A bond indenture is the legal contract under which a bond is issued. It includes standard and restrictive provisions and sinking-fund provisions, and identifies and describes any security held. The bond trustee is a third party whose responsibility it is to protect the interest of the bondholders.

A bond may be convertible, which means that the holder has an option of converting it into a specified number of shares of common stock; it may be callable, which means that the issuer can retire the bond at a specified call price prior to maturity; or it may have warrants, which allow the holder to purchase a specified number of shares of common stock at a specified price. Bond ratings, which are issued by independent companies such as Moody's and Standard and Poor's, are important indicators of the risk of a proposed or existing bond. The higher the risk, the lower the rating, and, therefore, the higher the interest cost.

An unsecured bond, or debenture, may or may not be subordinated to other debt instruments. Income bonds, which pay interest only if sufficient earnings are available, represent another type of unsecured bonds. Secured bonds may be secured with one of many types of mortgages, which are claims on real property. Other types of secured bonds are collateral trust bonds, which are secured by stocks and bonds, and equipment trust certificates. Deep discount, floating rate, and junk bonds may be either secured or unsecured.

In order to refund bonds prior to maturity, a firm can issue serial bonds that provide for the repayment of a certain proportion of the bond issue during each year bonds are outstanding. As an alternative to serial bonds, firms can issue callable bonds which may be retired before their stated maturity date. Capital budgeting techniques can be used to evaluate whether or not a firm should call its existing bonds and replace these securities with a new issue of debt. Discounts and premiums, call premiums, flotation costs, interest costs, and associated taxes must be considered in making this decision. For a proposed refunding to be acceptable, the present value of the expected cash flow savings on the new bond (discounted at the after-tax cost of debt) must be greater than the outlay required to refund the old bond and issue a new one.

Investment bankers underwrite or sell new issues of securities, including both stocks and bonds. They receive compensation in the form of a spread between their selling price and the price given to the issuing firm for its securities. They advise corporations seeking to issue new securities, bear risk through underwriting new security issues, and distribute securities in the market through the use of underwriting syndicates. In addition to the public offering of new securities, firms may also use private placements in order to issue debt and equity securities.

CONCEPT OUTLINE

I.   **Long-term debt is an important component of the firm's capital structure.**

A.   It provides financial leverage, which magnifies the effects of increased operating profits on the owners' returns.

B.   Because debt is the cheapest form of long-term financing due to the tax-deductibility of interest expense, its presence tends to lower the firm's overall cost of capital.

C.   Long-term debt financing can be obtained either through term loans from various financial institutions or from the sale of marketable debt in the form of bonds.

D.   Long-term debt, by definition, has a maturity of more than one year, although most long-term debt has a maturity of five to twenty years.

E.   The current portion of long-term debt is shown as a current liability on the issuing firm's books.

F.   Standard debt provisions, which are intended to insure that a borrower operates in a respectable and businesslike manner, are normally included in a long-term debt agreement.

G.   Standard debt provisions, which are intended to force the borrower to maintain liquidity and operate as a going concern, often require that:

1.   The borrower must maintain satisfactory accounting records.

2.   The borrower must periodically render financial statements.

3.   The borrower must pay taxes and other liabilities when due.

4.   The borrower must keep assets in good repair and working order.

H.   Restrictive loan provisions, or restrictive covenants which place certain constraints on the borrower, are often included to provide the lender with additional risk protection.

I.   Although specific restrictive covenants depend on a lender's evaluation of a long-term borrower, some common covenants are as follows:

   1.   The long-term borrower must maintain a specified level of net working capital.

   2.   The borrower is limited with respect to liquidation, acquisition, and encumbrance of fixed assets.

   3.   The borrower may be prohibited from any additional borrowing unless it is subordinated.

   4.   The borrower cannot enter into financial (i.e., long-term) leases in excess of a certain dollar amount.

   5.   The borrower may be prohibited from merging or consolidating with other firms.

   6.   The borrower may be prohibited from increasing the compensation paid to key employees of the firm.

   7.   The borrower may have to retain certain key employees for the duration of the loan.

   8.   The borrower may be prohibited from making security investments.

   9.   The borrower may be regulated with respect to the disposition of the loan proceeds.

   10.   The borrower may be restricted with respect to future dividend payments.

J.   The cost of long-term financing is typically higher than the cost of short-term financing because of the unpredictable nature of future interest rates.

   1.   The longer the loan maturity, the higher the interest rate needed to compensate the lender for the risk of higher future interest rates.

   2.   The larger the size of the loan, the greater its cost.

   3.   The greater the business and financial risk of the borrower, the greater the cost of the loan.

   4.   The higher the basic cost of funds as measured by the current yield on Treasury securities of similar maturity, the greater the cost of the loan.

II.   **Term loans are long-term loans made by various financial institutions to business firms.**

    A.   Term loans are most often made for financing fixed financial needs or to retire existing debts.

        1.   Maturities are generally between five and twelve years, although shorter-term loans can be arranged.

        2.   The standard and restrictive loan provisions described earlier are likely to be included as part of a term loan agreement.

        3.   Term loans generally require monthly, quarterly, semiannual, or annual payments.

        4.   Some term loans require a lump-sum or balloon payment at maturity.

        5.   A term loan may be secured or unsecured, depending on the risk perceived by the lender.

        6.   Inclusion of stock purchase options or warrants as part of a term loan is common.

    B.   The major term lenders are commercial banks, insurance companies, pension funds, regional development companies, the Small Business Administration, small business investment companies, commercial finance companies, and equipment manufacturers.

III.   **A bond is a negotiable certificate indicating that a corporation has borrowed a certain amount of money that it promises to repay at some future date.**

    A.   Most bonds have a $1,000 par value and are issued with initial maturities of ten to thirty years.

    B.   Because numerous unrelated persons may end up owning a portion of a bond issue, the issuer must provide certain legal protection to the owners.

        1.   The bond indenture is the legal contract that states the rights of the bondholders and the obligations of the issuing corporation.

        2.   The indenture will include various standard and restrictive loan provisions.

        3.   A sinking-fund requirement and some type of security may also be specified in the bond indenture.

4.   The bond trustee is a third party hired by the issuer to act as a watchdog on behalf of the bondholders.

5.   The bond trustee must enforce the bond indenture and take necessary action if any provisions are violated.

C.   A number of special features may be included as part of a bond issue.

1.   The bond may be convertible, which means that the holder can convert the bond into common stock at a specified price.

2.   The bond may have a call feature, which permits the issuer to retire the bond at a prespecified call price.

3.   The bond may have warrants, which are options to purchase the borrower's common stock at a specified price.

D.   Bond ratings, issued by independent companies such as Moody's and Standard and Poor's, measure the risk of publicly traded bonds. Lower ratings indicate higher risk, and thus higher interest costs to the issuing firm.

E.   Bonds may be secured or unsecured.

1.   Unsecured bonds include debentures, subordinated debentures, and income bonds.

a.   Subordinated debentures have a junior claim against the firm's earnings.

b.   Income bonds pay interest only if the firm has sufficient earnings to meet the interest payment.

2.   Secured bonds include mortgage bonds, collateral trust bonds, and equipment trust certificates.

a.   Mortgage bonds are secured by real property.

b.   Collateral trust certificates are secured by stocks and bonds.

c.   Equipment trust certificates, used to make long-term installment purchases of equipment, are secured by the purchased equipment.

F.   Other contemporary bonds include zero coupon bonds, junk bonds, floating rate bonds, extendable notes, and putable bonds.

1. Zero coupon bonds are sold at deep discount, and pay no coupon interest.

2. Junk bonds, or high-risk bonds, are bonds rated BA and lower by Moody's or BB and lower by Standard and Poor's.

3. Floating rate bonds carry an adjustable coupon interest rate.

4. Extendable notes carry short initial maturities of one to five years, but these notes can be redeemed or renewed for a similar period at the borrower's option.

5. Putable bonds can be redeemed at par at the option of the lender.

G. Firms wishing to retire or refund bonds prior to their maturity can issue serial bonds or callable bonds.

1. Serial bonds represent a bond issue in which a certain portion of the total issue matures each year.

2. Callable bonds may be redeemed before their maturity at the option of the borrower.

   a. The call premium associated with callable bonds represents the amount by which the call price exceeds the par value of the bonds.

   b. When bonds are sold at discount or premium, the issuer is required to amortize the discount or premium over the life of the bond. The amortized discount represents a tax-deductible expense, while the amortized premium represents taxable income.

   c. Any flotation or issuance costs incurred in issuing a bond must be amortized over the life of the bond.

3. Capital budgeting techniques can be used to make bond refunding decisions when interest rates have declined and the reissue of a bond with a lower interest rate is planned. If the present value of the expected cash flow savings on the new bond exceeds the outlay required to refund the old bond and issue the new bond, the proposed refunding decision should be accepted.

IV. **Investment bankers act as financial middlemen and purchase securities from corporate and government issuers while planning to resell these securities to the public.**

    A.   The investment banker is responsible for finding buyers for new security issues.

        1.   The investment banker may agree to underwrite (or accept all the risks of sale), place privately, or sell new security issues on a best efforts basis.

        2.   The investment banker also provides the issuer with a great deal of advice.

    B.   A firm selects an investment banker through either a competitive bid or a negotiated offering.

        1.   Once selected, the investment banker advises the issuer; syndicates the issue, if necessary; forms a selling group; ensures that the firm meets the legal requirements of the Securities and Exchange Commission; sets the price; issues the securities; and stabilizes the price.

        2.   The cost of the investment banker's service, which is paid in the form of a discount, is dependent on the size and type of the issue being sold.

    C.   An alternative which may or may not require the use of an investment banker is private placement of a security in the hands of a single purchaser or small group of purchasers.

        1.   Private placements may be made through stock options or stock purchase plans.

        2.   Even in the case of a private placement, the advice of an investment banker may be required to price the issue correctly.

APPLICATIONS

DEFINITIONS

1.   Contractual clauses in long-term debt agreements that place certain operating and financial constraints on corporate borrowers are known as *restrictive covenants*.

2.   A *term* loan represents a loan made by a financial institution to a business having an initial maturity of more than one year.

3. A large lump-sum payment made at the maturity of a loan represents a _balloon_ payment.

4. Any assets against which a lender has a legal claim if the borrower defaults on some provision of the loan represent _Collateral_

5. Stock purchase warrants give their holder the right to _purchase_ a certain number of shares of the firm's common stock at a specified price over a certain period of time.

6. The legal document stating the terms and conditions under which a bond has been issued is known as a _bond indenture_

7. A restrictive provision often included in a bond indenture that calls for the systematic retirement of bonds before their maturity date represents a _sinking fund_

8. Convertible bonds allow bondholders to exchange each bond into a stated amount of _common stock_

9. A call feature included in almost all corporate bonds given the issuer the opportunity to _repurchase_ bonds prior to maturity at a stated price.

10. An investment banker represents a financial middleman that purchases securities from _businesses_ and resells them to the _public_

11. The direct sale of a new security to one or more purchasers represents a _private placement_

12. An investment banking firm that uses its resources to sell a given security without assuming any underwriting risk engages in a public offering of securities on a _best efforts_ basis.

* 13. The portion of a security registration statement filed with the SEC that details the firm's operating and financial position is known as a _prospectus_

14. A security issue that is sold out is known as an _oversubscribed_ issue, while an issue whose shares are not immediately sold is _undersubscribed_

15. Under _competitive_ bidding, the investment banker that submits the higher bid for a given security issue is awarded the issue.

MULTIPLE CHOICE

1. Long-term debt can be obtained with all but which of the following?
    a.   term loan.
    b.   sale of bonds.
    c.   commercial paper.
    d.   convertible bonds.

2. Standard debt provisions include requirements to:
    a.   maintain satisfactory accounting records and supply audited financial statements.
    b.   pay taxes and other liabilities when due.
    c.   maintain all facilities in good working order.
    d.   all of the above.

3. Restrictive covenants:
    a.   are just standard debt provisions.
    b.   do not normally place a burden on the financially sound business borrower.
    c.   allow the lender to monitor and control the borrower's activities.
    d.   are usually ignored by knowledgeable financial managers.

4. The cost of long-term debt will usually be higher:
    a.   the shorter the loan maturity.
    b.   the larger the loan size.
    c.   the better the borrower's credit rating.
    d.   the lower the basic cost of money.

5. Most corporate bonds have denominations of _____ and maturities of _____.
    a. $1,000, 10 to 20 years.
    b. $1,000, 1 to 10 years.
    c. $500, 1 to 5 years.
    d. $10,000, 10 to 20 years.

6. The relatively complex and lengthy legal document stating the conditions under which a bond has been issued is called the:
    a.   subordinate debenture.
    b.   bond indenture.
    c.   bond trustee.
    d.   restrictive covenant.

7. The purpose of a bond call feature is to:
    a.   allow the investor to call the borrower to check on current performance.
    b.   allow the investor to call back his investment prior to maturity.
    c.   give the issuer the opportunity to repurchase bonds prior to maturity.
    d.   amortize interest payments over the life of the bond.

8.   Bond X has an A rating from Standard & Poor's and Bond Y has a higher effective interest rate. Which of the following statements is consistent with these facts?
     a.   Bond Y has a BB rating.
     b.   Bond Y has a shorter maturity than Bond X.
     c.   Bond Y has an AA rating.
     d.   Bond X is a callable bond.

9.   A firm would consider refunding a bond issue when:
     a.   market rates are below the coupon rates on the outstanding bonds.
     b.   the present value of the annual cash flow savings from the new bond are expected to exceed the expected incremental cash outlay required to refund.
     c.   there has been a significant drop in interest rates after a bond has been issued.
     d.   all of the above.

10. The investment banker's functions include:
     a.   underwriting security issues and advising clients.
     b.   providing term loans and performing credit analysis.
     c.   acting as a "watchdog" on behalf of the bondholders.
     d.   maintaining a transactions record for the firm's checking account.

11. Subordination of debt contracts means that:
     a.   the firm renounces all its debt contracts.
     b.   the firm plans to accelerate the repayment of its bonds.
     c.   less important creditors agree to wait until all claims of the firm's senior debt are satisfied before they receive payment.
     d.   the firm pays its preferred stock dividends before repaying bondholder interest.

12. Financial instruments that give holders the rights to purchase a certain number of shares of the firm's common stock at a specified price over a certain period of time are known as:
     a.   equity privileges
     b.   stock debentures
     c.   preferred action rights
     d.   stock purchase warrants

13. Which of the following financial firms does not offer term loans to corporate borrowers?
     a.   investment bankers.
     b.   commercial finance companies.
     c.   commercial banks.
     d.   pension funds.

14.   What type of bond allows bondholders to exchange their bonds for a prespecified number of shares of common stock in the firm?
    a.   a reversible bond.
    b.   an income bond.
    c.   a convertible bond
    d.   a subordinated debenture.

15.   Which of the following statements regarding junk bonds is true?
    a.   junk bonds provide lenders with no rate of return.
    b.   junk bonds carry a lower rating of credit quality from Moody's and/or Standard and Poor's.
    c.   junk bonds are often used to finance the sale of preowned capital equipment.
    d.   junk bonds are available only from investment bankers with questionable ethical standards.

PROBLEMS

1.   The Abarnathy Company has $3,000,000 of unsecured debt outstanding. The breakdown of the firm's debt is as follows:

Debt	Amount	Subordination Clause
General Creditors	$ 800,000	None
Debenture A	300,000	None
Debenture B	900,000	None
Debenture C	1,000,000	Yes - To Debenture A
TOTAL	$3,000,000	

The firm has no secured debt outstanding and has recently filed for bankruptcy. After the liquidation of all the firm's assets, $1,800,000 has been recovered.

    a.   Determine the amount each debt holder would receive if all creditors were general creditors;
    b.   Based on the actual nature of the firm's indebtedness, determine how much, if any, each creditor would receive;
    c.   Determine the percentage of each claim recovered by the creditors in part (b); and
    d.   Explain why a particular lender might wish to have other corporate debt subordinate to its claim.

2. The initial proceeds per bond, size of issue, life of bond, and years remaining to maturity for two bonds are as follows:

Bond	Proceeds per bond	Size of issue	Life of bond	Remaining to maturity
A	$ 970	20,000 bonds	15 year	10 year
B	1,025	30,000 bonds	25 year	20 year

For each bond, assume that the issuer is in the 40 percent tax bracket and that the bonds have a $1,000 par value.

a. Indicate whether the bonds were sold at a discount or at a premium;
b. Determine the total dollar discount or premium for each issue;
c. Determine the annual amortization of the discount or premium in each case;
d. Calculate the unamortized discount or premium in each case; and
e. Determine the after-tax inflow or outflow if the bonds were retired today.

3. The Morton Company is contemplating calling an outstanding $15,000,000 bond issue and replacing it with a new $15,000,000 bond issue. The firm wishes to do this in order to take advantage of a decline in interest rates that has occurred since the initial bond issuance. The old and new bonds are described separately as follows:

Old Bond:

The outstanding bond has a $1,000 par value and a 10 percent coupon rate. The bond initially was issued ten years ago with a thirty-year maturity. Because of the high level of interest rates at the time of issue, the bond was sold at a $30 discount from face value. The initial flotation cost of the bond totals $240,000. The current call price of the bond is $1,000.

New Bond:

The proposed bond would have a $1,000 par value and an 8.5 percent coupon rate. It will have a twenty-year maturity and can be sold at its $1,000 par value. The issuance cost of the new bond is expected to be $300,000. Interest is expected to overlap on the bonds for three months.

a. Calculate the after-tax cash inflow expected to result from the unamortized portion of the old bond issuance cost;
b. Calculate the annual after-tax cash inflow effect of the amortization of the issuance cost of the new bond;
c. Calculate the after-tax cash outflow effect of the overlapping interest;

d. Calculate the after-tax cash outflow resulting from payment of the call premiur ω retire the old bond;

e. Calculate the after-tax cash inflow resulting from the unamortized portion of the discount on the old bond;

f. Determine the incremental initial outlay required to call the old bond and issue the new bond; and

g. Calculate the annual cash-flow savings, if any, expected to result from the bond refunding and reissue.

h. Finally, if the firm has a 5 percent after-tax cost of debt, would you recommend the proposed refunding and reissue? Explain.

4. Tower One Ltd. wishes to raise $18.5 million to finance needed expansion. The firm believes that after deducting all selling costs, it should net enough money from a $20 million bond issue to finance the expansion. The underwriters believe that the bonds can be sold in the marketplace for their $1,000 par value and expect their administrative cost to be $750,000. They must sell the bonds at a 1 percent discount to the selling group. The underwriters wish to earn 1 percent on the sale price.

a. Calculate the per-bond spread required by the underwriters to cover their costs.

b. How much will Tower One Ltd. net from the issue?

c. How much will the selling group and the underwriters receive?

SOLUTIONS

DEFINITIONS

1. restrictive covenants
2. term
3. balloon
4. collateral
5. purchase
6. bond indenture
7. sinking fund
8. common stock
9. repurchase
10. corporations; public
11. private placement
12. best efforts
13. prospectus
14. oversubscribed; undersubscribed
15. competitive

MULTIPLE CHOICE

1.	c	9.	d
2.	d	10.	a
3.	c	11.	c
4.	b	12.	d
5.	a	13.	a
6.	b	14.	c
7.	c	15.	b
8.	a		

PROBLEMS

1. If all the creditors were general creditors, they would recover the same percentage of their claims as the total recovery represents as a percentage of total claims. Because $1,800,000 was recovered to be distributed among the creditors, each unsecured creditor would receive 60 percent of the claim ($1,800,000 ÷ $3,000,000). Their individual claims are calculated in tabular form as follows:

Debt	Claim (1)	Percentage Recovered (2)	Amount Recovered [(1) x (2)] (3)
General Creditors	$ 800,000	60%	$480,000
Debenture A	300,000	60	180,000
Debenture B	900,000	60	540,000
Debenture C	1,000,000	60	600,000
TOTAL	$3,000,000		$1,800,000

  b. When considering the subordination of debentures, the recovery schedule will differ from that shown in part (a). Debenture C must allow the holders of debenture A to take enough from it, if available, to allow full satisfaction of debenture A's $300,000 claim. Because debenture A needs only an additional $120,000 (i.e., $300,000 claim minus $180,000 recovery) to have its claim fully satisfied, and debenture C would recover $600,000, debenture C must pass $120,000 of its recovery to debenture A. The result at this point is as follows: Debenture A recovers $300,000 ($180,000 from its own recovery and $120,000 from subordinated debenture C). Debenture C recovers $480,000 ($600,000 recovery less the $120,000 it must give A).

The recovery of each creditor after consideration of the subordination of debenture C's claim is as follows:

Debt	Amount recovered
General creditors	$ 480,000
Debenture A	300,000
Debenture B	540,000
Debenture C	480,000
Total	$1,800,000

c. The percentage of each unsecured creditor's claim recovered after consideration of the subordination provision is as follows:

Debt	Claim (1)	Percentage Recovered (2)	Amount Recovered [(1) x (2)] (3)
General Creditors	$ 800,000	60%	$480,000
Debenture A	300,000	100	300,000
Debenture B	900,000	60	540,000
Debenture C	1,000,000	48	480,000
TOTAL	$3,000,000		$1,800,000

Column (2) gives the percentage of recovery experience by each creditor. It can be seen that debenture (A), to which another debenture (C) was subordinated, had the greatest recovery, while the subordinated debenture had the lowest. The other creditors (i.e., general creditors and debenture B) which were not subordinated received exactly their proportional claim of the total recovery (60 percent).

d. It should be obvious from these results that a debt holder has more protection by having other debts subordinated to it, because it can use the subordinated debenture's claim against the firm to help satisfy its own claim. If funds are available to distribute to unsecured creditors in liquidation, any debts to which other debts have been subordinated receive a greater proportion of the bankruptcy settlement than debts which do not have other debts subordinated to them.

2. a. Because bond A was sold for $970, which is below its $1,000 par value, it was sold at a discount; because bond B was sold for $1,025, which is above its $1,000 par value, it was sold at a premium.

b.   The discount on Bond A was $30 ($1,000 - $970), while the premium on Bond B was $25 ($1,025 - $1,000). Multiplying these per-bond values by the number of bonds issued yields the total dollar discount for Bond A and the total dollar premium for Bond B:

Bond	Amount of Discount or Premium (1)	Size of Issue (2)	Total Dollar Discount or Premium [(1) x (2)] (3)
A	$30 discount	20,000 bonds	$600,000 discount
B	$25 premium	30,000 bonds	$750,000 premium

c.   The amortization of the discount for Bond A and the premium for Bond B can be found by dividing the total dollar discount or premium calculated in part (b) by the life of the bond:

Bond	Total Dollar Discount or Premium (1)	Life of Bond (2)	Annual Amortization (Expense or Income) [(1) x (2)] (3)
A	$600,000 discount	15 years	$40,000 expense
B	$750,000 premium	25 years	$30,000 income

d.   The unamortized portion of the discount or premium for each bond can be found by multiplying the number of years remaining to maturity by the corresponding annual amortization:

Bond	Annual Amortization (Expense or Income) (1)	Years Remaining Until Maturity (2)	Unamortized Discount or Premium [(1) x (2)] (3)
A	$40,000 expense	10	$400,000 discount
B	$30,000 income	20	$600,000 premium

e.   Because the amortization of a discount or premium does not require the payment or receipt of cash, but rather is a noncash item, the only cash-flow effect of these entries is a tax effect. For a discount, a noncash expenditure results, which reduces taxes and therefore creates a cash inflow that is equal to the tax rate times the amount of discount amortized, while a premium represents noncash income that raises taxes and therefore acts as a cash outflow equal -- the tax rate times the amount of premium amortized. If a bond is retired prior to maturity, any unamortized discount is expended and any unamortized premium is shown as income. Therefore, the after-tax cash-flow effects for each of the bonds can be calculated as follows:

Bond	Unamortized Discount or Premium (1)	Tax Rate (2)	After-Tax Cash Inflow or Outflow from Tax Effect [(1) x (2)] (3)
A	$400,000 discount	0.40	$160,000 cash inflow
B	$600,000 premium	0.40	$240,000 cash outflow

3. a. The portion of the old bond issuance cost that still is unamortized can be deducted currently if the bond is called. The effect of this noncash expenditure is to create a cash inflow that is equal to the tax rate times the unamortized issuance cost. Because the issuance cost is amortized on a straight-line basis over thirty years, the annual write-off would be:

$$\text{Annual Issuance Cost Amortization} - \frac{\$240,000}{30} - \$8,000 \text{ per year .}$$

Because twenty years (30 years - 10 years) of cost is still to be amortized, the unamortized issuance cost would be:

$$(\$8,000/\text{yr}) \times (20 \text{ yr}) = \$160,000.$$

Multiplying this noncash expenditure by the 40 percent tax rate yields a cash inflow:

After-Tax Cash Inflow from Unamortized Issuance Cost   =   (.40) x ($160,000) = $64,000.

b. Because the amortization is a noncash expenditure, the annual after-tax cash flow effect of the amortization of the new bond issuance cost is found by multiplying the annual amortization of the issuance cost by the tax rate. The resulting product represents the cash inflow resulting from the reduced taxes due to the deduction of the noncash expenditure from taxable income:

$$\text{Amortization of New Bond Issuance Cost} - \frac{\$300,000}{20 \text{ years}} - \$15,000 \text{ per year .}$$

Multiplying by the 40 percent tax rate yields the annual after-tax cash inflow from this deduction:

$$(\$15,000) \times (0.40) = \$6,000.$$

$$(\$15,000) \times (0.40) = \$6,000.$$

c.   Because interest must be paid on both the old and the new bonds for a period of three months, the old bond is said to overlap the new. The amount of interest paid on the old bond during the overlap period would be:

$$(\$15,000,000) \times (0.10) \times \left(\frac{3 \text{ months}}{12 \text{ months}} \right).$$

Because the interest is tax-deductible, the after-tax cash inflow associated with the overlapping interest can be found by multiplying the amount of overlapping interest by one minus the tax rate:

$$(\$375,000) \times (1 - 0.40) = \$225,000.$$

d.   In order to call the old bond, the firm must pay a premium of $50 per bond (i.e., the call price of $1,050/bond - the par value of $1,000/bond). The total premium paid on the old bond can be found by multiplying the number of bonds outstanding by the per-bond call premium:

$$\text{Number of Bonds Outstanding} - \frac{\$15,000,000}{\$1,000} - \$15,000 \text{ Bonds}.$$

Multiplying the number of bonds by the call premium per bond yields a total premium of:

$$(\$50 \text{ per bond}) \times (15,000) = \$750,000.$$

Because this premium is treated as a tax-deductible expenditure in the year of the call, multiplying by one minus the tax rate yields the after-tax cash outflow from the call premium:

$$(\$750,000) \times (1 - 0.40) = \$450,000.$$

e.   The unamortized portion of the old bond discount can be written off when the bonds are called. The total amount of the discount being amortized can be found by multiplying the discount by the number of bonds issued:

$$(\$30 \text{ per bond}) \times (15,000 \text{ bonds}) = \$450,000.$$

Because the discount was being amortized on a straight-line basis over the bond's thirty-year life, the annual amortization expense would be:

$$\frac{\$450,000}{30 \text{ years}} - \$15,000 \text{ per year .}$$

Because the last twenty years of this amortization remains to be deducted, the unamortized discount would be:

(20 year) x ($15,000 per year) = $300,000.

Because the $300,000 represents a noncash expenditure that can be deducted currently, the after-tax cash inflow from this deduction would equal the tax rate times the deduction:

($300,000) x (0.40) = $120,000.

f.   Using the information developed in parts (a), (c), (d), and (e), the incremental initial outlay required to call the old bond and issue the new bond is calculated in tabular form as follows:

After-Tax Cash Outflows	
Call Premium [from part (d)]	$450,000
Issuance Cost of New Bond [given]	300,000
Overlapping Interest [from part (c)]	225,000
[1] TOTAL AFTER-TAX CASH OUTFLOWS	$975,000
After-Tax Cash Inflows	
Unamortized Discount on Old Bonds [from part (e)]	$120,000
Unamortized Issuance Cost on Old Bonds [from part (a)]	64,000
[2] TOTAL AFTER-TAX CASH INFLOWS	$184,000
Incremental Initial Outlay [(1) - (2)]	$791,000

The table excludes the $15,000,000 payment to retire the old bond from the outflows and also excludes the $15,000,000 proceeds from the sale of the new bond from the inflows, because these entries would cancel each other out. The incremental initial outlay represents the actual cash outflow the firm would have to make at time zero in order to retire the old bonds and replace them with the new bonds.

g.   The annual after-tax cash savings can be calculated by using the initial information along with some of the data developed in earlier parts of this problem. The required calculations are presented in tabular form as follows:

Old Bonds	
Annual Interest Expense ($15,000,000) x (0.10)	$1,500,000
Less: Tax Savings Provided By:	
Interest ($15,000,000) x (0.10) x (0.40)	- 600,000
Amortization of Issuing Cost [($240,000 ÷ 30) x (0.40)	- 3,200
Amortization of Discount [($450,000 ÷ 30) x (0.40)	- 6,000
[1] ANNUAL CASH OUTFLOWS FROM OLD BONDS	$890,800
New Bonds	
Annual Interest Expense ($15,000,000) x (0.085)	$1,275,000
Less: Tax Savings Provided By:	
Interest ($15,000,000) x (0.085) x (0.40)	- 510,000
Amortization of Issue Cost [($300,000 ÷ 20) x (0.40)]	- 6,000
[2] ANNUAL CASH OUTFLOWS FROM NEW BONDS	$759,000
[3] Annual Cash Flow Savings from New Bond [(1) - (2)]	$131,800

h.   If the firm's after-tax cost of debt is 5 percent, the desirability of the proposed refunding can be evaluated. By using the results of parts f and g, the refunding decision can be set up as a simple capital budgeting problem. By spending $791,000 [from part (f)], the firm can now expect to receive annual cash inflows of $131,800 [annual cash-flow savings from part (g)] in each of the next twenty years.   The present value of this twenty-year $131,800 annuity at the 5 percent after-tax cost of debt is calculated as follows:

Present value of savings = (12.462) x ($131,800) = $1,642,492

The interest factor for the present value of a twenty-year annuity discounted at 5 percent is 12.462.

Because the present value of the savings ($1,642,492) is greater than the $791,000 cost, the proposed refunding and reissue should be implemented. As a result of this action, the firm will experience a net savings of $851,492 (i.e., $1,642,492 savings - $791,000 cost).

4. a.   For the underwriters to cover their $750,000 cost, they must receive a discount in purchasing the bonds from Tower One equal to:

$$\frac{\$750,000}{\$20,000,000} - 3.75\% \ .$$

   b.   Tower One's proceeds from the issue would be:

Gross Proceeds	$20,000,000
Less: Administrative cost of underwriting	-750,000
Underwriters' profit: ($20,000,000) x (0.01)	-200,000
Selling group's fee: ($20,000,000) x (0.01)	-200,000
Net Issuer's Proceeds	$18,850,000

   c.   The selling group would receive $200,000 and the underwriters would receive $950,000 (i.e., $750,000 administrative fee = $200,000 commission).

CHAPTER 14

COMMON STOCK AND DIVIDEND POLICY

SUMMARY

This chapter discusses the key features of equity capital, common stock, stock rights, and dividends. Equity capital differs from debt capital in four basic respects:

Stock Characteristics	Bond Characteristics
Investment never matures.	Set maturity date.
Voting rights attached.	No voting rights.
Secondary claim to income.	Primary claim.
Dividends not deductible.	Interest tax deductible.

The true owners of the firm are the common stockholders, who invest their money and receive a claim only on the residual that is left after all other claims are satisfied. Holders of common stock have no guarantee of return, but they cannot lose more than they have invested in the firm. Potential returns are unlimited.

Common stock financing's advantages include the ability to pass dividends, the fact that it does not mature, and its ability to increase borrowing power. The key disadvantages are the possible dilution its issuance may cause for existing owners and its high cost. Stock rights permit existing shareholders to avoid dilution of their ownership and earnings resulting from a new issue of common stock.

The amount of the cash dividend normally is a quarterly decision made by the board of directors. Beginning four business days before the date of record, the stock sells ex dividend (i.e., without the dividend); before this date, the stock is sold with the dividend. The residual theory suggests that the dividend paid by a firm should be viewed as the amount left over after all acceptable investment opportunities have been undertaken. This theory seems to imply that dividends are irrelevant, a point that Modigliani and Miller prove using a number of very restrictive assumptions. Another school of thought indicates that dividends are relevant and have a very real effect on the value of a firm's stock. The expected level of dividends is an important input in the valuation process used throughout the text.

A firm's dividend policy is affected by legal, contractual, growth prospects, stock market behavior, and other factors. Generally stockholders prefer a relatively fixed or increasing level of dividends. Sometimes firms pay stock dividends, as either a replacement for or a supplement to cash dividends. Stock splits, which involve exchanging a specified number of new shares for a given number of outstanding shares, are used to change a firm's share price in order to enhance its trading activity. Firms sometimes make stock repurchases in order to retire outstanding shares of stock in lieu of paying cash dividends. Retiring shares increases earnings per share and the market price of outstanding shares.

CONCEPT OUTLINE

I.   **Equity capital has key characteristics that differentiate it from debt capital.**

    A. Equity can be raised internally or externally, debt is raised only externally.

    B. Unlike debt holders, equity holders are the owners of the business firm.

        1. Equity is permanent capital in the firm.

        2. Equity holders are more likely to receive voting rights than are suppliers of debt capital.

    C. Suppliers of equity capital receive a claim on income and assets that is secondary to the claims of the firm's creditors.

        1. The dividend claims of equity holders cannot be satisfied until all scheduled interest and principal payments are made to creditors.

        2. In liquidation, the equity holders must wait until all creditor claims are settled before they receive any distribution of assets.

    D. Dividends are not tax deductible, but interest is.

II.   **Common stockholders are the residual owners of a business firm, because they invest their money and receive a claim only on what is left after all other claims are satisfied.**

    A. The common stockholder is the owner who takes all the risk because of an agreement to be the last recipient of earnings.

    B. Ownership can be private, closely held, or public.

    C. Some common stock has a par value. Frequently stock is issued without a par value. State laws determine which is most advantageous.

    D. The number of shares authorized for issuance is given in the corporate charter, although not all issued shares may be outstanding. The firm can repurchase shares, which are then held as treasury stock.

    E. Common stockholders are normally given voting rights that can be used in electing directors and in special elections.

1. To minimize the loss of control and avoid takeover dangers, firms may issue stock with lower voting rights or nonvoting stock. The result is that current shareholders hold supervoting shares.

2. When different common stock classes exist, one class generally has more voting power and the other one class has preference in terms of dividend distributions.

3. Stockholders may sign proxies that give their votes to another party, who can vote them at the annual stockholders' meeting.

4. Sometimes dissident stockholders attempt to take over control of the firm through a proxy battle.

5. A firm may use a majority voting system or the more democratic cumulative voting system.

F. Firms typically pay dividends quarterly in cash, stock, or, rarely, in merchandise. Although not guaranteed, the possible rewards can be great.

G. Stock rights are an important tool of common stock financing that allows existing shareholders to purchase additional shares at a price below the prevailing market price.

1. Stock rights are primarily used by small companies, where proportionate control is a concern.

2. Preemptive rights permit existing shareholders to maintain their voting control by allowing them to avoid dilution of their ownership and earnings resulting from a new issue of common stock.

3. The use of rights to sell a new issue is attractive to the firm, because it can avoid various issuance costs. Additional administrative expense must be absorbed by the firm when a public issue of securities is made through an investment banker.

4. When a rights offering is made, the corporation sets a date of record, which is the last day a person can be the legal owner of the stock and receive the right.

5. Because of the lag in bookkeeping, stock sells ex rights four business days before the date of record; before that, the stock is said to sell cum rights or rights on.

6. The subscription price of the right is set below the market price, and, for each share, one right is generally given to purchase a fraction of a share.

7. Although a right has a certain theoretical value, it generally sells above this value in the marketplace because of the leverage provided.

8. Rights offerings may be made through underwriters or directly by the issuing company.

9. For a fee, underwriters will agree to purchase all shares not bought, thereby guaranteeing that the issue will not be undersubscribed. An oversubscription privilege gives interested shareholders the opportunity to buy rights not exercised by other shareholders.

H. Certain stated advantages and disadvantages of common stock financing are cited.

1. Advantages of common stock include the lack of a binding dividend requirement, absence of a maturity date, and that its issuance increases borrowing power.

2. Its key disadvantages are possible dilution, reduced earnings per share, a negative "overvalued" signal, and relatively high cost.

III. **Dividend policy is important to the firm's overall objective of shareholders' wealth maximization.**

A. Retained earnings must be viewed as a source of funds to the firm.

1. Paying them out as cash dividends results in a reduction of available cash.

2. The dividend decision must therefore be viewed as a financing decision, because it has direct effects on the firm's funds needs.

B. The firm's directors set and declare the cash dividend.

1. They set the date of record, which indicates that all stockholders on the firm's stock ledger on the given date will receive the declared dividend.

2. The stock begins to sell ex dividend (i.e., without the dividend), four business days before the date of record because of certain lags in bookkeeping.

3. Prior to the ex dividend date, the stock sells plus dividends, or cum dividends, which means that purchasers of the stock receive the dividend.

4. The actual payment date generally is set a few weeks after the date of record.

C. Stock reinvestment plans provide shareholders with an automatic way to convert cash dividends into outstanding shares or new issues.

D. Several schools of thought exist with respect to the relevance of dividends to the wealth of a firm's owners.

   1. The residual theory argues that cash dividends should be paid out only after all acceptable investments have been undertaken.

   2. Dividend irrelevance theory, proposed by Modigliani and Miller, uses very restrictive assumptions to assert that the actual dividend is immaterial.

      a. In a perfect world, only the firm's earnings power and riskiness matters.

      b. Stock prices react to dividend announcements because of the report's informational content.

      c. The clientele effect suggests that a firm attracts stockholders whose preferences regarding the pattern and stability of dividend payments align with those of the firm.

   3. Dividend relevance theory asserts that dividends received today are relevant and have a very real effect on the value of a firm's stock.

   4. Though theoretically unproven, financial managers and investors behave in a manner consistent with dividend relevance.

IV. **A firm's dividend policy is affected by a number of constraints and considerations.**

   A. Legal constraints generally prohibit paying out original capital, prohibit paying more dividends than the firm's present and past earnings, prohibit an insolvent or bankrupt firm from paying dividends, and prohibit firms from accumulating excess earnings in order to avoid taxes.

      1. These constraints do not prohibit the solvent firm from paying dividends in an amount greater than current earnings.

      2. The Internal Revenue Service often levies a special excess earnings tax on firms that accumulate excess earnings in an amount greater than $250,000.

   B. Contractual constraints normally result from certain loan covenants that may limit the firm's dividend payment.

C. The firm's dividend paying ability is generally constrained by the amount of excess cash available.

D. The firm's growth prospects, as they relate to the firm's forecasted financial requirements and expected funds availability, must be considered when establishing dividend policy.

E. The tax status of owners, their investment opportunities, and the possible dilution of ownership must also be considered when establishing dividend policy.

F. A very important consideration regarding dividend policy is the behavioral aspects of the securities markets.

     1. Investors generally favor a fixed or increasing level of dividend payments.

     2. Investors generally favor a continuous pattern of dividend payments. Hence, firms prefer to withhold dividend increases until they are sure that the new higher level can be maintained.

V. **There are three common types of dividend policies - the constant-payout-ratio dividend, the regular dividend, and the low-regular-and-extra dividend.**

A. The constant-payout-ratio dividend policy is one in which the firm pays out a fixed percentage of its earnings each period.

     1. The constant-payout-ratio dividend policy could result in a very volatile pattern of dividends.

     2. Volatile earnings result in owner uncertainty, which can cause stock prices to drop.

B. A regular dividend policy is one in which a regular fixed-dollar dividend is paid each period. The target dividend-payout ratio may be increased once a proven increase in earnings occurs.

C. The low-regular-and-extra dividend policy is one in which a constant dollar dividend is paid, but, when earnings warrant it, an extra dividend is paid.

     1. The use of the low regular-and-extra designation allows the firm to make the owners aware of the fact that they should not expect the extra amount each period.

     2. The regular dividend and the low-regular-and-extra dividend policies are preferable, because they provide owners with positive information and low levels of uncertainty.

VI.   **The key ways a firm can pay noncash dividends are with stock dividends, which have some similarity to stock splits, and with stock repurchases.**

    A. Firms often pay stock dividends as either a replacement for or supplement to cash dividends.

        1. In an accounting sense, the payment of stock dividends results in the capitalization of retained earnings.

        2. The payment of stock dividends really involves no cost other than administration, and the recipients actually receive nothing of value.

        3. Administrative costs are higher for stock dividends than for cash dividends.

    B. Although they are not a type of dividend, stock splits, which involve exchanging a specified number of new shares of a given number of outstanding shares, have a similar effect on a firm's share price as do stock dividends.

        1. Stock splits are used to enhance trading activity in a firm's shares, since they most often increase the number of shares outstanding (and lower the per-share price) while not providing any inflow of new capital.

        2. In the case of reverse stock splits a certain number of outstanding shares are exchanged for a new share.

        3. In an accounting sense, the stock split does not affect retained earnings; it merely results in a notational entry related to the number of shares and the par value, if any. The common stock account would still have the same value.

    C. Stock repurchases made to retire outstanding shares in lieu of paying cash dividends can be viewed as a dividend payment.

        1. Stock repurchase is often done to enhance firm value or hinder unfriendly takeovers.

        2. In an accounting sense, a stock repurchase increases the asset, treasury stock, which typically is shown as a deduction from stockholders' equity.

        3. By repurchasing shares, the firm distributes cash to owners by reducing the number of shares outstanding, thereby increasing the earnings and market price per share of outstanding stock.

4. After a stock repurchase, the remaining owners receive a capital gain as a result of the increased share price, instead of the dividend income they would receive from the payment of cash dividends.

5. If the Internal Revenue Service thinks a firm is using stock repurchases to pay dividends and avoid taxes, it will take appropriate action.

6. Stock repurchases are made either in the open market, through the use of tender offers, or by arranging to purchase a large block of shares from one or more large stockholders.

APPLICATIONS

DEFINITIONS

1. _Privately owned_ stock is held by a single individual, while _closely held_ - stock is held by a small group of investors.

2. The authorized stock, or shares that a firm is allowed to issue, is stated in the _corporate charter_.

3. _Issued_ stock represents the shares made available to the investing public.

4. The number of shares issued less the number of shares outstanding results in the number of _treasury_ shares held by a firm.

5. Firms wishing to raise equity capital but not willing to relinquish voting control may issue _non-voting_ common stock.

6. Stockholders not attending the annual meeting may transfer their votes to a representative through a _proxy_ statement.

7. The one share, one vote rule is found in a _majority_ voting system.

8. _Preemptive_ rights are designed to eliminate the chance of _dilution_ of ownership when additional shares are issued.

9. Management may use stock _options_ to purchase a certain number of shares at a specified price.

10. The _ex dividend_ day is four business days before the date of record.

11. _Dividend_ _reinvestment_ plans enable stockholders to use dividends to acquire additional shares.

12. According to the _dividend_ _relevance_ theory, investors prefer certain dividends today to uncertain future dividends.

13. The IRS may level an _excess earning accumulation_ tax when the firm's is allowing owners to delay paying ordinary income taxes.

14. A _regular dividend_ policy consists of paying a fixed dollar dividend each period.

15. In a _reverse_ split investors will receive less shares than previously owned.

MULTIPLE CHOICE

1. Equity capital differs from debt because equity:
    a. has a claim on assets that has priority over debt.
    b. is permanent financing and debt is not.
    c. is tax deductible, while debt interest is not.
    d. two of the above.

2. Which of the following will always be the maximum number of corporation shares.
    a. authorized shares
    b. outstanding shares
    c. issued shares
    d. treasury shares

3. In order to maintain control, a firm should not issue:
    a. class A income-reference stock.
    b. nonvoting shares.
    c. normal common shares.
    d. supervoting shares.

4. A system of voting for directors which gives minority shareholders an opportunity to elect at least some directors is called:
    a. cumulative voting.
    b. majority rights.
    c. one man, one vote.
    d. proxy voting.

5.   A firm has issued rights and it will take nine rights to purchase a share of stock at the subscription price of $20. The stock is selling rights on for $24. What is the theoretical value of a right?

$$24 - 20 \over 10 = {4 \over 10} = .40$$

   a.) $ .40.
   b. $ .44.
   c. $2.00.
   d. $2.40.

6.   Because rights have very low value:
   a. most investors just throw them away.
   b. their value is less than transaction cost.
   c. they are rarely used in a new issue of common equity.
   d. none of the above.

7.   In order to be eligible for stock rights or stock dividends, the stock must be held:
   a. 5 business days before the date of record.
   b. 4 business days before the date of record.
   c. on the date of record.
   d. 4 business days after the date of record.

8.   A (an) _____ privilege gives interested shareholders the opportunity to buy a pro rata share of unexercised shares.
   a. broker
   b. oversubscription
   c. standby
   d. undersubscription

9.   Among the disadvantages of common equity financing are that it causes a:
   a. minimum of constraints on management.
   b. potential dilution of ownership.
   c. it can increase the firm's ability to use debt.
   d. all of the above.

10.   Initial public offerings are regulated by the:
   a. Federal Bureau of Investigation.
   b. Internal Revenue Service.
   c. Interstate Commerce Commission.
   d. Securities and Exchange Commission.

11.　　According to the residual theory of dividends:
　　　　a. dividends are irrelevant.
　　　　b. dividends are relevant.
　　　　c. dividends will always be paid.
　　　　d. two of the above.

12.　　Dividend irrelevance is based upon the assumption that:
　　　　a. firm value is a function of earnings and risk.
　　　　b. dividend impacts of stock prices are surrogating for an informational effect.
　　　　c. in the long run, clienteles obtain the dividend stream they desire, making interim changes irrelevant.
　　　　d. all of the above.

13.　　Important considerations in establishing a dividend policy include:
　　　　a. excess cash available.
　　　　b. legal constraints.
　　　　c. tax status of the owners.
　　　　d. all of the above.

14.　　Enhancement of shareholder value through stock repurchases is achieved by all of the following except:
　　　　a. increasing earnings per share.
　　　　b. increasing the number of shares outstanding.
　　　　c. sending a signal that the stock is underpriced.
　　　　d. providing a floor for stock with declining prices.

15.　　In a negotiated stock repurchase, stock is obtained:
　　　　a. from all investors.
　　　　b. from major stockholders.
　　　　c. from anyone responding to a tender offer.
　　　　d. in the stock market.

PROBLEMS

1.　　The Exciting Service Corporation is in the process of electing six new directors to its board. The company has 3500 shares of common stock outstanding. The management controls 62 percent of these shares and is backing candidates A through F, while the minority shareholders are backing candidates G through L.

a. If the firm uses a majority voting system, how many directors could each group elect?

b. If the firm uses a cumulative voting system, how many directors could each group elect?

c. Discuss the differences between these two voting systems and their outcomes.

2.   The Reddy Manufacturing Company wishes to raise $2,000,000 in new equity capital through a rights offering. The firm currently has 200,000 shares of common stock outstanding. The firm plans to set a subscription price of $50 per share and expects the stock to sell for $53 with the rights on.

a. Calculate the number of shares the firm must sell in order to raise the desired amount of funds.

b. How many shares will each right entitle each shareholder to purchase?

c. If Sandy Roberts holds 10,000 shares of Reddy's stock, how many additional shares can he purchase?

d. Determine the theoretical value of the rights when the stock is selling both rights on and ex rights.

e. Approximately how much could Sandy Roberts sell his rights for immediately after the stock goes ex rights? Explain.

f. If the date of record for Reddy's rights was Thursday, February 10, on what days would the stock sell rights on and ex rights?

3.   On July 15, the directors of Big Mama's Pizza, declared a dividend of $1 per share, to be paid on August 30 to all holders of record on Friday, August 15. The firm currently has $150,000 in cash and 100,000 shares of common stock outstanding. Its retained earnings total $500,000.

a. Show the entries and affected accounts after the July 15 dividend declaration.

b. What is the largest per-share dividend that the firm could legally pay?

c. What is the largest per-share dividend that they could actually pay now without borrowing?

d. On what day would the stock first sell ex dividend?

e. After payment of the dividend, what would the firm's accounts be? What effect, if any, would the dividend have on total assets?

4.   Hai Enterprises is considering using the residual theory of dividends to establish its
        dividend payment for 1992. The firm's estimated earnings after taxes (available retained
        earnings) for 1992 are $1,200,000. The IOS and WMCC ranges are as follows, and the
        firm's target weight for common equity is 50 percent.

Investment ($000s)	IOS	Range (000s)	Cost of Capital
$ 200	18 %	$ 0 to $500	10 %
$ 800	16 %	$501 to $1250	11 %
$ 600	14 %	$1,251 to $2,000	12 %
$ 400	13 %	$2,001 to $2,500	15 %
$ 200	10 %	$2,501 and over	20 %
$ 600	8 %		
$1,400	6 %		

        If the firm uses the residual theory, what level of cash dividends will the firm pay out?

5.   A firm has had the following earnings per share over the 1984-1992 period:

Year	Earnings per share
1984	1.50
1985	1.00
1986	.80
1987	1.20
1988	1.30
1989	1.60
1990	1.10
1991	.90
1992	1.60

a. If the firm's dividend policy is based on a constant payout ratio of 50 percent for all years with positive earnings, determine the annual dividend paid in each year.

b. If the firm has a regular dividend policy of paying $.60 per share per year, regardless of the per-share earnings, until the per-share earnings remain above $1.20 for two periods, at which time the dividend would be increased to $.80 per share, determine the annual dividend paid in each year.

c. If the firm's policy is to pay out $.20 per share each period, except in those periods when earnings are above $1.00, when they would pay out an extra dividend equal to 30 percent of the earnings above $1.00, determine the amount of regular and extra dividends paid each year.

d. Compare and comment on the results of parts a through c.

6. The Carney Corporation has 100,000 shares of common stock outstanding. The stock is currently selling in the marketplace for $50 per share. The firm, which has earnings of $250,000 available for common stockholders, intends to retain these earnings and pay, instead, a 5 percent stock dividend. This action is deemed necessary because of the firm's desperate need for funds to overhaul certain items of equipment. The firm's stockholders' equity, which includes current earnings, is as follows:

Preferred stock	$ 600,000
Common stock (100,000 shares @ $2 par)	200,000
Paid in capital in excess of par	2,800,000
Retained earnings	900,000
Stockholders' equity	$4,500,000

a. Show the resulting entries in the stockholders' equity account from the proposed 5 percent stock dividend.

b. How would the effect of the payment of a cash dividend on the stockholders' equity differ from the results found in part a?

c. How much did the firm earn per share?

d. If Chuck Black owns 1000 share of stock in Hai, what proportion of the firm does he own?

e. What proportion of the firm would Chuck Black own after the 5 percent stock dividend?

f. What would you expect the market price of a share to be after payment of the stock dividend?

g. What would the firm's earnings per share be after the stock dividend?

7.   The Southern Chair Company's stockholders' equity account currently appears as follows:

Common stock (300,000 shares @ $1 par)	$ 300,000
Paid in capital in excess of par	11,700,000
Retained earnings	2,000,000
Stockholders' equity	$15,000,000

    a. Indicate the changes, if any, expected to result if the firm declares a 4-for-1 stock
        split.
    b. Indicate the changes, if any, expected to result if the firm declares a 1-for-2 reverse
        stock split.

8.   York Company has $300,000 of earnings available for common stock and has 100,000
      shares outstanding at $40 per share. The firm is currently contemplating a dividend
      payment of $1.50 per share.
    a. Calculate the firm's current earnings per share and price-earnings ratio.
    b. If the firm's stock is expected to sell at $41.50 per share with dividends on, and the
        firm could repurchase shares at this price, how many shares could be purchased
        in lieu of the proposed cash dividend payout.
    c. How much would the earnings per share be after the proposed repurchase?
    d. Compare and contrast the earnings per share and the market price per share both
        before and after the proposed stock repurchase, assuming that the firm's price-
        earnings ratio remains at its current level (found in part a).
    e. How do the balance sheet effects of the stock repurchase differ from those of a cash
        dividend payment?

SOLUTIONS

DEFINITIONS

1.   Privately-owned; closely-held
2.   corporate charter
3.   Issued
4.   treasury
5.   nonvoting
6.   proxy

7.   majority
8.   Preemptive; dilution
9.   options
10. ex dividend
11. Dividend reinvestment
12. dividend relevance
13. excess earnings accumulation
14. regular dividend
15. reverse

MULTIPLE CHOICE

1. b	6. d	11. a
2. a	7. a	12. d
3. d	8. b	13. d
4. b	9. b	14. b
5. a {(24-20) ÷ 10}	10. d	15. b

PROBLEMS

1.   a. Because, under a majority voting system, each share can be voted for each director being elected, the majority shareholders would control 62 percent of the votes and can elect the directors they choose (i.e., A through F).

b. If the firm used a cumulative voting system, the number of shares needed to elect a given number of directors can be calculated using the following formula:

$$N = \frac{O \ X \ D}{T + 1} + 1$$

where N = number of shares needed to elect director(s)
       O = total number of shares of common stock outstanding
       D = number of directors desired
       T = total number of directors to be elected

Substituting O = 3500 and T = 6, the number of votes needed to elect one to six directors can be calculated. It takes 500 votes per director plus one. The results are as follows:

Number of directors	Number of votes needed to elect
1	501
2	1001
3	1501
4	2001
5	2501
6	3001

Because the minority stockholders have only 38 percent of the votes (100% - 62%), they have 1330 votes (.38 X 3500), which will permit them to elect two directors. The majority shareholders, who control the other 2170 votes, can elect the other four directors.

    c. The cumulative voting system is obviously fairer, because it gives the minority stockholders some voice in management. In this case, they can elect two of the six directors, whereas, under the majority voting system, they cannot elect any directors.

2.   a. If the firm wishes to raise $2,000,000 and each share will be sold for $50, it will have to issue 40,000 new shares ($2,000,000 ÷ $50/share).

    b. Because there are 200,000 shares outstanding and 40,000 additional shares will be issued, each right would entitle its holder to purchase one-fifth of a share (40,000 shares ÷ 200,000 shares) at the subscription price.

    c. If Mr. Roberts holds 10,000 shares of stock, he will receive 10,000 rights, each allowing him to purchase one-fifth of a share. In total, therefore, he could purchase 2000 shares (1/5 X 10,000 shares).

    d. The theoretical value of a right with rights on, R_o, can be found by substituting into the following formula:

$$R_o = (M_o - S) \div (N + 1)$$

where R_o =   theoretical value of a right when stock is selling rights on
              M_o =   market value of stock with rights on
              S   =   subscription price of the stock
              N   =   number of rights needed to purchase one share

Substituting M_o = $53, S = $50, and N = 5 into the formula, we obtain the theoretical value of a right with stock selling rights on: $.50 [($53-$50) ÷ (5+1)].

When the stock sells ex rights, the theoretical value of the stock selling ex rights, M_e, can be found using the following equation:

$$M_e = M_o - R_o$$

Substituting M_o = $53 and R_o = $.50 yields:

$$M_e = \$53 - \$.50 = \$52.50$$

The formula for the theoretical value of a right when the stock is selling ex rights is:

$$R_e = (M_e - S) \div N$$

Substituting M_e = $52.50, S = $50, and N = 5 yields the theoretical value when the stock is selling ex rights: $.50 [($52.50 - $50) ÷ 5].

e.   S. Roberts should be able to sell each right for at least its theoretical value of $.50. Because he has 10,000 rights, he should be able to get $5,000 ($.50 X 10,000). Generally, the rights would be selling above their theoretical value, and therefore, it is expected that he would get more than $5,000.

f.   If the date of record was Thursday, February 10, the stock would first sell ex rights four business days earlier. Because of the weekend, the first date the stock sells ex rights would be Friday, February 4. Before Friday, February 4, the stock would be selling with rights on.

3.   a.   When the dividend of $1 per share, or a total payment of $100,000, is declared (i.e., $1/share X 100,000 shares), the firm's retained earnings would be reduced, cash would be unaffected, and a current liability - dividends payable - would be created. Total assets would not change at this point.

b.   Legally, the firm could pay out no more than all earnings retained, which would be $500,000. Because 100,000 shares are outstanding, the largest dividend per share would be $5 (i.e., $500,000 ÷ 100,000 shares).

c.   The firm has only $150,000 in cash for paying dividends, and it is therefore internally constrained. Because 100,000 shares are outstanding, the maximum dividend per share is $1.50 (i.e., $150,000 ÷ 100,000 shares).

d.   Because a stock goes ex dividend four business days before the date of record, Big Mama's Pizza stock would go ex dividend on Monday, August 11. Before this date, the stock would have sold with dividends on.

e.   After the dividend is paid, the firm's cash and dividends payable would be affected. Cash would equal $50,000, Dividends payable would equal $ 0, and Retained earnings would still equal $400,00. The payment of the $100,000 in cash dividends would reduce the firm's total assets and liabilities and stockholders' equity by $100,000.

4.   You can either graph the IOS and WMCC ranges or carefully review the data to determine the level of capital expenditure.

The first $2,000,000 of investment offers returns of 13 %, or more. Over this range the cost of capital is 12 % or less. The next dollar will offer a return of 10% and cost 15%. Hence, the optimal level of capital expenditure is $2,000,000.

Next, multiply the capital expenditure by the weight for common equity to determine the needed equity.

$2,000,000 X .5 = $1,000,000 needed equity

Finally, compare available retained earnings (forecast for 1992) to needed equity.

$1,200,000 - $1,000,000 = $200,000

Thus, $200,000 is available to be paid in cash dividends.

5.   a. If the firm paid out 50 percent of each year's earnings in years with positive earnings, the dividends paid per share (DPS) would be as follows:

Year	1984	1985	1986	1987	1988	1989	1990	1991	1992
DPS	$.75	$.50	$.40	$.60	$.65	$.80	$.55	$.45	$.80

   b. If the firm paid out a fixed $.60 per share until earnings were above $1.20 for two years, at which time they raised the dividend to $.80 per share, the dividends paid would be as follows:

Year	1984	1985	1986	1987	1988	1989	1990	1991	1992
DPS	$.60	$.60	$.60	$.60	$.60	$.80	$.80	$.80	$.80

   c. If the firm paid a regular dividend of $.20 per share each period, except in those periods when earnings were above $1.00, when they paid out an extra dividend equal to 30 percent of the earnings above $1.00, the regular (RDPS), extra (EDPS), and total dividends per share (TDPS) per year would be as follows:

Year	1984	1985	1986	1987	1988	1989	1990	1991	1992
RDPS	$.20	$.20	$.20	$.20	$.20	$.20	$.20	$.20	$.20
EDPS	$.15	$.00	$.00	$.06	$.09	$.18	$.03	$.00	$.18
TDPS	$.35	$.20	$.20	$.26	$.29	$.38	$.23	$.20	$.38

   d. By comparing the dividend patterns in parts a, b, and c, it can be seen that both the regular policy of part b and the low-regular-and-extra policy of part c provide much positive information. Although the range in part c, $.18 ($.38 - $.20), is not as great as that found in part a, $.40 ($.80 - $.40), it still is a substantial percentage of the lowest total dividend payment. The low-regular-and-extra policy provides the lowest total dividend payment, and, hence, the highest level of retained earnings.

6.   a.   As a result of the stock dividend of 5 percent, the firm will issue an additional 5000 shares (i.e., .05 X 100,000 shares). On the books, the firm would capitalize an amount of retained earnings equal to the product of the prevailing share price and the number of new shares issued. In this case, that would be $250,000 (i.e., 5000 shares X $50/share). Of this $250,000, an amount equal to the par value of the stock times the number of new shares issued would be placed in common stock, and the remaining portion would be moved into paid-in capital in excess of par. In this case, $10,000 (i.e., $2/share par X 5000 shares) would be moved to common stock, and $240,000 (i.e., $250,000 - $10,000) would be moved to paid-in capital in excess of par. The resulting stockholders' equity account is as follows:

Preferred stock	$ 600,000
Common stock (105,000 shares @ $2 par)	210,000
Paid in capital in excess of par	3,040,000
Retained earnings	650,000
Stockholders' equity	$4,500,000

  b.   If the firm pays a cash dividend, the firm's stockholders' equity would be reduced by the amount of the cash dividend, as a result of a reduction in retained earnings. When a stock dividend is paid, retained earnings are shifted to other equity accounts - common stock and paid-in capital in excess of par.

  c.   If the firm has $250,000 of earnings available for common stock and has 100,000 shares of common stock outstanding, earnings per share would be $2.50 (i.e., $250,000 ÷ 100,000 shares).

  d.   If Chuck Black owns 1,000 of the 100,000 shares of Hai stock outstanding, he would own 1 percent of the firm (i.e., 1,000 shares ÷ 100,000).

  e.   After the stock dividend of 5 percent, Chuck would have 1,050 shares [i.e., 1000 shares + (.05 X 1000 shares)]. After the stock dividend, the firm would have an added 5 percent of shares outstanding, which would be 105,000 shares (i.e., 1.05 X 100,000 shares). Because Chuck Black would own 1,050 of these 105,000 shares, he would still own 1 percent of the firm (i.e. , 1,050 shares ÷ 105,000 shares).

f. Because the firm's pre-stock-dividend share price is $50 and it has 100,000 shares outstanding, its value is $5,000,000 (i.e., $50/share X 100,000 shares). There is no reason for this value to change as a result of the stock dividend; all that changes is the number of shares outstanding. After the stock dividend, 105,000 shares will be outstanding, but the firm's total value will still be $5,000,000, and the price per share should be approximately $47.62 (i.e., $5,000,000 ÷ 105,000 shares).

g. Because 105,000 shares would have a claim on the $250,000 of earnings available for common stock, the after-stock-dividend earnings per share would be $2.38 (i.e., $250,000 ÷ 105,000 shares). The stock dividend does not represent the distribution of anything the stockholder didn't already own.

7. a. If the firm declares a 4-for-1 stock split, the only entry to change in the stockholders' equity account would be common stock. It would become

(1,200,000 shares @ $0.25 par) = $300,000

The price of the stock in the marketplace initially would be one-fourth of the previous price, and there would be four times as many shares outstanding.

b. If a 1-for-2 reverse stock split were declared, the common stock entry in the stockholders' equity account would become

(150,000 shares @ $2 par) = $300,000

The price of the stock in the marketplace initially would double, and there would be half as many shares outstanding.

8. a. Currently, the firm's earnings per share would be $3 ($300,000 ÷ 100,000 shares). The firm's current price-earnings ratio would be 13.33 ($40/share ÷ $3 share).

b. The proposed cash dividend payment of $1.50 per share on 100,000 shares would involve an outlay of $150,000. Spending this $150,000 repurchasing shares at $41.50 each would allow the firm to repurchase approximately 3615 shares ($150,000 ÷ $41.50/share).

c. After the stock repurchase, the firm would have 96,385 shares outstanding (100,000 shares - 3,615 shares) and, if earnings available for common stock are $300,000, the earnings per share would be approximately $3.11 ($300,000 ÷ 96,385 shares).

d. It can be seen that, as a result of the stock repurchase, the firm's earnings per share would increase from $3 to $3.11, because there would be fewer shares outstanding. If the firm's stock continues to sell at the pre-repurchase price-earnings ratio of 13.33 (found in part a), the price of the stock would be approximately $41.46 ($3.11/share X 13.33). This increase in share price from $40 to $41.46 is also attributable to the fact that fewer shares would be outstanding. It should be noted that, except for a slight rounding error, the after-repurchase share price of $41.46 equals the share price of the stock with dividends on ($41.50/share). A stock repurchase is therefore another way of paying dividends. The real payoff comes in the sense that the stockholder does not have dividends on which to pay taxes but rather has a capital gain on which taxes would have to be paid only if the stock were sold.

e. The stock repurchase reduces the firm's stockholders' equity by the amount of treasury stock purchased, and its cash account is reduced by an equivalent amount. When a cash dividend is paid, cash would be reduced; however, instead of having treasury stock, the firm's outstanding shares would remain unchanged, while its retained earnings would be reduced by the amount of the cash dividend.

CHAPTER 15

PREFERRED STOCK, LEASING, CONVERTIBLES, WARRANTS, AND OPTIONS

SUMMARY

Preferred stockholders are given certain privileges that make them senior to common stockholders. Preferred stockholders must be paid all dividends owed before common stockholders are paid, and they usually receive payment in liquidation before common stockholders. The preferred stockholder normally is not given voting rights. Some people consider preferred stock a type of quasi-debt, because it has a fixed return (i.e., dividend) similar to a debt, but it is permanent ownership capital. A recent innovation is adjustable rate preferred stock in which the dividend rate adjusts to changes in a market index such as a U.S. government bond index.

When preferred stock is issued, a contract is created that specifies the issuer's obligations and various covenants. The common types of covenants concern passing preferred stock dividends; selling senior securities; mergers, consolidations, and sales of assets; working capital minimums; and constraints on common stock dividends and repurchases. Preferred stock can be cumulative, which provides for payment of all past dividends; participating, which allows the preferred stockholder to receive more dividends than the amount stated; callable, which allows the issuer to retire the preferred stock; or convertible, which allows the holder to exchange the preferred stock for common stock. Firms often retire outstanding preferred stock either on a planned basis or as part of a refinancing, or recapitalization, program. The advantages of preferred stock include its ability to give the firm added leverage, the financial flexibility it provides, and its use in mergers and consolidations. The disadvantages are the seniority of the preferred claim and the cost of preferred stock, which is generally above the cost of debt.

The two basic types of leases are operating leases and financial or capital leases. Operating leases are short-term, cancelable leases typically written for periods of time shorter than the asset's life. Financial or capital leases are long-term, noncancelable leases typically written for a period of time over which the total payment is often greater than the cost of the leased asset. It is the noncancelable feature that gives the financial lease the characteristics of long-term financing. Financial leases can be made either as direct leases, on a sale-leaseback basis, or as leveraged leases. The direct lease results when a lessor owns or acquires the assets that are leased; under the sale-leaseback arrangements, the leased assets are purchased from the lessee by the lessor then leased back to the lessee. Leveraged leases include one or more third-party lenders.

The lease-purchase, or lease-buy, decision requires that the cash outflows associated with each financing alternative be calculated, and that the stream of cash outflows that has the minimum present value (i.e., cost) be selected. The cash outflows are discounted at the after-tax cost of debt, because both leasing and borrowing are viewed as equally risky contractual obligations.

Because leasing is really a source of financing, any evaluation of a firm's financial position must consider the presence of any leases. The lessee firm is required by certain opinions of the Financial Accounting Standards Board (FASB) to disclose the existence of leases in its financial statements. For financial (or capital) leases, FASB Standard No. 13 requires and outlines detailed procedures for capitalization of the lease commitment as an asset and corresponding liability. For operating leases, a footnote to the firm's financial statements is required, indicating the key features of the lease. If a lease obligation is not capitalized, the calculation of various financial ratios, will provide misleading conclusions regarding the lessee's leverage and profitability.

The commonly cited advantages of leasing are the ability to depreciate land effectively, the increased liquidity leasing can provide, the ability to get 100 percent financing, the treatment of lease payments in bankruptcy and reorganization, the general lack of many restrictive covenants, and the flexibility provided by this financing alternative. The disadvantages of leasing are said to be its high interest cost, lack of salvage value, difficulty in making property improvements, and possible obsolescence risk.

A convertible bond represents a debt security that can be converted into a specified number of shares of common stock at some future time. The bond value of a convertible is the price at which a nonconvertible (or straight) bond would sell in the market. It is found by discounting the interest payments on the convertible security at the market rate of return for a straight security. The stock (or conversion) value of a convertible security is the value of the security measured in terms of the common stock into which it is convertible. The market value of a convertible security is normally above its straight value and conversion value, and the premium associated with this difference is called the market premium of the convertible.

A conversion feature, which can be included as part of a bond or preferred stock issue, permits the holder of the security to convert it into preferred or common stock. This feature, which increases a security's marketability, most commonly provides for conversion into common stock. Convertibles have a stated conversion ratio, which specifies the rate at which the convertible security can be exchanged. Given the number of shares, the conversion price can be found by dividing the conversion ratio into the security's face, or stated, value. The conversion period, representing the life of the conversion privilege, extends for a specific period of time during the life of the convertible security.

Convertibles are often used as a form of deferred common stock financing. The conversion feature is often used as a sweetener to make a bond issue more salable. Convertible financing is cheaper than using a straight security, because the conversion feature provides lenders with a means to acquire the firm's common stock. All convertibles have a call feature, which allows the issuer to encourage conversion if needed. When it is not feasible to force conversion, although the firm wishes to do so, the issue is said to be overhanging.

Stock purchase warrants are similar to stock rights. Both instruments give holders an option to purchase a certain number of common stock shares at a specified price, known as the exercise price. The exercise or option price of a warrant may increase over time, but it is initially set near the prevailing market price. Warrants may have a limited life, and are often listed and traded on stock exchanges and in the over-the-counter market. They are often attached to debt or preferred stock issues as a sweetener to enhance the salability of these claims. They provide the purchaser with a deferred equity interest in the firm. Warrants differ from convertibles in that their exercise decreases leverage by bringing in new equity capital to the firm; conversion only shifts the existing capital structure to a less highly levered position.

An option is a security which gives its holder the opportunity (choice) to purchase or sell another asset at a specified price on or before a specified expiration date. Rights, warrants, calls and puts are different forms of option securities. Individuals can buy or write calls and puts on common stock. Options are not used to obtain new financing for the firm, but they are important to financial managers because activity in the options market is related to activity in the stock market.

CONCEPT OUTLINE

I.   Preferred stock is like debt in that it has a stated dividend that is given priority over common stock dividends, and like equity in that it is a form of ownership with no maturity date.

    A.   Par value preferred stock has a stated face value, while no-par preferred stock does not have a stated face value.

    B.   Most preferred stock has a fixed dividend, but some firms issue adjustable rate preferred stock that adjusts the dividend payment with changes in interest rates.

        1.   The dividend may be stated as a percentage of the par value, or face value, of the preferred stock.

        2.   Sometimes the annual preferred dividend is stated as a fixed dollar amount.

        3.   Payment-in-kind preferred stock does not pay a cash dividend, but does pay a dividend in the form of additional shares of preferred stock.

    C.   Preferred stockholders receive certain basic rights with respect to voting and earnings and asset distributions.

        1.   Preferred stockholders are given a claim on income senior to that of common stockholders.

2. Preferred stockholders also have preference over common stockholders in the liquidation of the firm's assets.

3. The preferred stockholder normally does not receive any voting rights because of this senior payment position.

D. Preferred stock has a number of important features.

1. When preferred stock is issued, a contract is often included containing certain covenants on such items as passing preferred stock dividends; selling senior securities; mergers, consolidations, and sale of assets; working capital minimums; and constraints on common stock dividends and repurchases.

2. Violation of any of the covenants by the firm provides certain recourse to the preferred stockholders.

3. Preferred stock is often cumulative, which means that all dividends in arrears must be paid to the preferred stockholder before dividends are paid to common stockholders.

4. Occasionally, preferred stock is participating, which means that the preferred stockholder is given an opportunity to receive more dividends than the amount stated.

5. Preferred stock often has a call feature, which allows the owner to retire outstanding shares.

6. Preferred stock can be convertible into a specified number of shares of common stock at the preferred stockholders' option.

7. Firms often retire outstanding preferred stock either on a planned basis or as part of a refinancing, or recapitalization, program.

E. Certain advantages and disadvantages for the use of preferred stock financing are often cited.

1. Advantages of preferred stock include the ability to increase leverage because of the fixed dividend payment, the financial flexibility it provides, and its use in mergers and consolidations.

2. Disadvantages to the firm's common stockholders include the seniority of the preferred claim, the high cost of preferred stock, and the difficulty that investors face in attempting to resell their preferred stock investments.

II.   **Financial leases represent noncancelable long-term financing arrangements under which firms can obtain the use of certain assets in exchange for a series of lease payments.**

   A.   The lessee is the recipient of the assets provided in the lease contract, while the lessor is the owner of the assets.

   B.   The two basic types of lease contracts are the operating lease and the financial lease.

      1.   The operating lease is generally a short-term, cancelable arrangement in which the total lease payments generally are less than the cost of the asset.

      2.   The financial or capital lease is a noncancelable, long-term arrangement under which the total payments are greater than the cost of the leased asset.

      3.   The noncancelable feature of the financial lease makes it similar to a long-term debt, and it is therefore viewed as a source of long-term financing.

   C.   A number of different types of leasing arrangements are possible.

      1.   A direct lease results when the lessor either owns or acquires the assets.

      2.   A sale-leaseback arrangement is one in which the lessor purchases assets already owned by the lessee, and leases them back to the lessee.

      3.   Leveraged leases include one or more third-party lenders who provide financing to the lessor.

      4.   Operating leases generally include maintenance provisions, while financial leases normally do not.

      5.   Renewal options are most common in operating leases, although they are occasionally included in financial leases.

      6.   A lessor could be an equipment manufacturer, an independent leasing company, or a financial institution such as a bank or insurance company.

   D.   The lessor and lessee normally sign a lease contract that outlines all the provisions and requirements for each party.

   E.   The lease-purchase, or lease-buy, decision is one that commonly confronts firms contemplating the acquisition of new fixed assets.

1.   The lease-purchase decision is analyzed by determining the cash outflows associated with the lease and the buy (the buy alternative assumes that the firm must borrow to make the purchase), and determining which project has the lowest present value of cash outflows.

2.   The cash outflows associated with the lease can be determined by subtracting the tax savings expected in each year of the lease from the amount of the lease payment.

3.   The cash outflows associated with the purchase option require deducting the tax shields resulting from the interest on borrowing and depreciation in each year of the borrowing transaction from the loan payment.

4.   The alternative that has the minimum present value of cash outflows is preferred.

    a.   All cash outflows are discounted at the after-tax cost of debt, because both leasing and borrowing are considered equally risky contractual obligations of the firm.

    b.   By using the after-tax cost of debt, only the costs of a contractual obligation are considered.

F.   Because leasing can be considered a type of financing, its effects on future financing must be considered.

1.   The lessee firm is required by certain opinions of the Financial Accounting Standards Board (FASB) of the AICPA to disclose the existence of leases on its financial statements.

2.   In the case of financial (or capital) leases, FASB Standard No. 13 requires and outlines detailed procedures for capitalization of the lease commitment as an asset and corresponding liability.

3.   For operating leases, a footnote to the firm's financial statements is required, indicating the key features of the lease.

4.   If a lease obligation is not capitalized, the calculation of various financial ratios, such as debt-equity, times interest earned, total asset turnover, and return on investment, will provide somewhat misleading conclusions regarding the lessee's leverage and profitability.

5.   The capitalization of financial leases required by Standard No. 13 provides for a balance sheet that more accurately reflects the true financial condition of the lessee.

G.   A number of advantages and disadvantages of leasing as a source of financing can be cited.

1.   The key advantages of leasing are the ability to depreciate land effectively, the increased liquidity it can provide, the ability to get 100 percent financing, the treatment of lease payments in bankruptcy, the general lack of many restrictive covenants, and the flexibility provided.

2.   The disadvantages of leasing are said to be its high interest cost, lack of salvage value, difficulty in making property improvements, and possible obsolescence risk.

III.   **Convertible securities give their holders the right to convert the debt or preferred stock they own into a specified number of common stock shares.**

A.   Because the conversion feature provides investors with an option not available to holders of nonconvertible securities, the conversion feature normally increases the marketability of a security.

B.   The conversion ratio specifies the terms at which convertible securities can be exchanged for common stock.

1.   If the conversion ratio is stated as a certain number of shares, the conversion price can be found by dividing the conversion ratio into the face value of the security.

2.   If the conversion price is known, the number of shares can be found by dividing the conversion price into the security's face value.

D.   Convertibles often are in effect for only a specified conversion period.

1.   Sometimes the conversion period is delayed, not beginning until a certain number of years after the security's issue date.

2.   Sometimes, as a way of forcing conversion, the conversion price will be scheduled to increase during the conversion period.

E.   The conversion value is the value of the security measured in terms of the security into which it may be converted.

F.   The conversion premium, which is the percentage difference between the conversion price and the issuance price, is initially set in the range of 10 to 20 percent.

G.   Convertibles may be issued for a number of possible reasons.

   1.   Sometimes convertibles are used as a form of deferred equity financing.

   2.   The conversion feature is often used as a sweetener to make the firm's securities more attractive to investors.

   3.   Convertibles can be used to raise cheap funds temporarily, and later shift the issuing firm's capital structure as investors exercise their conversion option.

H.   All convertible securities have a call feature, which gives issuing firms the option to retire these securities at a specified price.

   1.   This feature encourages conversion to common stock, because investors who fail to convert their securities must return their bonds to the issuer.

   2.   A convertible security that cannot be forced into conversion using the call feature is known as an overhanging issue.

I.   The bond value of a convertible security is the price at which a straight bond would sell in the marketplace.

   1.   This value is found by discounting the interest cash flows of the convertible at the rate for a straight security.

   2.   The straight value of a convertible is considered to be a floor, or lower limit, for its market price.

   3.   This floor would be affected only by changes in certain firm or capital market factors.

J.   The stock, or conversion, value of a convertible is the value of the security measured in terms of the common stock into which it can be converted.

K.   The market value of a convertible is generally above both its straight and its conversion value.

   1.   The straight value tends to act as a floor.

2. The market premium, or the amount by which the market price of a convertible exceeds its straight or conversion value, is largest when the market price of common stock is near the conversion price.

3. The market premium exists because of certain speculative characteristics of the convertible security.

IV. **Stock purchase warrants, which give their holders an option to purchase a certain number of common stock shares at a specified price over a certain period of time, are often attached as an enhancement to a corporate debt issue.**

A. Warrants are similar to stock rights as they give the holder an option to purchase stock.

B. Warrants are often attached to debt as a sweetener.

1. Warrants are attractive to purchasers, because they provide a deferred common stock interest in the firm.

2. Warrants differ from convertibles in that their exercise decreases leverage by bringing in new equity capital, while convertibles only shift the existing capital structure of the issuer to a less highly levered position.

C. The price at which warrant holders can purchase a specified number of common stock shares is known as the exercise price or option price.

1. The exercise or option price of warrants may increase over time in order to provide the incentive to exercise them.

2. The exercise price usually is set 10 to 20 percent above the prevailing market price of the firm's stock.

3. Warrants may have a limited life, and are often separately listed on the organized security exchanges and in the over-the-counter market.

D. The implied price of a warrant, found by subtracting the value of the firm's bonds without the warrant attached from the value of the firm's bonds containing a warrant, represents the effective price for a warrant.

E. The theoretical value of a warrant, or TVW, represents the amount investors would expect the warrant to sell for in the marketplace. The theoretical value is:

$$TVW = (P_0 - E) \times N$$

where P_0 = the current market price per share of the firm's common stock;

E = the warrant's exercise price; and

N = the number of shares of common stock that can be obtained with one warrant.

F.   The market value of a warrant is generally above its theoretical value.

   1.   The warrant premium results from investors' ability to obtain much greater leverage by purchasing warrants as opposed to stocks.

   2.   The premium is generally greatest when the stock price and the warrant exercise price are very close.

   3.   Because the leverage that makes warrant trading attractive works in both directions, a higher degree of risk is inherent in trading warrants as opposed to stocks.

V.   **Options provide their holders with an opportunity to purchase or sell an asset at a specified price on or before a specified date.**

   A.   Today most interest in options centers on common stock options such as rights, warrants, calls and puts.

      1.   Calls and puts are common stock options traded over-the-counter or on organized exchanges.

      2.   A call is an option to purchase a specified number of common shares on or before some future (expiration) date at a specified (striking) price.

      3.   A put option gives the holder the right to sell a specified number of common shares on or before the expiration date.

      4.   Investors buy call options when they feel the price of the underlying security will go up.

      5.   Investors buy put options when they feel the price of the underlying security will go down.

   B.   Options usually plan no direct role in the fundraising activities of the firm.

1.   Options are typically not issued by the firm; they represent secondary market transactions.

2.   Option market activity may affect the trading activity of the underlying asset (common stock).

3.   Option holders have none of the ownership privileges of stockholders.

APPLICATIONS

DEFINITIONS

1.   Preferred stock that has a stated face value represents _par value_ preferred stock, while preferred stock that has no face value is known as _____ preferred stock.

2.   Payment-in-kind preferred stock pays dividends in the form of _stock_ rather than in _cash_.

3.   Preferred stock for which all unpaid dividends in arrears must be paid prior to the payment of dividends to common stockholders is known as _cumulative_ preferred stock.

4.   A _conversion_ feature allows holders of preferred stock or bonds to transfer their securities into a specified number of common stock shares.

5.   The recipient of the services provided by assets under a lease contract is known as a _lessee_.

6.   A cancelable contractual arrangement which calls for a lessee to make period payments to a lessor for a short period of time is known as an _operating_ lease.

7.   Under a sale-and-leaseback arrangement, a _lessee_ can sell an asset for cash and then lease back the same asset.

8.   In a leveraged lease, the _lessor_ acts as an equity participant, supplying about 20 percent of the cost of an asset, while a _lender_ supplies the balance.

9.   A financial lease that has the present value of all its lease payments included as an asset and a liability on the firms' balance sheet represents a _capitalized_ lease.

10.   A bond that can be converted into a specific number of common stock shares at some future date is known as _convertible_ debt.

11.   The conversion value of a convertible security is measured in terms of the _~~market~~_ value of the common stock into which the security can be converted.

12.   The price at which holders of stock purchase warrants can purchase a certain number of common stock shares represents the _____ price.

13.   The price effectively paid for a particular warrant attached to a debt security represents the _____ price.

14.   A call option represents an option to _____ a given number of common stock shares, while a put option represents an option to _____ a specified number of common stock shares.

15.   Options and warrants are very similar to one another, except _____ can provide new financing to the firm, while _____ are not a source of financing for the firm.

MULTIPLE CHOICE

1.   The three primary techniques for obtaining assets to be leased include all but which of the following?
   a.   reversion lease.
   b.   direct lease.
   c.   sale-leaseback.
   d.   leveraged lease.

2.   In considering a lease-versus-purchase decision, one discounts the differences in cash outflows at:
   a.   the before-tax cost of capital.
   b.   the after-tax cost of capital.
   c.   the after-tax cost of debt.
   d.   the before-tax cost of debt.

3.   A new $1,000 face value corporate bond has been issued with a conversion price of $25. This means it can be converted into _____ shares of common stock?
   a.   2,500
   b.   25,000.
   c.   40.
   d.   not enough information to answer.

4.   Precious Metals, Inc. has outstanding warrants exercisable at $80 per share that entitle holders to purchase two shares of stock. The common stock is currently selling at $85 per share, and the warrants will expire in 5 years. Which of the following is the most likely price for the warrants to currently sell?
      a. $10.00.
      b. $14.00.
      c. $5.00.
      d. $800.00

5.   If an investor expects the market price of a company's common stock to fall, he or she might:
      a.   purchase a warrant.
      b.   purchase a call option.
      c.   purchase a put option.
      d.   purchase the stock.

6.   Call and put options differ from warrants and rights because the former are:
      a.   not a source of financing to the firm.
      b.   only traded on organized exchanges.
      c.   issued by the firm.
      d.   undervalued by investors.

7.   Preferred stock is like debt because:
      a.   both interest expense and preferred stock dividends are tax deductible.
      b.   like debt service payments, preferred stock dividends are given priority over common stock dividends.
      c.   the cost of debt and the cost of preferred stock are approximately equal.
      d.   both preferred stock issuance and debt issuance raise the firm's chances of default.

8.   Preferred stock which offers to pay dividends in the form of preferred shares rather than cash is known as:
      a.   adjustable rate preferred stock.
      b.   cumulative preferred stock.
      c.   payment-in-kind preferred stock.
      d.   junk stock.

9.   A capitalized lease:
      a.   is only used to acquire capital assets.
      b.   qualifies for special tax treatment under current tax law.
      c.   is the same as an operating lease.
      d.   requires the lessee to report the present value of all lease payments as an asset and a liability on the firm's balance sheet.

10. Which of the following is not a motive for the issuance of convertible securities?
    a. convertibles reduce default risk.
    b. convertibles provide deferred common stock financing.
    c. convertibles allow the deferred sale of common stock without excessive ownership and earnings dilution.
    d. convertibles can often be sold with lower interest rates than nonconvertibles.

11. An overhanging convertible issue represents:
    a. an issue with a maturity beyond twenty years.
    b. an issue with a variable interest rate.
    c. an issue that cannot be forced into conversion using a call feature.
    d. an issue for which the firm is unable to order currently due interest payments.

12. The market value of a convertible security is likely to be:
    a. greater than both the straight value and conversion value of the security.
    b. greater than the straight value of the security, but less than its conversion value.
    c. greater than the conversion value of the security, but less than its straight value.
    d. equal to the conversion value of the security.

13. The price at which holders of warrants can purchase a specified number of shares of common stock is known as the:
    a. trigger price.
    b. conversion price.
    c. exercise price.
    d. market price.

14. Most warrants are detachable, which means that:
    a. the issuer can redeem its warrants without redeeming the security to which the warrants are attached.
    b. bond holders may sell the warrants without selling the security to which they are attached.
    c. warrants mature before the security to which they are attached.
    d. warrants carry coupon interest payments which must be separated from the interest payments on the security to which they are attached.

15. A call option represents:
    a. an option to sell a given number of new warrants.
    b. an option to telephone corporate executives during the firm's annual meeting.
    c. an option to transfer security ownership without the use of a stockbroker.
    d. an option to purchase a specified number of shares on or before some future date at a stated price.

PROBLEMS

1. Barry's Pizza has a 10 percent, $80 preferred stock issue outstanding.

    a. How much is the annual preferred stock dividend? *$8*

    b. If the preferred stock is noncumulative and the dividends have been passed for the past two years, how much would have to be paid prior to payment of the common stockholders' dividend? *$8*

    c. If the preferred stock is cumulative and the situation in part (b) occurs, how much would have to be paid to the preferred shareholders prior to payment of dividends to the common stockholders? *$24*

    d. Compare and explain the results in parts (b) and (c).

    e. Assume that the preferred stockholders participate with the common stockholders on an equal basis once the latter have received dividends of $5 per share. If the firm has paid dividends to the preferred stockholders and intends to pay an additional $70,000 in dividends, how much of this, if any, would the preferred stockholders receive? The firm has 10,000 shares of common stock outstanding.

2. The Landslide Leasing Company wishes to determine the size of the lease payments it must charge on an asset for which it must make a current outlay of $100,000. The asset will be leased for eight years, after which it can be sold for $24,000. The lessee will be required to make equal beginning-of-year payments over the eight-year period. Landslide Leasing has a required return on investment of 12 percent.

    a. Calculate the present value of Landslide's initial investment in the leased asset.

    b. Determine the annual lease payment based on the results of part (a) and Landslide's 12 percent required return.

3. Rounding the lease payments charged by the Landslide Leasing Company in Problem (2) to $16,230 and assuming a 40 percent tax rate, calculate the lessee's after-tax outflows over the proposed eight-year duration of the lease.

4. The Wisconsin Widget Company (WWC) wishes to sell and lease back a piece of equipment. Two leasing companies have expressed a willingness to extend a sale-leaseback arrangement. Both firms will purchase the equipment for $140,000 and extend a ten-year lease to WWC. Industrial espionage has indicated the following additional information regarding each lessor:

Lessor	Expected salvage value	Required Return on Lease
A	$30,000	14%
B	$14,000	12%

    a.   Calculate the initial investment required of each lessor in present dollars.

    b.   Determine the annual lease payments charged by each lessor.

    c.   From which lessor should WWC lease? Explain your answer.

5.   The LTW Company has a ten-year lease requiring beginning-of-year payments of $30,000 per year. If the firm wishes to capitalize the lease at its 10 percent cost of capital, determine the amount of the capitalized value, and describe how this would be incorporated into the firm's balance sheet.

6.   The Ludlow Tool Company is attempting to determine whether to lease or purchase a new conveyor system. The firm is in the 40 percent tax bracket, and the after-tax cost of debt currently is 6 percent. The terms of the lease and the purchase are as follows:

    Lease: Annual advance lease payments of $19,744 are required over the four-year usable life of the asset. The lease payments are not deductible for tax purposes until the service of the new conveyer system is actually received.

    Purchase: The conveyor could be purchased for $70,000. Normal ACRS depreciation for a five-year recovery period would apply. The purchase would be financed with a $70,000, 9 percent loan requiring four annual end-of-year payments of $21,605. Even though the conveyor will have a positive book value at the end of year four, it is expected to have zero salvage value.

        a.   Calculate the after-tax cash outflows associated with each alternative.

        b.   Calculate the present value of each of these cash-flow streams using the after-tax cost of debt.

        c.   Which alternative would you recommend that Ludlow implement? Explain your answer.

7.   The Open Air Company has convertible bonds outstanding that have a face value of $1,000. Each bond is convertible into 25 shares of common stock for the next five years, and 22 shares thereafter until the maturity of the bonds.

     a.   Calculate the conversion price per share for each bond for (1) the first five years, and (2) the period beyond the fifth year.

     b.   If the stock is currently selling for $35 per share, calculate the conversion premium for each bond as a percentage of the firm's current stock price.

     c.   Calculate the conversion value of a bond at Open Air's current stock price, and also calculate the conversion value at a price of $40, $45, and $50 for the firm's stock.

8.   The Botch Manufacturing Company wishes to determine whether it is better to raise $3,000,000 by selling common stock, which currently has a depressed price, or by selling convertible bonds. New common stock can be sold for $50 per share, while the firm's outstanding equity is currently selling for $53 per share. The $3 price differential is explained by underpricing and flotation costs associated with the issuance of new stock. The firm currently has 200,000 shares of common stock outstanding. Convertible bonds can be sold for their $1,000 par value, and these bonds would be convertible into the firm's common stock at $68 per share. The firm expects its current level of earnings available for common stockholders to remain at $400,000.

     a.   Calculate the firm's earnings per share on common stock in each of the following cases:

         (1)   Common stock is sold now in order to raise the needed $3,000,000.

         (2)   The convertible bonds are sold, but not converted to common stock. Ignore the impact of convertible bond interest.

         (3)   The convertible bond is sold now, and conversion has taken place.

     b.   Which of the two financing methods is preferable? Explain your answer.

9.   The Rinehart Development Company has an issue of convertible, $1,000 par-value bonds outstanding. Each bond is convertible into 40 shares of common stock. The bonds, which have just been issued, offer a 7 percent coupon and thirty-year maturity. The interest rate on a straight bond of similar risk would be 9 percent.

a.   Calculate the conversion value of each bond when the market price of Rinehart's common stock is $15, $20, $25, $30, and $35.

b.   Calculate the straight bond value of this convertible security.

c.   What is the lowest price at which you would expect the bond to sell? Explain your answer.

d.   Given the following market values of the bond associated with various common stock values, draw on the same set of axes and label:

(1)   The straight bond value;
(2)   The conversion value;
(3)   The market value; and
(4)   The market premium.

Price of Common Stock	Market Value of Bond
$15	$ 800
20	870
25	1,050
30	1,230
35	1,420

10.   The Pioneer Company has warrants to purchase four shares of its common stock outstanding at $30 per share. The stock price per share and the associated warrant values are as follows:

Stock Price Per Share	Market Value of Warrant
$22	$ 4
26	10
30	16
34	24
38	36
42	50
46	64

a.   For each of the share prices given, calculate the theoretical warrant value.

b.   Graph the theoretical value and market value of the warrant on a set of stock price-warrant price axes. Label the warrant premium.

c.   Why does the warrant premium exist?

11.   Ann Ryan has an opportunity to invest $8,000 in either the stock or the warrants of the Texas Refining Company. The company's stock is currently selling for $40 per share, while its warrants, which provide for the purchase of three shares of common stock at $46 per share, are currently selling for $4 each.

a.   If Ann buys the stock today, holds it for one year, and sells it for $50, how much would she earn on her investment. You may ignore brokerage fees in your answer.

b.   If Ann buys the warrants today, holds them for one year, and sells them for $15, how much would she earn on her investment? Once again, you may ignore brokerage fees in your answer.

c.   Compare these alternatives, and discuss the trade-offs that confront Ann.

SOLUTIONS

DEFINITIONS

1.   par value; no-par
2.   stock; cash
3.   cumulative
4.   conversion
5.   lessee
6.   operating
7.   lessee
8.   lessor; lender
9.   capitalized
10.   convertible
11.   market
12.   exercise or option
13.   implied
14.   buy; sell
15.   warrants; options

MULTIPLE CHOICE

1.	a	9.	d
2.	c	10.	a
3.	c	11.	c
4.	c	12.	a
5.	c	13.	c
6.	a	14.	b
7.	b	15.	d
8.	c		

PROBLEMS

1. a. The annual preferred stock dividend can be found by multiplying the dividend percentage by the stated value of the preferred. This gives a preferred dividend per share of $8:

$$(\$80) \times (0.10) = \$8 \text{ per share.}$$

   b. If the preferred stock is noncumulative, only the current dividend of $8 per share would have to be paid prior to payment of dividends to common stockholders.

   c. If the preferred stock is cumulative, all dividends in arrears plus the current dividend must be paid to the preferred shareholders before the common stockholders can receive dividends. Because two past dividends plus the current dividend must be paid, the firm must pay three years of preferred stock dividends, which, at $8 per year, total $24 per share.

   d. Cumulative preferred stock obviously places the preferred stockholder in a better position, and the common stockholder in a worse position than does noncumulative preferred stock. In the cumulative case, the preferred stockholder must receive $24 before the common stockholder receives any dividends, while, in the noncumulative case, the preferred stockholder must receive only $8 per share prior to payment of dividends to the common stockholder.

2. a. The initial investment required by Landslide can be found by subtracting the present value of the projected salvage value of $24,000 to be received eight years from now from the current outlay of $100,000. The present value of the salvage value is calculated using the firm's 12 percent required return. Using Table A-3 in the Appendix, the present-value interest factor for 12 percent and eight years is found to be 0.404. Calculation of the initial investment is as follows:

Current outlay for initial purchase $100,000
Less: Present value of salvage value [($24,000) x (0.404)]   - 9,696
Initial investment $90,304

Landslide's initial investment in today's dollars is therefore $90,304.

b.   Because the lease payments are made in advance (at the start of the year), the cash inflows from the unknown payments to the lessor would be as follows:

End of Year	Beginning of Year	Payment Amount
0	1	$X
1 - 7	2 - 8	$X

To determine the eight beginning-of-year payments which will amortize the initial investment of $90,304 while providing the required 12 percent return, the following equation can be used:

$$\$90,304 = 1.000X + \$4.564X.$$

Because the payments are received at the beginning of the year, the first payment is received now, as shown by the coefficient 1.000. The remaining seven beginning-of-year payments can be treated as a seven-year annuity. The interest factor from Table A-4 in the Appendix for the present value of a seven-year annuity at 12 percent is 4.564, which is the coefficient of the last term in the equation shown above. Simplifying the equation yields the following expression:

$$\$90,304 = 5.564X.$$

Solving for X yields an annual beginning-of-year lease payment.

$$X = \frac{\$90,304}{5.564} = \$16,230.05 \ .$$

By charging eight annual beginning-of-year lease payments of $16,230.05 and selling the asset for $24,000 at the end of this eight-year period, the Landslide Leasing Company will earn its required 12 percent return on the lease investment.

3.   Because lease payments are made in advance, but the Internal Revenue Service does not permit their deduction for tax purposes until the service provided by the lease is received, the tax benefit (or shield) from each lease payment is not received until the year <u>after</u> the payment is actually made. The required calculations are presented in tabular form as follows:

Year-End	Lease Payment (1)	Tax Benefit [(1) x (0.40)] (2)	After-Tax Cash Flow [(1) - (2)] (3)
0	$16,230	$ 0	-$16,230
1	16,230	6,492	-9,738
2	16,230	6,492	-9,738
3	16,230	6,492	-9,738
4	16,230	6,492	-9,738
5	16,230	6,492	-9,738
6	16,230	6,492	-9,738
7	16,230	6,492	-9,738
8	0	6,492	+6,492

4.   a.   The initial investment for each lessor can be found by subtracting the present value of the salvage value from the $140,000 purchase outlay. The present value interest factor used in each case is found in Table A-3 in the Appendix for ten years at the rate of return appropriate to each lessor. The initial investment of each lessor is calculated as follows:

<u>Lessor A</u>

Current outlay to purchase equipment	$140,000
Less: Present value of salvage value ($30,000 x 0.270)	- 8,100
Initial investment in warehouse	$131,900

<u>Lessor B:</u>

Current outlay to purchase equipment	$140,000
Less: Present value of salvage value ($14,000 x .322)	- 4,508
Initial investment in warehouse	$135,492

Lessor A's initial investment would be $131,900, while lessor B's initial investment would be $135,492.

b. The annual lease payments charged by each lessor can be established by finding the payment that will allow each lessor to earn its required return on its initial investment. Because the lease payments are made in advance, each of these calculations considers the first payment to be received now and the remaining payments to be a nine-year annuity discounted at the lessor's required rate of return. Letting X represent the unknown lease payment, the solution for X for each lessor is as follows:

Lessor A:

$$\$131,900 \ = \ 1.000X + 4.946X,$$

where 4.946 is the interest factor for the present value of a nine-year annuity at 14 percent. Solving for X yields:

$$X \ - \ \frac{\$131,900}{5.946} \ - \ \$22,182.98 \ .$$

Lessor B:

$$\$135,492 \ = \ 1.000X + 5.328X,$$

where 5.328 is the interest factor for the present value of a nine-year annuity at 12 percent. Solving for X yields:

$$X \ - \ \frac{\$135,492}{6.328} \ - \ \$21,411.50 \ .$$

The lease payments charged by Lessor A and Lessor B would be $22,182.98 and $21,411.50, respectively.

c. Because the annual lease payment charged by Lessor B is less than that charged by Lessor A ($21,182.98), Lessor B would be preferred.

5. The stream of payments for this lease would consist of a payment now (i.e., at time zero), followed by a nine-year annuity. The capitalized value of the lease would be the present value of these cash outflows at the 10 percent rate:

Present value of lease payments = [(1.000) x ($30,000)] + [(5.759) x ($30,000)].

The first term on the right-hand side of the equation represents the present value of the present payment, while the second term represents the present value of the remaining nine payments. The number 5.759 represents the interest factor for the present value of a nine-year annuity at 10 percent obtained from Table A-4 in the Appendix. Solving the equation yields:

Present value of lease payments = (6.759) x ($30,000) = $202,770.

To adjust the firm's balance sheet correctly for the presence of the lease, the firm's assets and liabilities would be increased by $202,770. This adjustment extends to the lease an accounting treatment similar to that of a purchase that has been financed by borrowing.

6.   a. Lease Cash Flows:

To determine the after-tax cash outflows of the lease, the tax shield received for each year must be deducted from the lease payment. This is done in tabular form as follows:

End of Year	Lease Payment (1)	Tax Savings from Lease Payment (2)	Lease Cash Outflows [(1) - (2)] (3)
0	$19,744	$ 0	$19,744
1	19,744	7,898	11,846
2	19,744	7,898	11,846
3	19,744	7,898	11,846
4	0	7,898	-7,898

The resulting lease cash outflows associated with the lease are as shown in column (3).

Purchase Cash Flows:

To determine the cash outflows associated with the purchase, the interest on the loan must be known, because this portion of the loan payment is treated as a tax-deductible expenditure. The annual loan interest is obtained from the following amortization schedule:

Year	Loan Payment (1)	Beginning-of Year Principal (2)	Interest [(2) x (0.09)] (3)	Principal [(1) - (3)] (4)	End-of Year Principal [(2) - (4)] (5)
1	$21,605	$70,000	$6,300	$15,305	$54,695
2	21,605	54,695	4,923	16,682	38,013
3	21,605	38,013	3,421	18,184	19,829
4	21,605	19,829	1,785	19,820	0

Note that the year-end principal payment in year 4 does not reduce the principal balance exactly to zero, because of rounding. The annual depreciation expense associated with asset ownership is calculated as:

ACRS Year	ACRS Percentage (1)	Depreciable Value (2)	Annual Depreciation [(1) x (2)] (3)
1	20%	$70,000	$14,000
2	32	70,000	22,400
3	19	70,000	13,300
4	12	70,000	8,400
5	12	70,000	8,400
6	5	70,000	3,500

Now that we have the annual interest and depreciation associated with the loan, cash outflows are calculated in tabular form:

Year	Loan Payment (1)	Depreciation (2)	Interest (3)	Total Deductions [(2) + (3)] (4)	Tax Shield [.40 x (4)] (5)	Purchase Cash Outflows [(1) - (5)] (6)
1	$21,605	$14,000	$6,300	$20,300	$8,120	$13,485
2	21,605	22,400	4,923	27,323	10,929	10,676
3	21,605	13,300	3,421	16,721	6,688	14,917
4	21,605	20,300*	1,785	22,085	8,834	12,771

* Year 4 depreciation includes the write-off of the loss on the asset's remaining book value.

Column (6) presents the approximate cash outflows associated with the purchase alternative.

b.   The present value of the cash outflows associated with the lease and purchase alternatives is calculated in tabular form as follows, using the 6 percent after-tax cost of debt:

Lease

Year	Cash Outflows (1)	6% Present Value Interest Factors (Table A-3) (2)	Present Value of Outflows [(1) x (2)] (3)
0	$19,744	1.000	$19,744
1	11,846	0.943	11,171
2	11,846	0.890	10,543
3	11,846	0.840	9,951
4	- 7,898	0.792	- 6,255
Present value of cash outflows			$45,154

Purchase

Year	Cash Outflows (1)	6% Present Value Interest Factors (Table A-3) (2)	Present Value of Outflow [(1) x (2)] (3)
1	$13,485	0.943	$12,716
2	10,676	0.890	9,502
3	14,917	0.840	12,530
4	12,771	0.792	10,115
Present value of cash outflows			$44,863

The results indicate that the present value of cash outflows associated with the lease and the purchase are $45,154 and $44,863, respectively.

c.   The purchase alternative would be recommended because of its lower cost (i.e., $44,863 for the purchase versus $45,154 for the lease). In other words, the cheaper alternative for obtaining the conveyor's service over the four-year period would be to purchase the asset and finance it with the 9 percent loan.

7.   a.   The conversion price per share for the bond can be found by dividing its face value by the number of shares into which it is convertible:

$$\frac{\$1,000}{25} - \$40 \text{ per share .}$$

The conversion price beyond the fifth year will be:

$$\frac{\$1,000}{22} - \$45.45 \text{ per share .}$$

b.   When the stock is currently selling for $35 per share and the convertible bond can be converted at a price of $40 per share [from part (a)], the conversion premium is $5 per share (i.e., $40 per share). Stated as a percentage of the market price:

$$\text{Conversion Premium} - \frac{\$5}{22} - 14.3\% \text{ .}$$

c.   When the stock is selling for a given price, the conversion value of the bond can be found by multiplying the number of shares of stock into which the bond can be converted by the market price of the common stock. In this case, the bond can be converted into 25 shares of common stock. The conversion values are calculated as follows:

Market Price of Common Stock (1)	Conversion Ratio in Shares (2)	Conversion Value of Bond [(1) x (2)] (3)
$35	25	$ 875
40	25	1,000
45	25	1,125
50	25	1,250

8.   a-1.   If common stock is sold now, the firm would have to sell 60,000 new shares (i.e., $3,000,000 ÷ 50 per share) to raise the needed $3,000,000. This would leave the firm with a total of 260,000 shares outstanding (200,000 shares now + 60,000 new shares). If earnings available for common stockholders remain at $400,000, earnings per share would be:

$$\frac{\$400,000}{260,000 \text{ shares}} - \$1.54 \text{ per share} .$$

a-2. If the convertible bonds were sold, and bondholders did not convert their bonds to common stock, only the current 200,000 shares would be outstanding. If earnings available for the common stockholders remain at $400,000, ignoring the impact of convertible bond interest, the earnings per share would be:

$$\frac{\$400,000}{200,000 \text{ shares}} - \$2.00 \text{ per share} .$$

a-3. If the convertibles are sold, each bond can be converted into:

$$\frac{\$1,000}{\$68 \text{ per share}} - 14.7 \text{ shares} .$$

Because the firm will have to sell a total of 3,000 bonds ($3,000,000 ÷ $1,000 per bond), upon conversion of the bonds an additional 44,100 shares of stock would be issued (3,000 bonds x 14.7 shares of common stock per each bond). This would leave the firm with a total of 244,100 shares of common stock outstanding (200,000 shares now + 44,100 new shares). If earnings available for common stockholders remain at $400,000, the firm's earnings per share would be:

$$\frac{\$400,000}{244,100 \text{ shares}} - \$1.64 \text{ per share} .$$

b. The best way to compare the two financing methods is to compare the earnings per share under each alternative. The earnings per share calculated in part (a) are summarized as follows:

Financing Alternative	Earnings per share
Common stock	$1.54
Convertible bond	
Before conversion (ignoring interest)	2.00
After conversion	1.64

Comparing these values, it can be seen that the use of the convertible bond appears preferable, because earnings per share are higher both before and after conversion. Of course, other factors, such as the interest burden and other leverage effects, would have to be considered when making this financing decision.

9.   a.   Because each bond is convertible into 40 shares of common stock, the conversion value at each of the given prices can be found by multiplying the stock price by the 40 shares. This is done in tabular form as follows:

Market Price of Common Stock (1)	Conversion Ratio (in shares) (2)	Conversion Value of Bond [(1) x (2)] (3)
$15	40	$ 600
20	40	800
25	40	1,000
30	40	1,200
35	40	1,400

b.   To find the straight bond value, the present value of the convertible's cash flows must be calculated using the interest rate for a straight bond. The bond's cash flows are as follows:

Year	Item	Cash Flow Amount
1 through 30	Interest	($1,000) x (0.07) = $70
30	Principal	$1,000

Because a straight bond would have a 9 percent required return, the present value of the cash flows at 9 percent must be found. This is done in tabular form as follows:

Year	Cash Flow (1)	Present Value Interest Factor (2)	Present Value [(1) x (2)] (3)
1 through 30	$ 70	10.274[1]	$719.18
30	1,000	0.075[2]	75.00
			$794.18

1. From Table A-4 (in the Appendix), 30 years at 9 percent.
2. From Table A-3 (in the Appendix), year 30 at 9%.

The resulting straight bond value is $794.18.

c.   The bond would not be expected to sell for less than its straight value of $794.18. The straight value acts as a floor below which the bond is not expected to sell unless the firm's risk level changes or economic conditions change.

d.   The various functions are plotted and labeled as follows:

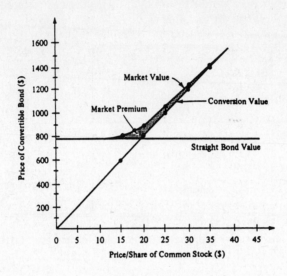

10. a.   The theoretical value of the warrant, TVW, is found using the following equation:

$$TVW = (P - E) \times N,$$

where: TVW =   the theoretical value of a warrant;

P   =   the market price of a share of common stock;

E   =   the exercise price of the warrant; and

N   =   the number of shares of common stock obtainable with one warrant.

Letting E = 30 and N = 4, the theoretical values of the warrants for various stock prices are calculated as follows:

Stock Price per Share (P) (1)	Warrant Exercise Price (E) (2)	[(1) - (2)] (3)	Theoretical Value (TVW) [4 x (3)] (4)
$22	$ 30	$ (8)	$(32)
26	30	4	(16)
30	30	0	0
34	30	4	16
38	30	8	32
42	30	12	48
46	30	16	64

b.   The theoretical value of the warrant (for stock prices above $30 per share), the market value of the warrant, and the warrant premium are graphed as follows:

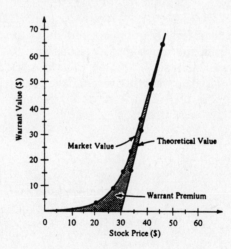

c.   The warrant premium exists because of the high degree of leverage investors can realize by trading warrants rather than the associated stock. Because of this leverage, investors are willing to pay a premium for the warrants -- especially when the market price of the stock is close to the warrant's exercise price.

11. a.   If Ann sells the stock for $50 per share, she will have earned $10 per share, because the stock would have been purchased originally for $40 per share. Because Ann had $8,000 to invest, she would have purchased 200 shares (i.e., $8,000 ÷ $40 per share). Because she realizes a return equal to $10 per share, her total profit would be $2,000 (i.e., $10 per share x 200 shares). Stated as a percentage, Ann's return on investment would be:

$$\frac{\$2,000}{\$8,000} - 25\% \ .$$

   b.   If Ann spends her $8,000 purchasing the warrants at $4 each, she would purchase 2,000 warrants (i.e., $8,000 ÷ $4 per warrant). If she is able to sell the warrants for $15 each, she would make $11 per warrant (i.e., $15 - $4). On the 2,000 warrants, her total earnings would be $22,000. Stated as a percentage of Ann's investment, her return on investment would be:

$$\frac{\$22,000}{\$8,000} - 275\% \ .$$

   c.   Ann would make a considerably greater profit by trading in warrants. This larger profit would result from the much greater sensitivity of the warrant to equity price changes than the stock itself has. Of course, had the stock price dropped over the year, the loss experienced with the warrants would have been considerably greater than the loss on the stock.

CHAPTER 16

NET WORKING CAPITAL AND SHORT-TERM FINANCING

SUMMARY

This chapter provides an in-depth look at the broad area of working capital management, the management of current assets and current liabilities. Firms generally maintain positive net working capital, the difference between current assets and current liabilities, to provide a cushion between cash outflows and cash inflows. $CA-CL$

Since low levels of net working capital indicate a higher probability of insufficient liquidity, or technical insolvency, net working capital is a very useful measure of risk. The lower a firm's ratio of current-to-total assets, reducing the proportion of lower-yielding (i.e., current) assets, the more profitable and more risky the firm is. An increase in the ratio of current liabilities to total assets would result in increased profitability because of the use of cheaper financing, while the risk of technical insolvency would increase. These trade-offs must be considered in evaluating a firm's net working capital position.

The firm's financing requirements consist of a permanent need, which is attributable to both fixed assets and the permanent portion of current assets, and a seasonal need, which is attributable to the existence of temporary current assets. Firms employing an aggressive financing strategy finance seasonal needs with short-term funds and long-term needs with long-term funds. This approach results in interest being paid only on needed funds; in exchange, however, the firm will have high risk, as virtually no net working capital would result. There is also a risk of being unable to obtain funds in an emergency. The conservative financing strategy consists of the firm financing all projected needs with long-term funds. The conservative strategy does not maximize profit, because the firm often would be paying interest on unneeded funds, but results in lower risk. A trade-off between the aggressive and conservative approaches would most likely be used.

Accounts payable and accruals are spontaneous sources of unsecured short-term financing, because they result from the normal business process. By accepting goods on account, a firm accepts the credit or repayment terms, which are stated on the supplier's invoice. A firm's credit terms state the credit period, the size of the cash discount, the cash discount period, and the credit period beginning. Because the use of accruals is virtually free, the firm should attempt to stretch them by paying for services on as infrequent a basis as possible.

The key supplier of unsecured short-term loans is the commercial bank. The three arrangements under which such loans are made are a single payment note, a line of credit, and a revolving credit agreement. A note is a single-payment loan on which the borrower pays interest. These notes may be fixed-rate loans, or, more commonly, floating-rate loans, with the interest rate changing as the bank's prime rate changes. On a line of credit, which is not guaranteed, the bank approves in advance a borrower's credit worthiness up to the stated limit. Most line-of-credit agreements require the borrower to maintain a compensating balance. This raises the effective rate or true cost of borrowing. A revolving credit agreement guarantees the availability of funds to the borrower, who must pay a commitment fee on the unused portion.

Commercial paper, which is short-term unsecured promissory notes, can be sold by large financially sound firms.

Secured loans extend to the lender a legal claim on certain collateral, or assets, of the borrower. Accounts receivable provide an attractive source of short-term loan collateral. The borrower is required to forward payments received on pledged accounts to the lender, who reduces the loan balance.

Factoring is the outright sale of accounts receivable. The factor (or bank or finance company) normally purchases accounts on a nonrecourse basis (i.e., accepts all credit risks) and notifies the customers to remit directly to itself. Factoring may be done on a continuing basis to turn accounts receivable immediately into cash and eliminate both credit and collection departments. Inventory is also frequently used as collateral. A floating inventory lien is sometimes used to secure inventories of small, difficult-to-identify items. A more secure type of inventory loan is the trust receipt loan, which is a loan against specific items that are left in the hands of the borrower (in trust). A warehouse receipt loan is one in which the lender obtains control of the inventory by having it guarded by a warehousing company. The warehouse used may be a terminal warehouse or a field warehouse, the latter type being set up on the borrower's premises.

CONCEPT OUTLINE

I.   **Net working capital can be used to evaluate the liquidity of the firm over time.**

   A. Net working capital is defined as the difference between current assets and current liabilities, or simply current assets minus current liabilities. Current assets are 40 percent of total assets and current liabilities are 26 percent of total financing at the average manufacturing firm.

   1. Net working capital represents the portion of the firm's current assets financed with long-term funds.

   2. Most firms must maintain positive net working capital in order to account for imperfectly synchronized cash flows.

   3. High levels of net working capital protect the firm against technical insolvency, which occurs when a firm cannot meet its current obligations. Technical insolvency is possible when the firm has most of its nonpermanent wealth in the inventory or accounts receivable phase of the operating cycle.

   4. The more predictable a firm's cash flows, the lower the level of net working capital needed, and vice versa. Cash inflows are less predictable than outflows.

B. The higher the firm's net working capital, the more liquid and less risky it is, and vice versa.

II. **There is a trade-off between the profitability and the risk associated with various liquidity strategies.**

A. Profitability refers to the excess of revenues over costs, while risk refers to the probability of technical insolvency. Increased profitability results in increased risk, and vice versa.

B. The trade-off can be illustrated using the ratio of current assets to total assets.

1. By increasing the proportion of current assets, profits decline, because of the higher proportion of low-yielding current assets, and risk decreases, because of the high level of net working capital, and vice versa.

2. By increasing the proportion of current liabilities, profitability increases, because of the reduced financing cost, but risk also increases, because of the lower level of net working capital, and vice versa.

3. Combined strategies of increasing current assets and decreasing current liabilities attempt to minimize the risk of technical insolvency at the expense of the firm's profits, and vice versa.

III. **An important working capital decision concerns the financing mix - the method by which the firm uses its current liabilities to finance its current assets.**

A. The firm's financing requirements can be broken into a permanent and a seasonal need.

1. The permanent need, consisting of fixed assets plus the permanent portion of the firm's current assets, remains unchanged over the year.

2. The seasonal need, which is attributable to the existence of certain temporary current assets, varies over the year.

B. Aggressive financing consists of funding seasonal needs with temporary funds and permanent needs with permanent funds.

1. This approach helps maximize profits through minimizing interest cost by paying interest only on required financing.

2. Using the aggressive approach would be risky, though because the firm would have minimum net working capital, since only the permanent portion of the firm's current assets would be financed with permanent funds.

3. The firm may also find it difficult to obtain funds when needed.

C. The conservative approach is based on financing virtually all of the firm's funds requirements with long-term funds.

1. The conservative approach minimizes the risk of technical insolvency by providing for high net working capital, because all seasonal and permanent needs are financed with permanent funds.

2. This approach does not use any of the firm's short-term borrowing capacity, which can be used to satisfy unexpected fund needs.

3. From a profitability standpoint, this approach is deficient. Interest is paid on unneeded funds, which are unlikely to earn more than their interest cost.

D. A trade-off between the aggressive and conservative approaches is usually made.

IV.   **Spontaneous sources of unsecured short-term financing can result from the normal business operation.**

A. Accounts payable are a spontaneous source of short-term financing that result from the purchase of goods on open account.

1. Open-account purchases represent the major source of short-term financing to business.

2. By accepting the merchandise, a purchaser of goods on open account agrees, in effect, to pay the supplier the required amount under the supplier's terms of sale.

B. The credit terms on accounts payable described the various aspects of repayment required by a supplier of open-account credit.

1. The credit period represents the number of days after which payment in full is required.

2. The cash discount represents the percentage reduction the purchaser can take from the purchase price if the payment is remitted before the end of the cash discount period.

3. Credit terms are normally stated in a form such as 2/10 net 30 EOM, which indicates that the purchaser can take a 2 percent cash discount if payment is made within 10 days of the credit period beginning, which is the end of month; otherwise, the full amount must be paid within 30 days of the credit period beginning.

4. Alternatively, the credit period could begin on the date of invoice.

C. When cash discounts are offered, there is an explicit cost of forgoing the discount.

1. If a firm forgoes a cash discount, it is, in effect, paying an amount equal to the cash discount in order to keep its money for a period of time equal to the difference between the net period and the cash discount period.

2. The annual percentage cost of forgoing the cash discount can be calculated using the following expression:

$$\frac{CD}{100\% - CD} \times \frac{360}{N}$$

where   CD = the stated cash discount in percentage terms
         N = number of days payment can be delayed by forgoing the cash discount

3. One effectively multiplies the cash discount as a percentage of the reduced price by the number of delayed payment periods in a year.

4. If a firm needs funds and can borrow at a rate lower than the cost of forgoing the cash discount, it should take the discount.

5. It is generally expensive to forgo the cash discount.

6. The effective cost of forgoing a cash discount can be reduced by stretching accounts payable, but will probably reap supplier displeasure.

D. Accruals, which represent obligations of the firm for services received but not yet paid for, are another spontaneous source of short-term financing.

1. Accrual of taxes cannot be manipulated.

2. Prolonged accrual of wages might curtail productivity.

E. The firm should take advantage of spontaneous sources or "interest free" sources of unsecured short-term financing whenever possible.

V. **Commercial banks are the primary provider of unsecured short-term loans to business.**

A. The major types of loans made by banks are short-term, self-liquidating loans.

1. These unsecured loans are self-liquidating in the sense that the reason for which the funds are borrowed furnishes the funds used for repayment.

2. These loans typically are made to finance seasonal buildups of inventory or accounts receivable.

B. A note is generally a single-payment unsecured short-term loan on which interest and principal are paid at maturity.

1. The interest rate on a note is either a fixed or floating rate that is typically tied to the prime rate, which is the lowest rate of interest charged on business loans made to the best borrowers. Floating rate loans are more common, but produce interest uncertainty.

2. The effective, or actual, rate of interest on the loan depends upon whether interest is paid at maturity or in advance.

a. In the cheaper case of payment at maturity, the effective rate is obtained by simply dividing the interest payment by the amount borrowed.

b. When interest is paid in advance, the effective rate is obtained by dividing the interest payment by the amount available to the firm (i.e., amount borrowed - interest).

c. If interest is deducted in advance, the firm will have to borrow more than required for operating needs.

C. A line of credit is an agreement under which a bank allows a borrower to owe up to a certain amount at any time during the year.

1. The line of credit can be considered an advance loan approval, usually granted for a period of one year.

2. The line of credit is not a guaranteed loan; rather, the lender agrees that, if sufficient funds are available, a customer can borrow up to a certain amount.

3. The interest rate on a line of credit is generally stated as the prime rate plus X, generally less than 2, percent.

D. Two features commonly included as part of a line of credit agreement are the compensating balance and the annual cleanup.

1. A compensating balance is a minimum deposit (usually 10 to 20 percent of the outstanding loan) that must be held against any borrowing.

2. The compensating balance raises the effective borrowing cost, because the borrower does not get the full use of borrowed funds.

3. The annual cleanup, which requires a borrower to have a zero loan balance for a specified period of time during the year, is often included in order to assure the lender that borrowed funds are being used for short-term purposes.

E. A revolving credit agreement is a line of credit for which the lender guarantees the availability of funds.

1. Occasionally, these agreements are made for two or three years.

2. A commitment fee is charged to the borrower on the unused portion of the revolving credit agreement.

F. Commercial paper, a nonbank source of unsecured financing is a short-term unsecured promissory note (3- to 270-day maturities) issued by a firm with a high credit rating.

1. It is a cheap form of financing for firms that can issue it, frequently less than the prime rate.

2. Commercial paper is sold at a discount from face value.

3. Commercial paper may be sold directly or through middlepersons known as commercial paper houses.

VI. **A firm may exhaust its unsecured short-term borrowing capacity. That is, beyond some level of borrowing, lenders consider a firm too risky to be given an unsecured short-term loan. The next step is to arrange for secured short-term financing.**

A. Most secured short-term borrowing is obtained by small, growing firms that have yet to become financially mature.

B. Secured loans extend to the lender a legal claim on certain collateral or assets of the borrower.

1. Holding collateral reduces the risk of loss on the loan.

2. Accounts receivable and inventories are preferred collateral.

3. Lenders prefer less risky loans, even if interest revenue is lower, rather than be in a position where collateral acquisition is likely.

4. Collateral has no impact on the risk of default.

C. Credit terms include a percentage advance, or statement of the percentage of the collateral that can be borrowed.

1. Interest rates are typically greater than the rates on unsecured loans.

2. Administrative costs also increase the effective rate.

D. The primary institutions making secured short-term loans to businesses are commercial banks and commercial finance companies.

1. Although commercial banks do make secured short-term loans, the primary type of loan they make is the unsecured short-term loan.

2. A commercial finance company is a financial institution that makes only secured loans.

E. Accounts receivable are a common form of short-term loan collateral.

1. A pledge or assignment of accounts receivable involves securing a short-term loan with certain accounts receivable.

2. Factoring of accounts receivable is another arrangement whereby the firm may receive cash for its accounts receivable. The factor generally purchases selected accounts without recourse, which means that they accept all credit risks from unpaid accounts.

3. Many firms factor all accounts in order to receive certain benefits believed to outweigh the costs.

a. The key benefits of factoring are the ability to turn accounts receivable into immediate cash and to add predictability to cash flows.

    b. If all accounts are factored, both the credit and collection departments can be eliminated.

    c. The chief disadvantages of factoring are its high cost, the potential sacrifice of liquidity, and the associated implication of financial weakness.

F. Inventory is commonly used as collateral for short-term loans.

    1. When evaluating inventory as loan collateral, the most important concerns are its marketability and market-price stability.

    2. A trust receipt is a loan against specific items that remain in the hands of the borrower (in trust). Upon sale, the proceeds must be remitted to the lender.

    3. A warehouse receipt is a loan against collateral that is under the control of the lender. The collateral is released by a third party only with the lender's approval, which normally is not given unless a payment has been received.

APPLICATIONS

DEFINITIONS

1. Short-term financial management consists of managing *current assets* and *current liabilities*.

2. During a firm's operating cycle, working capital is shifted from *cash* to *inventories* to *accounts receivable* and back to *cash*.

3. If firm's current assets exceed its current liabilities, it has *positive* net working capital.

4. Permanent financing requirements include *fixed* assets plus the *permanent* portion of current assets.

5. A firm using an *aggressive* financing strategy finances its seasonal needs with short-term funds.

6. *Spontaneous* financing does not have to be obtained from external sources, but instead arises from normal business operations.

7. The number of days until full payment of an account payable is required is referred to as the *credit period*.

8. The buyer may be able to take a _____cash_____ discount, or pay less than full price, if payment is made within the _____cash_____ discount _____period_____

9. The _____prime_____ rate is the lowest interest rate charged by leading banks for business loans to their more creditworthy borrowers.

10. Interest on a _____fixed rate_____ loan remains constant until maturity, while the interest on a _____floating rate_____ loan varies with changes in the prime rate until maturity.

11. To receive a guaranteed line of credit, also known as a _____revolving_____ credit agreement, a _____commitment fee_____ frequently is paid.

12. Short-term, unsecured promissory notes issued by firms with high credit standings are called _____Commercial paper_____

13. Secured short-term financing loans are obtained by pledging specific assets as _____Collateral_____

★ 14. If a firm's customers remits payment to its lender rather than the firm itself the accounts receivable were pledged on a _____notification basis_____

15. A _____floating_____ inventory loan gives the lender a claim to the borrower's general inventory as loan collateral.

MULTIPLE CHOICE

1. The portion of a firm's current assets financed with long-term funds is its:
    a. current ratio.
    b. deferred liabilities.
    c. net working capital.
    d. net worth.

★ 2. The greater the margin by which a firm's current assets cover its short-term obligations:
    a. the better able it will be to pay its bills as they come due.
    b. the greater the portion of its current assets financed by long-term funds.
    c. the less likely the firm is to become technically insolvent.
    d. all of the above.

3.   If a firm could hold constant its level of total assets but increase the ratio of current liabilities to total liabilities, the result would likely be:
    a. a decrease in both profit and risk.
    b. a decrease in profit and an increase in risk.
    c. an increase in both profit and risk.
    d. an increase in profit and a decrease in risk.

4.   Permanent financing needs include all but which of the following?
    a. current assets that vary with the seasons.
    b. fixed assets.
    c. the permanent portion of the firm's current assets.
    d. two of the above.

5.   A financing strategy that requires the firm to finance its seasonal needs with short-term funds and its permanent needs with long-term funds is called:
    a. the aggressive strategy.
    b. the conservative strategy.
    c. the matching strategy.
    d. the trade-off strategy.

6.   The financing strategy that requires the firm to finance all its financing needs with long term funds is called:
    a. the aggressive strategy.
    b. the conservative strategy.
    c. the seasonal strategy.
    d. the trade-off strategy.

7.   The aggressive strategy is a lower cost, higher profit strategy because:
    a. it does not borrow funds unless needed.
    b. it exposes the firm to higher risk.
    c. it uses more short-term financing.
    d. two of the above.

8.   The two major spontaneous sources of short-term financing are:
    a. accounts payable and accruals.
    b. inventory and accounts receivable.
    c. retained earnings and deferred taxes.
    d. short-term notes and dividends payable.

9.   A firm facing credit terms of (1/10 net 30 EOM) is forgoing the discount if:
      a. it fails to pay 10 days before the end of the month.
      b. it fails to pay 10 percent by the end of the month.
      c. it fails to pay within one day of the tenth of the month.
      d. it fails to pay within 10 days of the end of the invoice month.

10.   The cost of not taking the discount if the terms are (1/10 net 30 EOM) is:
      a. 10.00 percent.
      b. 12.00 percent.
      c. 18.18 percent.
      d. 36.73 percent.

$$\frac{1}{99} \cdot \frac{360}{20} =$$

11.   A firm wants to borrow $100,000 at a stated rate of interest of 10 percent. If the firm must leave a 10 percent compensating balance, what is the effective interest rate?
      a. 10.00 percent
      b. 11.11 percent
      c. 12.50 percent
      d. 20.00 percent

$$\frac{10,000}{90,000}"$$

12.   Collateral can reduce losses if the borrower defaults:
      a. and it reduces the risk of default.
      b. and this explains why lenders prefer secured loans over unsecured loans, regardless of risk.
      c. but it encourages default.
      d. but it has no impact on the risk of default.

13.   Lending institutions that make only short-term loans and generally charge a higher interest rate because they end up with high risk-borrowers are:
      a. commercial banks.
      b. commercial finance companies.
      c. factors.
      d. savings and loan associations.

14.   Which of the following is not a secured short-term borrowing arrangement?
      a. factoring accounts receivable — are sold outright
      b. floating inventory lien
      c. pledging accounts receivable
      d. warehouse receipt loan

15.   Which of the following is <u>not</u> true about warehouse receipt loans:
         a. Only upon lender approval can secured inventory be released.
         b. The lender receives control of the pledged collateral.
         c. The warehousing company places a guard over the inventory.
         d. Under a field warehousing agreement, a central warehouse is used to store merchandise.

PROBLEMS

1.   Morris Lipski Products, maker of facial creams, has the following asset and liability structures.

Assets		Liability and Equity	
Current Assets	$10,000	Current liabilities	$ 5,000
Fixed Assets	$30,000	Long-term funds	$35,000
Total	$40,000	Total	$40,000

The firm's current assets earn 3 percent, current liabilities cost 10 percent, fixed assets earn 18 percent, and long-term funds cost 14 percent.
         a. Calculate the level of the firm's net working capital.
         b. Calculate the dollar return on total assets and the ratio of current assets to total assets.
         c. Calculate the cost of financing and the ratio of current liabilities to total assets.
         d. Calculate the net profitability (i.e., dollar return on assets - cost of financing) of the current plan.

2.   Assume that the Morris Lipski (in problem 1) simultaneously shifted $2000 of current assets to fixed assets and $3000 of long-term funds to current liabilities.
         a. Calculate the level of the firm's net working capital.
         b. Calculate the dollar return on total assets and the ratio of current assets to total assets.
         c. Calculate the cost of financing and the ratio of current liabilities to total assets.
         d. Calculate the net profitability of the proposed plan.
         e. Compare and contrast the results with respect to risk and return of this problem and problem 1.

3. Calculate the average loan balance and annual loan cost associated with a 12 percent loan and the following monthly loan balances:

Month	Amount	Month	Amount
January	$30,000	July	$15,000
February	40,000	August	10,000
March	45,000	September	0
April	45,000	October	0
May	20,000	November	5,000
June	20,000	December	10,000

4. The R. M. Cook Company has forecast its monthly funds requirements for the coming year as follows:

Month	Amount	Month	Amount
January	$10,000,000	July	$ 5,000,000
February	9,000,000	August	7,000,000
March	8,000,000	September	8,000,000
April	6,000,000	October	10,000,000
May	4,000,000	November	11,000,000
June	3,000,000	December	12,000,000

The firm's cost of short- and long-term financing is expected to be 12 percent and 16 percent, respectively. Assume that the firm's seasonal needs are equal to its current assets and that its permanent needs are equal to its fixed assets. In other words, the firm has no permanent current assets.

a. Calculate the cost of financing the firm's funds needs using the aggressive approach. (The permanent portion of long-term funds is equal to the minimum fund requirement.)

b. Calculate the cost of financing the firm's funds needs using the conservative approach.

c. Calculate the peak net working capital associated with each of these plans.

d. Tabulate and discuss the basic risk-return trade-off associated with aggressive and conservative financing approaches. Risk is used here to refer to the peak net working capital requirement.

5. For the R. M. Cook Company (in problem 4):

a. Calculate the cost of financing the firm's funds requirements using fixed long-term financing of $8,000,000 and short-term funds for the remaining needs.

b. Calculate the peak net working capital associated with this plan.

c. Discuss this trade-off plan in light of the aggressive and conservative financing approaches.

6. The L. F. Company wishes to evaluate the credit terms offered by three suppliers of an undifferentiated product. The credit terms offered by each of the suppliers are as follows:

Supplier	Credit terms
A	2/20 net 60 EOM
B	1/30 net 60 EOM
C	2/10 net 90 EOM

a. Calculate the cost of forgoing the cash discount in each case.

b. Evaluating each supplier separately, would you recommend taking the cash discount if the firm could borrow at 10 percent? Explain.

c. If the firm were certain it would take the cash discount, from which supplier would you recommend purchasing? Explain.

d. If the firm is in desperate need of funds and is certain it will forgo the cash discount, from which supplier would you recommend it make the purchase? Explain.

e. If the firm knew it could stretch an account payable to supplier A by 20 days, what effect, if any, would this have on the cost of forgoing the discount from supplier A?

7. A firm currently pays its employees every two weeks. The total payroll is normally $2,000,000. The firm is considering paying employees on a monthly basis. The firm has a 12 percent opportunity cost of funds.

a. How much, if any, could the firm save annually by paying monthly instead of every two weeks?

b. If the change in payment period will cost the firm $50,000 per year, would you recommend the proposed change?

8. The Harrison-Monroe Bank loaned Guatemala Glass (GG) $100,000 on a 90-day note at 2.5 percent over the annual prime rate. The day the loan was made, the prime rate was 16 percent. It went to 17 percent on day 30, 18 percent on day 60, and 19 percent on day 90.
    a. What amount of interest would GG pay if this were a fixed-rate loan?
    b. What amount of interest would GG pay if this were a floating-rate loan?
    c. Discuss the difference between the two loans.

9. Calculate the annual percent interest cost on a $150,000, six-month loan with a stated interest rate of 12 percent if:
    a. Interest is paid at maturity.
    b. Interest is paid in advance.

10. Calculate the effective interest cost on a $300,000 line of credit with a 14 percent stated interest rate and a 15 percent compensating balance requirement.

11. A firm is changed a 0.4 percent commitment fee on the average unused portion of a revolving credit agreement. If the agreement is for $2,000,000 and the firm's average borrowing is $1,400,000, calculate the dollar amount of the commitment fee.

12. If commercial paper maturing to a value of $500,000 in 90 days can be sold for $480,000, what annual interest (percent) is paid on this issue?

13. The Bank of Jackson is considering making a loan secured by accounts receivable to the Fast Fix Company, who wishes to borrow as much as it can. The bank's policy is to accept as collateral the accounts of customers that pay within 15 days of the end of the 45-day credit period and have an average account age that is no more than 8 days beyond the customer's average payment period. The Fast Fix Company's accounts receivable balances, ages, and average payment period for each credit customer are given below. The Fast Fix Company extends net 45-day credit terms.

Customer	Accounts Receivable	Average age of account (days)	Average payment period of customer (days)
A	$10,000	65	70
B	25,000	40	50
C	40,000	50	60
D	20,000	20	45
E	30,000	10	55
F	15,000	60	50
G	20,000	50	65
H	25,000	12	50

    a. Calculate the dollar amount of acceptable accounts receivable collateral held by the Fast Fix Company.

    b. If the bank reduces acceptable collateral by 5 percent for returns and allowances, how much acceptable collateral does the firm have?

    c. If the bank will advance 70 percent against the adjusted acceptable collateral, how much can the firm borrow?

14.   The L & L Manufacturing Company has factored eight accounts to the World Factoring Company. The factored accounts are all due April 30, and the factor has taken a 3 percent discount on all factored accounts. Given the information below, indicate the dates and amount that World Factoring should remit to L & L by April 30.

Account	Amount	Status
A	$20,000	Uncollected
B	40,000	Collected April 27
C	10,000	Collected April 10
D	25,000	Collected April 15
E	105,000	Uncollected
F	80,000	Uncollected
G	5,000	Collected April 20
H	50,000	Uncollected

15. The Frankle Company operates in a seasonal business and currently faces a severe liquidity crisis. The firm has a maximum need of $60,000 for the next sixty days. The firm has exhausted all unsecured sources of short-term funds and wishes to find a secured short-term lender. The firm's accounts receivable are quite low, but its inventory, which is believed to be reasonably active, is considered good collateral. The firm through its research has found that the following lending arrangements against inventory are available. The book value of inventory is $120,000, of which $90,000 is finished goods.

Plan 1: Mercantile Bank will advance 60 percent of the book value of collateral for an 18 percent, 60-day note. The firm must borrow the maximum needed, since prepayment penalties will eliminate any reduction over the loan period.

Plan 2: The Republic Bank will make a trust receipt loan against the $90,000 of finished-goods inventory. The cost of this loan will be 17 percent interest plus a 0.50 percent administrative fee charged on the $90,000 collateral. The average loan will be $50,000.

Plan 3: The First Bank will lend 80 percent of the finished goods balance and will charge 19 percent on the outstanding loan balance. The average loan balance is expected to be $50,000 over the 60-day period. A 1.0 percent warehousing fee will be charged on the total finished goods that will be warehoused.

a. Assuming that $60,000 is the initial amount borrowed in each case, calculate the cost of each plan.

b. Which of the plans do you recommend that the firm accept?

c. If the firm were extended credit terms of 1/10 net 40 on a $60,000 purchase, with a 1.50 per month late charge, would it be better to forgo the discount than to take the action recommended in part b?

SOLUTIONS

DEFINITIONS

1.   current assets; current liabilities.
2.   cash; inventories; accounts receivable; cash
3.   positive
4.   fixed; permanent
5.   aggressive
6.   Spontaneous
7.   credit period
8.   cash; cash; period
9.   prime
10. fixed-rate; floating-rate
11. revolving; commitment fee
12. commercial paper
13. collateral
14. notification basis
15. floating

MULTIPLE CHOICE

1. c
2. d
3. c
4. a
5. a
6. b
7. d   (a+c)
8. a

9. d
10. c   (1/99) X (360/20) = .0101 X 18 = .1818
11. b $10,000 ÷ $90,000 = .1111
12. d
13. b
14. a   factored accounts have been sold
15. d

PROBLEMS

1.   a. Net working capital:

Current assets	$10,000
Less: Current liabilities	5,000
Net working capital	$ 5,000

   b. Dollar return on total assets:

   $(.03) \times (\$10,000) + (.18) \times (\$30,000) = \$5,700$

   Ratio of current to total assets:

   $\$10,000 \div \$40,000 = 0.25$, or twenty-five percent

   c. Cost of financing:

   $(.10) \times (\$5,000) + (.14) \times (\$35,000) = \$5,400$

   Ratio of current liabilities to total assets:

   $\$5,000 \div \$40,000 = 0.125$

   d. Net profitability:

   $\$5700 - \$5400 = \$300$

2.   Based upon the proposed changes, the firm's balance sheet will look like this:

Assets		Liability and Equity	
Current Assets	$ 8,000	Current liabilities	$ 8,000
Fixed Assets	$32,000	Long-term funds	$32,000
Total	$40,000	Total	$40,000

   a. Net working capital:

Current assets	$ 8,000
Less: Current liabilities	8,000
Net working capital	$ 0

b. Dollar return on total assets:

   (.03) x ($8,000) + (.18) X ($32,000) = $6,000

   Ratio of current to total assets:

   $8,000 ÷ $40,000 = 0.20 or twenty percent

c. Cost of financing:

   (.10) X ($8,000) + (.14) X ($32,000) = $5,280

   Ratio of current liabilities to total assets:

   $8,000 ÷ $40,000 = 0.20

d. Net profitability:

   $6000 - $5280 = $720

e. The results of measuring the risk of technical insolvency by the level of net working capital and comparing this to the profitability of each plan are given in tabular form:

Plan	Risk cushion as measured by net working capital	Profitability
Current	$ 5000	$ 300
Proposed	$ 0	$ 720

The higher a firm's net working capital is, the less risky the firm. It can be seen that the current plan has less risk ($5000 vs. $0 net working capital) and lower profit potentially ($300 vs. $720) than the proposed plan. The risk-return trade-off should be obvious. One other conclusion is that both a decrease in the ratio of current assets to total assets and an increase in the ratio of current liabilities to total assets tend to increase profits and risk. In this example, the change in both asset and liability structures tends to increase profits and risk.

3.   To calculate average plan loan balance, first, sum monthly loan balances:

$30,000 + $40,000 + $45,000 + $45,000 + $20,000 + $20,000 + $15,000 + $10,000 + $0 + $0 + $5,000 + $10,000 = $240,000

Then divide by 12 months:
   $240,000 ÷ 12 = $20,000

Annual loan cost:
   ($20,000) X (.12) = $2,400

4.   a. The long-term and short-term financing breakdown associated with this plan, which finances permanent needs with long-term funds and seasonal needs with short-term funds, is given in tabular form as follows:

Month	Total Funds needed (1)	Permanent Portion using long-term funds (2)	Seasonal portion using short-term funds (3)
January	$ 10,000,000	$ 3,000,000	$ 7,000,000
February	9,000,000	3,000,000	6,000,000
March	8,000,000	3,000,000	5,000,000
April	6,000,000	3,000,000	3,000,000
May	4,000,000	3,000,000	1,000,000
June	3,000,000	3,000,000	0
July	5,000,000	3,000,000	2,000,000
August	7,000,000	3,000,000	4,000,000
September	8,000,000	3,000,000	5,000,000
October	10,000,000	3,000,000	7,000,000
November	11,000,000	3,000,000	8,000,000
December	12,000,000	3,000,000	9,000,000
Average		$ 3,000,000	$ 4,750,000

Cost = (.16) X ($3,000,000) + (.12) X ($4,750,000)
     = $480,000 + $570,000 = $1,050,000

b. Using the conservative approach, the firm's peak funds need, which in this case is $12,000,000, is financed with long-term funds.

Cost = (.16) X ($12,000,000) = $1,920,000

c. Peak net working capital can be found by subtracting the minimum total funds needed (i.e., $3,000,000 in June) from the corresponding fixed financing.

Aggressive approach:
  $3,000,000 - $3,000,000 = $0

Conservative approach:
  $12,000,000 - $3,000,000 = $9,000,000

d. The risk-return trade-off of each plan is as follows:

Financing plan	Peak net working capital	Risk ranking*	Financing cost	Profit ranking*
Aggressive	0	2	$1,050,000	1
Conservative	$9,000,000	1	$1,920,000	2

*It can be seen that, although the aggressive approach is more desirable from a profitability standpoint, the conservative approach is more desirable from a risk standpoint (i.e., has higher net working capital) and is therefore more liquid and carries a lower chance of technical insolvency. The aggressive approach is therefore a high-profit, high-risk approach, while the conservative approach is a low-profit, low-risk alternative.

5.   a. The breakdown of the proposed financing into its long- and short-term components is as follows:

Month	Total Funds needed (1)	Permanent Portion using long-term funds (2)	Seasonal portion using short-term funds (1) - (2)
January	$10,000,000	$ 8,000,000	$ 2,000,000
February	9,000,000	8,000,000	1,000,000
March	8,000,000	8,000,000	0
April	6,000,000	8,000,000	0
May	4,000,000	8,000,000	0
June	3,000,000	8,000,000	0
July	5,000,000	8,000,000	0
August	7,000,000	8,000,000	0
September	8,000,000	8,000,000	0
October	10,000,000	8,000,000	2,000,000
November	11,000,000	8,000,000	3,000,000
December	12,000,000	8,000,000	4,000,000
Average		$ 8,000,000	$ 1,000,000

$$\text{Cost} = (.16) \times (\$8,000,000) + (.12) \times (\$1,000,000)$$
$$= \$1,280,000 + \$120,000 = \$1,400,000$$

b. Under this plan, the peak net working capital would occur during June:
   $$\$8,000,000 - \$3,000,000 = \$5,000,000$$

c. Comparing the results of this trade-off plan to the aggressive and conservative approaches, it can be seen that both the risk and profitability of this plan fall between the extremes of the aggressive and conservative approaches. This trade-off plan is less risky and less profitable than the aggressive and more risky than the conservative approach. The financial manager must also consider the potential return on investment of temporarily idle funds.

6.   a.   The cost of forgoing the cash discount from each supplier is calculated using the formula:

$$\frac{CD}{100\%-CD} \text{ X } \frac{360}{N}$$

where   CD = the stated cash discount in percentage terms
N = number of days payment can be delayed by forgoing the cash discount

Supplier A:

$$\frac{.02}{1-.02} \text{ X } \frac{360}{60-20} = \frac{.02}{.98} \text{ X } \frac{360}{40} = .0204(9) = 18.36\%$$

Supplier B:

$$\frac{.01}{1-.01} \text{ X } \frac{360}{60-30} = \frac{.01}{.99} \text{ X } \frac{360}{30} = .0101(12) = 12.12\%$$

Supplier C:

$$\frac{.02}{1-.02} \text{ X } \frac{360}{90-10} = \frac{.02}{.98} \text{ X } \frac{360}{80} = .0204(4.5) = 9.18\%$$

b.   Evaluating each supplier separately in light of the firm's 10 percent borrowing rate, it would be advisable to forgo the cash discount only from supplier C, because only in that case is the cost cheaper than their 10 percent bank rate (i.e., 9.18 percent).

c.   If a firm is certain it is going to take the cash discount, it would want to determine which supplier could be paid the least the latest. The cost of forgoing the discount calculated in part a. is not relevant to this decision. Supplier C can be eliminated, because purchasing from supplier A allows the firm to pay the same percentage (98 percent) ten days later than with supplier C. The decision between suppliers A and B must be made by determining whether or not it is worthwhile for the firm to forgo a 1 percent discount difference in order to pay supplier B ten days later than supplier A (i.e., day 30 as opposed to day 20). The cost of this ten-day delay stated as an annual percentage rate would be calculated in the same fashion as the cost of forgoing a discount.

$$\text{Cost of delay} = \frac{.01}{1-.01} \times \frac{360}{10} = .0101(36) = 36.36\%$$

Because the marginal cost of choosing supplier B over supplier A is so high, the firm should purchase form supplier A if it is sure it will take the cash discount.

d. If the firm must forgo the cash discount, it would purchase from the supplier that could be paid the latest. The cost of forgoing the discount would not be relevant to this decision. If the firm does not take the discount, it would be best to choose supplier C, because payment is not required for 90 days, while suppliers A and B must be paid after 60 days.

e. If the firm could stretch its payable to supplier A by 20 days, supplier A's credit terms could be viewed as 2/20 net 80 EOM, because full payment could be delayed an additional 20 days to day 80. The cost of forgoing the cash discount in this case could be calculated as:

$$\frac{.02}{1-.02} \times \frac{360}{80-20} = \frac{.02}{.98} \times \frac{360}{60} = .0204(6) = 12.24\%$$

The cost would be 12.24 percent, which is lower than the 18.36 percent cost when stretching of accounts payable was not considered. However, such a practice is not ethical, and would not be viewed with favor by the firm's supplier.

7.   a. The average accrual under the present and proposed plans can be calculated by dividing the payroll by 2. The payroll under the present plan is $2,000,000; under the proposed plan it would be $4,000,000 (assuming a four-week month).

Average accrual:

    Present plan   = $2,000,000 ÷ 2 = $1,000,000

    Proposed plan   = $4,000,000 ÷ 2 = $2,000,000

The added accrual (or interest-free loan to the firm) would be $1,000,000 ($2,000,000 - $1,000,000). Because the firm has a 12 percent opportunity cost, its added accrual would allow it to save or earn $120,000 (.12 X $1,000,000) per year.

b. If the firm must pay $50,000 annually to implement the proposed plan, which saves $120,000 per year, implementation of the plan would be recommended, because an annual net savings of $70,000 ($120,000 - $50,000) would result.

8. a. If this were a fixed-rate loan, the interest rate would be set on the day of the loan.

Annual interest rate = Prime + 2.5% = 18.5%
Interest due = (18.5%) X (90/360) X $100,000 = $4,625

b. With a floating rate loan, the interest rate changes each time the prime rate changes. Here, there are three 30-day periods to consider:

Period 1: Interest = 2.5% + 16% = 18.5%
Period 2: Interest = 2.5% + 17% = 19.5%
Period 3: Interest = 2.5% + 18% = 20.5%

Interest due = (18.5%) X (30/360) X ($100,000)
       + (19.5%) X (30/360) X ($100,000)
       + (20.5%) X (30/360) X ($100,000)
       = $1,541.67 + $1,625.00 + $1,708.33 = $4,875

c. With the floating-rate loan, interest is higher by $250. Floating-rate loans protect the financial institutions during periods of rising interest rates.

9. a. If interest is paid at maturity, the stated rate and the effective annual percentage cost are equal. The annual interest cost would be 12 percent.

b. If interest is paid in advance, the amount for the six months would be:
       1/2 yr. X (.12) X ($150,000) = $9,000

The firm would therefore receive the use of

   $150,000 - $9,000 = $141,000

The annual interest cost would therefore be

   ($9,000 ÷ $141,000) X 2 = .0638 X 2 = 12.76%

The calculation uses "2" to translate six months' interest into yearly terms. This problem illustrates that interest paid in advance increases the effective interest rate.

10.   If the firm borrows the full amount, it actually will receive only 85 percent of the funds, since 15 percent of the money must be held in a compensating balance. The annual interest in dollars on the loan would be $42,000 (i.e., .14 X $300,000) for a year. The effective interest cost can be found by dividing the interest by the amount of money the firm actually receives:

$$\text{Effective interest rate} = \frac{\$42,000}{.85(\$300,000)} = \frac{\$42,000}{\$255,000} = 16.47\%$$

A means to double-check this figure is to divide the stated interest rate by the percent of the loan not left in a compensating balance, as follows:

$$\text{Effective interest rate} = \frac{.14}{1-.15} = \frac{.14}{.85} = 16.47\%$$

11.   Applying the .4 percent commitment fee to the average unused balance of $60,000 yields a commitment cost of $2,400 (i.e., .4 x [$2,000,000 - $1,400,000]).

12.   The issuer will be paying $20,000 (i.e., $500,000 - $480,000) to borrow $480,000 for 90 days, or one-fourth of a year. The interest for one-fourth of a year would be:

$20,000 ÷ $480,000 = 4.17%

To find the annual interest rate, 4.17 percent must be multiplied by 4, because the year consists of four 90-day periods. The resulting annual interest cost is

4 x 4.17% = 16.68%

13.   a. The acceptable accounts are those that are paid within 15 days of the end of the credit period, which would be within 60 days, and that, on the average, are not more than 8 days beyond the customer's average payment period. For each customer, the account balance, if acceptable, and its disposition are given below.

Customer	Disposition	Account Balance
A	Age greater than 60 days	
B	OK	$25,000
C	OK	40,000
D	OK	20,000
E	OK	30,000
F	Ten days beyond average pay period	
G	Age greater than 60 days	
H	OK	25,000
	TOTAL ACCEPTABLE ACCOUNTS	$140,000

b. The acceptable collateral would be 95 percent of the amount of acceptable accounts, because a 5 percent reserve is maintained.

Acceptable collateral = (.95) X ($140,000) = $133,000

c. The firm can borrow 70 percent of the acceptable collateral.

Borrowing = (.70) X ($133,000) = $93,100

14. Accounts B, C, D, and G will be paid (minus the discount) by the factor to the firm on the days they are collected. All uncollected accounts must be paid by the factor at the end of the April 30 credit period; therefore, the firm would receive payment for accounts A, E, F, and H on April 30 (minus the discount). Although L and L gives up $10,050 ($355,000 X .03) in discounts, it receives payment on the four past due accounts equalling $ 247,350 ($255,000 X .97). World Factoring will aggressively seek to collect from the past due accounts.

15. Financing needs ($60,000) are less than funds offered ($72,000 = 0.6 X 120,000) by Plan 1, which has a cost of

$$(2/12) \text{ X } (.18) \text{ X } (\$60,000) = \$1,800$$

Since this is a 60-day note, the maximum and average loan amounts are the same.

The cost of Plan 2 would be:

Plan 2 interest:	(2/12) X (.17) X ($50,000)	=	$1,417
Plan 2 administrative fee:	(.005) X ($90,000)	=	450
Plan 2 cost:			$1,867

The cost of Plan 3 would be:

Plan 3 interest:	(2/12) X (.19) X ($50,000)	=	$1,583
Plan 3 warehouse fee:	(.01) X ($90,000)	=	900
Plan 3 cost:			$2,483

b. The firm should accept Plan 1, because its cost ($1,800) is less than that of either Plan 2 or Plan 3. Plan 2 also has appeal, in that it does not force the firm to give up control of the inventory.

c. If the firm forgoes the discount, it will pay 1 percent of the purchase price in order to borrow the money for 30 days, plus 1.5 percent for the next 30 days. The cost would be:

$$(.01) \text{ X } (\$60,000) + (.015) \text{ X } (\$60,000) = \$1,500$$

Because the $1,500 cost of this arrangement is below the $1,800 cost of plan 1, forgoing the discount in this case is a better alternative for raising the needed $60,000. However, simply paying the late fee may not satisfy the supplier offering trade credit, and other, implicit costs may result from poor supplier relations.

CHAPTER 17

CASH AND MARKETABLE SECURITIES

SUMMARY

This chapter is devoted to two important items of working capital: cash and marketable securities. Transactions, safety, and speculative motives exist for holding these assets. Because marketable securities are relatively safe investments that can be readily converted into cash, they provide an excellent interest-earning outlet for temporarily idle funds.

By reducing the minimum cash requirement, the firm can release money for more productive investments. If these balances are too low technical insolvency is more likely. The proportion of a firm's liquid assets that is made up of near-cash securities depends on the trade-off between the interest earned during the holding period and the brokerage costs associated with purchasing and selling marketable securities. The Baumol Model helps identify the appropriate level of cash to be transferred from marketable securities, under conditions of certainty, using a model similar to the EOQ model of inventory management presented in Chapter 18. When much cash flow uncertainty exists, the Miller-Orr model should be used.

Cash management strategies can be viewed in light of the cash cycle. The cash cycle is found by determining the average number of days the firm has its money tied up. By attempting to minimize the average age of inventory and the collection period and to maximize the payment period, the firm's minimum cash requirement can be reduced.

Cash management techniques available to financial managers are aimed at taking advantage of imperfections in the collection and payment system. Specifically, float, the time when funds have been dispatched by the payer but not fully transferred to the payee, provides profit opportunities. Collection float represents the delay in use of funds, while disbursement float represents the delay in the actual withdrawal of funds. Both types of float have three basic components: mail float, processing float, and clearing float. Several techniques exist to minimize collection float and maximize disbursement float. Good banking relationships are required for effective cash management.

A firm holds marketable securities in order to earn interest on temporarily idle funds. For a security to be considered marketable, it must have a ready market, which has both breadth and depth. In addition, the risks associated with the safety of the principal must be very low.

Government-issued marketable securities include Treasury bills and federal agency issues. Non-government issues are negotiable certificates of deposit, commercial paper, banker's acceptances, Eurodollar deposits, money market mutual funds, and repurchase agreements. Government issues are the least risky but have the lowest yield.

CONCEPT OUTLINE

I.   **Management of cash and marketable securities is one of the key areas of working capital management, allowing the financial manager to reduce the risk of technical insolvency.**

    A. Cash is the ready currency to which all liquid assets can be reduced. Because idle cash in a checking account does not earn a high rate of interest, firms purchase marketable securities in order to increase the yield on idle funds.

    B. Marketable securities are short-term investments made in order to earn a return on temporarily idle funds.

    C. Motives for holding cash and near-cash balances include:

        1. Transactions motive balances provide liquidity during normal business operations.

        2. Safety motive balances provide liquidity when cash outflows exceed cash inflows during normal business operations.

        3. Speculative motive balances allow the firm to take advantages of unforseen opportunities. This motive provides the lowest contribution to cash and near-cash balances.

II.   **Efficient management of cash is important for long-run maximization of owners' wealth.**

    A. Excess cash balances are likely to reduce firm profitability, while too little cash increases the chance of technical insolvency.

    B. The Baumol and Miller-Orr models provide insight to the optimal level of transactional balances.

        1. The Baumol model treats cash as a supply of funds that is replenished by marketable securities as needed.

           a. Its economic conversion quantity (ECQ) is a variation of the EOQ model used in inventory management. The model is:

$$ECQ = \sqrt{\frac{2 \ X \ \text{conversion cost} \ X \ \text{demand for cash}}{\text{opportunity cost (decimal form)}}}$$

b. The conversion cost is the clerical and brokerage costs of transferring funds to the cash account. There are economies of scale.

c. The opportunity cost is the interest rate foregone by holding cash instead of higher interest-bearing securities. In decimal form, opportunity cost represents a per-dollar cost.

d. Total cost of maintaining a cash balance equals the sum of conversion costs and opportunity costs, as shown in the following equation:

$$\text{Total Cost} = \frac{ECQ}{2}(OC) + \frac{TC}{ECQ}(CC)$$

where: OC = opportunity cost per dollar
          TC = total annual cash requirement
          CC = fixed conversion costs

Effectively, one is multiplying the average cash balance by the opportunity cost of cash and adding the sum of the frequency of cash transfer times the conversion cost.

e. If safety stocks are held, total cash costs also include the safety stock, in dollar terms, times the opportunity cost.

f. The Baumol model assumes that future demand can be perfectly predicted and that there is a constant cash usage.

2. The Miller-Orr model is more accurate when uncertainty surrounds future cash flows.

a. In addition to the conversion and opportunity costs considerations of the ECQ model, the Miller-Orr model considers the variance in daily net cash flows.

b. The return-point equation is:

$$\sqrt[3]{\frac{3 \text{ X conversion cost X cash flow variance}}{4 \text{ X daily opportunity cost (decimal form)}}}$$

c. The upper limit on the cash balance is three times the return point.

d. When the cash balance exceeds the upper limit two times the return point (or the upper limit less the return point) is converted to marketable securities. When the cash balance reaches zero, the return point amount is converted from near-cash to cash.

C. Marketable securities serve as a liquidity cushion.

1. The financial manager sets the liquidity level and assigns a portion to cash to cover transactional needs (with input from the Baumol or Miller-Orr models) and speculative needs.

2. A line of credit is often substituted for a portion of the portfolio of marketable securities.

III. **There are three basic strategies for efficient cash management.**

A. In order to understand the cash management strategies, a firm's operating and cash conversion cycles are reviewed first in the text.

1. A firm's cash cycle (CCC) represents the amount of time a firm has its money tied up in inventory and accounts receivable. The CCC can be calculated by subtracting the average accounts payable payment period from the sum of the average age of inventory and the average collection period. That is,

$$CCC = AAI + ACP - APP$$

where: AAI = average age of inventory
        ACP = average collection period
        APP = average payment period

a. A positive CCC indicates that supplier credit periods are not sufficiently long enough to cover the firm's operating cycle.

b. A negative CCC means that suppliers are implicitly financing the firm's inventory and receivable accounts. In fact, the sales proceeds are not immediately due to the supplier.

B. The three basic strategies for minimizing the cash conversion cycle are:

1. Manage the production-inventory function as efficiently as possible, avoiding stockouts that might result in shutting down the production line or in losing sales. Yet, do not carry excess inventory. Techniques include:

   a. Increasing raw materials turnover through more sales or reduced inventory levels.

   b. Shortening the production cycle.

   c. Increase finished goods turnover, again through more sales or reduced inventory levels.

2. Collect accounts receivable as quickly as possible without losing future sales because of high-pressure collection techniques.

3. Pay accounts payable as late as possible, so long as the firm's credit rating is not damaged; cash discounts, if favorable, are taken.

C. Dividing cash turnover into estimated annual cash outlays results in an estimate of the firm's minimum cash requirement (or minimum working capital requirement).

D. By minimizing the average age of inventory and the collection period and maximizing the average payment period, the firm will minimize its cash requirement, thereby permitting funds to be employed in more productive investments.

IV. **Cash management techniques exist to take advantage of float and certain imperfections in the collection and payment system.**

A. Float can be categorized as either collection or disbursement.

1. Collection float refers to funds dispatched by the payer, but not yet under the control of the payee.

2. Disbursement float refers to funds dispatched but over which the payee still has control.

B. Float may be categorized by stages in the collection and payment systems.

1. Mail float refers to the period between a payer placing payment in the mail and the payee receiving the check.

2. Processing float refers to the period between a payee receiving payment and depositing that payment in a bank.

3. Clearing float refers to the period between a payee depositing a payment in a bank and actually getting the use of the funds. Funds must be available within two or five days for local and out-of-town checks, respectively.

C. Collection techniques exist to minimize collection float.

1. Concentration banking, which involves collecting money through geographically dispersed collection centers, attempts to reduce both mail and transit float.

2. A lock-box system, which involves geographically dispersed post office boxes that are empties and deposited into the firm's account by its bank, further reduces mail and transit float. In addition, it also reduces processing float.

3. Direct sends, bypassing the Federal Reserve and directly presenting large checks for payment, works to reduce transit float.

4. Other techniques are preauthorized checks (PACs), depository transfer checks (DTCs), and wire transfers.

5. Automated clearing house debits, or preauthorized electronic withdrawals, reduce collection float to one day.

D. Disbursement techniques are designed to maximize disbursement float, allowing the firm to keep funds in an interest-earning form for as long as possible.

1. Controlled disbursing involves placing payments in the mail at locations from which it is known it will take a long time to reach the payee. This increases mail float.

2. Lengthening clearing time by playing the float may refer to writing checks against money not currently in the firm's checking account.

3. In order to take advantage of the float in the banking system, firms can pay from distant banks, because more time will be involved in check-clearing.

4. Scientific check-cashing analysis involves estimating the proportion of checks clearing the account each day and then depositing only enough money to cover these checks, or exercising staggered funding.

5. Overdraft and zero balance accounts allow firms to maintain minimum cash balances in disbursing accounts.

6. Many firms use automated clearinghouse credits to directly deposit payroll into employee or payee accounts. The loss of float is supposedly offset by greater goodwill on the part of employees and suppliers.

7. Although banks offer a variety of cash management services, they should only be used if the benefits exceed the costs.

V. **Marketable securities are short-term money market instruments that can easily be converted into cash.**

A. To be considered truly marketable, a security must have two key characteristics.

1. There must be a ready market that is willing to absorb these securities if their quick sale is desired.

2. The price obtained should not differ greatly from the initial purchase price (i.e., safety of principal).

B. The proportion of marketable securities held by a firm depends on a trade-off between brokerage fees and the length of time and resulting interest earned on holding the marketable security.

VI. **A large number of marketable securities are available, differing with respect to issuer, maturity, risk and return.**

A. A number of government issues of marketable types of securities are available.

1. Treasury bills and Treasury notes are virtually risk-free, lowest-yielding marketable securities issued by the U.S. Treasury.

2. Federal agency issues are marketable securities issued by various agencies of the federal government, such as the Federal Home Loan Bank. Investors believe they are implicitly backed by the federal government.

B. There is a group of nongovernment issues of marketable securities that has slightly higher risk and return.

1. Negotiable certificates of deposit are the marketable securities most commonly issued by commercial banks. Average denomination is $100,000.

2. Commercial paper - short-term, unsecured promissory notes issued by large, financially strong businesses - are very popular because of their high yields.

3. Banker's acceptances are very safe marketable securities issued by banks. They arise from international trade transactions requiring the buyer to issue a letter of credit to the seller.

4. Eurodollars are deposits in foreign banks denominated in U.S. dollars. Deposits are used to make loans denominated in U.S. dollars. Interest rates are frequently highest due to less foreign bank regulation and foreign exchange risk.

5. Money market mutual funds offer low brokerage fees, high returns, and great liquidity. They are simply managed portfolios of the commonly purchased marketable securities.

6. Repurchase agreements are tailor-made marketable securities issued by banks or security dealers.

C. Although each of the marketable securities has some individual characteristics, all are easily marketable and relatively safe short-term investments.

APPLICATIONS

DEFINITIONS

1. *Marketable securities* are short-term, interest-earning instruments used by the firm to obtain a return on temporarily idle funds.

2. A *safety* motive for holding cash or near-cash securities is to protect the firm against being unable to satisfy unexpected demands for cash.

3. The *Baumol* model estimates cost-efficient transactional cash balances; the amount of marketable securities to be liquidated.

4. Funds dispatched by a payer that are not yet in a form that can be spent by the payee are known as *float*

5. *Processing* float is the delay between the receipt of a check by the payee and its deposit in the firm's bank account.

6. The delay between the deposit of a check by the payee and the actual availability of funds is the *clearing* float.

7. A _lockbox system_ reduces collection float by having payments sent to nearby post offices boxes which are emptied by the firm's bank several times daily.

8. _Wire transfers_ remove funds from the payer's account and deposit them in the payee's account through electronic bookkeeping entries.

9. Controlled disbursing from strategic locations is designed to increase _mail float_.

10. Firms that are _playing the float_ keep funds in an interest-earnings form past the point when a check is written against them.

11. A _payable-through draft_ requires approval by the payer before the bank pays the payee.

12. A technique to generate employee goodwill by automatically depositing payroll directly into employee's accounts is known as _ACH credit / automated clearing house_

13. A _broad market_ is characterized by having many participants.

14. _Banker's acceptance_ arise from bank guarantees of business transactions.

15. In a _repurchase agreement_ a bank sells specific securities and agrees to buy them back at a specified price and time.

MULTIPLE CHOICE

1. When a firm holds cash and near-cash assets to provide as source of funds for normal business operations it is satisfying its _d_ motive.
   a. cash
   b. safety
   c. speculative
   d. transactions

2. The least common motive for holding cash is the:
   a. safety.
   b. speculative.
   c. transactions.
   d. trick question, they provide equal motivation.

3.   The _____ provides the economic cost-minimizing quantity (ECQ) in which to convert marketable securities to cash under conditions of certainty.
      a. Baumol Model
      b. Miller-Orr Model
      c. Minimal Cost Model
      d. Upper Limit Model

4.   The _____ cost can be reduced through increasing the efficiency of transferring marketable securities to cash.
      a. conversion
      b. inventory
      c. opportunity
      d. return point

5.   The return point, in the Miller-Orr Model, represents the:
      a. original level of the cash account
      b. the level the cash account is returned to after the cash balance reaches zero.
      c. the level the cash account is returned to after the cash balance exceeds the upper limit.
      d. all of the above.

6.   Basic strategies for the efficient management of cash include:
      a. collecting accounts receivable as late as possible.
      b. paying accounts payable as soon as possible.
      c. selling inventory as quickly as possible.
      d. all of the above.

7.   A firm with an average age of inventory of 80 days, an average collection period of 60 days, and an average payment period of 50 days, has a cash turnover of:
      a. 1.6 times.
      b. 2.8 times.
      c. 90 days.
      d. 190 days.

8.   A negative cash conversion cycle:
      a. allows the firm to use spontaneous financing to support the purchase of fixed assets.
      b. is common among manufacturing firms.
      c. is less desirable that a positive conversion cycle.
      d. requires the usage of nonspontaneous financing to support the cash conversion cycle.

9.   The three basic components of collection and/or disbursement float are:
      a. deposit float, receipt float, endorsement float.
      b. lock box float, draft float, Federal Reserve float.
      c. mail float, processing float, clearing float.
      d. all of the above.

10.   Concentration banking is superior to a lockbox system, because:
      a. it reduces clearing float.
      b. it reduces mail float.
      c. it reduces processing float.
      d. none of the above.

11.   _____ are preauthorized electronic withdrawals from payer's accounts.
      a. Automated clearinghouse credits
      b. Automated clearinghouse debits
      c. Payable-through drafts
      d. Preauthorized checks

12.   A firm using controlled disbursing would be more likely to send checks from:
      a. Los Angeles.
      b. Manitowish Waters.
      c. New York.
      d. St. Louis.

13.   Marketable securities must have all but which of the following characteristics?
      a. high yield.
      b. ready market.
      c. safety of principal.
      d. none of the above.

14.   U.S. dollar denominated deposits in banks outside the U.S. are called:
      a. illegal tender.
      b. high risk foreigns.
      c. Eurodollar deposits.
      d. International banker's acceptances.

15.   Advantages of repurchase agreements include:
      a. guaranteed repurchase.
      b. high return.
      c. standardized maturity dates.
      d. all of the above.

PROBLEMS

1. Every year D & D Designs takes in $3 million dollars from sales. Of this amount $1.75 million is needed for cash payments. Each time D & D Designs transfers funds into its cash account it incurs a charge of approximately $45.00, which covers brokerage expenses as well as its own clerical costs.
    a. If D & D Designs can alternatively hold marketable securities which yield 7 percent, what is the economic conversion quantity.
    b. What would be the total cost for one year of holding the economic conversion quantity according to the Baumol model.

2. After reviewing its cash flows, Damon and Debi noticed a great deal of fluctuation in D & D's cash flows. The variance of daily net cash flows equaled $10,000, or more than twice the average daily cash usage. Consequently, D & D replaced the Baumol model with the Miller-Orr model.
    a. What is the cash return point.
    b. What is the upper limit.
    c. Discuss the cash management procedure used when the cash balance exceeds the upper limit or equals zero.

3. Assume a firm currently has an average inventory age of 80 days, an average collection period of 70 days and an average payment period of 60 days.
    a. Calculate the firm's cash cycle.
    b. Calculate the firm's cash turnover, or frequency of its cash cycle, assuming a 360-day year.
    c. Does this firm have a positive or negative cash conversion cycle. Discuss.

4. Assume the firm in Problem 3 contemplates all of the following changes in cash management. Evaluate the effects of each of the following on the firm's cash cycle and the cost of carrying cash assuming that the firm spends $10 million annually on operating cycle investments.
    a. The firm stretches its average payment period by 10 days.
    b. The firm decreases the average age of inventory to 60 days.
    c. The firm decreases the average collection period by 15 days.
    d. The actions described in parts a, b, and c occur simultaneously.

5.   T-Mark, Inc., a large diversified chain of department stores, currently bills and collects its credit customers' accounts from a central location. Because of the high cost of financing, the firm recently hired a consultant to examine its current collection procedures and to suggest possible improvements. The two plans proposed by the consultant are as follows:

Plan A: Concentration banking system at an annual cost of $200,000, expected to reduce collection time by two days.

Plan B: Lock-box system at an annual cost of $320,000, expected to reduce the average collection time by three days.

If the firm's average daily collections are $1,000,000 and its opportunity cost of funds is 15 percent, which of the proposed plans would you recommend?

6.   Never Fail Products has just received four checks for large amounts, each drawn on a distant bank. The amounts of these checks and their expected transit time are presented below:

Check from	Amount (in 000's)	Number of days transit float expected
Shirley Supply	$ 300	5 days
Monroe Matic	1,600	6 days
Bozo Flunkall	100	3 days
Git-N-Mann	500	7 days

The firm has an opportunity cost of 15 percent. They can contract with Burgess Air to have a jet fly to each city and present the checks for immediate payment, having the funds wired directly to the home office in Tulsa. The cost for Burgess Air is $5,200 and the funds will be available in one day.

Should Never Fail Products use direct sends in this case?

7.   If a firm must pay $500 in brokerage fees to purchase and sell $20,000 of marketable securities yielding 12 percent annual interest, would you recommend the investment if the securities would be held for the following periods?

    a. One month
    b. Two months
    c. Three months
    d. Four months
    e. Six months
    f. Eight months

SOLUTIONS

DEFINITIONS

1.   Marketable securities
2.   safety
3.   Baumol
4.   float
5.   Processing
6.   clearing
7.   lockbox system
8.   Wire transfers
9.   mail float
10.   playing the float
11.   payable-through draft
12.   ACH (Automated clearinghouse) credits
13.   broad market
14.   Banker's acceptances
15.   repurchase agreement

$$\begin{array}{r} 140 \\ -50 \\ \hline 90 \end{array}$$

MULTIPLE CHOICE

1. d	6. c	11. b
2. b	7. d (80+60-50)	12. b
3. a	8. a	13. a
4. a	9. c	14. c
5. d	10. d	15. a

PROBLEMS

1.   a.   The economic conversion quantity (ECQ) is given by the following equation:

$$ECQ = \sqrt{\frac{2 \ X \ \ \text{conversion cost} \ \ X \ \ \text{demand for cash}}{\text{opportunity cost (decimal form)}}}$$

Note that the level of sales has no direct impact on the ECQ. Inserting the proper values for this equation results in a $47,434 cost-minimizing quantity in which to convert marketable securities to cash, as shown below:

$$ECQ = \sqrt{\frac{2 \ X \ \$45 \ X \ \$1,750,000}{.07}} = \$47,434$$

The maximum cash balance would be $47,434.

   b.   The total cost of holding cash instead of marketable securities equals both the total conversion cost plus the total opportunity cost. The total cost equation is:

$$\text{Total Cost} = \frac{ECQ}{2}(OC) + \frac{T}{ECQ}(CC) = 1660 + 1660 = \$3320$$

Note that the total annual cost of the average $23,717 cash balance is $1660. The total annual cost of approximately thirty-seven conversions is $1660. At the optimal ECQ level, opportunity costs equal conversion costs.

2.   a.   The cash return point is the amount of cash remaining after every cash adjustment. It is obtained using the following formula.

$$\sqrt[3]{\frac{3 \ X \ \text{conversion cost} \ X \ \text{cash flow variance}}{4 \ X \ \text{daily opportunity cost (decimal form)}}}$$

The marketable securities portfolio earns a .000194 (7%/360) daily rate. Applying the data from D & D Designs results in a return point of $1202, as calculated below.

$$\sqrt[3]{\frac{3 \times \$45 \times \$10,000}{(4 \times .000194)}} = \sqrt[3]{\frac{\$1,350,000}{.000776}} = \$1,202$$

b. The upper limit is three times the return point or \$3,606 (3 X \$1202).

c. The cash balance would originally be placed at \$1202. If cash outflows exceeded cash inflows, when the cash balance equaled \$0, an another \$1202 worth of marketable securities would be sold. If the cash balance reached \$3,606, \$2,404 (\$3606-\$1202) of cash would be invested in marketable securities.

3. a. The cash cycle can be found by adding the average age of inventory and the average collection period and subtracting the average payment period.

Cash cycle = 80 days + 70 days - 60 days = 90 days

b. Cash turnover is found by dividing the cash cycle into the number of days in the year.

Cash turnover = 360 days ÷ 90 days = 4 times

c. This firm has a positive cash conversion cycle, but in this instance being "positive" is not as satisfying as being "negative." The operating cycle exceeds the spontaneous financing offset, and hence financing will have to be obtained for cash conversion cycle period.

4. a. If the firm stretches its accounts payable by 10 days, the firm's cash conversion cycle (CCC) would be:

CCC = 80 days + 70 days - 70 days = 80 days

b. If the firm decreases the average age of inventory to 60 days, the firm's CCC would be:

CCC = 60 days + 70 days - 60 days = 70 days

c. If the firm decreases the average collection period by 15 days, the firm's cash cycle would be:

CCC = 80 days + 55 days - 60 days = 75 days

d. If all three changes occurred simultaneously, the resulting cash cycle would be:

   CCC = 60 days + 55 days - 70 days = 45 days

5.   For plan A, the savings, if any, can be found by calculating the amount of cash freed, calculating the savings, and subtracting the cost of the plan.

   Cash freed = 2 days X $1,000,000/day = $2,000,000

   Savings on freed cash = (.15) X ($2,000,000) = $300,000

   Net annual savings = $300,000 - $200,000 = $100,000

   For plan B, using the same procedure as those applied to plan A yields:

   Cash freed = 3 days X $1,000,000/day = $3,000,000

   Savings on freed cash = (.15) X ($3,000,000) = $450,000

   Net annual savings = $450,000 - $320,000 = $130,000

Both plans are acceptable, but plan B is preferred because it provides a higher net annual savings.

6.   The benefits of direct sends come from obtaining the use of the funds more quickly and earning their 15 percent opportunity cost.

   The computation required to determine the benefits are as follows:

Amount	X	Days Saved	=	Funds Made Available	X	Opp. Cost	X	Days Saved ÷ 360	=	Benefit
$ 300	x	4	=	$ 1,200	x	.15	x	4/360	=	$ 2.00
1,600	x	5	=	8,000	x	.15	x	5/360	=	16.67
100	x	2	=	200	x	.15	x	2/360	=	.17
500	x	6	=	3,000	x	.15	x	6/360	=	7.50
									Total	$26.34

The total benefits exceed $26,000 while the cost is only $5,200, so direct sends would be appropriate.

NOTE: It is unclear whether the $100,000 check should be part of the direct sends group. The benefit is only $170, but the specific cost is unknown.

7.   For each of the cases presented, the interest earned over the holding period is calculated below:

a. 1/12 X .12 X $20,000 = $ 200

b. 2/12 X .12 X $20,000 = $ 400

c. 3/12 X .12 X $20,000 = $ 600

d. 4/12 X .12 X $20,000 = $ 800

e. 6/12 X .12 X $20,000 = $1,200

f. 8/12   X .12 X $20,000 = $1,600

Comparing the resulting interest earned for each case to the $500 brokerage fees, it can be seen that the marketable security investment would be desirable for all but the one- and two-month holding periods. The actual annual yields, after transactions costs, are:

a. {($200 - $500) ÷ $20,000} X 12/1   =   -18%

b. {($400 - $500) ÷ $20,000} X 12/2   =   - 3%

c. {($600 - $500) ÷ $20,000} X 12/3   =   2%

d. {($800 - $500) ÷ $20,000} X 12/4   =   4.5%

e. {($1200 - 500) ÷ $20,000} X   2   =   7%

f. {($1600 - 500) ÷ $20,000} X   1.5   =   8.25%

CHAPTER 18

ACCOUNTS RECEIVABLE AND INVENTORY

SUMMARY

This chapter covers the two dominant current assets - accounts receivable and inventory. Credit policies focus on credit selection, credit terms, and collection policies. The financial manager considers inventory an investment of funds and must recognize and consider the interrelationship that exists between inventory and accounts receivable.

Credit selection has two dimensions: credit standards and credit analysis. The basic trade-offs from relaxed credit standards are the profit contribution from increased sales, offset by the cost of investment in accounts receivable and the cost of bad debts. The opposite effects would be expected from a tightening of credit standards.

Credit analysis involves the collection and evaluation of credit information on credit applicants to determine whether they can meet the firm's credit standards. The manager's analysis of credit information is both objective (i.e., credit scoring based upon financial characteristics and ratios) and subjective (i.e., based upon a "feel" for creditworthiness). The credit manager or review committee usually also considers economic conditions and availability of the sale item.

Credit terms have three components: the cash discount, the cash discount period, and the credit period. These affect the firm's sales, average collection period, bad debt expenses, and profit per unit. Collection policies determine the type and degree of effort exercised to collect overdue accounts. With the wide-spread use of computers, a large portion of the accounts receivable management process has been automated.

The financial manager should attempt to make sure that the investment in all types of inventory--raw materials inventory, work-in-process inventory, and finished goods inventory--is optimal. The financial manager's general disposition is to keep inventory levels low, without impairing production, to minimize the chance of carrying excess resources.

Several techniques to manage inventory are presented. The ABC system is aimed at determining which inventories require the most attention. The economic order quantity (EOQ) is the order quantity that minimizes the firm's total inventory cost, which consists of order cost and carrying cost components. Order cost is the fixed cost per order, accounting for writing a purchase order, processing the paperwork, checking orders against invoices, and any brokerage fees. Carrying costs include storage, insurance, deterioration and obsolescence, and a financial component representing an opportunity cost of funds invested in inventory.

Once the optimal order quantity has been determined, the firm must set a reorder point. Materials requirement planning (MRP) is a computerized system for making sure every part or material is available when needed. Just-in-time systems are also discussed.

CONCEPT OUTLINE

I.   **Accounts receivable and inventory are the two dominant current assets.**

    A. Accounts receivable average slightly over one-third of current assets and one-seventh of total assets of manufacturing firms.

    B. Inventory accounts for slightly over forty percent of current assets and one-sixth of total assets of manufacturing firms.

    C. To maximize shareholder wealth, a financial manager must attempt to minimize the investment in these assets while maintaining an adequate level of service.

II.   **Credit policy consists of three important aspects of accounts receivable management: credit policies, credit terms, and collection policies.**

    A. The credit policy of a firm represents the guidelines used to determine whether or not credit is to be extended to a customer, and how much.

        1. The 5 C's of creditworthiness are:

           a. Character--past payment history.

           b. Capacity--ability to repay based upon times interest earned and net working capital.

           c. Capital--debt/equity ratio, profitability.

           d. Collateral--lienable assets.

           e. Conditions--economic and inventory circumstances.

           f. Both character and capacity play major roles in credit selection.

        2. Credit selection begins with gathering credit information.

           a. Credit information normally is obtained from such sources as the applicant's financial statements, Dun and Bradstreet, Inc., credit interchange bureaus, direct credit information exchanges, and bank checking.

           b. The analysis of credit information normally is performed by calculating various ratios.

c. Sometimes the firm will establish a line of credit for a customer, which represents a maximum credit limit.

d. The credit decision normally is made not only on the basis of calculated ratios but with the aid of certain subjective managerial judgements.

e. The costs of credit analysis should not exceed the benefits.

3. Credit scoring is a computer-based procedure for ranking or scoring credit accounts.

4. Credit policies can be evaluated by estimating the effects of changes in credit standards on the key variables of sales, average investment in accounts receivable, and bad debt expense.

B. A firm's credit terms represent the repayment terms extended to credit customers.

1. Credit terms are commonly stated in a form such as 2/10 net 30, in which each number represents an important aspect of the firm's terms.

a. A customer would be allowed to take a 2 percent cash discount if payment is made within the 10-day cash discount period.

b. If the customer does not take the cash discount, payment must be made within the 30-day credit period.

2. An increase in the cash discount would be expected to result in an increase in sales and decreases in the average investment in accounts receivable, bad debts, and per-unit profits. (A decrease in the cash discount would be expected to have the opposite effects.)

3. An increase in the cash discount period would be expected to result in an increase in sales, decreases in bad debt expense and per-unit profit, and a change in the average investment in accounts receivable. (A decrease in the cash discount period would be expected to have the opposite effects.)

4. An increase in the credit period would be expected to result in increases in sales, average investment in accounts receivable, and bad debt expense. (A decrease in the credit period would be expected to have the opposite effects.)

C. A firm s collection policies are the procedures that are followed in attempting to collect accounts receivable as promptly as possible when they are due.

1. The level of collection policy effort should not be so aggressive that it offends good customers, nor should it be so lax that it allows slow-paying customers to become bad debts.

2. An increase in collection effort would be expected to result in decreases in bad debts and the average investment in accounts receivable and an increase in collection expenditures. (A decrease in collection effort would be expected to have the opposite effects.)

3. Aging accounts receivable, specifying the period of time over which they have been outstanding, highlights credit and collection problems.

4. Computers are very useful in all aspects of credit management.

III. **Inventory is an important current asset that typically requires a large dollar investment by the manufacturing firm.**

A. Although each type of inventory is not shown separately on the firm's balance sheet, an understanding of the basic types is important.

1. Although one firm's finished goods may be another firm's raw materials, it should be clear that all manufacturing firms have raw materials inventory.

2. The work-in process inventory represents all items currently in the production process.

3. Finished-goods inventory represents items that have been produced but not sold.

4. A trade-off generally exists between the production cost per unit and the level of finished-goods inventory, because large production runs lower per-unit cost but increase average inventory, and vice versa.

B. Conflicting opinions about the appropriate levels of the various types of inventory often exist within the business firm.

1. The financial manager generally favors low levels of inventory, because, the lower the inventory, the less money is tied up in this nonearning asset.

2. The marketing manager is primarily concerned with finished goods and prefers high levels in order to minimize stockouts and avoid lost sales.

3. The manufacturing manager generally is concerned with raw materials and work in process and prefers high levels of these inventories in order to keep the production line moving smoothly.

4. The purchasing manager is primarily concerned with raw materials and would generally prefer high levels in order to receive quantity discounts when purchasing in large quantities.

C. A firm's inventory must be viewed as an investment in the same sense as accounts receivable or fixed assets are investments.

1. The financial manager must recognize and consider the interrelationship that exists between inventory and accounts receivable, and not consider them separately.

2. The cost of carrying an item in inventory typically exceeds the cost of carrying the item in accounts receivable.

3. Due to storage, insurance, deterioration, obsolescence, and financing costs the cost of carrying an item in inventory ranges from twenty to thirty percent.

D. Various methods for controlling inventory are available to the firm.

1. Because inventory often consists of numerous items, it is often useful to group them using the ABC system.

2. The A items would be controlled using sophisticated techniques, while the B and C items would be controlled using less sophisticated techniques, such as the red-line method.

E. The basic economic order quantity (EOQ) model provides a simple approach for determining the optimum quantity to order of a specified inventory item.

1. The EOQ is a sophisticated approach that, in its simplest form, relies on certain basic assumptions.

a. A firm knows with certainty its annual usage of an item.

b. The firm uses inventory at a constant rate over time.

c. Orders placed to replenish inventory are received at the same time that the inventory level reaches zero.

d. In the absence of the certain environment provided by these assumptions, the firm would have to maintain a safety stock of inventory which is inventory in excess of that necessary to meet expected usage in view of the expected lead times to receive orders.

2. The EOQ represents the order quantity that minimizes total inventory cost, which consists of order cost and carrying cost components.

   a. The order cost is fixed, representing the clerical cost of writing an order, processing the paperwork, receiving and checking the order against the invoice, and brokerage costs.

   b. The carrying cost is a variable per unit, per year expense and is made up of a number of components, such as storage, insurance, deterioration and obsolescence, and, most important, the financial cost, which is the opportunity cost of investing funds in inventory.

   c. As the order quantity increases, the total fixed order cost will decrease, because fewer orders will be placed, while the carrying cost will increase because of the higher levels of inventory, and vice versa.

3. Given annual usage, order cost per order, and carrying cost per unit per year, the EOQ can be found either graphically or mathematically, using a simple formula. The model is:

$$EOQ = \sqrt{\frac{2 \times \text{Annual usage} \times \text{Cost per order}}{\text{Carrying Cost}}}$$

4. Total cost equals the average order cost times the number of orders plus the carrying cost times the average inventory. EOQ equates ordering and carrying costs, as shown in the following model:

$$\text{Total Inventory Cost} = \frac{EOQ}{2}(\text{Cost per Order}) + \frac{TC}{EOQ}(\text{Carrying Cost})$$

The EOQ model is similar to the Baumol model used in making the optimal transfer from marketable securities to cash, which was discussed in Chapter 17.

5. Even if it knows the quantity to be ordered, a firm must still determine the reorder point, or level at which an order for additional inventory should be placed.

a. A simple approach consists of multiplying the estimated lead time to receive an order in days by the daily usage of the given time.

b. Difficulty in predicting lead times and daily usage motivates usage of in safety stocks.

c. Materials requirement planning (MRP) is a computerized analysis of production needs, inventory, and lead-time needed to get materials.

d. Just-in-Time (JIT) systems rely upon timely delivery of quality raw materials to minimize raw materials inventories.

APPLICATIONS

DEFINITIONS

1. Credit policy consists of the determination of credit _selection_, credit _terms_, credit _standards_, and _collection_ policy.

2. Credit _selection_ concerns whether to extend credit to a customer.

3. A line of credit is the _maximum_ amount a credit customer can owe the lending institution.

4. Credit standards are the _minimum_ requirements for extending credit.

5. The ranking of an applicant's overall credit strength is called _credit scoring_.

6. _Collection policy_ procedures include letters, telephone calls, personal visits, and legal action.

7. _Aging_ is a technique for providing information on the proportion of accounts receivable that have been outstanding for a specified period of time.

8. The cost of carrying an item in inventory is _greater_ than the cost of carrying an account receivable.

9. Inventory items progress from the _raw material_ inventory, to the _work in process_ inventory, before entering the _finished goods_ inventory.

10. The _C_ group, when using ABC inventory management, consists of a large number of items but a relatively small dollar investment.

Economic Order Quantity

11.   While the red-line method specifies the ___*timing*___ of an inventory purchase, EOQ specifies the ___*size*___ of the purchase.

12.   Total inventory cost consists of ___*order*___ cost and ___*carrying*___ cost.

13.   Extra finished goods inventories, or ___*safety stocks*___, can be drawn down when actual sales exceed expectations.

14.   In ___*Materials requirement planning*___ a computer is used to determine order frequency based on production schedules and inventory balances.

15.   The ___*just in time*___ system of inventory management minimizes inventory investment by having needed items arrive at exactly the time they are needed.

MULTIPLE CHOICE

1.   Which of the following is not one of the five C's of credit:
       a.   capacity.
       b.   cash
       c.   character
       d.   capital   *b) Cash*

2.   The primary source of credit ratings and estimates of overall strength is:
       a.   Dun & Bradstreet.
       b.   Merrill Lynch.
       c.   Value Line.
       d.   Wall Street Journal.

3.   Relaxation of credit standards:
       a.   Increases bad debt expenses.
       b.   Increases investment in accounts receivable.
       c.   Increases sales volume.
       d.   All of the above.

4.   The portion of accounts receivable to be considered when adjusting credit standards is:
       a.   all costs.
       b.   fixed costs.
       c.   sunk costs.
       d.   variable costs.

5.   Happy Farmer's credit terms are 1/10 net 20. What is the cash discount?
      a. One percent
      b. Ten percent
      c. Twenty percent
      d. Some other value

6.   Increasing cash discounts:
      a. Decreases the number of new accounts receivable.
      b. Increases bad debt expenses.
      c. Increases profit per unit.
      d. Increases sales volume.

7.   Changes in _____ will have a negative impact upon profits when the credit period is reduced.
      a. bad debt expenses
      b. investment in accounts receivable
      c. sales volume
      d. a and b

8.   Increasing collection efforts will:
      a. decrease bad debt expenses.
      b. decrease collection expenditures.
      c. increase account receivable.
      d. increase sale volume.

9.   Which of the following sequences ranks collection techniques from lenient to strict:
      a. collection agency, telephone calls, legal action
      b. legal action, personal visits, collection agencies
      c. letters, personal visits, legal action
      d. personal visits, letters, telephone calls

10.   Inventory carrying costs for one year range from _____ percent of the cost (value) of the item.
      a.   0 to 10
      b. 10 to 20
      c. 20 to 30
      d. 30 to 40

11.   Assume a firm uses 100 units of an item each year, its order costs are $10 per order and carrying costs of $5 per unit per year. What is the economic order quantity for the firm?
        a. 10 units
        b. 20 units
        c. 200 units
        d. 400 units

12.   Under the assumptions underlying the EOQ model, at the optimal economic order quantity (EOQ):
        a. carrying costs are minimized.
        b. ordering costs are minimized.
        c. total costs inventory costs are minimized.
        d. all of the above are true.

13.   If the firm in problem 11 orders the EOQ, what total inventory costs will it have?
        a. $ 100
        b. $ 200
        c. $1,500
        d. None of the above

14.   A firm uses 720 units of an item per year, It takes 12 days to receive an order. Assume a 360 day year, and determine the reorder point.
        a. 6 units
        b. 12 units
        c. 24 units
        d. 240 units

15.   Just-in-time systems require the commitment of:
        a. firm employees.
        b. suppliers.
        c. transportation companies.
        d. all of the above.

PROBLEMS

1.   T.J. Peterson Cooking Oil sold 10,000 units of its product last year, but, based on proposed changes in credit terms, the firm anticipates that sales will increase by 10 percent, to 11,000 units, in the coming year. The firm's total fixed cost is $120,000, its variable cost per unit is $16, and the sale price per unit is $40. The firm expects the costs and the sales price to remain unchanged in the coming year.

    a. Calculate the average cost per unit under both the present and the proposed plans. Discuss the calculated difference in these values.

    b. Calculate the additional profit contribution from sales expected to result from implementation of the proposed plan.

2.   Assume that under both the current and proposed plans, the T.J. Peterson Company (in problem 1) makes all sales on credit. Under the present plan, the average collection period is 36 days; under the proposed plan, it would be 72 days. The firm's required return on investment is 20 percent.

    a. Calculate the firm's average investment in accounts receivable under both the present and proposed plans.

    b. Determine the firm's cost of the marginal investment in accounts receivable, based on the required return of 20 percent.

    c. If bad debts are unaffected by the proposal, would you recommend the proposed plan? Explain.

3.   Assume that, under the present and proposed plans, the T.J. Peterson Company (in problems 1 and 2) has bad debt expense of 1 percent and 3 percent, respectively.

    a. Calculate the cost of the marginal bad debts associated with implementation of the proposed plan.

    b. Would this added information change the decision found in problem 2c? Explain.

4.   The Karing Company, which currently makes all sales on terms of net 30 days, is contemplating offering a 2 percent cash discount on early payment. The firm currently sells 40,000 units at $10 per unit. Its variable cost per unit is $6, and the average cost per unit at the $400,000-unit sales level is $7.50. The firm expects that the relaxation in credit terms will results in a 15 percent increase in sales to 46,000 units and will reduce the average collection period to 18 days from its current level of 45 days. The firm expected that the cash discount will be taken on 70 percent of its sales that the bad debt expenses will be unchanged. The firm has a 15 percent required return on investment. Determine whether or not the proposed plan should be implemented.

5.   Duds, Inc., expects to have sales this year of $15 million under its current credit policy. The present terms are net 30, the average collection period is 60 days, and the bad debt percentage is 5 percent. The variable cost percentage is sixty percent (.6) and the firm's required rate of return is fifteen percent (.15).

Duds is considering hiring the Thug Collection Agency to collect past due accounts on Duds' behalf. The average collection period would decline to 40 days, with bad debts falling to one percent. Of course, this would drive away some customers, reducing sales to $14 million. Thug's charge would be $250,000, which Duds obviously always plans to pay on time. Should Duds hire Thug? Explain.

6.   The M. M. Adams Company has ten different items in its inventory. The average number of these items in inventory and their associated unit costs are given below. If the firm wishes to apply an ABC inventory control system, indicate a suggested breakdown of these items into A, B, and C classifications.

Item Number	Average Number of units in inventory	Average cost per unit
1	60	$ 1.00
2	150	9.00
3	400	0.90
4	1,000	25.00
5	3,000	4.00
6	620	10.00
7	30	200.00
8	25,000	.02
9	100	10.00
10	20,000	.08

7.   The Empire Manufacturing Company uses 2,400 units of a key raw material each year. The firm's order cost is $100 per order, and its carrying cost per unit per year is $2.50. Calculate values of the following variables for order quantities of 2,400, 1,200, 600, 300, and 100 units:
   a. Number of orders per year
   b. Annual ordering cost
   c. Average inventory
   d. Annual carrying cost
   e. Total inventory cost

8. The Twidwell Company uses 100,000 gallons of oil each year in its manufacturing process. The oil is used at a constant rate and can be purchased and received within 15 days. The 1 firm has sufficient storage capacity for up to 50,000 gallons. The firm has analyzed its inventory costs and has found that its order cost is $250 per order and its carrying cost is $2 per gallon per year.
    a. Calculate the EOQ for the company's oil.
    b. Calculate the total cost of the plan suggested by the EOQ.
    c. Calculate the firm's reorder point in terms of gallons.

9. Rework problem 8 above assuming that the firm intends to maintain a safety stock of 500 gallons.

SOLUTIONS

DEFINITIONS

1. selection, standards, terms, collection
2. selection
3. maximum
4. minimum
5. credit scoring
6. Collection policy
7. Aging
8. greater
9. raw materials; work-in-process; finished goods
10. C
11. timing; size
12. order; carrying
13. safety stocks
14. materials requirement planning
15. just-in-time system

MULTIPLE CHOICE

1. a
2. a
3. d
4. d
5. a
6. d
7. c
8. a
9. c
10. c.

11. b

$$\sqrt{\frac{2 \text{ X Units used X Order cost per order}}{\text{Carrying cost}}} = \sqrt{\frac{2 \text{ X } 100 \text{ X } \$10}{\$5}} = 20$$

12. c
13. a Total cost = [$10 X (100÷20)] + [$5 X(20÷2)]
                = $100
14. c Reorder point = [720 ÷ 360] X 12 = 24 units
15. d

PROBLEMS

1.   a. The average cost per unit under each plan can be found by dividing the total cost, based upon the expected sales, by the unit level of sales.

Present plan:

Total cost = $120,000 + ($16) X (10,000 units)
            = $120,000 + $160,000 = $280,000

Average cost/unit = $280,000 ÷ 10,000 units = $28/unit

Proposed plan:

Total cost = $120,000 + ($16) X (11,000 units)
            = $120,000 + $176,000 = $296,000

Average cost/unit = $296,000 ÷ 11,000 units = $26.91/unit

The lower average cost per unit of the proposed plan results because, under the proposed plan, the fixed cost is spread over more units (i.e., 11,000 versus 10,000), thereby lowering the per-unit fixed cost allocation, which lowers the average cost per unit.

b. The additional profit contribution from sales expected to result from implementation of the proposal is most easily calculated by multiplying the added units of sales by their per-unit profit contribution, which can be found by subtracting the variable cost per unit from the sale price per unit.

Additional profit   =   (11,000 - 10,000 units) X ($40 - $16)
                             =   1,000($24) = $24,000

2.   a. The simplest way to find the average investment in accounts receivable is to divide the total cost of the firm's annual sales by the turnover of accounts receivable.

Present plan:

Cost of sales = 10,000 units X $28/unit = $280,000

or $120,000 + [10,000 units X $16/unit] = $280,000

Turnover of accounts receivable = 360 days ÷ 36 days = 10

Average investment in A/R = $280,000 ÷ 10 = $28,000

Proposed plan:

Cost of sales = 11,000 units X $26.91/unit = $296,000

or $120,000 + [11,000 units X $16/unit] = $296,000

Turnover of A/R = 360 days ÷ 72 days = 5

Average investment in A/R = $296,000 ÷ 5 = $59,200

b. The cost of the marginal investment in accounts receivable is found by multiplying the marginal investment in accounts receivable by the firm's required return on investment.

Marginal investment = $59,200 - $28,000 = $31,200

Cost of the marginal investment in A/R = .20($31,200) = $6,240

c. The proposal would be highly acceptable, because the additional profit contribution from sales of $24,000 (calculated in problem 1b) exceeds the cost of the marginal investment in accounts receivable of $6,240 (calculated in problem 2b).

3.   a. The cost of the marginal bad debts is found by calculating the cost of bad debts under each plan and then taking their difference.

Proposed plan: (.03) (11,000 units) ($40/unit) = $13,200

Present plan: (.01) (10,000 units) ($40/unit) = $ 4,000

Cost of marginal bad debts: $ 9,200

b. Adding the cost of the marginal bad debts, $9,200, to the cost of the marginal investment in accounts receivable, $6,240 (calculated in problem 2b) results in a total costs of the proposed plan equalling $15,440. Comparing this cost to the $24,000 additional profit contribution from marginal sales indicates that the proposed plan would still be acceptable. The marginal profit would be $8,560($24,000 - $15,440).

4.   To determine whether or not the Karing Company should implement the proposed cash discount, the additional profit contribution from marginal sales and the savings on the reduced average investment in accounts receivable must be compared to the cost of the cash discount. If the savings are greater than the costs, the plans should be implemented; otherwise, it should be rejected.

Additional profit contribution from marginal sales =
($46,000 units - $40,000 units) X ($10/unit-$6/unit) =
    6,000 units X $4 = $24,000

The savings from reduced average investment in accounts receivable are calculated as follows:

(a) Present average A/R investment =

$$\frac{(\$7.50/\text{unit}) \ X \ (40,000 \ \text{units})}{360 \ \text{days}/45 \ \text{days}} = \frac{\$300,000}{8} = \$37,500$$

(b) Proposed average investment in accounts receivable =

$$\frac{(\$7.50/\text{unit} \times 40,000 \text{ units}) + (\$6/\text{unit} \times 6,000 \text{units})}{360 \text{ days}/18 \text{ days}}$$

$$= \frac{(\$300,000 + \$36,000)}{20} = \frac{\$336,000}{20} = \$16,800$$

(c) Reduced average investment in accounts receivable =
[(a) - (b)] = [\$37,500 - \$16,800] = \$ 20,700.

(d) Savings from reduced average investment in A/R =
0.15 X \$20,700 = $\underline{\$\ 3,105}$

The cost of the cash discount is calculated by multiplying the cash discount percentage by the portion of dollar sales in which the cash discount is taken:

$$(.02) \times (.70) \ (\$10/\text{unit}) \times (46,000 \text{ units}) = \$\ 6,440$$

The net effect is as follows:

Added revenues:
Additional profit from marginal sales	$24,000
Savings from reduced A/R investment	3,105
Total added revenues	$27,105
Added cost:	
Cost of cash discount	- 6,440
Net Profit	**$20,665**

Because the added revenues of \$27,105 resulting from the additional profit contribution from sales and reduced investment in accounts receivable exceeds the cost of the cash discount, the proposed plan is acceptable. The net effect on profits of implementing the proposed plan is \$20,665.

5.   To determine whether or not Duds should hire Thug, the lost sales and $250,000 charge
        must be compared to the reduced investment in accounts receivable and increased bad
        debt collection. If savings exceed costs, Thug should be hired.

        (a) Reduced profit contribution from lost sales =
            -$1,000,000 X (1.0 - 0.6) =   -$ 400,000

        (b) Reduced investment in accounts receivable =

            Present average investment in A/R
                ($15,000,000) ÷ (360/60) = $ 2,500,000

            Proposed investment in A/R
                ($14,000,000) ÷ (360/40) =   1,555,556

            Reduced average investment in A/R $ 944,444

            X Cost of capital   X   .15
            Savings from reduced A/R   141,667

        (c) Increased Collections

            Present collection loss =
                ($15,000,000 X .05) $ 750,000

            Less: Proposed Collection loss =
                ($14,000,000 X .01)   - $ 140,000   610,000

        (d) Collection agency fee: - 250,000

            Net effect on profit of hiring Thug $ 101,667

The gain resulting from increase collections and reduced investment in accounts receivable
($751,667) exceed the loss of profits on sales and collection agency fee ($650,000). Hiring
Thug Collection Agency will increase net profit by $101,667.

6.   Although there is no absolutely correct answer to this problem, a reasonable classification
        can be made by first determining the average dollar investment in each item by
        multiplying the average number of units by their average unit cost.

Item Number	Average dollar investment
1	$ 60
2	1,350
3	360
4	25,000
5	12,000
6	6,200
7	6,000
8	5,000
9	1,000
10	1,600

From a subjective evaluation of the average dollar investments, the following classification can be made.

Class	Item Number
A	4, 5
B	6, 7, 8
C	1, 2, 3, 9, 10

The A items are in the range of $12,000 to $25,000 average dollar investment; the B items are in the range of $5,000 to $6,200 average dollar investment; and the C items are $1,600 or less in average dollar investment.

7.   a.   The number of orders can be found by dividing the annual usage (2,400 units) by the order quantity.

Order Quantity (units)	Number of Orders
2,400	1
1,200	2
600	4
300	8
100	24

b. The annual ordering cost can be found by multiplying the number of orders by the $100 cost per order.

Order Quantity (units)	Number of Orders	Annual Ordering Cost
2,400	1	$ 100
1,200	2	200
600	4	400
300	8	800
100	24	2400

c. The average inventory can be found by dividing the order quantity by 2.

Order Quantity (units)	Average Inventory	Annual Carrying Cost
2,400	1,200	$ 3,000
1,200	600	1,500
600	300	750
300	150	375
100	50	125

d. The annual carrying cost can be found by multiplying the average inventory by the annual carrying cost of $2.50/unit, as shown above.

e. The total inventory cost can be found by adding the annual ordering cost calculated in part b to the annual carrying cost calculated in part d.

Order Quantity (units)	Annual Ordering Cost	Annual Carrying Cost	Total Inventory Cost
2,400	$ 100	$ 3,000	$ 3,100
1,200	200	1,500	1,700
600	400	750	1,150
300	800	375	1,175
100	2,400	125	2,525

8.   a. In order to calculate the EOQ, the values of S = 100,000 gallons, 0 = $250, and C = 2 must be substituted into the formula for the EOQ.

$$ EOQ = \sqrt{\frac{2SO}{C}} = \sqrt{\frac{(2)(100,000)(\$250)}{\$2}} = 5,000 \text{ gallons} $$

b. Each component of the total inventory cost can be estimated separately. It is best to determine the order cost first, because we must round off for an even number of orders.

Order cost: Dividing the annual usage by the EOQ results in the number of orders.

Number of orders = 100,000 ÷ 5,000 gallons = 20 orders

Annual order cost = 20 X $250 = $5,000

Carrying cost: Multiplying the average inventory by the carrying cost per unit.

Average inventory = 5,000 gallons/2 = 2,500 gallons

Annual carrying cost = 2,500 X $2 = $5,000

Annual Inventory cost = ordering cost + carrying cost

$$= \$5,000 + \$5,000 = \underline{\$10,000}$$

We know that EOQ and total cost were correctly calculated because annual ordering cost equals annual carrying cost.

c. The reorder point can be calculated by multiplying daily usage by the lead time, given as 15 days. Daily usage is annual usage of 100,000 gallons divided by 360 days in a year.

Daily usage = 100,000 gallons ÷ 360 days = 277.78 gals/day

Reorder point = 277.78 X 15 = 4166.67 gallons

Rounding to the next higher number, we determine that 4,167 gallons is the reorder point.

9.   a. The EOQ does not change due to safety stock 5,000 gals.

b. The total inventory cost will increase because it is expected that an extra 500 units will be carried over the period.

Cost of carrying safety stock = 500 x $2 = $1,000

Total inventory cost = $1,000 + $10,000 = $11,000

c. The reorder point will now be 500 units higher (the amount of the safety stock).

Reorder point = 4,167 + 500 = 4,667 gallons

CHAPTER 19

MERGERS, LBOs, DIVESTITURES, AND FAILURE

SUMMARY

This chapter discusses business combinations and business failure. Firms often find that external expansion is more attractive than internal growth. Firms commonly combine in order to achieve growth in either their size or the diversity of their products. Economies of scale frequently allow the firm to lower overhead. Other reasons for combination include increasing fund-raising ability, acquiring certain managerial skills, obtaining certain tax benefits, or providing owners with increased liquidity.

In evaluating possible business combinations, the financial manager must act in accordance with the long-run goal of owners' wealth maximization, using capital budgeting techniques. The manager must determine the net cash outlay and subsequent cash benefits expected and find the net present value at the appropriate discount rate. Prior to discounting cash inflows in such cases, any impacts on risk resulting from the acquisition must be considered.

The ratio of exchange, which is the ratio of the amount paid per share of the target firm to the market price of the acquiring firm, must be determined when merging firms use an exchange of stock. The long-run effect of a merger on earnings per share is largely dependent on the expected growth rate of the earnings of the merged firm. A merger may not positively affect earnings per share initially but do so over the long run. The price at which the merged firm will sell can be estimated by multiplying the expected price-earnings ratio by the forecasted earnings per share.

If the management of the merger candidate does not want to merge, the acquiring firm may attempt to gain control by buying the firm's stock in the marketplace or using tender offers for a certain number of shares at a specified price, which is set above the prevailing market price. Numerous takeover defenses for fighting hostile takeovers were developed during the 1980s.

The primary causes of business failure are mismanagement, downturns in economic activity, and corporate maturity. The creditor committee may recommend: extension, composition, creditor control, or some combination of these techniques. If the creditors do not accept the plan, then the firm will be liquidated, privately or under bankruptcy law.

The Bankruptcy Reform Act of 1978 contains two chapters of key importance for failed firms. Chapter 7 covers liquidation, and Chapter 11 deals with voluntary or involuntary reorganization. A reorganization plan must be judged fair, equitable, and feasible to the court and approved by the creditors.

If reorganization under Chapter 11 is not filed, if the courts determine that reorganization is not feasible, or if the reorganization plan is not accepted, the bankrupt firm will be liquidated. When the firm is deemed bankrupt, a judge may appoint a trustee to handle administrative duties.

CONCEPT OUTLINE

I.   **Business combinations allow firms to expand externally and increase productivity capacity, earnings, market price, or liquidity.**

   A. The key types of business combinations are consolidations, mergers, and holding companies.

   1. A consolidation involves the combination of two or more companies to form a completely new company.

   2. A merger is a combination of two or more companies in such a way that the resulting firm maintains the identity of one of the merged firms.

   3. A holding company is a corporation that has voting control over one or more corporations or subsidiaries. It is a group of corporations, rather than a single merged firm.

   B. Common motives for strategic mergers include:

   1. Rapid growth in either the firm's size or the diversity of its range of products.

   2. To achieve synergistic effects, or economies of scale, that allow a firm to lower its overhead.

   3. To increase fund-raising ability by acquiring cash-rich or low-levered firms.

   4. To acquire certain managerial skills, technology, or patent rights.

   5. To provide owners with increased liquidity through the enhanced marketability of shares.

   C. Motives for financial mergers, which normally include a restructuring of the capital structure, include:

   1. Take advantage of certain tax benefits, possibly in the form of tax-loss carryforwards.

   2. Increase earnings by cutting costs and selling low NPV assets.

   3. Enhance earnings per share by replacing shareholders with junk bond financing.

   4. Strategic and financial advantages resulted in a "merger mania" during the 1980s.

D. The high level of merger activity has resulted in the coinage of several new terms to describe participants and strategies.

   1. Acquiring firms generally identify, evaluate, and negotiate with the management and/or shareholders of the target firm.

   2. In a friendly merger, target management is receptive to the acquirer's proposal.

   3. If target management is not receptive, the acquiring firm may make a tender offer for shares at a premium price or buy them in the stock market.

   4. There are four types of mergers based upon the relative product line of the companies.

      a. Horizontal mergers join two firms in the same line of business, such as two beer producers.

      b. Vertical mergers occur when a firm acquires a supplier or a customer, such as a beer producer acquiring a distributor.

      c. Congeneric mergers occur when a firm acquires another in the same general industry, such as a beer producer acquiring a mineral water firm.

      d. Conglomerate mergers occur when a firm acquires another in an unrelated business, such as a beer producer acquiring an insurance agency.

E. Leveraged buyouts (LBOs) are an acquisition technique involving a large amount of debt.

   1. The goal of an LBO is to create a high-debt private corporation with improved cash flow.

   2. Typically 90 percent of the purchase price is financed with debt. Management often use LBOs to take firms private.

   3. To be an attractive LBO, a firm must:

      a. Be in a good industry position with a solid profit record.

      b. Have low debt and many bankable assets.

      c. Have stable and predictable cash flows.

F. Divestiture, the selling of some of one firm's assets, is often the source of another firm's external expansion.

1. Firms divest to generate cash for expansion, get rid of poorly performing operations, or to restructure lines of business.

2. The divestment methods most frequently used are:

a. Sale of a line of business to another business.

b. Sale of a unit to existing management. This is frequently through a leveraged buyout (LBO).

c. A spin-off wherein the unit becomes a new independent company.

d. Liquidation of the operating unit's individual assets.

II. **When analyzing prospective mergers, the financial manager must consider whether the firm is being acquired for cash or in exchange for stock.**

A. When a firm is acquiring another firm for cash, certain capital budgeting techniques are readily applicable.

1. If a firm is acquiring another firm for its assets, it must determine the net cash outlay and subsequent cash benefits expected and, using the appropriate discount rate, find the net present value.

2. If the net present value of the acquisition cash flows is greater than or equal to zero, the acquisition is feasible.

3. Cash acquisitions of going concerns are treated in the same manner as cash acquisitions of assets.

4. In acquisitions of going concerns for cash, it is difficult to estimate cash inflows, and the discount rate used must be chosen in light of any change in risk resulting from the acquisition.

B. Mergers involving the exchange of stock, referred to frequently as stock swap transactions, are more difficult to analyze.

1. Stock exchange transactions take place using a ratio of exchange, which is the ratio of the amount paid per share of the target firm (T) to the market price of the acquiring firm (A).

The equation is:

$$\text{Offer Price}_T \div \text{Market Price}_A = \text{Ratio of Exchange}$$

where: Offer Price$_T$ = price/share offered to T
        Market Price$_A$ = premerger market price of A

2. The earnings per share of the merged firm are likely to change as a result of the merger.

3. The effects on the earnings per share of both the acquiring and target firm can be evaluated by comparing the price-earnings ratio paid by the acquiring firm to acquire the company to the acquiring firm's own price-earnings ratio.

4. The long-run effect of the merger on earnings per share is largely dependent on the rate of growth of earnings of the merged firm.

C. The effects of a merger on the market price of the surviving firm can be evaluated by using the ratio of exchange in market values, which is the ratio of the market value paid by the acquiring firm to the premerger market value of the target firm.

1. The price at which a merged firm will sell can be estimated by multiplying the expected price-earnings ratio by the forecasted earnings per share.

2. Although both the earnings and market price effects resulting from a proposed merger are paramount, some attention normally is directed to dividends, book value, and the business and financial risks of a proposed merger.

III. **Mergers can be negotiated with the target's management or shareholders.**

A. Investment bankers often assist in identifying suitable candidates, evaluating the benefits of the combination, and handling negotiations.

B. In a hostile takeover, a two-tier tender offer has terms that are more attractive to those tendering their shares early.

C. Several defenses exist for fighting a hostile takeover.

1. A white knight defense involves finding a more suitable acquirer.

2. A greenmail defense consists of buying the stock of the hostile suitor at a premium.

3. A leveraged recapitalization defense involves the payment of a large debt-financed dividend, increasing financial leverage.

4. Golden parachutes give key executives bonuses in the event of takeover, resulting in an additional burden to the acquirer.

5. Shark repellents constrain the Board of Directors ability to transfer control, effectively entrenching management.

IV. **Holding companies have voting control of other companies.**

A. A holding company can gain control by holding as little as 10 percent of a firm's outstanding shares.

B. The holding company gains control of a subsidiary by making open-market purchases of its shares or by using tender offers.

C. The holding company arrangement has a number of stated advantages.

1. It enables a firm to get leverage to control a large amount of assets for a small dollar investment.

2. Other advantages include the risk protection available from diversification, the legal benefits resulting from having separate suitable entities, firm-specific state tax savings, and the ease with which the holding company gains control of a subsidiary.

D. Disadvantages of the holding company arrangement include double taxation of a portion of their income, the high risk from loss magnification, and the high administrative cost of maintaining numerous corporate entities.

V. **A number of basic types and causes of business failure exist.**

A. There are three basic types of business failure.

1. Firms have failed when returns on capital are consistently less than the cost of capital.

2. Technical insolvency is a situation in which a firm is unable to pay its liabilities as they come due. Because the firm has become illiquid, it cannot conduct its business.

3. Bankruptcy, which occurs when a firm's liabilities exceed the fair value of its assets, results in negative stockholders' equity.

B. There are several common causes of business failure.

1. The primary cause is mismanagement, resulting in overexpansion, poor financial actions, a poor sales force, and high production costs.

2. Prolonged economic downturns often contribute to the failure of business firms, especially those with high fixed costs.

3. Corporate maturity can cause business failure. If a firm does not plan ways to prolong its life, it can fall into decline.

VI. **A firm that is technically insolvent or bankrupt may make certain arrangements with creditors for an out-of-court or voluntary settlement to keep the firm operating.**

A. A voluntary settlement normally is initiated by the debtor, who arranges to meet with all creditors, possibly with the aid of a key creditor.

B. A number of possible arrangements may be recommended by the creditor committee.

1. An extension can be arranged.

2. Composition provides the creditors with a pro rata settlement.

3. Creditor control is an arrangement by which creditors manage the firm until their claims are settled.

C. If the creditors do not accept the plan presented by the creditor committee, the firm will be liquidated, either voluntarily or under bankruptcy law.

VII. **If a firm is not sustained under a voluntary settlement, it can be reorganized under bankruptcy law.**

A. The Bankruptcy Reform Act of 1978 is the legal basis.

1. Chapter 7 covers liquidations.

2. Chapter 11 covers both voluntary and involuntary reorganization. Involuntary reorganization may be filed by one or more creditors

B. The debtor in possession (DIP) must first value the firm in order to determine whether or not reorganization is appropriate.

C. If reorganization is appropriate, the DIP must draw up a fair, equitable, and feasible plan of recapitalization.

D. Once the DIP's reorganization plan is found acceptable by the court, it must be approved by creditors and stockholders.

VIII. **If reorganization under Chapter 11 is not filed, if the courts determine that reorganization is not feasible, or if the reorganization plan is not accepted, the bankrupt firm will be liquidated.**

A. When the firm is deemed bankrupt, the judge appoints a trustee to handle the administrative duties of the bankruptcy and temporarily take charge of property. The trustee's responsibilities include keeping records, examining creditors' claims, disbursing money, and making a final liquidation report.

B. The trustee's most important function is the liquidation of assets and the payment of all provable claims. The priority of claims, which must be observed when distributing the proceeds from liquidation of assets is as follows:

1. Expenses of administering the bankruptcy.

2. Interim business expenses incurred between filing and the appointment of the trustee.

3. Wages of not more than $2,000 per worker earned in the three-month period preceding the bankruptcy proceedings.

4. Unpaid employee benefit plan contributions due in the six-month period preceding the filing or business termination (whichever occurred first).

5. Unsecured deposits of customers up to $900.

6. Taxes due.

7. Claims of secured creditors.

8. Claims of unsecured creditors.

9. Claims of preferred stockholders, up to the par value of their shares.

10. Claims of common shareholders, who receive anything that remains. (It is not unusual for the common stockholders to receive nothing as a result of the liquidation process.)

C. Once the court approves the final accounting, liquidation is complete.

APPLICATIONS

DEFINITIONS

1.   The resulting combination maintains the identity of one of the original firms in a _____.

2.   A _____ _____ has voting control of its subsidiaries.

3.   The acquiring firm acquires a supplier or a customer in a _____ merger.

4.   An acquisition technique involving the use of a large amount of debt to purchase a firm is referred to as a _____ _____.

5.   A ____-____ results in an operating unit becoming an independent company by issuing shares of the new firm on a proportionate basis to the parent company's shareholders.

6.   Shareholders who tender their shares early receive a greater payment in a ____-____ tender offer.

7.   A _____ takeover defense consists of a target firm repurchasing a large block of stock at a premium from the shareholders attempting a hostile takeover.

8.   _____ _____ provide key executives sizable compensation if the firm is taken over.

9.   A firm unable to pay its liabilities as they come due is _____ _____.

10. If a firms' creditors agree to defer receipt of payment, the firm has received a (an) _____.

11. _____ _____ arrangements permit the creditor committee to replace the firm's operating management.

12. Chapter ____ of the Bankruptcy Act of 1978 details the procedures to follow when liquidating a firm.

13.   In _____ reorganizations, the petition for reorganization or payment of creditors
        is initiated by an outside party.

14.   A failed firm's debts are exchanged for equity in a _____.

15.   _____ creditors have specific assets pledged as collateral.

MULTIPLE CHOICE

1.   Key forms of business combinations include all but which one of the following?
        a. consolidation.
        b. divestment.
        c. holding company.
        d. merger.

2.   Which of the following is an example of a financial merger?
        a. merger of a low debt firm and high debt firm
        b. merger of a wholesaler and retailer
        c. merger of two producers of beer
        d. merger of two firms in the same industry

3.   Horizontal growth results from the combination of:
        a. a supplier and a customer.
        b. firms in the same line of business.
        c. firms in unrelated lines of business.
        d. two of the above.

4.   A _____ merger's key benefit is its ability to reduce risk by merging firms with different
        seasonal or cyclical patterns.
        a. congeneric
        b. conglomerate
        c. horizontal
        d. vertical

5.   Which of the following is not true of a typical leveraged buyout?
        a. cash flows are expected to improve
        b. it results in a public corporation
        c. the bonds issued are backed by all firm assets
        d. the firm is purchased with almost all debt

6.   The basic difficulty of applying the capital budgeting techniques to the acquisition of going concerns is estimating:
     a. cash flow and risk.
     b. life-cycle of the firm.
     c. working capital requirements.
     d. yield-to-maturity.

7.   Smith Drug wants to acquire Monroe Tire. Smith's stock sells for $50 and Monroe's at $80. Smith has offered Monroe $100 per share in a stock transaction. What is the ratio of exchange?
     a. .625
     b. 1.00
     c. 1.60
     d. 2.00

8.   If a firm in a stock-exchange acquisition pays a greater P/E multiple than its current multiple, it will initially experience a _____ in EPS, and the target firm's shareholders will experience a _____ in EPS.
     a. decrease, decrease.
     b. decrease, increase.
     c. increase, decrease.
     d. increase, increase.

9.   When the ratio of exchange in market price is greater than 1:
     a. a stock's price earnings ratio will decline.
     b. owners of the target firm receive a premium.
     c. owners of the acquiring firm cannot gain.
     d. two of the above.

10. A formal offer to purchase a given number of shares of a firm's stock at a given price is called:
     a. a negotiated bid.
     b. a tender offer.
     c. a white knight.
     d. greenmail

11. _____ could entrench existing management, by limiting the shareholders' rights to transfer managerial control.
     a. Golden parachutes
     b. Poison pills
     c. Shark repellents
     d. White knights

12.   The primary advantage of the holding company arrangement is the:
      a. leverage effect.
      b. risk reduction.
      c. tax effect.
      d. all of the above.

13.   The primary cause of business failure is:
      a. failure to use this textbook and study guide.
      b. lack of a business degree.
      c. mismanagement.
      d. undercapitalization.

14.   When a company must be liquidated, creditors prefer it to be voluntary because of:
      a. lower bankruptcy costs.
      b. potential publicity.
      c. the ethical issues involved.
      d. all of the above.

15.   In the event of a liquidation under Chapter 7 of the Bankruptcy Reform Act of 1978, highest priority for payment is for:
      a. common equity.
      b. taxes due the U.S. Government.
      c. the company's workers, up to $2,000.
      d. the expenses of administrating the bankruptcy.

Problems

1.   The Newport Pipe Company is contemplating acquisition of the Akron Tire Company, which currently has a tax-loss carryforward of $800,000. The tax loss is broken into the following components:

Years remaining to carry forward	Amount
1	$ 200,000
2	300,000
3	80,000
4	120,000
5	100,000
Total loss	$ 800,000

The firm expects that its earnings before taxes in the five years following the acquisition will be as follows:

Years after acquisition	Earnings before taxes
1	$180,000
2	200,000
3	100,000
4	100,000
5	200,000

Newport is in the 40 percent tax bracket. Assume the tax-loss carryforward is within the limits of the Tax Reform Act of 1986.
  a. Calculate the firm's tax payments without the acquisition.
  b. Calculate the firm's tax payments for each year with the proposed acquisition.
  c. Determine the total tax benefit from the proposed acquisition.
  d. What is the most you would pay for the firm if its only value was the tax loss?

2. The Fendwick Company is contemplating acquisition of the Graves Company for a cash price of $275,000. The Fendwick Company currently is very highly levered and therefore has a cost of capital of 13 percent. As a result of acquiring Graves, which is entirely financed with equity, Fendwick expects its cost of capital to drop to 11 percent. Acquisition of the Graves Company is expected to increase Fendwick's cash inflows by $40,000 per year for the next 15 years.
  a. Determine whether or not the proposed cash acquisition is desirable.
  b. If the firm's capital structure were to remain unchanged as a result of the proposed acquisition, how would this affect your decision?

3. Pierce Company is interested in acquiring the Bellmon Company by exchanging 0.9 shares of its stock for each share of Bellmon's stock. Some financial data for these companies are as follows:

	Pierce Company	Bellmon Company
Earnings available for common stock	$500,000	$300,000
Number of shares of common stock outstanding	200,000	100,000
Earnings per share	$2.50	$3.00
Market price per share	$25.00	$24.00
Price-earnings ratio	10	8

Pierce Company has sufficient authorized but unissued shares to carry out the proposed acquisition.

    a. How many shares of stock will Pierce have to issue in order to implement the proposed acquisition?

    b. If the earnings from each firm remain unchanged, how much would the postmerger earnings per share be?

    c. How much has been effectively earned on behalf of each of the original shares of Bellmon's stock?

    d. Comment on the effects of the, merger on the per-share earnings of both the old and the new shareholders. Explain what has happened in light of the price-earnings ratio paid for Bellmon's stock.

4.   The Brewer Company wishes to evaluate the effects of a proposed merger on its long-run earnings per share. The firm's 1990 earnings were $600,000, and the firm has 200,000 shares of common stock outstanding. The firm is considering acquiring the Server Company, which has 50,000 shares of common stock outstanding on which it earned $250,000. The earnings of Brewer are expected to grow at a rate of 4 percent each year, while Server's earnings are expected to grow at an annual rate of 10 percent. The proposed ratio of exchange is 2.0.

    a. Calculate Brewer's earnings per share for each year in the 1990-1997 period, assuming that it does not merge.

    b. Calculate Brewer's earnings per share for each year in the 1990-1997 period, assuming that it does merge.

    c. What recommendation would you make? Explain.

5.   The following data are given for the Ames Company and the Baker Company, which Ames is considering acquiring for a 1.4 ratio of exchange.

	Ames	Baker
Number of shares of common stock outstanding	50,000	10,000
Earnings available for common stock	$175,000	$40,000
Market price per share	$30	$40

a. Calculate the ratio of exchange in market price.
b. Calculate the earnings per share and price-earnings ratio for each company.
c. ⌐alculate the price-earnings ratio paid to purchase the Baker Company.
d. Calculate the postmerger earnings per share for the Ames Company.
e. Calculate the expected market price per share of the merged firm, assuming that it continue to sell at its premerger price-earnings ratio.

6. Hold'em Incorporated holds enough stock to give it voting control of both companies X and Y. The simplified balance sheets for these companies are shown on the next page.
    a. What percentage of the total assets controlled by Hold'em Incorporated does its stockholders' equity represent?
    b. If the Charles Company owns 15 percent of the stock in Hold'em and this gives it voting control, what percentage of the total assets controlled does the Charles Company's equity represent?

7. Classify each of the following voluntary settlements as an extension, a composition, or a combination of the two. Explain the resulting classifications.
    a. One group of creditors is paid in full now, and the remaining creditors receive full payment in four future installments.
    b. Each creditor receives $.70 on the dollar, to be received immediately.
    c. Creditors receive $.60 on the dollar now and will be paid the remaining $.40 on the dollar within two years.
    d. One group of creditors is paid in full now, and the remaining creditors are paid $.80 on the dollar in two installments-$.40 now and $.40 in the future.

Hold'em Incorporated			
Assets		Liabilities and stockholders' equity	
Common stock holdings:		Long-term debt	$200,000
Company X	$200,000	Preferred stock	100,000
Company Y	300,000	Common stock	200,000
Total	$500,000	Total	$500,000

Company X			
Assets		Liabilities and stockholders' equity	
Current assets	$ 500,000	Current liabilities	$ 200,000
Fixed assets	1,000,000	Long-term debt	500,000
		Common stock	800,000
Total	$1,500,000	Total	$1,500,000

Company Y			
Assets		Liabilities and stockholders' equity	
Current assets	$1,000,000	Current liabilities	$ 500,000
Fixed assets	3,000,000	Long-term debt	1,500,000
		Common stock	2,000,000
Total	$4,000,000	Total	$4,000,000

8.   The T. Hollingsworth Corporation's liquidation value is estimated to be $650,000. The firm's after-tax earnings are estimated to remain indefinitely at $90,000 per year, and the firm's cost of capital is estimated to be 13 percent. The firm's current and proposed capital structures are as follows:

Capital Structures		
Type of capital:	Current	Proposed
Debentures	$ 350,000	$100,000
Mortgage bonds	200,000	100,000
Income bonds	0	200,000
Preferred stock	50,000	0
Common stock	400,000	200,000
Total capital	$1,000,000	$600,000

a. Calculate the going-concern value of the firm, and indicate whether or not the firm should be reorganized.
b. Calculate and discuss the degree of leverage present in the current and proposed capital structures.
c. Discuss the exchanges that would result from implementing the proposed recapitalization. Indicate what amount, if any, and type of capital each of the original fund suppliers would receive.

9.   The Fail Never Company has recently failed and has been liquidated by a court-appointed trustee. The trustee, who has charged $180,000 for his services, managed to liquidate the firm for $1,800,000, which consisted of $1,000,000 from current assets and $800,000 from fixed assets. There were no interim business expenses between the bankruptcy petition and the appointment of the trustee. The firm's preliquidation balance sheet is given on the next page.
   a. Prepare a table indicating the amount, if any, to be distributed to each claimant except unsecured creditors.
   b. After satisfying all claims other than unsecured creditors, how much, if any, is owed to the second mortgage holder? Explain.
   c. Prepare a table showing how the funds, if any, would be distributed to the firm's unsecured creditors.
   d. Do the firm's owners receive any distribution of funds?
   e. What effect, if any, does the presence of the subordinated debentures have on the payment of the notes to the bank (Notes payable-bank)?

The Fail Never Company
Preliquidation Balance Sheet

Cash	$ 50,000	Accounts payable	$ 400,000
Marketable securities	50,000	Notes payable -bank	250,000
Accounts receivable	500,000	Accrued wages[a]	90,000
Inventory	550,000	Unpaid employee benefits[b]	50,000
Prepaid expenses	50,000	Accrued rent[c]	60,000
Total current assets	$1,200,000	Taxes payable	100,000
Land	$1,000,000	Total current liabilities	$ 950,000
Equipment	500,000	First Mortgage[d]	700,000
Plant	450,000	Second Mortgage[d]	300,000
Total fixed assets	$1,950,000	Subordinated mortgages[e]	150,000
		Long-term debt	$1,150,000
		Preferred stock (10,000 shares)	200,000
		Common stock (20,000 shares)	80,000
		Paid-in capital in excess of par	670,000
		Retained earnings	100,000
		Shareholders' equity	$1,050,000
Total assets	$3,150,000	Total	$3,150,000

[a]Represents wages of $900 per employee earned within three months of filing bankruptcy for 100 of the firm's employees.

[b]Unpaid employee benefits that should have been paid in the preceding six months.

[c]Rent owed for use of machinery received within three months prior to filing for bankruptcy.

[d]The first and second mortgages are on the firm's total fixed assets.

[e]The debentures have been subordinated to the notes payable to the bank.

SOLUTIONS

DEFINITIONS

1. merger
2. holding company
3. vertical
4. leveraged buyout
5. spin-off
6. two-tier
7. greenmail
8. Golden parachutes
9. technically insolvent
10. extension
11. Creditor control
12. 7
13. involuntary
14. recapitalization
15. Secured

MULTIPLE CHOICE

1. b
2. a
3. a
4. b
5. b

6. a
7. d ($100 ÷ $50)
8. b
9. b
10. b

11. c
12. a
13. c
14. a
15. d

PROBLEMS

1. a. Without the acquisition, the tax payments in each year would equal 40 percent before-tax earnings as follows:

Years	Tax payment
1	$72,000
2	80,000
3	40,000
4	40,000
5	80,000

 b. If the firm were to make the acquisition, it would use the tax losses to lower its tax liabilities. The required calculations are given in tabular form as follows:

Year	Earnings before taxes (1)	Application of tax loss (2)	Taxable income [(1) - (2)] (3)	Tax payment [.40 x (3)] (4)
1	$180,000	$180,000	$ 0	$ 0
2	200,000	200,000	0	0
3	100,000	100,000*	0	0
4	100,000	100,000	0	0
5	200,000	100,000	100,000	40,000

*Represents $80,000 from portion with three years remaining and $20,000 from portion with four years remaining.

 c. The total tax benefit of the proposed acquisition can be found by calculating the difference in tax payments without and with the acquisition, from parts a and b, respectively.

Year	Taxes without acquisition (1)	Taxes with acquisition (2)	Reduction in taxes [(1) - (2)] (3)
1	$ 72,000	$ 0	$ 72,000
2	80,000	0	80,000
3	40,000	0	40,000
4	40,000	0	40,000
5	80,000	40,000	40,000
Total	$312,000	$40,000	$272,000

The tax savings are given in column (3). Total savings over the five years is $272,000.

d. The most the firm should pay to make the acquisition (ignoring administrative costs) is $272,000. The individual savings occur at different points over the next five years, so the true amount would be less, because, by using an appropriate discount rate, the present value of the tax savings would be less than $272,000.

2.   a. The acceptability of the proposed acquisition can be treated as a simple capital budgeting problem. Finding the net present value by using the 11 percent postmerger cost of capital yields the following:

Net present value = [(7.191) X ($40,000)] - $275,000

   = $287,640 - $275,000 = $12,640

The 7.191 value is the interest factor for the present value of a 15-year discounted annuity at 11 percent. The net present value of $12,640 indicates that the proposed acquisition is acceptable.

b. If the firm's capital structure remained unchanged, the cash inflows would be discounted at a 13 percent cost of capital. The net present value at 13 percent is calculated as follows:

Net present value = [(6.462) X ($40,000)] - $275,000

   = $258,480 - $275,000 = -$16,520

The 6.462 value is the interest factor for the present value of a 15-year annuity discounted at 13 percent. The net present value of -$16,520 indicates that the proposed acquisition is not acceptable. Because the firm's cost of capital did not drop in this case, the resulting negative net present value makes the project unacceptable.

3.   a. Because the ratio of exchange is .9 (i.e., .9 share of Pierce would be given for each of the 100,000 shares of Bellmon), Pierce will have to issue an additional 90,000 shares (.9 X 100,000 shares).

      b. If the earnings from each firm remain unchanged, the total postmerger earnings available for common stockholders would be $800,000 ($500,000 from Pierce + $300,000 from Bellmon). After the merger, there will be a total of 290,000 shares of common stock outstanding (200,000 old shares of Pierce + 90,000 new shares exchanged for Bellmon shares). The postmerger earnings per share, therefore, would be $2.76 ($800,000 ÷ 290,000 shares).

      c. Because an original share of Bellmon is .9 share of Pierce, the original share of Bellmon would reap earnings of $2.48 (.9 X $2.76/share).

      d. The result of the merger is that Pierce Company owners experience an increase in per-share earnings (from $2.50 to $2.76/share), while Bellmon Company owners experience an effective decrease in per-share earnings (from $3 to $2.48/share). This occurs because the price-earnings ratio of 7.5 paid to acquire Bellmon [(.9 X $25) ÷ $3] is less than the Pierce Company's price-earnings ratio of 10.

4.   a. In 1990, Brewer earned $600,000 on its 200,000 outstanding shares, giving it earnings per share of $3 ($600,000 ÷ 200,000 shares). Applying an annual growth rate of 4 percent yields the following earnings per share for the 1990-1997 period:

Year	Earnings per share
1990	$3.00
1991	3.12
1992	3.24
1993	3.37
1994	3.51
1995	3.60
1996	3.80
1997	3.95

b. If the Brewer and Server Companies merge, using a 2.0 ratio of exchange, an additional 100,000 shares would be issued (2.0 X 50,000 shares of Server), resulting in a total of 300,000 shares outstanding after the merger (200,000 shares + 100,000 shares). To find the earnings per share after the merger, the differing growth rates must be applied to the earnings streams, and then these earnings must be summed to get total earnings. Dividing the total earnings by the 300,000 shares then outstanding would give the postmerger earnings per share, calculated in tabular form as follows:

Year	Brewer Company earnings* (1)	Server Company earnings** (2)	Total earnings [(1) + (2)] (3)	Postmerger earnings per share [(3) ÷ 300,000] (4)
1990	$600,000	$250,000	$ 850,000	$ 2.83
1991	624,000	275,000	899,000	3.00
1992	648,960	302,500	951,460	3.17
1993	674,918	332,750	1,007,668	3.36
1994	701,925	366,025	1,067,940	3.56
1995	729,992	402,628	1,132,620	3.78
1996	759,192	442,891	1,202,083	4.01
1997	789,560	487,180	1,276,740	4.26

*Earnings grow at a 4 percent annual rate.
**Earnings grow at a 10 percent annual rate.

   c. It is difficult to make a definitive recommendation, but it can be seen that, although the earnings per share are largest initially without the merger, after 1993 the merged firm would be expected to have greater earnings per share.

5.   a. The ratio of exchange in market price is found by dividing the product of the ratio of exchange and the market price of the acquiring firm by the market price of the target firm.

Market price ratio of exchange $= \dfrac{(1.4)(\$30)}{\$40} = \dfrac{\$42}{\$40} = 1.05$

     b. The earnings per share of the Ames Company is $3.50 (i.e., $175,000 ÷ 50,000 shares), and its price-earnings ratio is 8.57 ($30 ÷ $3.50). The earnings per share for the Baker Company is $4 ($40,000 ÷ 10,000 shares), and its price-earnings ratio is 10 ($40 ÷ $4).

     c. Because the ratio of exchange is 1.4, the price paid per share of Baker Company's stock would be $42 (1.4 X $30/share). Because Baker earns $4 per share (from part b), the price-earnings ratio paid would be 10.50 ($42 ÷ $4).

d. The postmerger earnings of the Ames Company would be $215,000 ($175,000 from Ames + $40,000 from Baker). In order to acquire Baker, an additional 14,000 shares would have to be issued (1.4 X 10,000 shares), leaving a total of 64,000 shares outstanding. The postmerger earnings per share would be $3.36 ($215,000 ÷ 64,000 shares).

e. If the stock of the merged firm sells for its premerger price-earnings ratio, a multiple of 8.57 (found in part b), the expected market price can be found by multiplying this price-earnings ratio by the expected earnings per share of $3.36 (found in part d). The resulting market price would be $28.80 ($3.36 X 8.57), which is below the premerger market price because of the high dilution of ownership resulting from the market price ratio of exchange, which is greater than one.

6.   a. With its $200,000 of common stock equity, Hold'em Incorporated controls the assets of both company X and company Y, totaling $5,500,000 ($1,500,000 of company X and $4,000,000 of company Y). Stated as a percentage, Hold'em Incorporated's stockholders' equity represents 3.64 percent of the total assets it controls ($200,000 ÷ $5,500,000).

b. If the Charles Company owns 15 percent of Hold'em's stock, it would have an investment of $30,000 (.15 X $200,000), which would give it control over the $5,500,000 of assets. Stated as a percentage, the $30,000 of Charles Company equity would represent .55 percent of the total assets it controls.

7.   a. Because the creditors will receive full payment, but not immediately, this is a form of extension. The creditors paid in full now are obviously dissident creditors who would not go along with the voluntary settlement.

b. This is a composition, because, the creditors have agreed to discharge the firm's debts by accepting less than full payment.

c. This is an extension, because the creditors will receive full payment of their claims over a future period of time.

d. This plan is a combination of composition and extension, because some creditors receive only partial payment that is spread over the future. Nonreceipt of full payment is a characteristic of composition, while payment over the future is a characteristic of extension. There obviously are some dissident creditors who would not accept the plan and therefore had to be paid in full.

8. a. The going-concern value of T. Hollingsworth can be found by capitalizing the expected $90,000-per-year after-tax earnings at the firm's 13 percent cost of capital. Because the $90,000 per year is expected to be received indefinitely, the present value of this $90,000 annuity discounted at 13 percent must be found. Because the is a perpetuity, the present-value interest factor can be found by dividing 13 percent into $90,000. The firm's going-concern value is:

$$\$90,000 \div .13 = \$692,308$$

The firm is therefore worth $692,308 as a going concern and could be liquidated for $650,000. Because the firm's going-concern value is greater than its liquidation value, it should be reorganized. Had the going-concern value been less than $650,000, liquidation would have been recommended, because the firm would have been worth more dead than alive.

b. The current capital structure has a debt-equity ratio of 1.22 ($550,000 ÷ $450,000); the debt-equity ratio under the proposed plan is .50 ($200,000 ÷ $400,000). It should be noted that the income bonds are included as part of the equity, because their interest does not have to be paid unless earnings are available to pay it. The proposed recapitalization lowers the firm's leverage considerably (from 1.22 to .50), which should allow the firm to function more smoothly.

c. The exchange of the capital would be carried out in such a way that the priority of each fund supplier is maintained. The order in which the types of capital were listed in the statement of the problem is their order of priority. Therefore, the $350,000 of debentures would have to receive new capital first; once their claim is met, the mortgage bondholders would have their $200,000 claim satisfied, and so on. This process would be continued until the $600,000 was exhausted. The following table shows how the securities would be exchanged for the T. Hollingsworth Corporation.

Original capital ownership		New capital ownership	
Type	Amount	Type	Amount
Debentures	$350,000	Debentures Mortgage bonds Income bonds Total new capital	$100,000 100,000 150,000 $350,000
Mortgage bonds	$200,000	Income bonds Common stock Total new capital	$ 50,000 150,000 $200,000
Preferred stock	$ 50,000	Common stock	$50,000
Common stock	$400,000		$ 0

It can be seen that the debenture holders, the mortgage bondholders, and the preferred stockholders would each receive the same amount of capital (but of a different type) than they had before the recapitalization, while the common stockholders would be completely written off the books. After the exchange, the old mortgage bondholders and preferred stockholder would become the new common stockholders.

9.   a.   The satisfaction of the claims on the firm must follow the order of priority that is set down by law. The only obligation of the firm not shown on the balance sheet is the $180,000 expense for administering the bankruptcy. The following table shows how the proceeds of the liquidation would be distributed. The payments are listed in order of priority. Note that the eligibility of a number of these payments (wages, taxes, and lease expense) was made clear in the footnotes to the firm's balance sheet.

Proceeds from liquidation	$1,800,000
-Expenses of administering bankruptcy	180,000
-Wages owed workers	90,000
-Unpaid employee benefits	50,000
-Rent owed lessor	60,000
-Taxes owed governments	100,000
Funds available for creditors	$1,320,000
-First mortgage, paid from $800,000 proceeds from sale of fixed assets	700,000
-Second mortgage, partially paid from remaining $100,000 of fixed asset proceeds	100,000
Funds available for unsecured creditors	$ 520,000

It can be seen that, after satisfying all prior claims, $520,000 is available for distribution to unsecured creditors.

b. Once all claims other than those of unsecured creditors are satisfied, it can be seen in the table in part a that only $100,000 of the $300,000 of second mortgage claims are satisfied.   Therefore, the second mortgage creditors are still owed $200,000 (i.e., $300,000 - $100,000). They become unsecured creditors for the $200,000 still owed them.

c. The distribution of the $520,000 to the firm's unsecured creditors, which includes the unpaid balance of the second mortgage, accounts payable, notes payable-bank, and subordinated debentures, is shown in tabular form as follows:

Unsecured creditors claims	Amount Due	Settlement at 52 percent*	After subordinated adjustment
Unpaid balance of second mortgage	$ 200,000***	$ 104,000	$ 104,000
Accounts payable	400,000	208,000	208,000
Notes payable-bank	250,000	130,000	208,000
Subordinated debentures	150,000	78,000	0
Total	$1,000,000	$520,000	$520,000

*The 52 percent rate is calculated by dividing the $520,000 available for unsecured creditors by the $1,000,000 owed unsecured creditors. Each creditor is entitled to a pro rata share.

**The subordination adjustment concerns the notes payable-bank, to which certain debentures were subordinated. The debenture holders must pay the notes payable from their proceeds up to an amount sufficient to permit the notes payable holder (the bank) to have its claims fully satisfied.

***This figure represents the difference between the $300,000 second mortgage and the $100,000 payment on the second mortgage from the sale of the fixed-asset collateral remaining after satisfying the first mortgage.

d. The firm's owners - both preferred and common stockholders - will not receive any distribution of funds in this case, because not even the unsecured creditors had their claims fully satisfied. Had there been sufficient funds to cover all unsecured creditor claims, then preferred stockholders would have had their claims satisfied; if any funds were still remaining, they would have gone to the common stockholders.

e. From the table in part c, it can be seen that the presence of the subordinated debentures allows the bank to recover 83 percent of its claim (i.e., $208,000 of $250,000) rather than its 52 percent pro rata share of $130,000. Because the debentures are subordinated to the notes payable-bank, the bank is able to recover more than its pro rata share, because, until its claims are satisfied, the subordinated debenture holders do not receive anything. Subordination is a contractual requirement that was included in the bank loan as a restrictive covenant.

CHAPTER 20

INTERNATIONAL FINANCIAL MANAGEMENT

SUMMARY

This chapter expands the principles of managerial finance to cover multinational companies (MNCs). MNCs are those firms that have assets and operations in foreign markets and draw part of their revenues and profits from such markets. They differ from domestic firms in four key ways. MNCs may have some foreign ownership or partners. They have opportunities to use multinational capital markets. Accounting rules differ for multinationals due to the existence of different national currencies. Foreign exchange risks can affect revenues and profits.

Joint-venture agreements with either private investors or government-based agencies are often essential for an MNC to operate. Many governments require this, and it does reduce political risks. The combination of the European Community into one economic unit in 1992 provides both the ability to more efficiently do business across national boundaries and greater competition.

Several factors concerning international taxation must be considered. The level of taxes (high or low rates) differs by country. Taxable income is defined differently by various governments. Tax agreements between the United States and other governments also affect the total tax liability of the MNC.

Multinationals can also use the Euromarkets to obtain needed financing and to invest temporarily idle funds. The Euromarkets provide for depositing and lending of currencies outside their countries of origin. Multinationals use the Euromarkets to raise both long-term and short-term funds.

The three key differences between domestically-oriented and internationally-based financial reports are consolidation, translation, and international profit repatriation limitations. Financial statements of subsidiaries are consolidated, based on the percentage ownership by the parent firm. Individual accounts on the financial statements must be converted from foreign currency to U.S. dollars. American MNC's use the current rate method to translate foreign subsidiary accounts. The financial statements of foreign subsidiaries are translated into U.S. dollars at the current exchange rate (balance sheet) or average exchange rate over the period (income statement). This process may cause exchange rate gains or losses.

Foreign exchange risk is the risk that a MNC's revenues or costs in foreign currencies may change when the exchange rate between these foreign currencies and the U.S. dollar changes. The exchange rate is the value of two currencies with respect to each other; for example, US$1.00 = Sf 1.40. Exchange rates can be floating or fixed. Most major currencies float against one another. Foreign exchange risk exists because the future exchange rate is not known. The exposure to foreign exchange risk can be considered accounting exposure, reflecting possible changes to the financial statements, or economic exposure, considering changes to all future revenues and costs.

Some foreign exchange risks can be minimized through the manipulation of accounts receivable and accounts payable.

Political risk refers to host government rules and regulations that can result in a discontinuity or a complete seizure of the operations of a foreign company in that country. Political risk can be macro, which applies to all foreign operations, or micro, which is specific to certain industries or individual countries.

Capital structures of multinational firms differ from those of domestic firms due to access to international capital markets, international diversification, and country factors. London is the center of Euroequity activity. International cash management consists of hedging undesirable exposures with options or other tools, and adjustments in operations, such as reduction of liabilities if the currency of payment is appreciating. Credit and inventory management problems are more pronounced in less developed nations. However, multinational operations frequently provide additional opportunities to maximize shareholder wealth.

CONCEPT OUTLINE

I.   **The principles of managerial finance apply to multinational companies (MNCs).**

A. Factors unique to MNCs add challenges and opportunities.

1. Often a portion of equity is owned by foreign investors.

2. Foreign and international capital markets expand opportunities for financing.

3. The existence of different currencies, and specific translation, consolidation, and profit reporting rules for MNCs makes their financial statements different.

4. MNCs face foreign exchange risk due to fluctuations in exchange rates.

B. A major change in the multinational environment is the transformation of the European Economic Community into a single market by year-end 1992. The new EEC will offer challenges and opportunities to MNCs.

1. MNC will face higher levels of competition, especially from merged European firms.

2. MNC success will require:

a. Correct product mix for customer differences.

b. Taking advantage of the European Currency Unit and Euroequities markets.

    c. Staff operations with proper combination of local and foreign personnel.

C. Foreign business organizations generally take the form of subsidiary or affiliate.

    1. Two general forms of organization exist.

        a. In German-speaking countries, the two forms are the Aktiengesellschaft (A.G.) or the Gesellschaft mit beschrankter Haftung (GmbH).

        b. In other countries, the forms are the Societe Anonyme (S.A.) or the Societe a Responsibilite Limitee (S.A.R.L.).

        c. The A.G. or the S.A. are the most common forms but there are more limitations on them than on the alternative forms.

    2. Joint-venture agreements with either private investors or government-based agencies are becoming increasingly essential.

        a. Several nations, including Brazil and Mexico, require that the majority of ownership be held by domestically based investors.

        b. Foreign ownership results in a substantial degree of management and control by host countries over day-to-day operations, reinvestment, and repatriation.

    3. International taxation is very complex, but four areas must be considered.

        a. The rate of tax differs between high-tax and low-tax countries; and some, but not all, countries have withholding taxes.

        b. The definition of taxable income may differ by country.

        c. Tax agreements between the United States and a foreign government affect when and where taxes are paid.

        d. Local taxes, such as the unitary tax laws, also will reduce the profitability of expanding into certain areas.

D. The Euromarkets provide multinationals with external opportunities to obtain funds or invest surplus funds.

    1. The Euromarkets have grown rapidly and now have currency deposits of over $3.0 trillion, with the U.S. dollar the dominant currency.

a. The markets started with Russian deposits of dollar earnings outside the U.S. jurisdiction.

b. The U.S. balance of payments deficits have left large dollar balances scattered around the world.

c. Specific U.S. banking regulations, such as interest rate ceilings, encouraged foreign deposits.

d. Because of the lack of control and regulation, the size of this external financial market cannot be determined accurately.

2. The market is concentrated in several cities - so-called off-shore centers - such as London, Singapore, Bahrain, Nassau, Hong Kong, and Luxembourg, in which the main factors are availability of communication and transportation facilities, language, costs, time zones, taxes, and local banking regulations.

3. The major participants are banks.

a. U.S. bank branches in London and other off-shore centers are the most important participants.

b. European and Japanese banks have increased their importance in recent years.

c. Both short-term and long-term financing is available through the Euromarkets.

II. **The three key differences between domestically oriented and internally based financial reports are consolidation, translation, and international profits.**

A. Consolidation of foreign subsidiaries depends on the percentage of ownership of the parent.

1. From 0-20 percent ownership requires only reporting of dividends received.

2. From 20-50 percent ownership requires reporting of profits or losses on a pro rata basis.

3. Over 50 percent ownership requires full consolidation.

B. According to FASB No. 52, any items on the financial statements of the subsidiary that are not in U.S. dollars must be translated into dollars using the all-current-rate method.

1. Accounts are kept in the functional currency of the local economy.

2. The balance sheet is translated at the current exchange rate.

3. On the income statement, revenues and expenses must be translated at the average rate over the period.

C. International profitability is affected by translation of accounts at current rates, which may change.

1. Most profits and losses from exchange rate changes are not reflected on the income statement of the MNC.

2. These are reflected in the equity accounts on its balance sheet.

D. Foreign exchange risk results from having revenues and costs based on foreign currencies.

1. The major currencies have a floating relationship, whereas the minor currencies are fixed, or pegged, to one or more major currency.

2. The foreign exchange rate between two currencies, or their value with a respect to each other, is usually expressed as a ratio, for example, Sf1.35/US$, meaning that one must pay 1.35 Swiss francs to purchase one U.S. dollar.

3. Floating rates fluctuate on a daily basis, while fixed rates change only when one or both governments officially change them.

a. An increase in the value of a floating currency is called appreciation; for a fixed currency, it is called an official revaluation.

b. A decrease in the value of a floating currency is called depreciation; for a fixed currency, it is called an official devaluation.

4. A spot exchange rate is the rate for a foreign exchange transaction today; a forward exchange rate is the rate for a future transaction contracted for today.

5. International supply and demand, as well as economic and political elements, help shape spot and forward exchange rates.

6. Foreign exchange risk can be either accounting exposure or economic exposure.

a. Accounting exposure refers to changes in the financial statements resulting from changes in foreign exchange rates.

b. Economic exposure considers the effects of currency changes on the present value of foreign operations.

III. **Political risk come from potential actions by the host government.**

A. A government may cause discontinuity or even seize the operations of a foreign company in its country, with or without compensation.

B. Macro political risk refers to governmental actions that affect all foreign operations within the country.

C. Micro political risk refers to actions that affect specific industries, firms, or firms of specific countries.

D. The greatest political risk is thought to exist in the less-developed countries, because of their political instability.

1. These countries also have very attractive markets.

2. Thus, the risk-return decision must be considered.

E. Several approaches exist to reduce political risks.

1. Positive approaches, involving prior negotiations and local involvement, yield the best results.

2. Negative approaches, such as control of transportation and markets, may work in extractive industries.

3. External approaches, such as local financing, provide little risk reduction.

IV. **Financial decisions on long-term investments must be viewed differently for MNCs.**

A. Foreign direct investment (FDI) is the transfer of capital, managerial, and technical assets to another country.

1. Such investments are subject to the risks of all business plus political and foreign exchange risk.

2. Foreign direct investment into the U.S. exceeds U.S. FDI abroad.

B. Firms undertake FDI for a variety of reasons. However, it is difficult to estimate future cash inflows and risk.

V.   **Financing decisions for MNCs face some unique factors.**

A. Capital structures vary with both whether the firm is a MNC and the location of the MNC's domicile.

   1. International diversification reduces the volatility of cash flows, but this advantage may be offset by political risks.

   2. Legal, tax, political and other aspects of the host country may cause divergence in capital structures.

B. To finance long-term debt requirements, MNCs can sell international bonds in the international capital markets.

   1. Such bonds are either foreign bonds or Eurobonds.

      a. Foreign bonds are sold in the country of the currency of issue.

      b. Eurobonds are sold in countries other than that of the currency of issue.

   2. Non-U.S. multinationals dominate the Eurobond market, and these bonds are primarily issued in U.S. dollars.

   3. Foreign bonds are primarily issued in Swiss francs.

   4. Underwriting institutions in the country of issue handle underwriting.

      a. Underwriting fees are comparable to domestic fees.

      b. Interest rates on international bonds are comparable to those in the country of the currency of issue.

C. International capital markets provide a setting for acquiring international equity funds.

   1. The Euroequity market has greatest activity in London and is a source of international equity financing for MNCs.

2. MNCs prefer to have as little international equity stock and as much debt as possible.

    a. This removes the chance of takeover as a result of local government changes.

    b. There are less restrictions in interest payments than dividend repatriation.

D. Subsidiaries of MNCs can use local money markets and Euromarkets for short-term financing.

    1. The rates on Eurocurrency financing depend on home-country nominal interest rates and the exchange rate between the home currency and other major currencies.

    2. The effective rate takes into account not only the nominal rate but also gains or losses on foreign exchange.

        a. Borrowing in an appreciating currency results in an effective rate above the nominal rate, and vice versa.

        b. Lending in an appreciating currency results in an effective yield greater than the nominal yield, and vice versa.

E. Managing cash and marketable securities denominated in several currencies may require hedging or operating adjustments to reduce foreign exchange risk.

    1. Common hedging tools available to offset short-term foreign exchange risk include:

        a. Borrowing and lending in different currencies.

        b. Forward contracts to buy or sell foreign currency.

        c. Futures contracts to buy or sell foreign currency.

        d. Options contracts to buy or sell foreign currency. Options eliminates downside risk, yet retains upside potential.

        e. Interest rates and currency swaps.

    2. Relationships with other firms - third parties - can be altered.

        a. Accounts payable should be increased in a currency that is expected to depreciate, and vice versa.

      b. Accounts receivable should be decreased in a currency that is expected to depreciate, and vice versa.

   3. Intra-MNC accounts can be paid so as to maximize the value of the parent firm.

      a. Accounts payable should be paid rapidly to divisions in devaluation-prone countries, and vice versa.

      b. Accounts receivable should be paid rapidly to divisions in upvaluation-prone countries, and vice versa.

   4. Other factors must be considered.

      a. Tax status may affect the adjustments.

      b. Local regulations may affect the adjustments.

F. Foreign government cooperation is an important ingredient in both credit and inventory management.

   1. Respective governments can help by identifying target markets and extending credit.

   2. Inventory concerns include having the proper level of inventory spread globally, while minimizing exchange rate fluctuations, tariffs, and the chance of expropriation.

VI. Multinationals form combinations for the same reasons as domestic firms, and for other international considerations as well.

A. International joint ventures and mergers increased during the 1980s.

   1. Developing countries have become increasingly involved.

   2. Direct foreign investment in the United States has increased.

   3. Joint ventures with Japanese firms have increased rapidly in the 1980s.

B. Developing countries have historically required foreign MNCs to form joint ventures with host country firms or the government.

   1. Such combinations are less attractive to foreign MNCs.

2. Recent activities suggest this practice may be relaxed somewhat.

C. International holding companies organize in countries such as Liechtenstein and Panama which have favorable business and tax laws.

APPLICATIONS

DEFINITIONS

1. _____ _____ have international assets and operations in foreign markets.

2. _____ ____ _____ tax multinationals on a percentage of their worldwide income.

3. The _____ provides companies currencies for borrowing outside the currency of their country of origin.

4. FASB No. 52 requires U.S. MNCs to convert the financial statements of foreign subsidiaries into their _____ _____ and then translate the accounts into the parent's firm currency using the ____-_____-____ method.

5. _____ _____ _____ is caused by varying exchange rates between two countries.

6. The value of Japanese yen with respect to U.S. dollars is its _____ _____ _____.

7. If the values of two currencies are allowed to fluctuate with respect to each other they have a _____ _____.

8. The rate of exchange between two currencies at some specified future date is their _____ _____ _____.

9. Nationalization, expropriation, and confiscation are examples of _____ risk.

10. Rules aimed at regulating inflows of foreign direct investment are referred to as _____ _____ _____ _____.

11. Whereas a _____ _____ is often distributed in many countries, a _____ _____ is sold primarily in the country of the currency of the issue.

12. The capital market that deals in international equity issues is called the _____ _____.

13.   In the international context, the nominal interest rate is charged on financing when only the ___'s _____currency is involved.

14.   Adjusting the nominal interest rate for relative fluctuations in foreign currency value results in the _____ interest rate.

15.   Forward contracts, futures contracts, options, and interest rate swaps are examples of _____ _____ used to eliminate international accounting exposure risk.

MULTIPLE CHOICE:

1.   Multinational companies are based in:
       a. Europe.
       b. Japan.
       c. United States.
       d. all of the above.

2.   Which of the following is not true for MNCs?
       a. Consolidated financial statements are based on one currency.
       b. Fluctuations in foreign exchange markets can affect foreign revenues and profits.
       c. Fluctuations in foreign exchange markets can affect the overall value of the firm.
       d. Portions of equity of foreign investments are frequently owned by foreign partners.

3.   Expected outcomes of the transformation of the European Economic Community into a single market by 1992 include:
       a. Fewer restrictions and regulations.
       b. New MNCs arising from mergers by companies within the European Community.
       c. The European Community will enjoy greater economic growth rates.
       d. All of the above.

4.   Features differentiating a MNC's environment from that of the purely domestic firm include all of the below, except:
       a. financial markets.
       b. goal of the corporation.
       c. taxes.
       d. trick question, all vary significantly.

5.   Off balance sheet financing is possible prior to the point where full consolidation of subsidiary in parent financial statements is required, or ___ ownership.
     a. 19 percent
     b. 20 percent
     c. 50 percent
     d. 76 percent

6.   If the US $/DM exchange rate is $.50/DM, what is the DM/US $ exchange rate?
     a. DM .25/US $.
     b. DM .50/US $.
     c. DM 2/US $.
     d. DM 4/US $.

7.   Floating exchange rates imply the value of two currencies:
     a. are officially tied.
     b. may fluctuate on a daily basis.
     c. move up and down together.
     d. two of the above.

8.   On November 1, 1990 the US $/Sfr exchange rate was US $ .60/Sfr. If the Sfr depreciates by 10 percent, what will the exchange rate be?
     a. US $ .54/Sfr.
     b. US $ .66/Sfr.
     c. Sfr 1.67/US $.
     d. some other value.

9.   Foreign exchange fluctuations that affect the firm's value are called:
     a. accounting exposure.
     b. economic exposure.
     c. political exchange exposure.
     d. systematic exchange risk.

10. Political risk:
     a. cannot take place in the U.S.
     b. is probably greatest in developed countries.
     c. is probably greatest in third world countries.
     d. two of the above.

11. Seizure of Company ABC's assets in a foreign country is an example of a _____ risk.
     a. firm specific
     b. macro political
     c. micro political
     d. systematic

12.   An example of an indirect approach to reduce political risk would be:
      a. international insurance.
      b. joint venture with host government.
      c. use of locals in management.
      d. two of the above.

13.   If a U.S. firm borrows in Swiss francs at 6 percent interest, and the value of the Swiss franc appreciates by 2 percent, its nominal rate is ____ percent but its effective rate is ____ percent.
      a. 2, 6.
      b. 6, 2.
      c. 6, 4.
      d. 6, 8.

14.   If a U.S.-based MNC with a subsidiary in Italy expected the Italian currency to appreciate in value relative to the U.S. dollar:
      a. accounts payable should be reduced.
      b. accounts receivable should be reduced.
      c. nothing should be done, since exchange rates are out of the control of the financial manager.
      d. sales to Italian customers should be cut back.

15.   An example of a foreign exchange hedging tool that can eliminate downside risk is:
      a. currency option contract.
      b. forward contract.
      c. futures contract.
      d. all of the above.

PROBLEMS

1.   International Grub has two subsidiaries abroad, as follows: subsidiary 1 (S1) is 49 percent owned by the MNC, with a taxable income of $20 million and local taxes of $8 million; subsidiary 2 (S2) is 25 percent owned by the MNC and has a taxable income of $10 million and local taxes of $2 million. Assume that the MNC can only take foreign income taxes paid by Subsidiary 1 as a direct credit against its U.S. tax liabilities. Further assume that a ten percent foreign dividend withholding tax applies in both instances. Calculate the tax credits and taxes due the MNC if all the taxable income and taxes represent the <u>share</u> belonging to the MNC. Assume a 40 percent U.S. tax rate.

2. Parr Drilling has a subsidiary in S. Newland. The present exchange rate is US $.004/peso or 0.4 cents (U.S.) per 1 peso. Parr makes cash outlays of 20 million pesos per year to S. Newland suppliers. The subsidiary has an average collection period of 60 days, an average age of inventory of 40 days, and an average payment period of 30 days. Parr can adjust operations to change any of the three periods by 10 days (longer or shorter).

    a. What is the present peso minimum cash balance and the dollar equivalent?
    b. If the peso is expected to appreciate to US$.0045/peso, what adjustment should be made in the time periods?
    c. Calculate the foreign exchange gain in U.S. dollars for both the present cash cycle and the cycle indicated in part b. Ignore financing costs.

3. A U.S.-based MNC, Chocolate Goodies, has a subsidiary in Switzerland. The balance sheet and income statement of the subsidiary are shown below. On 12/31/90, the exchange rate is Sfr1.50/US$. Assume that the local (Swiss france, Sfr) figures remain the same on 12/31/91. The average Sfr/$ rate for 1990 is Sfr1.50/US$ and for 1991 is Sfr1.55/US$. Assume all profits are paid out (repatriated) as dividends.

    a. Complete the US$ translated figures for 12/31/90.
    b. Complete the US$ translated figures for 12/31/91 assuming the US dollar appreciates to Sfr1.60/US$.

	12/31/90 Sfr	12/31/90 US$	12/31/91 US$
Cash	50.00		
Inventory	250.00		
Plant and Equip.	350.00		
	650.00		
Total			
Debt	300.00		
Paid-in Capital	150.00		
Retained Earnings	200.00		
Total	650.00		
Sales	4000.00		
Cost of Goods Sold	3200.00		
Operating Profits	800.00		

4.   A U.S. based MNC has two subsidiaries:
        West German Lifting (local currency, Deutsche mark, DM) and United Kingdom
        Hoists (local currency, British pound sterling, L). Forecasts of business operations
        indicate the following short-term financing position for each subsidiary (in equivalent
        U.S. dollars).

        W. Germany: $20 million funds to be raised
        U.K.: $30 million excess cash to invest

        Financial analysts have prepared the following data:

Item	US$	Currency DM	L
Spot exchange rates		DM1.65/US$	L.55/US$
Forecast % change in rate		-2.5%	+2.0%
Interest rates			
Nominal			
Euromarket	10.0%	7.4	11.5
Domestic	9.5%	6.85	11.3
Effective			
Euromarket	10.0%		
Domestic	9.5%		

        a. Complete the table to show the effective interest rate for each currency in the
            Euromarket and domestic market.
        b. Where should the funds be raised and invested? Why?

SOLUTIONS

DEFINITIONS:

1.   multinational companies
2.   unitary tax laws
3.   Euromarket
4.   functional currency; all-current-rate
5.   foreign exchange risk
6.   foreign exchange rate
7.   floating relationship
8.   forward exchange rate
9.   political
10.   national entry control systems

11.   international bond; foreign bond
12.   Euroequity market
13.   MNC's parent
14.   effective
15.   hedging strategies

MULTIPLE CHOICE:

1. d	6. c (1 / 0.5) = 2	11. c
2. a	7. b	12. c
3. d	8. a $.60 X (1.0-.1) = $.54	13. d 6+2 = 8
4. b	9. b	14. a
5. c	10. c	15. d

PROBLEMS

1.   As shown in the following table, International Grub will have $14 million dollars available after paying domestic and foreign taxes. Even though Subsidiary 2 has earnings which are 67 percent of Subsidiary 1, after adjustment for U.S. taxes, the net available from Subsidiary 2's operations is under half of that provided by Subsidiary 1.

	Subsidiary 1	Subsidiary 2
Subsidiary income before local taxes	$20,000,000	$10,000,000
Foreign income tax	8,000,000	2,000,000
Earnings	$12,000,000	$ 8,000,000
Foreign dividend withholding tax	(1,200,000)	(800,000)
MNC's receipt of dividends	$10,800,000	$ 7,200,000
U.S. Tax Liability	8,000,000	$ 4,000,000
Total Foreign Taxes to be used as a credit	$9,200,000	$ 0
U.S. Taxes Due	$ 0	$ 4,000,000
Net Funds Available	$10,800,000	$ 3,200,000

2.   a.   The cash cycle is

$$60 + 40 - 30 = 70 \text{ days}$$

The cash turnover is

$$(360 \div 70) = 5.14$$

In pesos, the minimum cash balance is

$$20{,}000{,}000 \div 5.14 = 3{,}891{,}051 \text{ pesos}$$

In U.S. dollars, the minimum cash balance is

$$3{,}891{,}050 \text{ pesos X US\$ } .004 = \text{US\$15,564}$$

b.   In a currency that is expected to appreciate, the firm should increase assets and decrease liabilities. Here, the subsidiary should increase the collection period to 70 days, increase the average age of inventory to 50 days, and reduce payables to 20 days.

The new cash cycle is

$$70 + 50 - 20 = 100 \text{ days}$$

The new cash turnover is

$$(360 \div 100) = 3.6$$

In pesos, the minimum cash balance is

$$20{,}000{,}000 \div 3.6 = 5{,}555{,}556 \text{ pesos}$$

In U.S. dollars, the minimum cash balance is

$$5{,}555{,}556 \text{ pesos X US\$ } .0045 = \text{US\$25,000}$$

c.   Compare the foreign exchange gain that would have been received in part a with the gain that would have been received in part b. In both cases, the gain is \$US.005 (\$.045-\$.040) per peso times the minimum cash balance.

Present (part a):

$$3{,}891{,}051 \text{ X US\$}.005 = \text{US\$1,946}$$

Change (part b):

$$5,555,556 \text{ X US\$.005} = \text{US\$2,778}$$

Net gain on adjustment:

$$\text{US\$2,778 - US\$1,946} = \text{US\$832}$$

Of course, this requires an accurate prediction of the relative exchange rates--no small feat!

3.

	12/31/90 Sfr	12/31/90 US$	12/31/91 US$
Cash	$ 50.00	$ 33.33	$ 31.25
Inventory	250.00	166.67	156.25
Plant and Equip.	350.00	233.33	218.75
Total	650.00	433.33	406.25
Debt	300.00	200.00	187.50
Paid-in Capital	150.00	100.00	93.75
Retained Earnings	200.00	133.33	125.00
Total	650.00	433.33	406.25
Sales	4000.00	2666.67	2580.65
Cost of Goods Sold	3200.00	2133.33	2064.52
Operating Profits	800.00	533.33	516.13

Notice that U.S. equity (retained earnings) has decreased due to the depreciation of the Swiss franc.

4.   a.   The effective rate equals the nominal rate adjusted for exchange rate changes. The table specifies changes in the exchange rate, so here one subtracts the forecast exchange rate change from the relevant stated interest rate from a U.S. perspective. The completed table given below contains the results.

Item	US$	Currency DM	L
Spot exchange rates		DM1.65/US$	L.55/US$
Forecast % change in rate		-2.5%	+2.0%
Interest rates			
Nominal			
Euromarket	10.0%	7.4	11.5
Domestic	9.5%	6.85	11.3
Effective			
Euromarket	10.0%	9.9	9.5
Domestic	9.5%	9.35	9.3

b. The lowest effective rate is 9.3% domestic rate in Britain. If possible, borrow $20 million in that market. The highest rate is the Euromarket dollar rate available in the U.S., invest there.

```
  $30 million  X  .10    =  $ 3.0 million
- $20 million  X  .093   =  $ 1.86
        Net gain            $ 1.14 million
```

Note that in this case, netting the funds and investing the $10 million net surplus at 10 percent yields only a gain of $1 million. This illustrates an advantage that the MNC has over a domestic firm.

APPENDIXES

Financial Tables

Table A-1   Future-Value Interest Factors for One Dollar Compounded at k Percent for n Periods: $FVIF_{k,n} = (1 + k)^n$

Period	1%	2%	3%	4%	5%	6%	7%	8%	9%	10%
1	1.010	1.020	1.030	1.040	1.050	1.060	1.070	1.080	1.090	1.100
2	1.020	1.040	1.061	1.082	1.102	1.124	1.145	1.166	1.188	1.210
3	1.030	1.061	1.093	1.125	1.158	1.191	1.225	1.260	1.295	1.331
4	1.041	1.082	1.126	1.170	1.216	1.262	1.311	1.360	1.412	1.464
5	1.051	1.104	1.159	1.217	1.276	1.338	1.403	1.469	1.539	1.611
6	1.062	1.126	1.194	1.265	1.340	1.419	1.501	1.587	1.677	1.772
7	1.072	1.149	1.230	1.316	1.407	1.504	1.606	1.714	1.828	1.949
8	1.083	1.172	1.267	1.369	1.477	1.594	1.718	1.851	1.993	2.144
9	1.094	1.195	1.305	1.423	1.551	1.689	1.838	1.999	2.172	2.358
10	1.105	1.219	1.344	1.480	1.629	1.791	1.967	2.159	2.367	2.594
11	1.116	1.243	1.384	1.539	1.710	1.898	2.105	2.332	2.580	2.853
12	1.127	1.268	1.426	1.601	1.796	2.012	2.252	2.518	2.813	3.138
13	1.138	1.294	1.469	1.665	1.886	2.133	2.410	2.720	3.066	3.452
14	1.149	1.319	1.513	1.732	1.980	2.261	2.579	2.937	3.342	3.797
15	1.161	1.346	1.558	1.801	2.079	2.397	2.759	3.172	3.642	4.177
16	1.173	1.373	1.605	1.873	2.183	2.540	2.952	3.426	3.970	4.595
17	1.184	1.400	1.653	1.948	2.292	2.693	3.159	3.700	4.328	5.054
18	1.196	1.428	1.702	2.026	2.407	2.854	3.380	3.996	4.717	5.560
19	1.208	1.457	1.753	2.107	2.527	3.026	3.616	4.316	5.142	6.116
20	1.220	1.486	1.806	2.191	2.653	3.207	3.870	4.661	5.604	6.727
21	1.232	1.516	1.860	2.279	2.786	3.399	4.140	5.034	6.109	7.400
22	1.245	1.546	1.916	2.370	2.925	3.603	4.430	5.436	6.658	8.140
23	1.257	1.577	1.974	2.465	3.071	3.820	4.740	5.871	7.258	8.954
24	1.270	1.608	2.033	2.563	3.225	4.049	5.072	6.341	7.911	9.850
25	1.282	1.641	2.094	2.666	3.386	4.292	5.427	6.848	8.623	10.834
30	1.348	1.811	2.427	3.243	4.322	5.743	7.612	10.062	13.267	17.449
35	1.417	2.000	2.814	3.946	5.516	7.686	10.676	14.785	20.413	28.102
40	1.489	2.208	3.262	4.801	7.040	10.285	14.974	21.724	31.408	45.258
45	1.565	2.438	3.781	5.841	8.985	13.764	21.002	31.920	48.325	72.888
50	1.645	2.691	4.384	7.106	11.467	18.419	29.456	46.900	74.354	117.386

Table A-1 Future-Value Interest Factors for One Dollar Compounded at k Percent for n Periods: $FVIF_{k,n} = (1 + k)^n$ (continued)

Period	11%	12%	13%	14%	15%	16%	17%	18%	19%	20%
1	1.110	1.120	1.130	1.140	1.150	1.160	1.170	1.180	1.190	1.200
2	1.232	1.254	1.277	1.300	1.322	1.346	1.369	1.392	1.416	1.440
3	1.368	1.405	1.443	1.482	1.521	1.561	1.602	1.643	1.685	1.728
4	1.518	1.574	1.630	1.689	1.749	1.811	1.874	1.939	2.005	2.074
5	1.685	1.762	1.842	1.925	2.011	2.100	2.192	2.288	2.386	2.488
6	1.870	1.974	2.082	2.195	2.313	2.436	2.565	2.700	2.840	2.986
7	2.076	2.211	2.353	2.502	2.660	2.826	3.001	3.185	3.379	3.583
8	2.305	2.476	2.658	2.853	3.059	3.278	3.511	3.759	4.021	4.300
9	2.558	2.773	3.004	3.252	3.518	3.803	4.108	4.435	4.785	5.160
10	2.839	3.106	3.395	3.707	4.046	4.411	4.807	5.234	5.695	6.192
11	3.152	3.479	3.836	4.226	4.652	5.117	5.624	6.176	6.777	7.430
12	3.498	3.896	4.334	4.818	5.350	5.936	6.580	7.288	8.064	8.916
13	3.883	4.363	4.898	5.492	6.153	6.886	7.699	8.599	9.596	10.699
14	4.310	4.887	5.535	6.261	7.076	7.987	9.007	10.147	11.420	12.839
15	4.785	5.474	6.254	7.138	8.137	9.265	10.539	11.974	13.589	15.407
16	5.311	6.130	7.067	8.137	9.358	10.748	12.330	14.129	16.171	18.488
17	5.895	6.866	7.986	9.276	10.761	12.468	14.426	16.672	19.244	22.186
18	6.543	7.690	9.024	10.575	12.375	14.462	16.879	19.673	22.900	26.623
19	7.263	8.613	10.197	12.055	14.232	16.776	19.748	23.214	27.251	31.948
20	8.062	9.646	11.523	13.743	16.366	19.461	23.105	27.393	32.429	38.337
21	8.949	10.804	13.021	15.667	18.821	22.574	27.033	32.323	38.591	46.005
22	9.933	12.100	14.713	17.861	21.644	26.186	31.629	38.141	45.923	55.205
23	11.026	13.552	16.626	20.361	24.891	30.376	37.005	45.007	54.648	66.247
24	12.239	15.178	18.788	23.212	28.625	35.236	43.296	53.108	65.031	79.496
25	13.585	17.000	21.230	26.461	32.918	40.874	50.656	62.667	77.387	95.395
30	22.892	29.960	39.115	50.949	66.210	85.849	111.061	143.367	184.672	237.373
35	38.574	52.799	72.066	98.097	133.172	180.311	243.495	327.988	440.691	590.657
40	64.999	93.049	132.776	188.876	267.856	378.715	533.846	750.353	1051.642	1469.740
45	109.527	163.985	244.629	363.662	538.752	795.429	1170.425	1716.619	2509.583	3657.176
50	184.559	288.996	450.711	700.197	1083.619	1670.669	2566.080	3927.189	5988.730	9100.191

Table A-1 Future-Value Interest Factors for One Dollar Compounded at k Percent for n Periods: $FVIF_{k,n} = (1 + k)^n$ (continued)

Period	21%	22%	23%	24%	25%	26%	27%	28%	29%	30%
1	1.210	1.220	1.230	1.240	1.250	1.260	1.270	1.280	1.290	1.300
2	1.464	1.488	1.513	1.538	1.562	1.588	1.613	1.638	1.664	1.690
3	1.772	1.816	1.861	1.907	1.953	2.000	2.048	2.097	2.147	2.197
4	2.144	2.215	2.289	2.364	2.441	2.520	2.601	2.684	2.769	2.856
5	2.594	2.703	2.815	2.932	3.052	3.176	3.304	3.436	3.572	3.713
6	3.138	3.297	3.463	3.635	3.815	4.001	4.196	4.398	4.608	4.827
7	3.797	4.023	4.259	4.508	4.768	5.042	5.329	5.629	5.945	6.275
8	4.595	4.908	5.239	5.589	5.960	6.353	6.767	7.206	7.669	8.157
9	5.560	5.987	6.444	6.931	7.451	8.004	8.595	9.223	9.893	10.604
10	6.727	7.305	7.926	8.594	9.313	10.086	10.915	11.806	12.761	13.786
11	8.140	8.912	9.749	10.657	11.642	12.708	13.862	15.112	16.462	17.921
12	9.850	10.872	11.991	13.215	14.552	16.012	17.605	19.343	21.236	23.298
13	11.918	13.264	14.749	16.386	18.190	20.175	22.359	24.759	27.395	30.287
14	14.421	16.182	18.141	20.319	22.737	25.420	28.395	31.691	35.339	39.373
15	17.449	19.742	22.314	25.195	28.422	32.030	36.062	40.565	45.587	51.185
16	21.113	24.085	27.446	31.242	35.527	40.357	45.799	51.923	58.808	66.541
17	25.547	29.384	33.758	38.740	44.409	50.850	58.165	66.461	75.862	86.503
18	30.912	35.848	41.523	48.038	55.511	64.071	73.869	85.070	97.862	112.454
19	37.404	43.735	51.073	59.567	69.389	80.730	93.813	108.890	126.242	146.190
20	45.258	53.357	62.820	73.863	86.736	101.720	119.143	139.379	162.852	190.047
21	54.762	65.095	77.268	91.591	108.420	128.167	151.312	178.405	210.079	247.061
22	66.262	79.416	95.040	113.572	135.525	161.490	192.165	228.358	271.002	321.178
23	80.178	96.887	116.899	140.829	169.407	203.477	244.050	292.298	349.592	417.531
24	97.015	118.203	143.786	174.628	211.758	256.381	309.943	374.141	450.974	542.791
25	117.388	144.207	176.857	216.539	264.698	323.040	393.628	478.901	581.756	705.627
30	304.471	389.748	497.904	634.810	807.793	1025.904	1300.477	1645.488	2078.208	2619.936
35	789.716	1053.370	1401.749	1861.020	2465.189	3258.053	4296.547	5653.840	7423.988	9727.598
40	2048.309	2846.941	3946.340	5455.797	7523.156	10346.879	14195.051	19426.418	26520.723	36117.754
45	5312.758	7694.418	11110.121	15994.316	22958.844	32859.457	46897.973	66748.500	94739.937	134102.187
50	13779.844	20795.680	31278.301	46889.207	70064.812	104354.562	154942.687	229345.875	338440.000	497910.125

Table A-1 Future-Value Interest Factors for One Dollar Compounded at k Percent for n Periods: $FVIF_{k,n} = (1 + k)^n$ (continued)

Period	31%	32%	33%	34%	35%	36%	37%	38%	39%	40%
1	1.310	1.320	1.330	1.340	1.350	1.360	1.370	1.380	1.390	1.400
2	1.716	1.742	1.769	1.796	1.822	1.850	1.877	1.904	1.932	1.960
3	2.248	2.300	2.353	2.406	2.460	2.515	2.571	2.628	2.686	2.744
4	2.945	3.036	3.129	3.224	3.321	3.421	3.523	3.627	3.733	3.842
5	3.858	4.007	4.162	4.320	4.484	4.653	4.826	5.005	5.189	5.378
6	5.054	5.290	5.535	5.789	6.053	6.328	6.612	6.907	7.213	7.530
7	6.621	6.983	7.361	7.758	8.172	8.605	9.058	9.531	10.025	10.541
8	8.673	9.217	9.791	10.395	11.032	11.703	12.410	13.153	13.935	14.758
9	11.362	12.166	13.022	13.930	14.894	15.917	17.001	18.151	19.370	20.661
10	14.884	16.060	17.319	18.666	20.106	21.646	23.292	25.049	26.924	28.925
11	19.498	21.199	23.034	25.012	27.144	29.439	31.910	34.567	37.425	40.495
12	25.542	27.982	30.635	33.516	36.644	40.037	43.716	47.703	52.020	56.694
13	33.460	36.937	40.745	44.912	49.469	54.451	59.892	65.830	72.308	79.371
14	43.832	48.756	54.190	60.181	66.784	74.053	82.051	90.845	100.509	111.119
15	57.420	64.358	72.073	80.643	90.158	100.712	112.410	125.366	139.707	155.567
16	75.220	84.953	95.857	108.061	121.713	136.968	154.002	173.005	194.192	217.793
17	98.539	112.138	127.490	144.802	164.312	186.277	210.983	238.747	269.927	304.911
18	129.086	148.022	169.561	194.035	221.822	253.337	289.046	329.471	375.198	426.875
19	169.102	195.389	225.517	260.006	299.459	344.537	395.993	454.669	521.525	597.625
20	221.523	257.913	299.937	348.408	404.270	468.571	542.511	627.443	724.919	836.674
21	290.196	340.446	398.916	466.867	545.764	637.256	743.240	865.871	1007.637	1171.343
22	380.156	449.388	530.558	625.601	736.781	866.668	1018.238	1194.900	1400.615	1639.878
23	498.004	593.192	705.642	838.305	994.653	1178.668	1394.986	1648.961	1946.854	2295.829
24	652.385	783.013	938.504	1123.328	1342.781	1602.988	1911.129	2275.564	2706.125	3214.158
25	854.623	1033.577	1248.210	1505.258	1812.754	2180.063	2618.245	3140.275	3761.511	4499.816
30	3297.081	4142.008	5194.516	6503.285	8128.426	10142.914	12636.086	15716.703	19517.969	24201.043
35	12719.918	16598.906	21617.363	28096.695	36448.051	47190.727	60983.836	78660.188	101276.125	130158.687
40	49072.621	66519.313	89962.188	121388.437	163433.875	219558.625	294317.937	393684.687	525508.312	700022.688

Table A-1 Future-Value Interest Factors for One Dollar Compounded at k Percent for n Periods: $FVIF_{k,n} = (1 + k)^n$ (continued)

Period	41%	42%	43%	44%	45%	46%	47%	48%	49%	50%
1	1.410	1.420	1.430	1.440	1.450	1.460	1.470	1.480	1.490	1.500
2	1.988	2.016	2.045	2.074	2.102	2.132	2.161	2.190	2.220	2.250
3	2.803	2.863	2.924	2.986	3.049	3.112	3.177	3.242	3.308	3.375
4	3.953	4.066	4.182	4.300	4.421	4.544	4.669	4.798	4.929	5.063
5	5.573	5.774	5.980	6.192	6.410	6.634	6.864	7.101	7.344	7.594
6	7.858	8.198	8.551	8.916	9.294	9.685	10.090	10.509	10.943	11.391
7	11.080	11.642	12.228	12.839	13.476	14.141	14.833	15.554	16.304	17.086
8	15.623	16.531	17.486	18.488	19.541	20.645	21.804	23.019	24.293	25.629
9	22.028	23.474	25.005	26.623	28.334	30.142	32.052	34.069	36.197	38.443
10	31.059	33.333	35.757	38.337	41.085	44.007	47.116	50.421	53.934	57.665
11	43.793	47.333	51.132	55.206	59.573	64.251	69.261	74.624	80.361	86.498
12	61.749	67.213	73.119	79.496	86.380	93.806	101.813	110.443	119.738	129.746
13	87.066	95.443	104.560	114.475	125.251	136.956	149.665	163.456	178.410	194.620
14	122.763	135.529	149.521	164.843	181.614	199.956	220.008	241.914	265.831	291.929
15	173.095	192.451	213.814	237.374	263.341	291.936	323.411	358.033	396.088	437.894
16	244.064	273.280	305.754	341.819	381.844	426.226	475.414	529.888	590.170	656.841
17	344.130	388.057	437.228	492.219	553.674	622.289	698.859	784.234	879.354	985.261
18	485.224	551.041	625.235	708.794	802.826	908.541	1027.321	1160.666	1310.236	1477.892
19	684.165	782.478	894.086	1020.663	1164.098	1326.469	1510.161	1717.785	1952.252	2216.838
20	964.673	1111.118	1278.543	1469.754	1687.942	1936.642	2219.936	2542.321	2908.854	3325.257
21	1360.188	1577.786	1828.315	2116.445	2447.515	2827.496	3263.304	3762.633	4334.188	4987.883
22	1917.865	2240.455	2614.489	3047.679	3548.896	4128.137	4797.051	5568.691	6457.941	7481.824
23	2704.188	3181.443	3738.717	4388.656	5145.898	6027.078	7051.660	8241.664	9622.324	11222.738
24	3812.905	4517.641	5346.355	6319.656	7461.547	8799.523	10365.934	12197.656	14337.258	16834.109
25	5376.191	6415.047	7645.289	9100.305	10819.242	12847.297	15237.914	18052.516	21362.508	25251.164
30	29961.941	37037.383	45716.496	56346.535	69348.375	85226.375	104594.938	128187.438	156885.438	191751.000

Table A-2 Future-Value Interest Factors for a One-Dollar Annuity Compounded at k Percent for n Periods: $FVIFA_{k,n} = \sum\limits_{t=1}^{n} (1 + k)^{t-1}$

Period	1%	2%	3%	4%	5%	6%	7%	8%	9%	10%
1	1.000	1.000	1.000	1.000	1.000	1.000	1.000	1.000	1.000	1.000
2	2.010	2.020	2.030	2.040	2.050	2.060	2.070	2.080	2.090	2.100
3	3.030	3.060	3.091	3.122	3.152	3.184	3.215	3.246	3.278	3.310
4	4.060	4.122	4.184	4.246	4.310	4.375	4.440	4.506	4.573	4.641
5	5.101	5.204	5.309	5.416	5.526	5.637	5.751	5.867	5.985	6.105
6	6.152	6.308	6.468	6.633	6.802	6.975	7.153	7.336	7.523	7.716
7	7.214	7.434	7.662	7.898	8.142	8.394	8.654	8.923	9.200	9.487
8	8.286	8.583	8.892	9.214	9.549	9.897	10.260	10.637	11.028	11.436
9	9.368	9.755	10.159	10.583	11.027	11.491	11.978	12.488	13.021	13.579
10	10.462	10.950	11.464	12.006	12.578	13.181	13.816	14.487	15.193	15.937
11	11.567	12.169	12.808	13.486	14.207	14.972	15.784	16.645	17.560	18.531
12	12.682	13.412	14.192	15.026	15.917	16.870	17.888	18.977	20.141	21.384
13	13.809	14.680	15.618	16.627	17.713	18.882	20.141	21.495	22.953	24.523
14	14.947	15.974	17.086	18.292	19.598	21.015	22.550	24.215	26.019	27.975
15	16.097	17.293	18.599	20.023	21.578	23.276	25.129	27.152	29.361	31.772
16	17.258	18.639	20.157	21.824	23.657	25.672	27.888	30.324	33.003	35.949
17	18.430	20.012	21.761	23.697	25.840	28.213	30.840	33.750	36.973	40.544
18	19.614	21.412	23.414	25.645	28.132	30.905	33.999	37.450	41.301	45.599
19	20.811	22.840	25.117	27.671	30.539	33.760	37.379	41.446	46.018	51.158
20	22.019	24.297	26.870	29.778	33.066	36.785	40.995	45.762	51.159	57.274
21	23.239	25.783	28.676	31.969	35.719	39.992	44.865	50.422	56.764	64.002
22	24.471	27.299	30.536	34.248	38.505	43.392	49.005	55.456	62.872	71.402
23	25.716	28.845	32.452	36.618	41.430	46.995	53.435	60.893	69.531	79.542
24	26.973	30.421	34.426	39.082	44.501	50.815	58.176	66.764	76.789	88.496
25	28.243	32.030	36.459	41.645	47.726	54.864	63.248	73.105	84.699	98.346
30	34.784	40.567	47.575	56.084	66.438	79.057	94.459	113.282	136.305	164.491
35	41.659	49.994	60.461	73.651	90.318	111.432	138.234	172.314	215.705	271.018
40	48.885	60.401	75.400	95.024	120.797	154.758	199.630	259.052	337.872	442.580
45	56.479	71.891	92.718	121.027	159.695	212.737	285.741	386.497	525.840	718.881
50	64.461	84.577	112.794	152.664	209.341	290.325	406.516	573.756	815.051	1163.865

Table A-2 Future-Value Interest Factors for a One-Dollar Annuity Compounded at k Percent for n Periods: $FVIFA_{k,n} = \sum_{t=1}^{n} (1 + k)^{t-1}$ (continued)

Period	11%	12%	13%	14%	15%	16%	17%	18%	19%	20%
1	1.000	1.000	1.000	1.000	1.000	1.000	1.000	1.000	1.000	1.000
2	2.110	2.120	2.130	2.140	2.150	2.160	2.170	2.180	2.190	2.200
3	3.342	3.374	3.407	3.440	3.472	3.506	3.539	3.572	3.606	3.640
4	4.710	4.779	4.850	4.921	4.993	5.066	5.141	5.215	5.291	5.368
5	6.228	6.353	6.480	6.610	6.742	6.877	7.014	7.154	7.297	7.442
6	7.913	8.115	8.323	8.535	8.754	8.977	9.207	9.442	9.683	9.930
7	9.783	10.089	10.405	10.730	11.067	11.414	11.772	12.141	12.523	12.916
8	11.859	12.300	12.757	13.233	13.727	14.240	14.773	15.327	15.902	16.499
9	14.164	14.776	15.416	16.085	16.786	17.518	18.285	19.086	19.923	20.799
10	16.722	17.549	18.420	19.337	20.304	21.321	22.393	23.521	24.709	25.959
11	19.561	20.655	21.814	23.044	24.349	25.733	27.200	28.755	30.403	32.150
12	22.713	24.133	25.650	27.271	29.001	30.850	32.824	34.931	37.180	39.580
13	26.211	28.029	29.984	32.088	34.352	36.786	39.404	42.218	45.244	48.496
14	30.095	32.392	34.882	37.581	40.504	43.672	47.102	50.818	54.841	59.196
15	34.405	37.280	40.417	43.842	47.580	51.659	56.109	60.965	66.260	72.035
16	39.190	42.753	46.671	50.980	55.717	60.925	66.648	72.938	79.850	87.442
17	44.500	48.883	53.738	59.117	65.075	71.673	78.978	87.067	96.021	105.930
18	50.396	55.749	61.724	68.393	75.836	84.140	93.404	103.739	115.265	128.116
19	56.939	63.439	70.748	78.968	88.211	98.603	110.283	123.412	138.165	154.739
20	64.202	72.052	80.946	91.024	102.443	115.379	130.031	146.626	165.417	186.687
21	72.264	81.698	92.468	104.767	118.809	134.840	153.136	174.019	197.846	225.024
22	81.213	92.502	105.489	120.434	137.630	157.414	180.169	206.342	236.436	271.028
23	91.147	104.602	120.203	138.295	159.274	183.600	211.798	244.483	282.359	326.234
24	102.173	118.154	136.829	158.656	184.166	213.976	248.803	289.490	337.007	392.480
25	114.412	133.333	155.616	181.867	212.790	249.212	292.099	342.598	402.038	471.976
30	199.018	241.330	293.192	356.778	434.738	530.306	647.423	790.932	966.698	1181.865
35	341.583	431.658	546.663	693.552	881.152	1120.699	1426.448	1816.607	2314.173	2948.294
40	581.812	767.080	1013.667	1341.979	1779.048	2360.724	3134.412	4163.094	5529.711	7343.715
45	986.613	1358.208	1874.086	2590.464	3585.031	4965.191	6879.008	9531.258	13203.105	18280.914
50	1668.723	2399.975	3459.344	4994.301	7217.488	10435.449	15088.805	21812.273	31514.492	45496.094

Table A-2 Future-Value Interest Factors for a One-Dollar Annuity Compounded at k Percent for n Periods: $FVIFA_{k,n} = \sum_{t=1}^{n} (1 + k)^{t-1}$ (continued)

Period	21%	22%	23%	24%	25%	26%	27%	28%	29%	30%
1	1.000	1.000	1.000	1.000	1.000	1.000	1.000	1.000	1.000	1.000
2	2.210	2.220	2.230	2.240	2.250	2.260	2.270	2.280	2.290	2.300
3	3.674	3.708	3.743	3.778	3.813	3.848	3.883	3.918	3.954	3.990
4	5.446	5.524	5.604	5.684	5.766	5.848	5.931	6.016	6.101	6.187
5	7.589	7.740	7.893	8.048	8.207	8.368	8.533	8.700	8.870	9.043
6	10.183	10.442	10.708	10.980	11.259	11.544	11.837	12.136	12.442	12.756
7	13.321	13.740	14.171	14.615	15.073	15.546	16.032	16.534	17.051	17.583
8	17.119	17.762	18.430	19.123	19.842	20.588	21.361	22.163	22.995	23.858
9	21.714	22.670	23.669	24.712	25.802	26.940	28.129	29.369	30.664	32.015
10	27.274	28.657	30.113	31.643	33.253	34.945	36.723	38.592	40.556	42.619
11	34.001	35.962	38.039	40.238	42.566	45.030	47.639	50.398	53.318	56.405
12	42.141	44.873	47.787	50.895	54.208	57.738	61.501	65.510	69.780	74.326
13	51.991	55.745	59.778	64.109	68.760	73.750	79.106	84.853	91.016	97.624
14	63.909	69.009	74.528	80.496	86.949	93.925	101.465	109.611	118.411	127.912
15	78.330	85.191	92.669	100.815	109.687	119.346	129.860	141.302	153.750	167.285
16	95.779	104.933	114.983	126.010	138.109	151.375	165.922	181.867	199.337	218.470
17	116.892	129.019	142.428	157.252	173.636	191.733	211.721	233.790	258.145	285.011
18	142.439	158.403	176.187	195.993	218.045	242.583	269.885	300.250	334.006	371.514
19	173.351	194.251	217.710	244.031	273.556	306.654	343.754	385.321	431.868	483.968
20	210.755	237.986	268.783	303.598	342.945	387.384	437.568	494.210	558.110	630.157
21	256.013	291.343	331.603	377.461	429.681	489.104	556.710	633.589	720.962	820.204
22	310.775	356.438	408.871	469.052	538.101	617.270	708.022	811.993	931.040	1067.265
23	377.038	435.854	503.911	582.624	673.626	778.760	900.187	1040.351	1202.042	1388.443
24	457.215	532.741	620.810	723.453	843.032	982.237	1144.237	1332.649	1551.634	1805.975
25	554.230	650.944	764.596	898.082	1054.791	1238.617	1454.180	1706.790	2002.608	2348.765
30	1445.111	1767.044	2160.459	2640.881	3227.172	3941.953	4812.891	5873.172	7162.785	8729.805
35	3755.814	4783.520	6090.227	7750.094	9856.746	12527.160	15909.480	20188.742	25596.512	32422.090
40	9749.141	12936.141	17153.691	22728.367	30088.621	39791.957	52570.707	69376.562	91447.375	120389.375
45	25294.223	34970.230	48300.660	66638.937	91831.312	126378.937	173692.875	238384.312	326686.375	447005.062

Table A-2 Future-Value Interest Factors for a One-Dollar Annuity Compounded at k Percent for n Periods: $FVIFA_{k,n} = \sum_{t=1}^{n} (1 + k)^{t-1}$ (continued)

Period	31%	32%	33%	34%	35%	36%	37%	38%	39%	40%
1	1.000	1.000	1.000	1.000	1.000	1.000	1.000	1.000	1.000	1.000
2	2.310	2.320	2.330	2.340	2.350	2.360	2.370	2.380	2.390	2.400
3	4.026	4.062	4.099	4.136	4.172	4.210	4.247	4.284	4.322	4.360
4	6.274	6.362	6.452	6.542	6.633	6.725	6.818	6.912	7.008	7.104
5	9.219	9.398	9.581	9.766	9.954	10.146	10.341	10.539	10.741	10.946
6	13.077	13.406	13.742	14.086	14.438	14.799	15.167	15.544	15.930	16.324
7	18.131	18.696	19.277	19.876	20.492	21.126	21.779	22.451	23.142	23.853
8	24.752	25.678	26.638	27.633	28.664	29.732	30.837	31.982	33.167	34.395
9	33.425	34.895	36.429	38.028	39.696	41.435	43.247	45.135	47.103	49.152
10	44.786	47.062	49.451	51.958	54.590	57.351	60.248	63.287	66.473	69.813
11	59.670	63.121	66.769	70.624	74.696	78.998	83.540	88.335	93.397	98.739
12	79.167	84.320	89.803	95.636	101.840	108.437	115.450	122.903	130.822	139.234
13	104.709	112.302	120.438	129.152	138.484	148.474	159.166	170.606	182.842	195.928
14	138.169	149.239	161.183	174.063	187.953	202.925	219.058	236.435	255.151	275.299
15	182.001	197.996	215.373	234.245	254.737	276.978	301.109	327.281	355.659	386.418
16	239.421	262.354	287.446	314.888	344.895	377.690	413.520	452.647	495.366	541.985
17	314.642	347.307	383.303	422.949	466.608	514.658	567.521	625.652	689.558	759.778
18	413.180	459.445	510.792	567.751	630.920	700.935	778.504	864.399	959.485	1064.689
19	542.266	607.467	680.354	761.786	852.741	954.271	1067.551	1193.870	1334.683	1491.563
20	711.368	802.856	905.870	1021.792	1152.200	1298.809	1463.544	1648.539	1856.208	2089.188
21	932.891	1060.769	1205.807	1370.201	1556.470	1767.380	2006.055	2275.982	2581.128	2925.862
22	1223.087	1401.215	1604.724	1837.068	2102.234	2404.636	2749.294	3141.852	3588.765	4097.203
23	1603.243	1850.603	2135.282	2462.669	2839.014	3271.304	3767.532	4336.750	4989.379	5737.078
24	2101.247	2443.795	2840.924	3300.974	3833.667	4449.969	5162.516	5985.711	6936.230	8032.906
25	2753.631	3226.808	3779.428	4424.301	5176.445	6052.957	7073.645	8261.273	9642.352	11247.062
30	10632.543	12940.672	15737.945	19124.434	23221.258	28172.016	34148.906	41357.227	50043.625	60500.207
35	41028.887	51868.563	65504.199	82634.625	104134.500	131082.625	164818.438	206998.375	259680.313	325394.688

Table A-2 Future-Value Interest Factors for a One-Dollar Annuity Compounded at k Percent for n Periods: $FVIFA_{k,n} = \sum_{t=1}^{n} (1 + k)^{t-1}$ (continued)

Period	41%	42%	43%	44%	45%	46%	47%	48%	49%	50%
1	1.000	1.000	1.000	1.000	1.000	1.000	1.000	1.000	1.000	1.000
2	2.410	2.420	2.430	2.440	2.450	2.460	2.470	2.480	2.490	2.500
3	4.398	4.436	4.475	4.514	4.552	4.592	4.631	4.670	4.710	4.750
4	7.201	7.300	7.399	7.500	7.601	7.704	7.807	7.912	8.018	8.125
5	11.154	11.366	11.581	11.799	12.022	12.247	12.477	12.710	12.947	13.188
6	16.727	17.139	17.560	17.991	18.431	18.881	19.341	19.811	20.291	20.781
7	24.585	25.337	26.111	26.907	27.725	28.567	29.431	30.320	31.233	32.172
8	35.665	36.979	38.339	39.746	41.202	42.707	44.264	45.874	47.538	49.258
9	51.287	53.510	55.825	58.235	60.743	63.352	66.068	68.893	71.831	74.887
10	73.315	76.985	80.830	84.858	89.077	93.494	98.120	102.961	108.028	113.330
11	104.374	110.318	116.586	123.195	130.161	137.502	145.236	153.383	161.962	170.995
12	148.168	157.651	167.719	178.401	189.734	201.752	214.497	228.007	242.323	257.493
13	209.916	224.865	240.837	257.897	276.114	295.558	316.310	338.449	362.062	387.239
14	296.982	320.308	345.397	372.372	401.365	432.514	465.975	501.905	540.471	581.858
15	419.744	455.837	494.918	537.215	582.980	632.470	685.983	743.819	806.302	873.788
16	592.839	648.288	708.732	774.589	846.321	924.406	1009.394	1101.852	1202.390	1311.681
17	836.903	921.568	1014.486	1116.408	1228.165	1350.631	1484.809	1631.740	1792.560	1968.522
18	1181.034	1309.625	1451.714	1608.626	1781.838	1972.920	2183.667	2415.974	2671.914	2953.783
19	1666.257	1860.666	2076.949	2317.421	2584.665	2881.461	3210.989	3576.640	3982.150	4431.672
20	2350.422	2643.144	2971.035	3338.084	3748.763	4207.926	4721.148	5294.422	5934.402	6648.508
21	3315.095	3754.262	4249.574	4807.836	5436.703	6144.566	6941.082	7836.742	8843.254	9973.762
22	4675.281	5332.047	6077.887	6924.281	7884.215	8972.059	10204.383	11599.375	13177.441	14961.645
23	6593.145	7572.500	8692.375	9971.957	11433.109	13100.195	15001.434	17168.066	19635.383	22443.469
24	9297.332	10753.941	12431.090	14360.613	16579.008	19127.273	22053.094	25409.730	29257.707	33666.207
25	13110.234	15271.582	17777.445	20680.270	24040.555	27926.797	32419.027	37607.387	43594.965	50500.316
30	73075.500	88181.938	106315.250	128058.125	154105.313	185273.000	222540.625	267055.375	320172.750	383500.000

Table A-3　Present-Value Interest Factors for One Dollar Discounted at k Percent for n Periods: $PVIF_{k,n} = \dfrac{1}{(1+k)^n}$

Period	1%	2%	3%	4%	5%	6%	7%	8%	9%	10%
1	.990	.980	.971	.962	.952	.943	.935	.926	.917	.909
2	.980	.961	.943	.925	.907	.890	.873	.857	.842	.826
3	.971	.942	.915	.889	.864	.840	.816	.794	.772	.751
4	.961	.924	.888	.855	.823	.792	.763	.735	.708	.683
5	.951	.906	.863	.822	.784	.747	.713	.681	.650	.621
6	.942	.888	.837	.790	.746	.705	.666	.630	.596	.564
7	.933	.871	.813	.760	.711	.665	.623	.583	.547	.513
8	.923	.853	.789	.731	.677	.627	.582	.540	.502	.467
9	.914	.837	.766	.703	.645	.592	.544	.500	.460	.424
10	.905	.820	.744	.676	.614	.558	.508	.463	.422	.386
11	.896	.804	.722	.650	.585	.527	.475	.429	.388	.350
12	.887	.789	.701	.625	.557	.497	.444	.397	.356	.319
13	.879	.773	.681	.601	.530	.469	.415	.368	.326	.290
14	.870	.758	.661	.577	.505	.442	.388	.340	.299	.263
15	.861	.743	.642	.555	.481	.417	.362	.315	.275	.239
16	.853	.728	.623	.534	.458	.394	.339	.292	.252	.218
17	.844	.714	.605	.513	.436	.371	.317	.270	.231	.198
18	.836	.700	.587	.494	.416	.350	.296	.250	.212	.180
19	.828	.686	.570	.475	.396	.331	.277	.232	.194	.164
20	.820	.673	.554	.456	.377	.312	.258	.215	.178	.149
21	.811	.660	.538	.439	.359	.294	.242	.199	.164	.135
22	.803	.647	.522	.422	.342	.278	.226	.184	.150	.123
23	.795	.634	.507	.406	.326	.262	.211	.170	.138	.112
24	.788	.622	.492	.390	.310	.247	.197	.158	.126	.102
25	.780	.610	.478	.375	.295	.233	.184	.146	.116	.092
30	.742	.552	.412	.308	.231	.174	.131	.099	.075	.057
35	.706	.500	.355	.253	.181	.130	.094	.068	.049	.036
40	.672	.453	.307	.208	.142	.097	.067	.046	.032	.022
45	.639	.410	.264	.171	.111	.073	.048	.031	.021	.014
50	.608	.372	.228	.141	.087	.054	.034	.021	.013	.009

Table A-3   Present-Value Interest Factors for One Dollar Discounted at k Percent for n Periods: $PVIF_{k,n} = \dfrac{1}{(1 + k)^n}$ (continued)

Period	11%	12%	13%	14%	15%	16%	17%	18%	19%	20%
1	.901	.893	.885	.877	.870	.862	.855	.847	.840	.833
2	.812	.797	.783	.769	.756	.743	.731	.718	.706	.694
3	.731	.712	.693	.675	.658	.641	.624	.609	.593	.579
4	.659	.636	.613	.592	.572	.552	.534	.516	.499	.482
5	.593	.567	.543	.519	.497	.476	.456	.437	.419	.402
6	.535	.507	.480	.456	.432	.410	.390	.370	.352	.335
7	.482	.452	.425	.400	.376	.354	.333	.314	.296	.279
8	.434	.404	.376	.351	.327	.305	.285	.266	.249	.233
9	.391	.361	.333	.308	.284	.263	.243	.225	.209	.194
10	.352	.322	.295	.270	.247	.227	.208	.191	.176	.162
11	.317	.287	.261	.237	.215	.195	.178	.162	.148	.135
12	.286	.257	.231	.208	.187	.168	.152	.137	.124	.112
13	.258	.229	.204	.182	.163	.145	.130	.116	.104	.093
14	.232	.205	.181	.160	.141	.125	.111	.099	.088	.078
15	.209	.183	.160	.140	.123	.108	.095	.084	.074	.065
16	.188	.163	.141	.123	.107	.093	.081	.071	.062	.054
17	.170	.146	.125	.108	.093	.080	.069	.060	.052	.045
18	.153	.130	.111	.095	.081	.069	.059	.051	.044	.038
19	.138	.116	.098	.083	.070	.060	.051	.043	.037	.031
20	.124	.104	.087	.073	.061	.051	.043	.037	.031	.026
21	.112	.093	.077	.064	.053	.044	.037	.031	.026	.022
22	.101	.083	.068	.056	.046	.038	.032	.026	.022	.018
23	.091	.074	.060	.049	.040	.033	.027	.022	.018	.015
24	.082	.066	.053	.043	.035	.028	.023	.019	.015	.013
25	.074	.059	.047	.038	.030	.024	.020	.016	.013	.010
30	.044	.033	.026	.020	.015	.012	.009	.007	.005	.004
35	.026	.019	.014	.010	.008	.006	.004	.003	.002	.002
40	.015	.011	.008	.005	.004	.003	.002	.001	.001	.001
45	.009	.006	.004	.003	.002	.001	.001	.001	*	*
50	.005	.003	.002	.001	.001	.001	*	*	*	*

*$PVIF$ is zero to three decimal places.

Table A-3 Present-Value Interest Factors for One Dollar Discounted at k Percent for n Periods: $PVIF_{k,n} = \dfrac{1}{(1 + k)^n}$ (continued)

Period	21%	22%	23%	24%	25%	26%	27%	28%	29%	30%
1	.826	.820	.813	.806	.800	.794	.787	.781	.775	.769
2	.683	.672	.661	.650	.640	.630	.620	.610	.601	.592
3	.564	.551	.537	.524	.512	.500	.488	.477	.466	.455
4	.467	.451	.437	.423	.410	.397	.384	.373	.361	.350
5	.386	.370	.355	.341	.328	.315	.303	.291	.280	.269
6	.319	.303	.289	.275	.262	.250	.238	.227	.217	.207
7	.263	.249	.235	.222	.210	.198	.188	.178	.168	.159
8	.218	.204	.191	.179	.168	.157	.148	.139	.130	.123
9	.180	.167	.155	.144	.134	.125	.116	.108	.101	.094
10	.149	.137	.126	.116	.107	.099	.092	.085	.078	.073
11	.123	.112	.103	.094	.086	.079	.072	.066	.061	.056
12	.102	.092	.083	.076	.069	.062	.057	.052	.047	.043
13	.084	.075	.068	.061	.055	.050	.045	.040	.037	.033
14	.069	.062	.055	.049	.044	.039	.035	.032	.028	.025
15	.057	.051	.045	.040	.035	.031	.028	.025	.022	.020
16	.047	.042	.036	.032	.028	.025	.022	.019	.017	.015
17	.039	.034	.030	.026	.023	.020	.017	.015	.013	.012
18	.032	.028	.024	.021	.018	.016	.014	.012	.010	.009
19	.027	.023	.020	.017	.014	.012	.011	.009	.008	.007
20	.022	.019	.016	.014	.012	.010	.008	.007	.006	.005
21	.018	.015	.013	.011	.009	.008	.007	.006	.005	.004
22	.015	.013	.011	.009	.007	.006	.005	.004	.004	.003
23	.012	.010	.009	.007	.006	.005	.004	.003	.003	.002
24	.010	.008	.007	.006	.005	.004	.003	.003	.002	.002
25	.009	.007	.006	.005	.004	.003	.003	.002	.002	.001
30	.003	.003	.002	.002	.001	.001	.001	.001	*	*
35	.001	.001	.001	.001	*	*	*	*	*	*
40	*	*	*	*	*	*	*	*	*	*
45	*	*	*	*	*	*	*	*	*	*
50	*	*	*	*	*	*	*	*	*	*

*$PVIF$ is zero to three decimal places.

Table A-3 Present-Value Interest Factors for One Dollar Discounted at k Percent for n Periods: $PVIF_{k,n} = \dfrac{1}{(1 + k)^n}$ (continued)

Period	31%	32%	33%	34%	35%	36%	37%	38%	39%	40%
1	.763	.758	.752	.746	.741	.735	.730	.725	.719	.714
2	.583	.574	.565	.557	.549	.541	.533	.525	.518	.510
3	.445	.435	.425	.416	.406	.398	.389	.381	.372	.364
4	.340	.329	.320	.310	.301	.292	.284	.276	.268	.260
5	.259	.250	.240	.231	.223	.215	.207	.200	.193	.186
6	.198	.189	.181	.173	.165	.158	.151	.145	.139	.133
7	.151	.143	.136	.129	.122	.116	.110	.105	.100	.095
8	.115	.108	.102	.096	.091	.085	.081	.076	.072	.068
9	.088	.082	.077	.072	.067	.063	.059	.055	.052	.048
10	.067	.062	.058	.054	.050	.046	.043	.040	.037	.035
11	.051	.047	.043	.040	.037	.034	.031	.029	.027	.025
12	.039	.036	.033	.030	.027	.025	.023	.021	.019	.018
13	.030	.027	.025	.022	.020	.018	.017	.015	.014	.013
14	.023	.021	.018	.017	.015	.014	.012	.011	.010	.009
15	.017	.016	.014	.012	.011	.010	.009	.008	.007	.006
16	.013	.012	.010	.009	.008	.007	.006	.006	.005	.005
17	.010	.009	.008	.007	.006	.005	.005	.004	.004	.003
18	.008	.007	.006	.005	.005	.004	.003	.003	.003	.002
19	.006	.005	.004	.004	.003	.003	.003	.002	.002	.002
20	.005	.004	.003	.003	.002	.002	.002	.002	.001	.001
21	.003	.003	.003	.002	.002	.002	.001	.001	.001	.001
22	.003	.002	.002	.002	.001	.001	.001	.001	.001	.001
23	.002	.002	.001	.001	.001	.001	.001	.001	.001	*
24	.002	.001	.001	.001	.001	.001	.001	*	*	*
25	.001	.001	.001	.001	.001	*	*	*	*	*
30	*	*	*	*	*	*	*	*	*	*
35	*	*	*	*	*	*	*	*	*	*
40	*	*	*	*	*	*	*	*	*	*
45	*	*	*	*	*	*	*	*	*	*
50	*	*	*	*	*	*	*	*	*	*

*$PVIF$ is zero to three decimal places.

Table A-3 Present-Value Interest Factors for One Dollar Discounted at k Percent for n Periods: $PVIF_{k,n} = \dfrac{1}{(1 + k)^n}$ (continued)

Period	41%	42%	43%	44%	45%	46%	47%	48%	49%	50%
1	.709	.704	.699	.694	.690	.685	.680	.676	.671	.667
2	.503	.496	.489	.482	.476	.469	.463	.457	.450	.444
3	.357	.349	.342	.335	.328	.321	.315	.308	.302	.296
4	.253	.246	.239	.233	.226	.220	.214	.208	.203	.198
5	.179	.173	.167	.162	.156	.151	.146	.141	.136	.132
6	.127	.122	.117	.112	.108	.103	.099	.095	.091	.088
7	.090	.086	.082	.078	.074	.071	.067	.064	.061	.059
8	.064	.060	.057	.054	.051	.048	.046	.043	.041	.039
9	.045	.043	.040	.038	.035	.033	.031	.029	.028	.026
10	.032	.030	.028	.026	.024	.023	.021	.020	.019	.017
11	.023	.021	.020	.018	.017	.016	.014	.013	.012	.012
12	.016	.015	.014	.013	.012	.011	.010	.009	.008	.008
13	.011	.010	.010	.009	.008	.007	.007	.006	.006	.005
14	.008	.007	.007	.006	.006	.005	.005	.004	.004	.003
15	.006	.005	.005	.004	.004	.003	.003	.003	.003	.002
16	.004	.004	.003	.003	.003	.002	.002	.002	.002	.002
17	.003	.003	.002	.002	.002	.002	.001	.001	.001	.001
18	.002	.002	.002	.001	.001	.001	.001	.001	.001	.001
19	.001	.001	.001	.001	.001	.001	.001	.001	.001	*
20	.001	.001	.001	.001	.001	.001	*	*	*	*
21	.001	.001	.001	*	*	*	*	*	*	*
22	.001	*	*	*	*	*	*	*	*	*
23	*	*	*	*	*	*	*	*	*	*
24	*	*	*	*	*	*	*	*	*	*
25	*	*	*	*	*	*	*	*	*	*
30	*	*	*	*	*	*	*	*	*	*
35	*	*	*	*	*	*	*	*	*	*
40	*	*	*	*	*	*	*	*	*	*
45	*	*	*	*	*	*	*	*	*	*
50	*	*	*	*	*	*	*	*	*	*

*$PVIF$ is zero to three decimal places.

Table A-4 Present-Value Interest Factors for a One-Dollar Annuity Discounted at k Percent for n Periods: $PVIFA_{k,n} = \sum_{t=1}^{n} \dfrac{1}{(1+k)^t}$

Period	1%	2%	3%	4%	5%	6%	7%	8%	9%	10%
1	.990	.980	.971	.962	.952	.943	.935	.926	.917	.909
2	1.970	1.942	1.913	1.886	1.859	1.833	1.808	1.783	1.759	1.736
3	2.941	2.884	2.829	2.775	2.723	2.673	2.624	2.577	2.531	2.487
4	3.902	3.808	3.717	3.630	3.546	3.465	3.387	3.312	3.240	3.170
5	4.853	4.713	4.580	4.452	4.329	4.212	4.100	3.993	3.890	3.791
6	5.795	5.601	5.417	5.242	5.076	4.917	4.767	4.623	4.486	4.355
7	6.728	6.472	6.230	6.002	5.786	5.582	5.389	5.206	5.033	4.868
8	7.652	7.326	7.020	6.733	6.463	6.210	5.971	5.747	5.535	5.335
9	8.566	8.162	7.786	7.435	7.108	6.802	6.515	6.247	5.995	5.759
10	9.471	8.983	8.530	8.111	7.722	7.360	7.024	6.710	6.418	6.145
11	10.368	9.787	9.253	8.760	8.306	7.887	7.499	7.139	6.805	6.495
12	11.255	10.575	9.954	9.385	8.863	8.384	7.943	7.536	7.161	6.814
13	12.134	11.348	10.635	9.986	9.394	8.853	8.358	7.904	7.487	7.013
14	13.004	12.106	11.296	10.563	9.899	9.295	8.745	8.244	7.786	7.367
15	13.865	12.849	11.938	11.118	10.380	9.712	9.108	8.560	8.061	7.606
16	14.718	13.578	12.561	11.652	10.838	10.106	9.447	8.851	8.313	7.824
17	15.562	14.292	13.166	12.166	11.274	10.477	9.763	9.122	8.544	8.022
18	16.398	14.992	13.754	12.659	11.690	10.828	10.059	9.372	8.756	8.201
19	17.226	15.679	14.324	13.134	12.085	11.158	10.336	9.604	8.950	8.365
20	18.046	16.352	14.878	13.590	12.462	11.470	10.594	9.818	9.129	8.514
21	18.857	17.011	15.415	14.029	12.821	11.764	10.836	10.017	9.292	8.649
22	19.661	17.658	15.937	14.451	13.163	12.042	11.061	10.201	9.442	8.772
23	20.456	18.292	16.444	14.857	13.489	12.303	11.272	10.371	9.580	8.883
24	21.244	18.914	16.936	15.247	13.799	12.550	11.469	10.529	9.707	8.985
25	22.023	19.524	17.413	15.622	14.094	12.783	11.654	10.675	9.823	9.077
30	25.808	22.396	19.601	17.292	15.373	13.765	12.409	11.258	10.274	9.427
35	29.409	24.999	21.487	18.665	16.374	14.498	12.948	11.655	10.567	9.644
40	32.835	27.356	23.115	19.793	17.159	15.046	13.332	11.925	10.757	9.779
45	36.095	29.490	24.519	20.720	17.774	15.456	13.606	12.108	10.881	9.863
50	39.196	31.424	25.730	21.482	18.256	15.762	13.801	12.233	10.962	9.915

Table A-4 Present-Value Interest Factors for a One-Dollar Annuity Discounted at k Percent for n Periods: $PVIFA_{k,n} = \sum_{t=1}^{n} \dfrac{1}{(1+k)^t}$ (continued)

Period	11%	12%	13%	14%	15%	16%	17%	18%	19%	20%
1	.901	.893	.885	.877	.870	.862	.855	.847	.840	.833
2	1.713	1.690	1.668	1.647	1.626	1.605	1.585	1.566	1.547	1.528
3	2.444	2.402	2.361	2.322	2.283	2.246	2.210	2.174	2.140	2.106
4	3.102	3.037	2.974	2.914	2.855	2.798	2.743	2.690	2.639	2.589
5	3.696	3.605	3.517	3.433	3.352	3.274	3.199	3.127	3.058	2.991
6	4.231	4.111	3.998	3.889	3.784	3.685	3.589	3.498	3.410	3.326
7	4.712	4.564	4.423	4.288	4.160	4.039	3.922	3.812	3.706	3.605
8	5.146	4.968	4.799	4.639	4.487	4.344	4.207	4.078	3.954	3.837
9	5.537	5.328	5.132	4.946	4.772	4.607	4.451	4.303	4.163	4.031
10	5.889	5.650	5.426	5.216	5.019	4.833	4.659	4.494	4.339	4.192
11	6.207	5.938	5.687	5.453	5.234	5.029	4.836	4.656	4.486	4.327
12	6.492	6.194	5.918	5.660	5.421	5.197	4.988	4.793	4.611	4.439
13	6.750	6.424	6.122	5.842	5.583	5.342	5.118	4.910	4.715	4.533
14	6.982	6.628	6.302	6.002	5.724	5.468	5.229	5.008	4.802	4.611
15	7.191	6.811	6.462	6.142	5.847	5.575	5.324	5.092	4.876	4.675
16	7.379	6.974	6.604	6.265	5.954	5.668	5.405	5.162	4.938	4.730
17	7.549	7.120	6.729	6.373	6.047	5.749	5.475	5.222	4.990	4.775
18	7.702	7.250	6.840	6.467	6.128	5.818	5.534	5.273	5.033	4.812
19	7.839	7.366	6.938	6.550	6.198	5.877	5.584	5.316	5.070	4.843
20	7.963	7.469	7.025	6.623	6.259	5.929	5.628	5.353	5.101	4.870
21	8.075	7.562	7.102	6.687	6.312	5.973	5.665	5.384	5.127	4.891
22	8.176	7.645	7.170	6.743	6.359	6.011	5.696	5.410	5.149	4.909
23	8.266	7.718	7.230	6.792	6.399	6.044	5.723	5.432	5.167	4.925
24	8.348	7.784	7.283	6.835	6.434	6.073	5.746	5.451	5.182	4.937
25	8.422	7.843	7.330	6.873	6.464	6.097	5.766	5.467	5.195	4.948
30	8.694	8.055	7.496	7.003	6.566	6.177	5.829	5.517	5.235	4.979
35	8.855	8.176	7.586	7.070	6.617	6.215	5.858	5.539	5.251	4.992
40	8.951	8.244	7.634	7.105	6.642	6.233	5.871	5.548	5.258	4.997
45	9.008	8.283	7.661	7.123	6.654	6.242	5.877	5.552	5.261	4.999
50	9.042	8.304	7.675	7.133	6.661	6.246	5.880	5.554	5.262	4.999

Table A-4 Present-Value Interest Factors for a One-Dollar Annuity Discounted at k Percent for n Periods: $PVIFA_{k,n} = \sum_{t=1}^{n} \dfrac{1}{(1+k)^t}$ (continued)

Period	21%	22%	23%	24%	25%	26%	27%	28%	29%	30%
1	.826	.820	.813	.806	.800	.794	.787	.781	.775	.769
2	1.509	1.492	1.474	1.457	1.440	1.424	1.407	1.392	1.376	1.361
3	2.074	2.042	2.011	1.981	1.952	1.923	1.896	1.868	1.842	1.816
4	2.540	2.494	2.448	2.404	2.362	2.320	2.280	2.241	2.203	2.166
5	2.926	2.864	2.803	2.745	2.689	2.635	2.583	2.532	2.483	2.436
6	3.245	3.167	3.092	3.020	2.951	2.885	2.821	2.759	2.700	2.643
7	3.508	3.416	3.327	3.242	3.161	3.083	3.009	2.937	2.868	2.802
8	3.726	3.619	3.518	3.421	3.329	3.241	3.156	3.076	2.999	2.925
9	3.905	3.786	3.673	3.566	3.463	3.366	3.273	3.184	3.100	3.019
10	4.054	3.923	3.799	3.682	3.570	3.465	3.364	3.269	3.178	3.092
11	4.177	4.035	3.902	3.776	3.656	3.544	3.437	3.335	3.239	3.147
12	4.278	4.127	3.985	3.851	3.725	3.606	3.493	3.387	3.286	3.190
13	4.362	4.203	4.053	3.912	3.780	3.656	3.538	3.427	3.322	3.223
14	4.432	4.265	4.108	3.962	3.824	3.695	3.573	3.459	3.351	3.249
15	4.489	4.315	4.153	4.001	3.859	3.726	3.601	3.483	3.373	3.268
16	4.536	4.357	4.189	4.033	3.887	3.751	3.623	3.503	3.390	3.283
17	4.576	4.391	4.219	4.059	3.910	3.771	3.640	3.518	3.403	3.295
18	4.608	4.419	4.243	4.080	3.928	3.786	3.654	3.529	3.413	3.304
19	4.635	4.442	4.263	4.097	3.942	3.799	3.664	3.539	3.421	3.311
20	4.657	4.460	4.279	4.110	3.954	3.808	3.673	3.546	3.427	3.316
21	4.675	4.476	4.292	4.121	3.963	3.816	3.679	3.551	3.432	3.320
22	4.690	4.488	4.302	4.130	3.970	3.822	3.684	3.556	3.436	3.323
23	4.703	4.499	4.311	4.137	3.976	3.827	3.689	3.559	3.438	3.325
24	4.713	4.507	4.318	4.143	3.981	3.831	3.692	3.562	3.441	3.327
25	4.721	4.514	4.323	4.147	3.985	3.834	3.694	3.564	3.442	3.329
30	4.746	4.534	4.339	4.160	3.995	3.842	3.701	3.569	3.447	3.332
35	4.756	4.541	4.345	4.164	3.998	3.845	3.703	3.571	3.448	3.333
40	4.760	4.544	4.347	4.166	3.999	3.846	3.703	3.571	3.448	3.333
45	4.761	4.545	4.347	4.166	4.000	3.846	3.704	3.571	3.448	3.333
50	4.762	4.545	4.348	4.167	4.000	3.846	3.704	3.571	3.448	3.333

Table A-4   Present-Value Interest Factors for a One-Dollar Annuity Discounted at k Percent for n Periods: $PVIFA_{k,n} = \sum_{t=1}^{n} \dfrac{1}{(1+k)^t}$ (continued)

Period	31%	32%	33%	34%	35%	36%	37%	38%	39%	40%
1	.763	.758	.752	.746	.741	.735	.730	.725	.719	.714
2	1.346	1.331	1.317	1.303	1.289	1.276	1.263	1.250	1.237	1.224
3	1.791	1.766	1.742	1.719	1.696	1.673	1.652	1.630	1.609	1.589
4	2.130	2.096	2.062	2.029	1.997	1.966	1.935	1.906	1.877	1.849
5	2.390	2.345	2.302	2.260	2.220	2.181	2.143	2.106	2.070	2.035
6	2.588	2.534	2.483	2.433	2.385	2.339	2.294	2.251	2.209	2.168
7	2.739	2.677	2.619	2.562	2.508	2.455	2.404	2.355	2.308	2.263
8	2.854	2.786	2.721	2.658	2.598	2.540	2.485	2.432	2.380	2.331
9	2.942	2.868	2.798	2.730	2.665	2.603	2.544	2.487	2.432	2.379
10	3.009	2.930	2.855	2.784	2.715	2.649	2.587	2.527	2.469	2.414
11	3.060	2.978	2.899	2.824	2.752	2.683	2.618	2.555	2.496	2.438
12	3.100	3.013	2.931	2.853	2.779	2.708	2.641	2.576	2.515	2.456
13	3.129	3.040	2.956	2.876	2.799	2.727	2.658	2.592	2.529	2.469
14	3.152	3.061	2.974	2.892	2.814	2.740	2.670	2.603	2.539	2.478
15	3.170	3.076	2.988	2.905	2.825	2.750	2.679	2.611	2.546	2.484
16	3.183	3.088	2.999	2.914	2.834	2.757	2.685	2.616	2.551	2.489
17	3.193	3.097	3.007	2.921	2.840	2.763	2.690	2.621	2.555	2.492
18	3.201	3.104	3.012	2.926	2.844	2.767	2.693	2.624	2.557	2.494
19	3.207	3.109	3.017	2.930	2.848	2.770	2.696	2.626	2.559	2.496
20	3.211	3.113	3.020	2.933	2.850	2.772	2.698	2.627	2.561	2.497
21	3.215	3.116	3.023	2.935	2.852	2.773	2.699	2.629	2.562	2.498
22	3.217	3.118	3.025	2.936	2.853	2.775	2.700	2.629	2.562	2.498
23	3.219	3.120	3.026	2.938	2.854	2.775	2.701	2.630	2.563	2.499
24	3.221	3.121	3.027	2.939	2.855	2.776	2.701	2.630	2.563	2.499
25	3.222	3.122	3.028	2.939	2.856	2.776	2.702	2.631	2.563	2.499
30	3.225	3.124	3.030	2.941	2.857	2.777	2.702	2.631	2.564	2.500
35	3.226	3.125	3.030	2.941	2.857	2.778	2.703	2.632	2.564	2.500
40	3.226	3.125	3.030	2.941	2.857	2.778	2.703	2.632	2.564	2.500
45	3.226	3.125	3.030	2.941	2.857	2.778	2.703	2.632	2.564	2.500
50	3.226	3.125	3.030	2.941	2.857	2.778	2.703	2.632	2.564	2.500

Table A-4 Present-Value Interest Factors for a One-Dollar Annuity Discounted at k Percent for n Periods: $PVIFA_{k,n} = \sum\limits_{t=1}^{n} \dfrac{1}{(1+k)^t}$ (continued)

Period	41%	42%	43%	44%	45%	46%	47%	48%	49%	50%
1	.709	.704	.699	.694	.690	.685	.680	.676	.671	.667
2	1.212	1.200	1.188	1.177	1.165	1.154	1.143	1.132	1.122	1.111
3	1.569	1.549	1.530	1.512	1.493	1.475	1.458	1.441	1.424	1.407
4	1.822	1.795	1.769	1.744	1.720	1.695	1.672	1.649	1.627	1.605
5	2.001	1.969	1.937	1.906	1.876	1.846	1.818	1.790	1.763	1.737
6	2.129	2.091	2.054	2.018	1.983	1.949	1.917	1.885	1.854	1.824
7	2.219	2.176	2.135	2.096	2.057	2.020	1.984	1.949	1.916	1.883
8	2.283	2.237	2.193	2.150	2.109	2.069	2.030	1.993	1.957	1.922
9	2.328	2.280	2.233	2.187	2.144	2.102	2.061	2.022	1.984	1.948
10	2.360	2.310	2.261	2.213	2.168	2.125	2.083	2.042	2.003	1.965
11	2.383	2.331	2.280	2.232	2.185	2.140	2.097	2.055	2.015	1.977
12	2.400	2.346	2.294	2.244	2.196	2.151	2.107	2.064	2.024	1.985
13	2.411	2.356	2.303	2.253	2.204	2.158	2.113	2.071	2.029	1.990
14	2.419	2.363	2.310	2.259	2.210	2.163	2.118	2.075	2.033	1.993
15	2.425	2.369	2.315	2.263	2.214	2.166	2.121	2.078	2.036	1.995
16	2.429	2.372	2.318	2.266	2.216	2.169	2.123	2.079	2.037	1.997
17	2.432	2.375	2.320	2.268	2.218	2.170	2.125	2.081	2.038	1.998
18	2.434	2.377	2.322	2.270	2.219	2.172	2.126	2.082	2.039	1.999
19	2.435	2.378	2.323	2.270	2.220	2.172	2.126	2.082	2.040	1.999
20	2.436	2.379	2.324	2.271	2.221	2.173	2.127	2.083	2.040	1.999
21	2.437	2.379	2.324	2.272	2.221	2.173	2.127	2.083	2.040	2.000
22	2.438	2.380	2.325	2.272	2.222	2.173	2.127	2.083	2.040	2.000
23	2.438	2.380	2.325	2.272	2.222	2.174	2.127	2.083	2.041	2.000
24	2.438	2.380	2.325	2.272	2.222	2.174	2.127	2.083	2.041	2.000
25	2.439	2.381	2.325	2.272	2.222	2.174	2.128	2.083	2.041	2.000
30	2.439	2.381	2.326	2.273	2.222	2.174	2.128	2.083	2.041	2.000
35	2.439	2.381	2.326	2.273	2.222	2.174	2.128	2.083	2.041	2.000
40	2.439	2.381	2.326	2.273	2.222	2.174	2.128	2.083	2.041	2.000
45	2.439	2.381	2.326	2.273	2.222	2.174	2.128	2.083	2.041	2.000
50	2.439	2.381	2.326	2.273	2.222	2.174	2.128	2.083	2.041	2.000